A Clash of Chiefs

rex militaris,

rex sacrorum

Carlos Quiles

A Clash of Chiefs

rex militaris,

rex sacrorum

Carlos Quiles

A Song of Sheep and Horses

Book 2

ACADEMIA PRISCA

2019

A SONG OF SHEEP AND HORSES:
EURAFRASIA NOSTRATICA, EURASIA INDOURALICA

Book One: A Game of Clans: *collectores venatoresque, agricolae pastoresque.*
Book Two: A Clash of Chiefs: *rex militaris, rex sacrorum.*
Book Three: A Storm of Words: *vetera verba, priscae linguae.*
Book Four: A Feat of Crowds: *hic sunt leones, hic sunt dracones.*

Version: 1.2 (first printed edition), June 1st, 2019
ISBN-13: 978-1-072-02353-1 paperback

ACADEMIA PRISCA
Avda. Sta. María de la Cabeza, 3, E-LL, Badajoz 06001, Spain.
European Union

Work based on Quiles, Carlos (2017). Indo-European demic diffusion model (3rd ed.). Badajoz, Spain: Universidad de Extremadura. DOI: 10.13140/RG.2.2.35620.58241

Official site: <https://indo-european.eu/asosah/>
Publisher's site: <https://academiaprisca.org/>
Full text and latest revisions: <https://indo-european.info>
Blog for images, discussion, and new findings: <https://indo-european.eu/>

Cover image *Bronzegießerei* by Gerhard Beuthner, appeared in Erdal-Bilderreihe Nr. 115 Bild 1 (1930).

Table of Contents

Guide to the reader

Abbreviations

AASI: Ancient Ancestral South Indian

AEA: Ancient East Asians

AHG: Anatolian Hunter-Gatherer

AME: Ancient Middle Easterner

ANA: Ancient North African

ANE: Ancient North Eurasian

ANI: Ancestral North Indian

ANS: Ancient North Siberian

ASI: Ancestral South Indian

AP: Ancient Palaeosiberian

BA: Bronze Age

BBC: Bell Beaker culture

BMAC: Bactria and Margiana Archaeological Complex

BE: Basal Eurasians

CA: Copper Age

CHG: Caucasus Hunter-Gatherer

CWC: Corded Ware culture

ENA: Eastern non-Africans

EWE: Early West Eurasians

EN: Early Neolithic

FBA: Final Bronze Age

IA: Iron Age

IE: Indo-European

IN: Iranian Neolithic

LBA: Late Bronze Age

LBK: Linearbandkeramik

LCA: Late Chalcolithic

LN: Late Neolithic

MBA: Middle Bronze Age

MCW: Multi-Cordoned Ware

MLBA: Middle–Late Bronze Age

MN: Middle Neolithic

NWAN: North-West Anatolian Neolithic

PCA: Principal Component Analysis

CWE: Common West Eurasian

CEU: Central European

GAC: Globular Amphora(e) culture

EBA: Early Bronze Age

EEA: Early East Asian

EEBA: Early European Bronze Age

EEF: Early European Farmer

EH: Early Helladic

EHG: Eastern Hunter-Gatherer

EIA: Early Iron Age

PIE: Proto-Indo-European

PU: Proto-Uralic

SNP: Single   Nucleotide Polymorphism

SRBW: Simple-Relief-Band Ware

TMRCA: Time to Most Recent Common Ancestor

TRB: Funnel Beaker culture

WHG: Western Hunter-Gatherer

WSHG: Western Siberian Hunter-Gatherer

Symbols

(x[SNP])   denotes "negative for [SNP]"

[SNP]⁺   marks an unofficial or probabilistic [SNP] call

[SNP]*   implies that the sample is of a "basal" [SNP] subclade

[N%]⁺   denotes an unofficial result of "N% ancestry"

[SNP]+   denotes "positive for [SNP]"

*[word]   denotes a reconstructed form

Conventions used in this book

This text is not a simple essay anymore. Even though I conceived it initially as a mere fourth revision at the end of 2017, it grew rapidly out of hand, as I intended to include as much relevant information as possible on published (and reported) population movements supported by genetic investigation. The association of genetic data with potential prehistoric ethnolinguistic communities required in turn the addition of all potentially relevant archaeological data.

The first two volumes of this series must be understood as a *detailed supplement* of the main work, which is the third volume concerning linguistic data. This order of relevance is not only related to this series' emphasis on languages over prehistoric cultures or genetics, but to the actual nature of the matter at hand: this a comprehensive work on reconstructed languages and the peoples who might have spoken them.

The work follows simple rules in its aim to achieve clarity and coherence.

It is an encyclopaedia-like text, free and organised in more or less isolated linguistic, archaeological, and genetic sections organised to facilitate future revisions by anyone, incorporating the latest research.

Unlike armchair work in linguistics or bioinformatics, where results and interpretations can be reviewed with knowledge and proper access to data, it is impossible to be an *armchair archaeologist* without ample experience in the specific field investigated. Therefore, secondary archaeological sources, giving proper interpretation and synthesis of primary research and fieldwork, are preferred over primary sources in the archaeological section, with little or no personal additions in this part, although primary sources and proper connections of the data have also been added whenever necessary. All archaeological summaries included are properly referenced, with the main author or authors behind the content of each paragraph properly cited—at least the author of the secondary source, often more relevant than primary sources— to allow for proper identification of the original text and for further reading.

A chronologically and regionally organised structure has been given to the full text, to allow for an easy searching of the content, and for the reading of the text in either a linear or non-linear manner.

Names of samples, their cultures or groupings, ancestries, or clusters do not necessarily follow the nomenclature systems used by the different authors, papers, research labs, or archaeological teams, but are made to fit into the coherent picture of this book (Eisenmann et al. 2018).

Haplogroup (hg.) will be frequently used to refer to Y-chromosome haplogroups, unless otherwise expressly stated. Y-DNA haplogroups and subclades will also be referred to as *line* or *lineage*, whereas common admixture components defined in recent papers will be referred to as *ancestry*. The preferred nomenclature system of haplogroups is *X-Y*, where *X* is the standard name by ISOGG (2018), and *Y* is one or more SNP mutations defining the haplogroup, using whenever possible the one preferred by YFull. An asterisk *X-Y** is used to represent a *basal lineage*, commonly understood as a subclade with different mutations from the most common, 'successful' ones.

Additional positive *Y*+ reported online in non-peer reviewed publications are represented in this text as $X\text{-}Y^+$. The originally published haplogroup for the samples, other reported positive and negative SNPs, as well as the author or authors of the additional information, can be found in online supplementary materials of this book.

For the sake of consistency, only YFull estimates for year formed and time to most recent common ancestor (TMRCA) of Y-chromosome haplogroups have been used[1], unless other sources are expressly stated. Years before present (ybp) have been approximated to BC assuming 2,000 years of difference, to round out estimates. Estimates were obtained by Vladimir Tagankin by applying the method published in Adamov et al. (2015) to the data received

---

[1] Dates were retrieved from the website <https://www.yfull.com/> during October-December 2018.

from voluntary users[2]. Also for the sake of consistency, dates expressed as years before present (YBP) have been simplistically approximated to BC.

TMRCA dates are used as gross approximations to expansions of Y-DNA lineages (see Figure 1). They can offer an inaccurate idea of the lineage evolution because a) the actual rate of mutation is unknown, and b) TMRCA estimates are based on the lineages that survived, which may obviate other previous expansions in the same trunk.

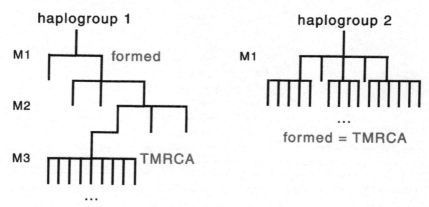

Figure 1. Simplistic example of SNP mutations in a haplogroup. Lines represent diverging male lineages. Haplogroup 1 is only successful after the third mutation, and is thus defined by mutations M1, M2, and M3, with M1 representing its formation date, and M3 its TMRCA. Haplogroup 2 is successful during its formation, and thus M1 defines it, as well as its formation and TMRCA date.

Modern physical maps are used to illustrate potential expansion routes of ancient cultures, peoples, and languages, even though they pose a significant danger to the development of a sound model, since they almost invariably involve "a concatenation of weakly supported links that corporately form an 'arrow' of dispersion" (Mallory 2014). Map routes are only depicted as a visual help to add movement to the otherwise stationary maps of ancient cultures,

---

[2] For details on the specific methodology used, see <https://www.yfull.com/faq/what-yfulls-age-estimation-methodology/>.

peoples, languages, and ancient DNA obtained from scattered burials. Eurasian biomes (Figure 2) and Suppl. Fig. 19) are commonly referenced to in this book to delimit cultural groups and migration routes.

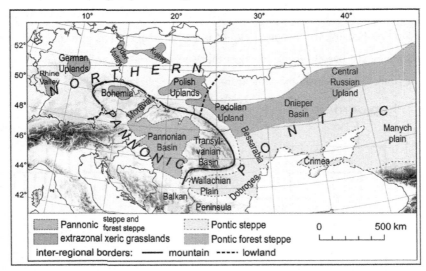

Figure 2. Simplified map of the distribution of steppes and forest-steppes (Pontic and Pannonian) and xeric grasslands in Eastern Central Europe (with adjoining East European ranges). Modified from Kajtoch et al. (2016).

List of Supplementary Figures

The following is an ordered list of supplementary graphics with their description and links to online sites for download. All supplementary data is also contained in the fourth volume of this series, *A Feat of Crowds.*

Maps

A list of available maps can be found at <https://indo-european.eu/maps/>.

Suppl. Fig. 1. Map of out-of-Africa migrations of anatomically modern humans (before ca. 35000 BC) with Y-DNA haplogroups, ADMIXTURE, and mtDNA haplogroups. <https://indo-european.eu/maps/out-of-africa/>.

Suppl. Fig. 2. Map of Upper Palaeolithic cultures (ca. 35000–20000 BC), with Y-DNA haplogroups, ADMIXTURE, and mtDNA haplogroups. <https://indo-european.eu/maps/palaeolithic/>.

Suppl. Fig. 3. Map of Epipalaeolithic cultures (ca. 20000-10000 BC), with Y-DNA haplogroups, ADMIXTURE, and mtDNA haplogroups. <https://indo-european.eu/maps/epipalaeolithic/>.

Suppl. Fig. 4. Map of Early Mesolithic cultures (ca. 10000–7500 BC), with Y-DNA haplogroups, ADMIXTURE, and mtDNA haplogroups. <https://indo-european.eu/maps/mesolithic-early/>.

Suppl. Fig. 5. Map of Late Mesolithic cultures (ca. 7500–6000 BC), with Y-DNA haplogroups, ADMIXTURE, and mtDNA haplogroups. <https://indo-european.eu/maps/mesolithic/>.

Suppl. Fig. 6. Map of Neolithic and hunter-gatherer pottery expansion (ca. 6000–5000 BC), with Y-DNA haplogroups, ADMIXTURE, and mtDNA haplogroups. <https://indo-european.eu/maps/neolithic/>.

Suppl. Fig. 7. Map of Early Eneolithic cultures (ca. 5000–4000 BC), with Y-DNA haplogroups, ADMIXTURE, and mtDNA haplogroups. <https://indo-european.eu/maps/eneolithic-early/>.

Graphics

A list of available graphics may be found at <https://indo-european.eu/pca/>.

VIII. Early Bronze Age

VIII.1. The European Early Bronze Age

The European Early Bronze Age (EEBA), although difficult to define for all cultures involved, may be said to have begun with changes in settlement systems, burial customs and material culture, in particular the mostly plain pottery. This process began ca. 2500 BC in the entire Carpathian Basin, Italy, and to the east, with a general decrease in decoration on pottery: Vessels are no longer messengers or symbols indicating an affiliation to an identity group; their functional aspect is emphasised. Begleitkeramik are common starting with the Classical Bell Beaker, including jugs, cups, and bowls, low and deep (Heyd 2013).

This innovation process progresses gradually ca. 2400–2250 BC in a wide area from the Lower Danube down to the Alps and northern Italy, and is recognised in the Carpathian Basin by a return to tell settlements as a development from south to north, affecting Vinkovci, then reaching the Danube, and finally early Nagyrév ca. 2250–2000 BC. Exotic objects that would later become iconic of the Bronze Age begin to appear (Heyd 2013). Continuous use or emergence of circular enclosures in central Europe, appearing (or being essentially improved) after ca. 2500 BC in northern

Germany, Iberia, the British Isles, or Bulgaria, suggest a renewed Europe-wide concept of sanctuary, and extensive communication networks with intellectual and religious contents circulating alongside raw materials (Spatzier and Bertemes 2018).

The regional organisation changes thus from trans-regional cultural phenomena prevalent ca. 2750–2500 BC, like Vučedol and Makó/Kosihý–Čaka, to a cultural fragmentation after ca. 2400 BC with 5 new regional units, apart from the continuing late Makó/Kosihý–Čaka, late Somogyvár–Nagýrev, Nyírség, Gyula-Roşia, Maros (Pitvaros), Ada, Gornea-Orleşt. Distinguished by a significant degree of similarity of material culture (burial ritual and pottery), they seem to be a sign of the birth of chiefdoms and tribal organisation (Heyd 2013).

This combination of graves with Bronze Age equipment, cultural fragmentation and tell resettling and expansion gradually expands in importance and consistency, from 2300 BC and especially 2200 BC onwards. This influence is appreciated rather soon in neighbouring cultures, such as the exotic objects appearing in the early/mid–23rd century BC in the Csepel group of the Bell Beaker culture, like a copper/bronze halberd and roll-headed pins or *Noppenringe* (Heyd 2013).

After the expansion of the Classical Bell Beakers ca. 2500 BC, the Middle and Lower Danube (up to central Germany) and Moravia turn into the cradle of the new Early Bronze Age Civilisation (Figure 48). This expansion and subsequent connected cultural developments are responsible for the creation of extensive sociocultural contacts that will last, with certain evolutionary changes, the whole European Bronze Age. Communities tend to concentrate along interregional trade routes, and long-range exchange becomes common, supporting the unifying, true pan-European nature of the Bell Beaker people, later intensified by certain regional centres (usually in central Europe) throughout the Bronze and Iron Ages (Heyd 2013).

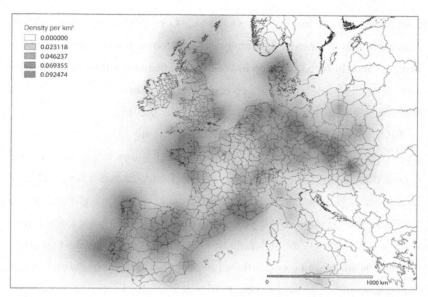

Density per km²
- 0.000000
- 0.023118
- 0.046237
- 0.069355
- 0.092474

0   1000 km

Figure 48. Density analysis of Bell Beaker distribution per region. Combination of different levels of B-spline interpolation. Modified from Bilger (2019). Values and analysis explained in the original open access paper.

Significant waves of regional fragmentation and emancipation from previous traditions are also seen over the 23rd century BC in Bell Beaker territories in the vicinity of the Carpathian Basin, such as Oggau-Wipfing in the Middle Danube, Proto-Únětice in the Moravian province, or Chłopice–Veselé in Lesser Poland. Apart from the fragmentation, the first centralisation waves appear with the first fortifications on hills in southern areas, and longhouses predominate as living places and foci of the new settlement planning (Heyd 2013).

After ca. 2200 BC, a gradual and continuous process involving the intensification of cultural subsystems is seen, and then massively in the 21st century BC. Metallurgy increases in regional centres. Eventually, the next stage of a full-fledged "European Bronze Age package" is reached from ca. 2000 BC on, when wide parts of temperate Europe develop a system of intensified exchange where trade becomes established, based on a hierarchically organised society, with many prestige and status objects belonging to the elites, culminating in their lavishly equipped graves (e.g.

Leubingen and Helmsdorf in Germany, Łęki Małe in Poland, Thun-Renzenbühl in Switzerland, Kermonen en Plouvorn and Saint Adrien in Brittany, and Bush and Clandon in Wessex), and large metal hoards. There are also precious metal vessels, economic specialisation, specialised craft production, and widely available tin–bronze (Heyd 2013).

EBA groups emerge therefore within a unifying framework established previously by expanding East Bell Beakers, which shows thus common cross-regional features, such as shared object forms, burial rites, and new technologies, like the introduction of tin–bronze, and the advent of complex metalworking techniques. All groups are connected from west to east, from north to south Europe, through farming communities that show the emergence of a leading social group of chieftains, characterised by rich single graves with votive depositions, as well as hoards with new kinds of ceremonial weapons, such as solid-hilted daggers (Vollgriffdolche) and halberds (Heyd 2013).

The Early European Bronze Age region becomes finally divided into three fundamentally distinct provinces of cultural material and burial rituals, which act as cultural centres that influence adjacent regions. Three supra-regional culture complexes formed by different groups appear between the Rhine in the West and Transdanubia in the east, the Alps to the south, and the line between Mittelelbe–Saale-region to Upper Silesia/Lesser Poland: its common basis is built by the East Bell Beaker group and regional European groups. Mainly along the Danube appears the Danube Early Bronze Age culture; to the north appears the Únětice complex, forming separated regional *Únětice cultures*; and the Eastern Early Bronze Age is formed by the Nitra, Mierzanowice and Košťany groups, to the north of the Danube and to the east of the Morava in East Moravia, in south-west Slovakia and Lesser Poland, including (with Košťany) the northern Carpathian Basin (Heyd 2013).

These central groups are delimited from Western Early Bronze Age cultures (Adlerberg and Rhône, based on the West Bell Beaker groups), from Carpathian cultures (Makó/Kosihý–Čaka, Somogyvár–Vinkovci, and

Vučedol), and from other northern traditions based on Bell Beaker cultures – like the Veluwe-type Beakers from the Netherlands and the Rhein – or Corded Ware – like Riesenbecher, apart from the developing Nordic Dagger period to the north. Lower Danube, Únětice, and Nordic BA, strongly unified in that they are saturated with huge amounts of diverse metal goods. This is interpreted as a response to a great demand for prestige objects by local communities, and indirect indication of their social differentiation and ranking, as part of the materialisation process of the transformation in ideology (Kadrow 1998).

During the evolution of this Early Bronze period, different shifting independent ("pan-European") centres of cultural and technological innovations can be seen in Central Europe, from the Upper Danube ca. 2200–2050 BC; to the northern ranges of Únětice ca. 2050–1900 BC; to the Bohemia and Moravian regions ca. 1900–1750 BC; and later, ca. 1750–1400 BC, to one centre in the north-eastern part of the Carpathian Basin (a complex of Füzesabony, Mad'arovce, and Věteřov cultures), in contact with the Aegean world, and another represented by the circle of Nordic cultures, with a singular culture. A different European centre, heir of an important Corded Ware culture influence on Bell Beakers, developed early (at least ca. 2300 BC) as the Epi-Corded Carpathian Cultural Circle, which manifested itself in the Mierzanowice culture (Kadrow 1998).

The real transformational change in Bell Beakers, shifting from a unifying expanding culture to the different regionalisation trends, starts when the centre of gravity shifts from expanding Bell Beakers ca. 2500/2400 BC to the *real* trade boosted by Aegean influence ca. 2300/2200 BC. The intermediate period sees both worlds meeting in their respective expansions, e.g. in the Adriatic, in the Carpathian Basin, and possibly even in Iberia (Heyd 2013).

viii.1. Old Europeans

Yamna admixed with local EEF-like populations from Hungary before (and during) their evolution into Classical or East Bell Beakers. During their explosive expansion, tens of thousands of Yamna/East Bell Beaker migrants[18] also admixed with local European populations through exogamy, revealing multiple male-biased migration waves, based on the prevalent Yamna R1b1a1b1-L23 (especially R1b1a1b1a1a-L151) lineages and the reported replacements of male lines in all European territories where it spread, in some cases—like the British Isles or Iberia—close to 100%, while the spread of Steppe ancestry was in many cases inferior to 50% and usually decreasing with distance (Olalde et al. 2018). Nevertheless, a reported early Bell Beaker sample from France, likely from the Eastern Swiss–Alsatian–Southwestern German province[19], shows elevated Steppe ancestry and clusters quite close to Yamna (Brunel 2018), showing that the Yamna-like cluster was still prevalent among expanding East Bell Beakers ca. 2500 BC (Suppl. Fig. 10.C).

The admixture of non-Iberian Bell Beakers relative to Yamna samples has been described as mainly with EEF populations with hunter-gatherer ancestry closer to Körös (in a La Braña–Körös WHG cline), higher than the one found in samples from Hungary LCA or Germany MN. The admixture in Iberian Bell Beakers shows a better fit with previous Iberian populations (from the Neolithic or Chalcolithic), except for Copper Age populations from the north, which harbour more hunter-gatherer ancestry.

In the case of Iberia, as is most likely the case at least in in south-western European samples, the best fit of a source population for Steppe ancestry are Bell Beakers from Germany (CEU BBC). Other sources such as Bell Beakers from France or the Netherlands failed, likely because they have slightly higher proportions of steppe ancestry than the true source population (Olalde et al. 2019). This further supports the admixture of Yamna settlers all over the Upper Danube before the transition to the Classical Bell Beaker culture and its expansion all over Europe.

---

[18] Estimate by Volker Heyd (2018) based on the number of barrows found to date.
[19] Informal report of the Ph.D. Thesis does not include the specific locations. Samples investigated come from northern France, Alsace, and the Mediterranean region, with Alsace having the earliest investigated Bell Beaker burials to date in France.

Similarly, early samples from the British Isles show high variability in ancestry compatible with recent admixture, like the Boscombe Bowmen collective burial, where two closely related individuals (ca. 2500-2140 BC), likely third-degree relatives, share ca. 13–43% ancestry and show the lowest and one of the highest amounts of Steppe-related ancestry, respectively (Olalde et al. 2018).

The reported Steppe ancestry in some later Bell Beaker samples from central, east-central, and northern European territories, and in the British Isles, is higher instead of lower (Olalde et al. 2018). Similar to the increase in Iberian farmer contribution found exclusively in Bell Beakers from Iberia, this increase in Steppe ancestry in certain late Bell Beaker groups compared to earlier ones from nearby regions is explained by exogamy, more specifically admixture with females of local Corded Ware peoples, who are the best fit for that increased ancestral component from the steppe.

So, for example, Bell Beakers from the Netherlands (and consequently the British Isles, see *§viii.5. Pre-Celts*) show elevated Steppe ancestry, in excess of that found in Central European Bell Beakers, who are the likely origin of expansions northward through the Rhine, and southward into Iberia and Italy (Olalde et al. 2019). This difference is also seen in the *northward* shift of the Dutch–British cluster, toward the earlier Corded Ware cluster.

The precise evolution of Yamna-derived vs. Corded Ware-derived Steppe ancestry in certain regions is difficult to describe with precision without detailed temporal and regional transects, since Yamna pioneer groups seem to have been in contact with Corded Ware groups from central Europe, who show an increased Yamna-like Steppe ancestry likely due to exogamy (see *§vii.1. Western and Eastern Uralians*), at the same time as these Yamna settlers may have also increased their Corded Ware-like Steppe ancestry around the Middle and Upper Danube through exogamy, prior to their emergence as East Bell Beakers

Unlike the admixture of peoples of Yamna descent with EEF populations found in Bell Beakers, where typical Early European farmer mtDNA subclades are found together with typical Yamna Y-DNA lineages (Olalde et al. 2018), it is difficult to pinpoint precise mtDNA subclades in Bell Beakers corresponding to their admixture with Corded Ware peoples, because of the shared mtDNA originally from the Pontic–Caspian steppes, and because of the previous admixture of central European Corded Ware peoples with EEF populations, too (Juras et al. 2018), similar to Yamna groups from Hungary (see *§vii.7. North-West Indo-Europeans*).

Main R1b1a1b1a1a-L151 subclades expanding with East Bell Beakers are R1b1a1b1a1a1-U106/S21/M405 (TMRCA ca. 2700 BC) and R1b1a1b1a1a2-P312/S116 (TMRCA ca. 2500 BC), with a comparatively earlier successful expansion of the former's surviving subclades. The earliest R1b1a1b1a1a1-U106 subclades are found during the late 3rd millennium BC in Scandinavia (Allentoft et al. 2015) and Bohemia, and slightly later in the Netherlands, while R1b1a1b1a1a2-P312 subclades are found everywhere in Europe (Olalde et al. 2018), except for northern Scandinavia, which suggests a bottleneck of hg. R1b1a1b1a1a1-U106 in migrating Bell Beakers in Jutland.

The main R1b1a1b1a1a2-P312 subclades R1b1a1b1a1a2b-U152, R1b1a1b1a1a2a-DF27, and R1b1a1b1a1a2c-S461 share an early TMRCA ca. 2500 BC. Nevertheless, only R1b1a1b1a1a2b-U152 lineages are found widespread in different EEBA provinces at the end of the 3rd millennium, including the Upper Danube, Iberia, Bohemia, Poland, and Hungary (Olalde et al. 2018). R1b1a1b1a1a2a-DF27 is found early in a sample from Quedlinburg[20] in central Europe (Mathieson et al. 2015), in Iberian Bronze Age samples (Valdiosera et al. 2018), and one much later among Longobards in Hungary (Amorim et al. 2018), with a clear bottleneck in south-western Europe, especially beyond the Pyrenées. R1b1a1b1a1a2c-S461 lineages are

---

[20] ZZ11+ equivalent (ancestral to DF27 and U152); DF27+? In 390k BAM file, but short, may actually belong to chromosomes 2 or 5. Additional information from Alex Williamson.

mainly found in Bell Beakers from Britain and later Bronze Age populations, in a bottleneck caused by the expansion to the British Isles (Olalde et al. 2018).

Rarer R1b1a1b1a1a2-P312 subclades include R1b1a1b1a1a2d-L238 (TMRCA ca. 2500 BC), reported in an old Icelander (Ebenesersdóttir et al. 2018), and present mainly among modern peoples of Scandinavian descent, which may suggest its early expansion to the north; R1b1a1b1a1a2e-DF19[+] (TMRCA ca. 2500 BC), found in a Roman individual from Britain (Martiniano et al. 2016), and among modern northern Europeans; and R1b1a1b1a1a2f-DF99 (TMRCA ca. 2000 BC), found in an early medieval Longobard (Amorim et al. 2018) and among modern northern-central Europeans.

Due to the early TMRCA of R1b1a1b1a1a-L151 lineages, and to the occasional finding of early subclades of the most common lineages in distant territories, the split of hg. R1b1a1b1a1a-L151 in expanding clans must have happened early during the Yamna Hungary–early East Bell Beaker society. It is impossible, then, to assign any R1b1a1b1a1a-L151 lineage to a specific Early Bronze Age community, in spite of the known majority distributions in certain regions. The association of certain subclades with specific linguistic communities needs to be understood, therefore, as the product of gradual and successive Y-chromosome bottlenecks, and a simplification of the ancient picture based on the limited data available.

Studies of ancient European hydronymy, reflected in the so-called Old European pattern (Krahe 1964, 1949; Nicolaisen 1957), reveals a quasi-uniform name-giving system for water courses that shows Indo-European water-words and suffixes following rules of Late Proto-Indo-European word formation (Adrados 1998). This points to an ancient wave of Late Indo-European speakers that spread over northern, western, and central Europe, before the proto-historic Celtic and Germanic expansions, including the British Isles, the Italian and Iberian peninsulas, the Balkans, and the Northern European Plains up to the Neman River in Lithuania.

The expansion of the Bell Beaker folk, originally from their North-West Indo-European homeland in the Yamna Hungary–East Bell Beaker community (Mallory 2013), and especially the expansion of R1b1a1b1-L23 lineages, under further Y-chromosome bottlenecks of R1b1a1b1a1a-L151 subclades (Cassidy et al. 2016), should therefore be associated with the spread of these *Old Europeans* throughout Europe, where their dialects would later evolve into the majority of the attested Indo-European branches of Europe.

VIII.2. Southern EEBA province

VIII.2.1. Northern Italy

Northern Italian regions south of the Alps show the evolution of Final Neolithic attributes to the earliest western Proto-Beaker package before ca. 2500 BC, which did not include wristguards, copper knives, ornaments of amber, and showed scarce arrowheads or V-buttons (using instead flat or round beads), but did include anthropomorphic stelae, such as those found in Sion and Aosta. Eventually, the eastern or Classical Beaker ideology imposed itself after ca. 2500 BC (ca. 2425 BC for Sion and Aosta), quickly and violently if we take the destruction of stelae by incoming groups as a representation of the wider social and cultural struggle between groups, which ended in the overthrowing of early Beaker peoples by the new immigrants (Harrison and Heyd 2007).

This province is associated with the rivers draining into the Po south of the Alps, and had thus links to the East Bell Beaker group to the north through the Danube; to the northern groups through the Rhine; and to western and south-western groups through the Rhône. Remedello societies of the north and Rinaldone in the west, heirs of the warrior ideology that had expanded earlier with the Yamna package (see *§VI.2. The Transformation of Europe*), were more receptive to Beaker novelties. Although the Alps have been considered a natural and cultural barrier since Roman times, they worked during prehistory as a bridge between central European and Mediterranean cultures (Harrison and Heyd 2007).

Northern Italy belonged thus from the very beginning, together with the East Bell Beaker groups, and possibly also the Middle-Elbe Saale region, to the core area of the expanding Classical Bell Beaker phenomenon (after ca. 2500 BC), reflected in the appearance of distinctive ornaments and fittings of polished shell to the south. However, after this disruptive and expansive Middle Bell Beaker period, later phases of the Bell Beaker culture reflect a reduction in range and volume. The Northern Italian EBA (starting ca.

2300/2200 BC) began probably delayed compared with south-central Hungary, through connections with innovations and ideas from the Adriatic. Communities showed new equipment, burial rules (the first proper individual graves), and material culture including globular cups and bone, shell, and metal jewellery, apart from *pithoi* graves of children (Heyd 2013).

Northern Italian groups resumed then their traditional contacts with the south and west, continuing customs of Beaker burials, as well as new fashions of dress and ornament introduced from a wide area of northern Italy, especially the Polada culture, which shows the beginning of its classical stage by the introduction of wetland and lakeside settlement sites ca. 2100 BC, with rich metal inventory including typical flanged axes, triangular daggers, and various forms of jewellery (Heyd 2013).

Polada marks an increase in population and settlement, and a remarkable expansion starting around the southern banks of Lake Garda and the small lakes in the neighbouring morainic hills, eventually covering large areas of northern Italy and influencing neighbouring regions. Such an increase results in two main settlement models: pile–dwellings and *Terramara* villages (*Palafitte* and *Terramare*), the latter probably representing an expansion of settlements to the plain, into the Po, southern Trentino, eastern Lombardy, and eastern Veneto (Nicolis 2013).

This culture shows a mix of East Bell Beakers from the Danubian cultures and a local substratum which continues the previous Copper Age traditions, like the Remedello culture. In the later phase, Polada was also affected by Danubian cultures, and a real population influx has been suggested, given the evidence from Gata–Wieselburg group in sites of eastern Veneto. Metallurgy was similar to the Únětice cultural area. In the east-central Alps, the Inner Alpine group inherits characteristics from the late Alpine EBA—such as wing-head pins (a variant of the disc-head pins), and pottery with plastic cordon applications—displaying a noticeable influence from the Terramare complex throughout the MBA and LBA (della Casa 2013).

Figure 49. Terramara di Montale (Modena), abitazioni ricostruite. Photograph by Reever, image from Wikipedia.

Simple graves, often primary burials, are normally grouped in small cemeteries, but there are examples of double or triple burials. Tombs are covered by stones, and bodies placed in a flexed position on one side, orientated in a north–south direction or vice versa (Nicolis 2013). The offerings continued in these sites ca. 2100–1850, including lighting fires and piling more stones on previously used cairns, but burials were remade again around 1800 BC. All these developments point probably to an emphasis on the legendary antiquity of a lineage, where it was important for the EBA elite to be associated physically with the founding members of the community, even if that connection was not real (Harrison and Heyd 2007).

Pile–dwellings were built both in the water, on the lake bank, and on dry land, and there is continuity of settlements—with minor shifts—in the original region of Polada until the Late Bronze Age. During the Middle Bronze Age, the Terramara phenomenon expanded, starting ca. 1700/1650 BC, with large settlements with banks and fortifications spreading from the Po plain south to the Apennines, constituting a genuine colonisation of areas that peaks ca. 1550/1500 BC (Bernabò Brea 2009).

Materials, especially pottery, belong to the late Poladian and pile-dwelling periods, the Grotta Nuova finds from central Italy, and to a lesser extent elements from the western area. Structures built directly on the ground with apses belong more to the peninsular than to the plain, where houses are built on raised platforms, as in the pile-dwelling settlements (Cardarelli 2009). Settlements were small (1-2 ha), built on dry land, housing 100–200 people, and new farming techniques are seen, such as plough pulled by animals, crop rotation, and stabling.

Social organisation includes elite areas within individual settlements, but no hierarchical distinctions are made between the different settlements, so they probably formed *confederations* of villages (Bernabò Brea 2009). During the MBA and LBA, only cremation is used in the west, but it is combined with inhumation in the east. Remains of the dead were placed in urns, generally covered with a bowl and placed in small shallow pits, without burnt earth, and with scarce goods if any. In the case of inhumations, bodies were placed in flat graves, usually in a supine position (Nicolis 2013).

The LBA or Peschiera phase (1350/1300–1200 BC) shows the maximum development of pile–dwelling villages, with true centres of production and commerce in bronze objects, as well as the standardisation of objects and circulation of metal products on a continental scale. At the same time, settlements begin to differentiate within the context of a population increase and economic development, with some villages being abandoned, others extended (up to 20 ha, housing up to 1000 people), and others constructed anew. Dwellings are structured like 'pile–dwellings on dry land'(Bernabò Brea 2009) and fortifications became imposing. Stability of the Terramara system was based on management of space, bartering, production and social relations (Nicolis 2013).

The Terramara system of pile–dwelling collapsed ca. 1200 BC, with the political instability brought about in the whole Mediterranean area. It has been traditionally argued that the radical depopulation of vast sectors of the Po Plain and the appearance of elements from the Po Plain/Terramare tradition in central-southern Italy in diminishing proportions resulted from the dispersal of groups, numerous or otherwise, of Terramare peoples from the north (Cardarelli 2009).

Some areas, like large valleys around Verona and the Po delta, were not affected by the crisis, and villages were relocated along main rivers and economies reorganised around complex production systems and wide-ranging trading networks. Mycenaean sherds are found in this area, probably from centres in Apulia which had Aegean craftsmen, or directly from the Greek mainland. In eastern Trentino, metallurgical production on a proto-industrial scale is seen ca. 1200–1000 BC, linked to the Luco/Laugen culture typical of the Alpine environment, and connected through centres of the Po plain with the Mediterranean (Nicolis 2013).

The Final Bronze Age shows the emergence of Frattesina in the north-eastern Po plain, the paramount centre of craftsmanship and trade, continuing the Terramare–Palafitte tradition on a much larger scale. Glass and antler artefacts, objects of bronze, faience, amber, and elephant ivory prove the central economic role of this site in a Cypriot–Phoenician trade system (Heyd 2013).

VIII.2.2. Central Italy

In central Italy (Etruria and neighbouring regions), the Early Bronze Age is defined Bell Beaker pottery of a style similar to the Polada culture. Settlements include open-air sites, along with rock shelters and caves that were used also for collective burial and cult practices. Pastoralism plays an important role, complemented by agriculture and hunting (Bietti Sestieri 2013).

Pre-Apennine facies dominate in central Italy ca. 2000–1500 BC. Settlements include open-air villages along the Adriatic and Tyrrhenian coasts in connection with lakes, while natural caves are used for settlement and collective burials featuring inhumation and cult practices. Subterranean multiple chamber tombs are considered exclusive to elite kin-groups. Pottery includes carinated or rounded cups and bowls, biconical or ovoid jugs, ovoid jars, and truncated-conical bowls. Grotta Nuova pottery appears in the earliest layers of the Capitoline Hill settlement in Rome. Copper ores were exploited during the Copper Age, and this activity intensifies during the Early Bronze Age, dominated by metallurgists and craftsmen who make them whole and distribute them (Bietti Sestieri 2013).

Apennine facies (Figure 50) define the final phase of the Middle Bronze Age (ca. 1500–1350 BC), and are widely distributed over the entire Italian peninsula. Pottery includes bowls, carinated and rounded cups, ovoid and biconical jars, with incised engraved decoration. Lake settlements increase, cave sites and shelters are still used in the Apennine regions and in the coastal Tyrrhenian area (Bietti Sestieri 2013).

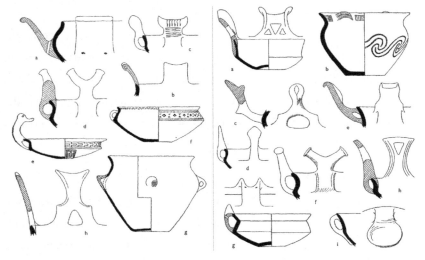

Figure 50. Characteristic Apennine pottery with northern (left) and southern (right) forms. Modified from Trump (2014).

The Late Bronze Age (starting ca. 1350 BC) shows the widespread distribution of Sub-Apennine pottery (until ca. 1000 BC)—with varied cups and bowls with plastic protrusions on handles—associated initially with Mycenaean pottery. In Etruria, the demographic crisis of Terramare is evidenced by the depopulation of the plains, although settlements continue in the Apennine area. Cremation cemeteries appear in Lazio and Apulia, with a close relationship with Palafitte–Terramare communities of the north, marked by formal features of northern type in the local pottery, which may signal the interest of northern communities in mining resources and access to the Adriatic. This period sees the widespread adoption of Peschiera bronzes—violin–bow fibulae, daggers, and flange-hilted swords—found in the Balkans, Aegean, Cyprus and the Levant. Use of metal intensifies, with bronze tools needed for all productive activities. Palafitte–Terramare appear up to southern Italy in small numbers (Bietti Sestieri 2013).

Large-scale interaction networks during the MBA and LBA between the Apennines and The Marches territories are supported in earlier times by the characteristic decorative motif of Apennine bowls, showing likely symbolic significance generically connected to family-group identities, possibly through marriage exchanges, rather than simple regional tradition. Exchange of raw materials (like flint) and perishable goods, as well as valuables like Baltic amber—shared with the Adriatic—also points to continued contacts. This close relationship is further supported by the shared mobile pastoralist economy, which may have allowed for the exploitation of nearby territories, reducing the perception of distance commonly travelled by shepherds (Moroni et al. 2019).

The Final Bronze Age facies ('Chiusi-Cetona') in Etruria shows formal similarities with north-eastern Po plain and Frattesina, with pottery decoration reminiscent of Terramare patterns. Inland settlements are mostly on hills and plateaus, and no evidence of occupation in future Villanovan centres along the Tyrrhenian coast is found. Funerary practices include small cremation cemeteries, with urns decorated with Vogelsonnenbarke ('bird-sun-boat') or birds' heads patterns. This region participated in the international trade of bronze artefacts between Frattesina to the north-east and south-western regions (Bietti Sestieri 2013).

At the Final Bronze Age–Early Iron Age transition (ca. 1200–850 BC), different groups emerge. The Picene emerge in the Marche with hill settlements near the coast, continuing the Final Bronze, and demographic growth is documented in the area. In the inland Apennine and Adriatic coastal areas, facies are initially close to Lazio and southern Etruria, but during the Early Iron Age they show a systematic connection with the Picene facies. In southern Etruria, the Proto-Villanovan pottery is characterised by engraved and plastic decoration. The settlement system aims at territorial control, and a sophisticated metal industry and trading system emerges. Funerary ritual shows the acceptance of the ideological implications of cremation, being based on the urn as the house of the deceased, connected to the destruction of the body by fire and transition to a different dimension. The Early Iron Age Villanovan, direct ancestor of the Etruscan culture, shows cultural homogeneity and synchronous emergence of central and peripheral sites (Bietti Sestieri 2013).

The ancient Lazio evolved during the Final Bronze Age under the influence of southern Etruria, shown in similarities in material culture, ritual, and settlement patterns, but this influence faded at the end of this period, probably due to the consolidation of the region's ethnocultural identity. Apparently, chiefs, priests, and possibly chiefly priests were entitled to an exclusive burial ritual, with miniature assemblages including the indicators of the main social roles: sword for military-political power; knife and a statuette in the form of an offer for religious role. During the Early Iron Age, initially territorial organisation shows a connection with Fossa–grave groups of Campania and Calabria, which probably evidences the close ethnolinguistic connection of these regions. This connection shifts later to southern Etruria, under the Etruscan influence. Cremation cemeteries appear in the region (Bietti Sestieri 2013).

VIII.2.3. Southern Italy

Chalcolithic *Laterza* facies continues up to southern Lazio until the turn of the 2nd millennium BC. Unlike Late Copper Age northern and western Italian cultures like Remedello or Rinaldone, which had already a symbolism similar to the Bell Beaker message, cultures like Conelle and Laterza in the Adriatic basin were less receptive to the new package, which resulted in a different distribution of Beaker pots. This is also visible far to the south in Sicily, where Bell Beakers established a Beaker core in the west of the island, in the previous Conca d'Oro area. Western Sicily, although not part of the core, had in the south a role of transmitter of impulses similar to the role of the Rhenish/Dutch Bell Beaker to the north (Heyd 2013).

Quite relevant for the situation of Bell Beakers in these regions is the direct exchange links of these regions with the Aegean during the Early Bronze Age. The social background is different from other Aegean-related cultures: there are less prestige goods made of precious metal, no direct evidence of local elites, and burial traditions show collective graves are found in artificial grottos and caves. In the period 3000–2500 BC different single burials are seen from regional cultures related to Gaudo, Rinaldone or Remedello, but they are absent ca. 2500–2000 BC (Heyd 2013).

All these findings range from traded goods to prestige objects to imitations, and seem to have been mediated by certain important ports, such as the Steno site on the Ionian island of Levkas, which shows southern Greek mainland and Cyclades objects that appeared later in the Adriatic, and in Apulia and Sicily. Chronologically, Sicily would have been affected in the 25th century BC, Apulia and Cetina in the 24th c., and northern Italy (Polada) in the 23rd c. while the western half of Italy was influenced starting in the 22nd c. (Heyd 2013).

Numerous Proto-Apennine settlements are found along the Adriatic and Ionian coasts, particularly concentrated on the south-eastern regions. The earliest Mycenaean pottery occurs in the late Proto-Apennine period of coastal sites, while the Tyrrhenian area maritime contacts are more limited. Interior sites are few and concentrated in the control of natural routes. Funerary practices include inhumation and multiple or collective burials, with burial complexes including caves and underground chamber tombs, which are seen as correlates of the individual elite kin-groups of the local communities, emphasising the principal role of weapon-bearers (Bietti Sestieri 2013).

Metal artefacts are rare until the end of the Middle Bronze Age, which points to the lack of relevance for local economies. Trans-Adriatic contacts are evidenced by the widespread presence of Bronzes in northern Apulia, paralleled in the eastern Adriatic region, but absent in the south, while Mycenaean pottery is absent in the north and present in the south. This points to a specialised exchange system through the eastern Mediterranean. The final phase of the Middle Bronze Age shows a deterioration of the local system of coastal trading in the west, scarcity of Apenine settlements, and sites with Sicilian–Aeolian Thapsos–Milazzese facies, which point to the occupation of marginal areas of the peninsula by inhabitants from the Aeolian Islands. In the centre and east, the Aegean presence intensifies, with the association of local *impasto* with imported Mycenaean pottery. However, no colonisation can be seen, but rather small groups of Aegean sailors integrating within the local system of trade and manufacture of metals and amber. There is continuity of funerary practices (Bietti Sestieri 2013).

During the Late Bronze Age, Aegean contacts intensify. Abundant Mycenaean pottery – imported closed vessels (probably with varied contents) – are traded. Mycenaean pottery of south Italian production is found up to northern Italy, while eastern Mediterranean cultures look for look for metal and amber. Local bronze artefacts of Aegean type indicate the presence of foreign groups, a trend observed up to the Final Bronze Age. The Final Bronze Age and Iron Age (1200–720 BC) start with the invasion of the Aeolian islands and parts of north-eastern Sicily from the southern Tyrrhenian coast, following a deterioration of relationship. Local Proto-Geometric pottery and wheel-turned dolia are technological legacy of Aegean contacts, with coastal sites being prevalent—with trans-Adriatic routes still in use, and close Balkan connection with Apulia—while inland settlements control territory and long-distance communication (Bietti Sestieri 2013).

VIII.2.4. Sicily, Malta and the Aeolian islands

The first contacts with Sicily are seen ca. 2750–2500 BC, but most exchanges must have taken place during the peak of the Early Helladic IIb period (ca. 2500–2200 BC), with different objects made of precious metals found in graves. The third period, after ca. 2200 BC, saw further Aegean imports, in lesser quantity. Different from these are the trans-Adriatic contacts in central and northern Italy with the western Balkans, related to Cetina (see *§VIII.9.1. Cetina*). The Tarxien cremation cemetery in Malta, with a description similar to that of a tumulus, also shows a Mediterranean connection in small finds, metal artefacts, and pottery links. Malta also belonged to the marginal area of Bell Beaker presence, against the cultural background of the 'cremation cemetery' of Tarxien, V-buttons made of Spondylus shell and horizontal band-like decorated beaker-like vessels (Heyd 2013).

The Early Bronze Age in Sicily (ca. 2200–1500 BC), represented by the Castelluccio culture, is characterised by a system of coastal trade involving a great part of the central Mediterranean, which shows similar material culture: handmade *impasto* pottery—jars, high-handled carinated cups, open vessels on a high conical stand—with incised decoration and similar shapes, related to the local Copper Age tradition and to the Middle Helladic matt-painted pottery production. Other local groups are also visible in Sicily and Malta: Rodì-Tindari-Vallelunga (RTV) shows similarities with Proto-Apennine pottery from the mainland, with sites found in the Tyrrhenian coast of Calabria; Moarda, in the west and sporadically in the south, shows pottery clearly related to Bell Beaker pottery with Castelluccio influence. Systematic trade routes with the Aegean and eastern Mediterranean are apparent ca. 1700–1500 BC (Bietti Sestieri 2013).

The Early Bronze Age shows an organisation in small villages, showing some degree of functional specialisation and interdependence, joined to form clusters, probably corresponding to tribal groups. Coast and inland, as well as hills, plateaus and plains are occupied, with caves and open-air settlements adapted to the local environment for their subsistence economy. Local goods are mixed with exotic objects obtained through the trade system. Funerary rite is inhumation, usually multiple or collective, with special features possibly showing competition between kin-groups in the same community (Bietti Sestieri 2013).

The Middle Bronze Age is defined by the Thapsos–Milazzese culture in Sicily, the Aeolian Islands and the coast of Calabria, featuring handmade impasto with no painted decoration, showing formal and functional similarities to the previous RTV culture with local imitations of Mycenaean and Cypriot pottery. This period coincides with the maximum intensity of Aegean contacts and east Mediterranean–Cypriot participation. A decrease in the number of sites and concentration in the east-central zone in Sicily shows a more centralised political and territorial organisation, with dwelling structures characterised by circular or rectangular huts with stone foundations. Tombs are plain *grotticelle* (Bietti Sestieri 2013).

Aeolian villages, a cultural extension of Sicily in this period, are small, and trade is concentrated with northern regions of the peninsula to procure raw materials and artefacts. Increasingly hostile relationships are seen in the coast of Calabria with the establishment of Thapsos–Milazzese groups, coinciding with a decrease in local Apennine occupation and a decrease in Apennine pottery in Sicily, which has been interpreted as raids carried out in the mainland involving seizing objects and potentially people (Bietti Sestieri 2013).

The Late Bronze Age (starting ca. 1250 BC) is marked by an invasion from the mainland, probably the coast of Calabria. The Ausonian I culture, on the north-eastern zone, follows the Sub-Apennine culture, and there is a limited continuity of contacts and trade with the Aegean. A small amount of Proto-Villanovan pottery can also be seen, with some evidence of cremation and typical Proto-Villanovan urnfield. The Pantalica culture continues the Thapsos–Milazzese tradition, of Aegean influence, moving from the eastern to the southern coast and the interior. Mediterranean trade gradually shifts from the Aegean focus to the eastern Mediterranean, and to Sardinia as the far west post. Long-distance trade systems connecting northern Italy with the eastern Mediterranean remain in place (Bietti Sestieri 2013).

The Final Bronze Age–Early Iron Age transition (1100–800 BC) is defined by the Ausonian II culture, showing a local elaboration integrating formal and functional features of peninsular and Sicilian origin, with a systematic, strong connection to the Calabrian coast regarding metal extraction (from mining resources of Calabria) and production. Pantalica tradition survives in the west with the S. Angelo Muxaro group (Bietti Sestieri 2013).

viii.2. Italic peoples and Etruscans

viii.2.1. Italic and Venetic peoples

The admixture of northern Italian Bell Beakers with female locals is evident in three samples from Gui, Parma (ca. 2200–1930 BC), where a female and a male sample (of hg. R1b1a1b1a1a2-P312) show Steppe ancestry (ca. 26-30%), whereas another female, buried together with the male, shows a common ancestry with Neolithic and Copper Age European populations (Olalde et al. 2018).

Pre-Celtic and Proto-Italic languages must have been spoken to the north and south of the Alps, respectively, still in close contact for the short common Italo-Celtic period, potentially through the known contacts of northern Italy with Danubian cultures. The strongest genetic connection found between both communities to date lies in the presence of R1b1a1b1a1a2b-U152 subclades: R1b1a1b1a1a2b1-L2 lineages (TMRCA ca. 2500 BC) are found widespread in ancient Bell Beaker samples of central and western Europe, including Iberia, while other R1b1a1b1a1a2b-U152 (xR1b1a1b1a1a2b1-L2) lineages are prevalent in certain Italian regions, probably due to later regional bottlenecks.

R1b1a1b1a1a2b1-L2 lineages are found mainly in the north-east, potentially associated with ancient Venetic-speaking peoples, but they are possibly due to later Celtic expansions, since a spread of early eastern Urnfield cultures from Transdanubia is attested in the Po Valley (Váczi 2013). On the other hand, R1b1a1b1a1a2b3-Z56 lineages (TMRCA ca. 2200 BC) are prevalent in the west, and in modern west European populations, hence probably associated with ancient Italic-speaking peoples (and their later spread with the Roman expansion). Other R1b1a1b1a1a2b-U152 lineages also present in Italy, like R1b1a1b1a1a2b2-Z36, those with the Z192 mutation, and other basal lineages, have an ancient split time coinciding with the spread of East Bell Beakers (TMRCA ca. 2500 BC), and cannot be associated with specific regions, which makes any connection with ancient linguistic communities speculative at this moment.

Based on the current lack of data supporting an ancient genetic connection in terms of modern lineages, the early Italo-Celtic community was possibly based on cultural diffusion between communities to the north (Pre-Celts) and south (Pre-Italo-Venetians) of the Alps, visible in archaeology (see above). Similarly, the separation of Venetic from the common Italic trunk may have been quite early, with continuous contacts between both communities allowing for the spread of common innovations (Figure 51).

While Bronze Age samples of west-central Italy show a clear homogenisation of the genetic pool, with a shift in the PCA towards central Europe (away from the previous CHG/Iran Neolithic influence), and thus close to the modern Sardinian cluster, the few investigated Iron Age samples from the Republican period (ca. 700–20 BC) show a widespread genetic cluster encompassing the modern Italian ones, overlapping North Italian (ca. 60%) or South Italian/Sicilian (ca. 40%) clusters. The arrival or increase of EHG-, Levant Neolithic-, or CHG/IN-related ancestry in samples from this period suggest influence from previous population movements during the LBA from the north or through the Mediterranean, respectively. The Imperial Period shows influence from CHG/IN-related ancestry, but only sporadically Levant Neolithic[21].

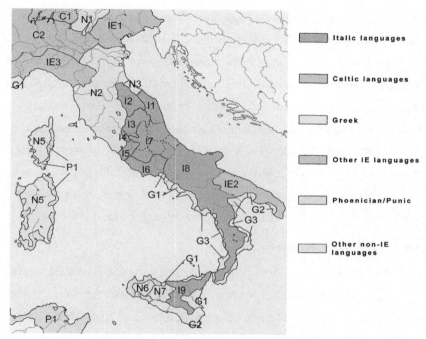

Figure 51. Languages of pre-Roman Italy and nearby islands: N1, Rhaetian; N2, Etruscan; N3, North Picene (Picene of Novilara); N5, Nuragic; N6, Elymian; N7, Sicanian; C1, Lepontic; C2, Gaulish; I1, South Picene; I2, Umbrian; I3, Sabine; I4, Faliscan; I5, Latin; I6, Volscian and Hernican; I7, Central Italic (Marsian, Aequian, Paeligni, Marrucinian, Vestinian); I8, Oscan, Sidicini, Pre-Samnite; I9, Sicel; IE1, Venetic; IE2, Messapian; IE3, Ligurian; G1-G2-G3, Greek dialects (G1: Ionic, G2: Aeolic, G3: Doric); P1, Punic. Image modified from Davius Sanctex.

The substantial genetic impact of the Roman conquest in Iberia can be seen in the shift of sampled Iberians from the Iron Age to the Classical period, including ten individuals from the site of L'Esquerda in the north-east (7th–8th

---

[21] Report from oral communication *A 12,000-year Genetic History of Rome and the Italian Peninsula*, by Hannah Moots, the 6th February 2019, at the Archaeology Center of Stanford University, about an unpublished study of 134 ancient samples from Lazio and surrounding areas spanning 12,000 years from the Upper Palaeolithic to the Renaissance.

c.), who show a central/eastern Mediterranean ancestry (ca. 25%) and corresponding shift in the PCA cluster, also observed in present-day Iberians outside of the Basque area. Interestingly, the first R1b1a1b1a1a2c-S461 lineage sampled in Iberia comes from the Roman site of Mas Gassol (ca. AD 200–500), likely representing population movements across the empire, including peoples from the northern Atlantic Façade (Olalde et al. 2019).

Preliminary reports from a forthcoming paper support this shift of Iberian samples from the Iron Age to the Roman and post-Roman period, closer to Iron Age samples from central Italy, which in turn show—like Etruscans—a position intermediate between Sardinians and central Europeans (see below). The reported Iron Age samples from Rome show a wide cluster including, possibly divisible in those of modern North and South Italians (Grugni et al. 2019). This also supports reports of how the city of Rome grew from a small city to become a mosaic of inhabitants from across the Mediterranean empire.

viii.2.2. Elymians and Sicels

A Bell Beaker sample from Per, western Sicily (ca. 2500–1900 BC) shows most of its ancestry from a NWAN source (ca. 93%) with few WHG-related ancestry, and none derived from the steppe (Olalde et al. 2018). The incursion of Steppe ancestry in Sicily (ca. 9%) appears only in Early Bronze Age samples from ca. 2300 BC on, coupled with the appearance of typical Bell Beaker R1b1a1b1a1a2-P312 lineages, four out of eight reported samples, with the other four being J-M304, at least one J2a1-L26 (Fernandes et al. 2019).

Two of the individuals of hg. R1b1a1b1a1a2-P312 (ca. 2300–2100 BC) are outliers, with ca. 40% and ca. 23% Steppe ancestry. At least two of the Bell Beaker lineages are R1b1a1b1a1a2a1-Z195, found in Iberian Bronze Age individuals. The origin of these Indo-European speakers in the north-west Mediterranean is further supported by the best fit of their source population found in Bell Beakers of high Steppe ancestry from Iberia, and those sampled from France (Fernandes et al. 2019).

Iranian-related ancestry is found in Sicily by the Middle Bronze Age (ca. 1800–1500 BC), with a consistent shift toward Mycenaeans in the PCA. Specifically, two of the three sampled individuals can only be fit with Iran Neolithic (ca. 15–18%) apart from NWAN- and WHG-related ancestry, with good fits obtained with Minoans. Of the two reported haplogroups, one from the Aegean-related group is G2a2b2a1a1c1a-Z1903, and another continuing the previous cluster is R1b1a1b1a1a2-P312. In the Late Bronze Age (ca. 1450–900 BC), a further incursion of Steppe-related ancestry (ca. 15%) is found, even though the two reported samples are one G2a2b2a1a1c1a-Z1903, and the other G2a2b2a1a1c1a2-FGC46572 (Fernandes et al. 2019).

Genetic shifts in Sicily reflect the complex history of the island during the Bronze Age, as described in archaeology. The Elymians represent the autochthonous people inhabiting west Sicily in the archaic period, and their fragmentary language is invariably considered Indo-European, most likely a Late Indo-European dialect (Marchesini 2012), probably not related to Greek (since Greek settlers would have recognized it). Given the findings of population genomics coupled with archaeology of west Sicily, it is quite possible that they represent the remnant population from the Sicilian EBA group, and their language would be related to the north-west Mediterranean (see below *viii.3. Ligurians and Iberians*).

The continued contacts of Sicily with the East Mediterranean are reflected particularly in the Middle Bronze Age, where archaeological contacts with the Aegean are more intense. The increase in Steppe ancestry in the Late Bronze Age is probably coincident with the arrival of Sicel-speaking peoples, which supports the close relationship of their language to Italic. Even though the chronological and regional transect of the available samples is limited, data seems to support the presence of a single language and writing culture from ca. 5th c. BC on, with several varieties roughly divided with archaeological cultures between the north-eastern part (more frequently subjected to innovations owing to contacts with other Italic dialects) and the southern one.

There is thus no linguistic or genetic reason to support a distinction between the *Sicels* and *Sicani*[22] (Poccetti 2012).

The term Sicanian as Pre-Indo-European remains thus a useful resource for the oldest stratum, geographically overlaid by the arrival of Indo-Europeans. This substrate does not survive into the 1st millennium BC, and there are no Sicanian inscriptions, but some recurring suffixes and topo-hydronymy may be classified as *Sicanian*, with a potential typological resemblance to Mediterranean names from Tartessus to Asia Minor, and in particular to the Aegean or 'Pre-Greek' toponymy (Simkin 2012).

viii.2.3. Etruscans

Preliminary reports from a forthcoming paper shows Etruscan Iron Age samples cluster close to Picentes, Samnites, and Umbri. This ancient Etruscan cluster appears to be intermediate between Central European and EEF populations, and in particular surrounded by modern Tuscans and North Italians (more Central European-like), Iberian Iron Age, modern Sardinians, and Iron Age Romans. The few reported Etruscans to date also cluster close to Italian Tuscans, but more shifted towards Sardinians (Ávila-Arcos 2015). While Etruscans may show the described LBA impact from the Eastern Mediterranean, the finding of one outlier closer to Central European Bell Beakers may show the described impact of an EHG-related population, potentially through Urnfield-related migrations.

---

[22] The term *Sicanian* as Pre-Indo-European remains thus a useful resource for the oldest stratum, geographically overlaid by the arrival of Indo-Europeans. This substrate certainly did not survive into the 1st millennium BC, and there are no Sicanian inscriptions or examples of the supposed language. However, some recurring suffixes (e.g. *-ssus*, *-ssa*) and topo-hydronymy may be classified as *Sicanian*, with a potential typological resemblance to Mediterranean names from Tartessus to Asia Minor, and in particular to the Aegean or 'Pre-Greek' toponymy (Simkin 2012).

The traditional association of Etruscans and the Tursēnoi of Lemnos in the Aegean seems supported by recent genetic research on the frequent contacts of Mediterranean peoples during the Bronze Age, and it is likely derived from a recent invasion of the Italian Peninsula by eastern peoples from Asia Minor, which justifies the recent Near Eastern cultural and linguistic influence of Etruscans (Magness 2001), as well as the indirect influence of the former in Latin and Osco-Umbrian through the expansion of the latter. The arrival of Tyrrhenian speakers may have been an infiltration of small elite groups with few material objects, which may be as difficult to pinpoint exactly as that of Proto-Greeks in the southern Balkans (Beekes 2003).

Nevertheless, it seems that the Proto-Villanova culture shows a break with the previous Bronze Age Apennine culture ca. 1200 BC (Briquel 1999; Torelli 2000), with Villanovan territory being mostly coincident with the later Etruscan-speaking zone, and no clear cultural break is seen between both cultures. This possibly implies the arrival of foreign peoples displacing or dominating Umbrians on their homeland around the River Umbro, with a timing fitting the famine among Tursēnoi in the Aegean, and the turmoil involving Sea Peoples (Beekes 2003). Increasing contacts between southern and central Italy and southern Greek mainland from the 13th c. BC on has been detected in terms of material culture, migrants, and also a potential transfer of livestock such as pigs (Meiri et al. 2019).

The language of Etruscans would then be closely related to that of the ancient Minoans. The concentration of J2a1b-M67 subclades in central-west and north-west Italians, with lesser presence in Provence and in northern Corsica (Di Cristofaro et al. 2018), may be associated with this migration, because haplogroup J2a1-L26 is found in Anatolian Neolithic-related populations. Even though this haplogroup is also found among Early European farmers from central Europe, the only ancient J2a1b-M67 subclade reported to date in Europe comes from Ludas-Varjú-dűlő (ca. 1200 BC), belonging to the Kyjatice group of the Urnfield culture (Gamba et al. 2014).

Since the Urnfield culture is also associated with the expansion of the Villanova culture, it is possible that this or similar contemporary samples of hg. J2a1b-M67 were associated with other expanding Tyrsenian peoples like the Raeti, from the central Alps, although this is too speculative at this moment. Based on modern populations, the diffusion of J2a1b-M67 lineages in Italy, with variance and coalescent time values comparable to those of the Middle East, has been described as potentially related to the 'Maritime Trojan Culture' involving the western Anatolian mainland and the eastern Aegean Sea. The high microsatellite variation age of J2a1b-M67 in Volterra, located in the core area of ancient Etruria, supports the ancestral source of the Etruscan gene pool in Asia Minor (Grugni et al. 2018).

A recent Anatolian connection was reported by examining mtDNA in modern populations of present day Tuscany (Brisighelli et al. 2009), but no major shift can be seen in the maternal ancestry of this region across 50 centuries, from the Eneolithic to modern Italians. The higher maternal diversity of Tuscany compared to neighbouring populations has been accumulating likely due to incoming peoples with a consistent social and sex (i.e. male) bias (Leonardi, Sandionigi, et al. 2018). The presence of Middle Eastern ancestry particularly in southern Italian and Sardinian populations, as a varying mixture of WHG, NWAN, CHG/IN and North African components depending on the specific region (Raveane et al. 2018), cannot be properly interpreted without access to a proper ancient DNA temporal and geographical transect.

An alternative possibility for Etruscans includes a resurge of a previous linguistic community, based on the potentially recent Chalcolithic migrations from Anatolia to the Italian Peninsula through southern Europe observed in the samples from Remedello (Kilinc et al. 2016). This situation would be therefore similar to the expansion of indigenous non-Indo-European languages in Iberia, in spite of the almost complete male population replacement. However, the close relationship with the population of Lemnos would require a movement of peoples in the opposite direction, which is not supported by the current archaeological and genetic investigation (Beekes 2003).

VIII.3. Mediterranean EEBA Province

VIII.3.1. El Argar

In south-east Iberia, the 22nd century BC sees the emergence of new residential, productive, and funerary practices known as "El Argar", a highly hierarchical and integrated regional polity. Its culture does not show typical Bell Beaker pottery, specialised flint production, decorated stone, round dwellings with stone foundations, walled or ditched enclosures, collective burial rites, or any other local Iberian or Central European Chalcolithic feature (Risch et al. 2015). Amber, for example, loses its relevant social value as a marker of identity in the Argaric burial norm (Murillo-Barroso and Montero-Ruiz 2017).

Argaric communities stand out as a complete ignorance or fundamental rejection of the meaning and ideology of these objects, probably the consequence of a rejection of the incoming foreign population with Bell Beaker symbology, and thus also a different language and *Weltanschauung* (Risch et al. 2015). Despite this discontinuity with Iberian Chalcolithic traditions, Argaric cultures continue the tradition of linen textiles of Los Millares, connecting it to the previous Chalcolithic population of south-east Iberia (Marin Aguilera et al. 2019).

This culture brings a more regionalised system of influence; a complex settlement organisation and architecture, with hill forts ca. 1–6 ha as focus, occupied and expanded over the next 650 years; specific intramural rite in cists, rock cut tombs, large pottery vessels (*pithoi*), and pits, with funerary contexts corresponding at least to three social classes during its economic peak; large array of macro-lithic tools, but limited set of metal weapons, tools and ornaments; highly standardised and finely burnished pottery production. The Argaric settlements become complex urban or proto-urban centres (Risch et al. 2015).

Its material culture shows new bone, antler, and ivory working techniques and artefacts. Flint arrowheads and blade production disappear completely, while flint was used almost exclusively for the preparation of sickle blades. Palmela and leaf-shaped projectile points continue, suggesting the use of arrows armed with metal tips or bone points. A more developed arrow technology is also suggested by sandstone polishers with a central groove, used for shaping or sharpening of bone or metal tools, possibly also as arrow shaft straighteners. All this suggest an increased precision of arrow shooting, probably related to combat rather than hunting (Risch et al. 2015).

A whole new set of macro-lithic tools appear related to the new economy: elongated narrow type of grinding slab with slightly convex transversal profile, operated with wooden manos, enables the production of finer flour in less time; a cylindrical polisher made of slate or schist to separate honey from beeswax; tools related to metal production and maintenance, such as moulds of fine sandstone for axes, awls, and ingots, or metalworking hammers; etc. The appearance of these metalworking tools in male burials supports the social and economic value of this activity in the new social and economic context (Ache et al. 2017).

Single or double burials became the most common funerary ritual in El Argar, where communal burials—typical of the previous Iberian Chalcolithic cultures, before the arrival of East Bell Beakers—disappeared. Old customs were gradually replaced by the placement of tombs underneath the settled area rather than on its margins, the use of carefully built burials (contrasting with poor Final Copper Age burials), and including new offerings alongside the body, such as metal artefacts, halberds and riveted daggers, and well-manufactured pottery, depending on the social class. Silver and gold appear first as metal ornaments in the tombs of the elite, interpreted as an example of the differential access to metal ornaments in the Argaric society, with copper and bronze ornaments becoming more frequent after ca. 1800 BC (Murillo-Barroso and Montero-Ruiz 2017). This change in essential social customs further support the emergence of a new social order, dominated by a form of power within the first stages of a state organisation (Risch et al. 2015).

El Argar achieved a dominant position over resources and communication routes including neighbouring societies, as reflected in a preference for settlements on protected promontories, a socially selective burial ritual within the living space, and the movement of important raw materials like copper, silver, or ivory. Hilltop settlements are usually smaller than 0.5 ha, with a demographic density estimated as similar to El Argar settlements. These settlements share the use of plain pottery, as well as individual graves under some of the dwellings, with no apparent restrictions of sex or age (Risch et al. 2015).

It seems that the new system brought about a stabilisation of settlements and a subsequent increase in population and production. Argaric-like groups dominated over centres of communal storage and production, starting what seems a violent expansion ca. 2150–1900 BC into neighbouring regions— including La Mancha, the east coast, and western Andalucia—which do not display a comparable degree of social exploitation as the core regions. Smaller groups expanded further ca. 1700–1500 BC, northward to Valencia and eastward into the Guadalquivir River region, where they tried to impose their funerary practices and political relations (Figure 52), without attaining the intensity or stability of El Argar core territory (Lull, Micó, Herrada, et al. 2013).

The late Argaric subsistence production was dominated by extensive barley cultivation, which had a severe environmental impact in the most arid region of the Iberian Peninsula. Due to the dependence on such poor-quality crops, access to animal fat and honey became crucial, with evidence showing elites consuming this kind of high energy foods, e.g. through the separation of honey from beeswax through "pressed honey" method, using specialised tools made for this task (Ache et al. 2017).

The economic and social hegemony of El Argar ended ca. 1550 BC, apparently by internal forces, as suggested by the suppression of its ideological superstructure—end of traditional funerary practices—and its economic system, probably because of a subsistence crisis caused by the over-exploitation of the environment. In the southern peninsula, ca. 50% of upland settlements were abandoned. Post-Argaric societies tried to maintain a vertical system of production but on a local scale, returning to systems of self-sufficiency, with regionally diverse stockbreeding, agriculture, and metallurgy. Specialised workshops for cereals and textiles disappear, and pottery copies decorative motifs originally from Cogotas I style. There are some traces of regional centres of power with local, perhaps hereditary aristocracy, controlling interregional communication and centralising surpluses (Lull, Micó, Herrada, et al. 2013).

After the Late Bronze Age, most settlements were abandoned, and small settlements—some on hilltops—comprising huts with oval bases made of stone or mud-brick are found, with evidence supporting that they were specialised in stockbreeding. Eventually, near the 1st millennium BC, new hilltop centres appear, or existing settlements were reorganised, which evidence the emergence of specialised metallurgy. The south-western corner becomes a producer and consumer of Atlantic metals and metals from Sierra Morena, and possibly Sardinia (Lull, Micó, Herrada, et al. 2013).

Figure 52. Settlement patterns in Iberia between c. 2200 and 1550 BC. Symbols simulate the form and density of settlement based on information derived from survey and excavation rather than indicating real locations. Notice, around the Argaric influence territory, the higher density of hilltop settlements (black triangles) and fortified settlements (blank triangles). Map by S. Gill and Lull, Micó, Herrada, et al. (2013).

VIII.3.2. North-West Mediterranean

Diverse pre-Beaker traditions overlapped in the north-western Mediterranean region, such as the Treïlles (3300–2800 BC) and the Véraza groups (3500–2500 BC). Lowland pit sites and cave occupations were common, and semi-nomadic farming was the main subsistence economy. There is no evidence of local metallurgy. During the Bell Beaker phase, Old Neolithic monuments were still reused; selected dead were interred with standardised mortuary assemblages in pits adapted for the purpose or individual cists (either laid flat, semi-flexed, or in very contracted positions), as well as *hypogea*, or caves. The first gold and copper smelting appear in the region, mainly found in funerary contexts, with its technology disconnected from the Iberian tradition. The *chaînes operatoires* and products on both sides of the Pyrenees—including Catalonia, Provence, Languedoc, and north-eastern Italy—were thus strikingly similar, with comparable atypical chemical compositions and characteristic metallic types, such as biconvex gold beads, copper tanged daggers, and breastplates (Blanco-González et al. 2018).

To the south-west, in the Middle Ebro basin, Chalcolithic groups show tumuli, multiple burial bits, megaliths, and natural caves, some later reused during the Bell Beaker phase, with settlements showing huts delimited by postholes, and elongated dug-out hearths. In Valencia, preferences continue since the Neolithic, with ditched enclosures and upland prominent sites. Burial practices show continued inhumations in pits and in caves. The Epi-Bell Beaker or late Bell Beaker fineware marks the onset of the Bronze Age ca. 2250 BC in the region. It is represented by the Arbolí, consisting of bowls with incised and impressed motifs (swags, garlands, suns, etc.), stemming from the south of the Pyrenees and reaching the Cantabrian fringe, the upper Duero, and

Alicante to the south. In the other direction, twin-bodied vessels expand from Valencia to the upper Ebro ca. 1900 BC (Blanco-González et al. 2018).

Metallurgy gains in importance, with the first bronze alloys concentrated in the Ebro / south Pyrenees area, and intense exchange networks are kept in the east Mediterranean, between groups belonging to Polada, Terramare, Únĕtice, and Rhône Basin Cultures, characterised by the production of polypod vases. Around 1600 BC, metallurgy had acquired social esteem akin to the Bell Beaker period, within a context of increasing social asymmetry evidenced by burials of metalworkers, although metallurgy is weakened in comparison with western and central European centres. There is an increase in agrarian production and sedentarisation, but mortuary customs continue to be—as in the Chalcolithic—highly varied, with cavities, orthostatic chambers and galleries, reused rock-cut caves or *hypogea*, and burials made in pits (Blanco-González et al. 2018).

This period ends with the start of the Late Bronze Age ca. 1600/1500 BC, coinciding with the appearance of the earliest Urnfield groups south of the Pyrenees, known as the Segre–Cinca I group (ca. 1650–1300 BC), showing contacts between Iberia and central Europe. It is associated with carinated button-handled vessels, akin to Italian Polada examples. Rectangular dwellings with stone foundations and the use of pottery vessels with fluted decoration (linked to the emergence of the funerary phenomenon of the Urnfields) buried in a pit along with grave goods in a pit, sometimes marked on the surface. Although this practice is found scattered in northern Portugal and the south-east, the greater density of graves in the north-east suggests that new populations may have crossed the Pyrenees bringing the Hallstatt culture, although certain previous forms of settlement and burial ritual remain (Lull, Micó, Herrada, et al. 2013). Reaching up to the Middle Ebro and Aragon, open-air nucleated sites become more frequent and stable. (Blanco-González et al. 2018).

Regions neighbouring north-east Iberia show different developments. In southern France, the funerary use of caves continues throughout the Bronze Age, with inhumations and cremations showing a more or less structure deposition, and collective family graves being also common, including small funeral monuments (mounds and/or enclosures). The Mailhacien culture shows huge cremation cemeteries. In east Iberia, however, the Bronce Mediterráneo or Iberian-Valencian Bronze Age from ca. 2200–1800 BC shows new upland permanent settlements, often fortified, probably due to the Argaric influence. Villages show rectangular dwellings with stony foundations; inhumations with burial furnishings (intramural and extramural), including dismembered human remains; agriculture with a focus on cereals and using irrigation; and an increase in settlements and human activity up to 1600 BC (Blanco-González et al. 2018). The influence of Post-Argaric settlements increases then to the north (see *§VIII.3.1. El Argar*).

VIII.3.3. Balearic Islands

The first phase of colonisation of the Balearic Islands started in Majorca ca. 2400–2300 BC, with populations probably from the north-western Mediterranean arc, judging by the affinities of its late Bell Beaker tradition with the Pyrenean style of north-eastern Iberia, Roussillon and Languedoc. Caves and rock shelters were used as settlements and occasionally as burial sites, and huts on open-air settlements were the most common construction. Settlements were occupied seasonally, and its subsistence economy was probably based on animal herding and slash–and–burn agriculture. Continuity with Iberian Bell Beakers is observed in pottery shapes (especially the typical Bell Beaker *Begleitkeramik*), bone manufacture, and funerary rites (Lull, Micó, Rihuete Herrada, et al. 2013).

During the next colonisation phase ca. 2100–1600 BC, the Epi-Bell Beaker–Dolmen archaeological group reaches Menorca and the Pine Islands. Settlements follow a similar pattern, with material culture showing pottery decorated with incised designs related to Bell Beaker style, hence 'Epi-Bell

Beaker'. The most striking change is perceived in funerary contexts, where new kinds of tombs are used: it starts with hypogea with a single circular or oval chamber, provided with a megalithic entrance, similar to Catalan late Chalcolithic and Early Bronze Age examples. Dolmens—similar to megalithic tombs in Languedoc—follow in the 19th century BC, with monuments facing west and south-west. This orientation is prevalent in monuments in Languedoc and Provence, in contrast to neighbouring regions, where monuments face south or south-east. Grave goods are scarce and are composed mainly of objects of everyday use, and human remains show no apparent pattern (Lull, Micó, Rihuete Herrada, et al. 2013).

All this data point to long-lasting contacts of the Pyrenées–Languedoc societies—of north-east Catalonia and much of Mediterranean France—with populations that settled the Balearic Islands (Sureda 2018). It is believed that advances in technology, such as production of food and metallurgy, allowed for the permanent settlement of the islands. Social violence and demographic pressure in the mainland may have been the triggering factor for the development of a safer, distant community, which is supported by the scarcity of fortifications, preference for lowland locations, absence of specialised weapons, and predominance of collective burial rites, as well as absence of gold and silver ornaments (Lull, Micó, Rihuete Herrada, et al. 2013).

The Naviform group (ca. 1600–1100 BC) is characterised by the emergence of large buildings with an elongated floor plan and Cyclopean stone walls, used for craft production, showing a moderate division of labour between buildings. This architecture coincides with the abandonment of natural caves and the appearance of new types of funerary structures alongside the previous types, with communal tombs reflecting autonomous social units. In its late phase, more diversity in the naviform pattern is seen, as well as growing relevance of bronze working and agriculture within their subsistence economy (Lull, Micó, Rihuete Herrada, et al. 2013).

The Proto-Talayotic period (ca. 1100–850 BC) represents the end of the naviform society, with settlements organised in compact urban areas, organised around a large, tall stone building possibly ancestral to the *talaiots*. Collective funerary practices continued the use of natural caves and funerary structures like *hypogea*, but also saw the emergence of the *navetas*, large stone buildings with a circular or apse-shaped plan, tombs used for the burials of up to hundreds of bodies. Grave goods become more numerous and varied, a feature shared across the islands. This unity comes to an end with the Talaiotic period, where the construction of compact settlements or *talaiots* represent the affirmation of the community rather than the celebration of the past and the ancestors at a distance from the settlements (Lull, Micó, Rihuete Herrada, et al. 2013).

VIII.3.4. Sardinia and Corsica

The Chalcolithic culture of Monte Carlo covers the whole island during the 3rd millennium BC, with an economy based on agriculture, animal husbandry, fishing, and trading with the central Mediterranean. The appearance and wide diffusion of the Bell Beaker pottery coincides with the Bonnanaro culture or Corona Moltana tradition (ca. 2200–1900 BC), and the appearance of thousands of Domus de Janas ('House of the Fairies / Witches'). Burial rituals involve monumental tombs, also with reused anthropomorphic menhirs; appearance of metal; and small number of settlements, possibly small farms over wide areas (Lo Schiavo 2013). Small, self-sufficient and autonomous groups probably dispersed throughout the territory to form single village groupings, organised along lines of kinship (Perra 2009).

In the second phase of the EBA, the limited expansion of S. Iroxi tradition evidences cultural contacts with Iberia, and especially El Argar, as seen in sword shapes, although the copper used for manufacture is local. Pottery is scarce, and settlements are unknown, but there is an explosion of local metallurgical production. There is some cultural continuity with the Nuragic period, represented strongly by the large flanged axes, very similar to a type found in the Lazio area. The shape does not change in Sardinia, though, contrary to the evolution on the mainland, which probably indicates the independent development on the island. The Sa Turricula culture shows renewed contacts with the Italian peninsula at the end of the EBA and beginning of the MBA (Lo Schiavo 2013).

The characteristic 'corridor nuraghi' or 'proto-nuraghi' and *tholos* nuraghi, together with villages, and the characteristic collective burials—and eventually worship places—called 'Giant's tombs', appear first, concentrated in the central and northern parts of the island, used as territorial markers. Metope patterns in pottery appearing slightly later. This society is interpreted as evolving from kinship-based during the previous period to communal-based, where there is a concentrated, common effort to erect great monuments in dominant positions, and there is an obvious spread of settlement nuclei (Lo Schiavo 2013).

Figure 53. Left: Nuragic density in Sardinia, from Wikipedia based on data from Kriek (2003). Right: Nuraghe, Sardinia 1600 BC. Design by Kenny Arne Lang Antonsen and Jimmy John Antonsen. From Wikipedia.

Eventually, the nuraghi evolve into a golden age within the MBA–FBA transition, with complex architecture showing multi-towered, polylobate, regular or irregular structures with stone enclosures and bastions. This needed a concentrated, communal local effort, where size, number and complexity of constructions were probably considered status symbols, showing an inherited awareness of earlier kinship tradition. Based on the expansion of monumental constructions, local communities seem to unify under a centralised power (Figure 53). The building technique and structure of tombs change into 'isodomic' constructions (in regular layers), also rising in complexity, although they remain large chambers for collective burials. Metallurgical production seems to also benefit from the new organisation. Storage silos are built inside the nuraghi, and advanced cultivation of cereals seem to have been the main subsistence economy. Characteristic 'Nuragic grey' pottery appears associated with Mycenaean pottery, and spreads through central-southern Sardinia. However, differences in pottery seem to reflect local productions, since the Nuragic Civilisation is homogenous throughout the island (Lo Schiavo 2013).

At the transition of the EBA – Early Iron Age (from ca. 11th century BC), the traditionally close connections with the Cypriot and the Agean world during the MBA shift again to the Iberian Peninsula. Territorial systems enlarge, and the ritual or religious dimension—reflected in the increasingly religious nature of the nuraghi—is used as means of expression and overcoming conflicts, reaffirming social unity, and legitimising the power of emerging groups (Perra 2009).

The funerary practice of individual inhumations in cist graves with grave goods, and shaft tombs with grave goods, begin to appear. This is probably connected with Phoenicians, Semitic peoples settling in the island and circulating copper in the form of oxhide ingots through Mediterranean routes. Contacts across the Tyrrhenian Sea with peninsular Italy intensify, strengthening their relationship, as evidenced in written sources with interconnected genealogies, mythologies, and common designations (Lo Schiavo 2013).

viii.3. Ligurians and Iberians

viii.3.1. Ligurians and Sorothaptic peoples

Bell Beaker samples from south-eastern France, from Haute-Savoie (ca. 2300 BC), of hg. R1b1a1b1a1a-L151, and Le Lauzet–Ubaye (ca. 2050 BC), of hg. R1b1a1b1a1a2b1-L2, show Steppe ancestry (50%) apart from France Middle Neolithic ancestry, indicating the presence of East Bell Beaker migrants (Olalde et al. 2018).

In Iberia, there are clear north–south and west–east clines of Central European ancestry in Iberia, with the highest values attested in the centre and north-west (around 65% to 90%), with slightly less and more variable reach in early samples from the south-west (ca. 16% to 61%), while samples from the north-east (ca. 30% to 50%) and especially the south-east around El Argar (ca. 20 to 35%) show lower values. The dates for samples with Steppe ancestry, appearing earlier in the Meseta, are also compatible with different waves that reached each region at a different pace, probably allowing for the survival of local languages in the most distant and isolated southern regions.

Early Bell Beakers from Cerdanyola, north-east Iberia (ca. 2800–2300 BC) show no Steppe ancestry and typical Neolithic haplogroups, among them one I2a1b-M436, three R1b1b-V88 (shared with earlier north-east Iberians and Sardinians), and two G2-P287. This is compatible with a late expansion of East Bell Beakers of R1b1a1b1-L23 lineages, which did eventually replace all indigenous male lines of Iberia after ca. 2000 BC. Among Bronze Age samples from the north-east (ca. 2000–1400 BC), all showing Steppe ancestry (ca. 30–50%), the four reported Y-chromosome haplogroups are R1b1a1b1a1a-L151, at least two of them R1b1a1b1a1a2a1-Z195 (Olalde et al. 2019).

The archaeological connection of Bell Beakers from the north-west Mediterranean (north-east Iberians and groups from southern France) with north Italian Bell Beakers is also supported by the expansion of R1b1a1b1a1a2b-U152 (xR1b1a1b1a1a2b1-L2) lineages, present today in west and north-west Italy, and by the expansion of R1b1a1b1a1a2a-DF27 lineages in France and (with subsequent bottlenecks) south of the Pyrenées.

Subclades particularly associated with Iberia include the consecutive subclades R1b1a1b1a1a2a1a-Z272 (TMRCA ca. 2300 BC) and R1b1a1b1a1a2a1b-Z198 (TMRCA ca. 2700 BC), both peaking in modern eastern Iberian populations (Solé-Morata et al. 2017). Later expansions of these haplogroups to the south with the Reconquista and repeopling of east and south-east Iberia by the north-eastern Iberian kingdoms do not let us reconstruct their ancient distribution without a proper sampling of ancient populations.

Ligurian is a fragmentary Indo-European language spoken in southern France and north-eastern Italy during the Iron Age. Little is known of the language, with certain phonological traits placing it likely outside the Italic or Celtic branches (Prósper 2017), but nevertheless more closely related to them than to other North-West Indo-European dialects. The Apuani tribe, bordering Etruria during Roman times, show half of the reported Y-DNA of R1b1a1b1a1a2b3-Z56 lineages[23].

Ligurian is probably the most closely related language to the ancestral Indo-European dialects spread with East Bell Beakers through ancient Liguria and north-eastern Iberia, as well as (probably) the Balearic Islands and Corsica, before the expansion of Iberian languages from south-east Iberia. The Pre-Celtic Sorothaptic language, believed to be behind certain toponyms and inscriptions around the Pyrenees (Coromines 1976), was therefore probably closely related to Ligurian.

vii.3.2. Iberians

Early samples from south-eastern Iberia also show no incursion of Steppe ancestry and continuity with Chalcolithic lineages, one non-I-M170 and two I-M170, at least one of them I2a1a2-M423. Similar to the north-east, Bronze

---

[23] Information by Richard Rocca (2018).

Age samples (ca. 2100–1000 BC) show Steppe ancestry, with those from El Argar in Cabezo Redondo and Pirulejo (ca. 2000–1500 BC) showing less Steppe ancestry (ca. 20–35%) than those on the periphery, most likely also connected to the culture (ca. 23–45%). There are at least eight R1b1a1b1a1a-L151 over nine reported haplogroups, among them one from Coveta del Frare (ca. 1840 BC) is positive for SNPs ZZ12$^+$ and BY3332$^+$ (Valdiosera et al. 2018; Olalde et al. 2019), confirms the expansion of this haplogroup also in the culture that most likely expanded Iberian languages to the north and west.

The expansion of East Bell Beakers in Iberia seems thus to have reached thus later south-eastern Iberia, with El Argar culture being preceded by a break in Chalcolithic cultural traditions, suggesting an upheaval of existing social structures or an influx of groups that cannot be distinguished from the local population at the present of genetic resolution, e.g. from south-eastern Europe (Szecsenyi-Nagy et al. 2017), possibly in part as a reaction to the spread of the Bell Beaker culture. The infiltration of Bell Beaker lineages, probably through exogamy among established chiefs of El Argar, must have led to the evident language shift in spite of the successful expansion of Yamna male lines over the indigenous ones, since ancient non-Indo-European speakers were genetically similar to Indo-European speakers (Olalde et al. 2019).

Nevertheless, one sample from Covacha del Ángel in southern Iberia (ca. 1700 BC), without clear archaeological context, shows a typical Neolithic haplogroup G2a2b2a1a1b-Z738 (formed ca. 8700 BC, TMRCA ca. 5200 BC), reported as xCTS4703 (González-Fortes et al. 2019), hence from an upper clade of a lineage widely distributed in modern European samples, which may be alternatively interpreted as a resurgence of a local population, or alternatively a haplogroup incorporated during the expansion of Central European Bell Beakers.

Proto-Iberian, probably surviving only in El Argar ca. 2000 BC, must have spread with this culture's early expansion to the west into Andalusia, to the north-west into the Meseta, and to the north into the Valencian Region, possibly representing eventually the most densely populated areas of Iberia during the Bronze Age, with the lesser proportion of Steppe ancestry being another clear data further supporting the gradual southward expansion of North-West Indo-European-speaking Bell Beakers that must have left a clear opportunity for local groups to thrive (Olalde et al. 2019).

The arrival of Celts with the Urnfield culture and their occupation of the south Pyrenees and the Meseta (see below *§viii.6. Celts*), with language change reaching up to south-west Iberia, must have caused population movements in the east, with Iberian-speaking populations retreating to the coast and possibly expanding slightly later to the north along the coast, replacing or displacing Ligurian-like speakers to their proto-historical territory. The arrival of Phoenician and Greek settlers, with increased trade and probably renewed demographic pressure (Matisoo-Smith et al. 2018; Zalloua et al. 2018), may have caused their expansion to inner territories again.

Iron Age samples from Iberians in north-east Spain show a variable increase of CEU BBC ancestry (32–98%) related to the previous period, with an increase related to the contribution of 'foreign' sources (from central European groups) shared with Celtiberian samples, although such contribution found in Iberians (ca. 18%) is lower than the one found in Celtiberians (ca. 35%), compared to the contribution of Bronze Age Iberian sources (Olalde et al. 2019). This increased ancestry found in Pre-Iberian and Iberian samples after the Urnfield period likely reveals the expansion of Iberian-speaking groups and Iberian languages over previous Celtic-speaking areas in north-eastern Spain and south-eastern France.

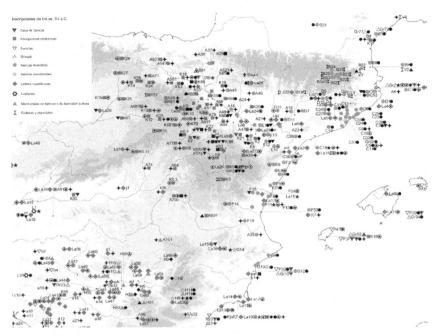

Figure 54. Inscriptions in Iberia ca. 2nd–1st c. BC. Purple squares show Celtiberian inscriptions, blue circles show Iberian inscriptions. Image modified from Hesperia – Banco de datos de lenguas paleohispánicas.

The first Balearic settlers of the Early Bronze Age, represented by an individual from Mallorca (ca. 2400-2300 BC) had substantial Steppe ancestry (ca. 37%), with the closest source being Iberian Bell Beaker individuals of high Steppe ancestry, hence likely from a north-western Mediterranean source. Two later individuals from the Middle Bronze Age show lower Steppe-related ancestry in Menorca (ca. 23%) and Formentera (ca. 26%). The source of this increase in indigenous ancestry may be linked to both Iberia Chalcolithic and Sardinia Nuragic ancestry, although the mtDNA haplogroup U5b1 found in the Menorca MBA sample is observed in multiple Iberia Chalcolithic individuals, but not in Sardinia. This may suggest that both Talaiotic peoples from the Balearic Islands and the ancestors of Nuragic Sardinians received gene flow from an unsampled Iberian Chalcolithic-related group (Fernandes et al. 2019).

The expansion or resurgence of Iberian languages in the west Mediterranean islands may be thus related to the appearance of megalithic structures, as a sign of resurging pre-Beaker customs (possibly under the influence of eastern Iberia), such as *talaiots* in the Balearic Islands, the *nuraghi* in Sardinia, and the *torri* from southern Corsica (Ugas 2005). While Iberian languages are attested in the Balearic Islands in proto-historic times, the relation of Iberian (and Basque) with the described Paleosardo substrate of Sardinian languages (Blasco Ferrer 2010) remains a controversial linguistic topic, and their shared connection may be much older.

The modern population of Ibiza, one of the Balearic Islands, shows a split from the mainland parallel to the divergence of Sardinia from mainland Italy, and a distance from modern Basques similar to that of modern Sardinians. This is not related to the Phoenician expansion, since their ancestry is not continuous with an ancient sample from Ca's Molí (ca. 260 BC), which can be modelled as an admixture of NWAN (ca. 19%) with Morocco Neolithic ancestry (ca. 81%), suggesting a recent Punic origin. Their modern Ibizan ancestry can therefore be explained by the consanguineous unions in the Island since the Catalan repopulation of the 13th century, and its population decline in the Middle Ages (Biagini et al. 2019). It probably reflects thus an ancient situation in north-east Iberia coupled with genetic drift.

viii.3.3. Palaeo-Sardinians

Ancient Sardinian individuals sit between early Neolithic Iberian and later Copper Age Iberian populations, roughly on an axis that differentiates WHG and EEF populations and embedded in a cluster that additionally includes Neolithic British individual. The most shared genetic drift of ancient Sardinians is found with Copper Age Iberia, while southern French Neolithic individuals are the most consistent with being a single source for Neolithic Sardinia (Marcus et al. 2019). In fact, ancient Sardinians harbour HG ancestry (ca. 17%) that is higher than early Neolithic mainland populations (including Iberia, ca. 8%), but lower than Copper Age Iberians (ca. 25%) and about the same as Southern French Middle-Neolithic individuals (ca. 21%).

It is not possible to reject major genetic continuity of the Neolithic population in Sardinia into the Bronze Age and Nuragic times, with a WHG proportion remaining stable (ca. 17%) throughout the three ancient time-periods. No haplogroups are reported before the Early Bronze Age, but from the late 4th millennium BC until the Nuragic period there are probably seven R1b1b-V88 samples, two G2a2a1a2a1a-L166, as well as six I2-M438 lineages shared with Neolithic and Chalcolithic populations from Iberia and the British Isles: five I2a1a2a-L161 and one I2a1a1-M26 (Marcus et al. 2019).

In samples attributed to the Nuragic period (ca. 2100–950 BC), there are seven R1b1b-V88, two I2a1a2a-L161, four G2a2a1a2a1a-L166, apart from four J2b2a1-L283, which may also be interpreted as remnants of the Neolithic expansion through the Mediterranean (Fernandes et al. 2019). The survival of I2a1a1-M423 lineages among modern Sardinians (ca. 39%) supports the continuity of this haplogroup during the Nuragic period, too (Chiang et al. 2018).

An Iron Age sample (ca. 300 BC) shows evidence of Iranian-related ancestry, which may be interpreted from the chronologically closest populations as Iberia Chalcolithic (ca. 12%) and Mycenaean ancestry (ca. 88%), with little if any ancestry from earlier Sardinians. This outlier and Late Antiquity samples from the south-east (AD 200–700), showing even higher Iranian farmer-related ancestry, are consistent with the genetic impact of Phoenician colonies in Sardinia. One of these samples (ca. AD 450) shows the first evidence of Steppe-related ancestry in Sardinia(Fernandes et al. 2019).

A connection of Paleosardo with a Basque-Iberian community may be supported thus by the survival of Neolithic farmer and pre-Neolithic hunter-gatherer ancestry in ancient Sardinians, also distinguished in modern Sardinians and shared particularly with modern Basques (Terradas et al. 2014), especially in samples from isolated populations of central and eastern regions (Chiang et al. 2018). Similarly, the presence of elevated WHG ancestry in modern southern Italian clusters (Raveane et al. 2018) supports an ancestral connection with Iron Age Basques, as remnant populations of Early European Farmers associated with Cardial pottery.

In light of the potential recent contacts between Sardinia and the north-west Mediterranean mainland, and with the Balearic Islands in particular, it is unclear if similarities of Paleosardo with Basque-Iberian languages are due to the Early Neolithic expansion or to a more recent connection, such as Middle or Late Neolithic population movements.

The presence of G2a2a1a2-L91 lineages (ca. 11.3% in Corsica, especially in the south) and G2a2a-PF3147 (xL91, xM286) subclades in present-day southern Corsica and Sardinia, apart from Tuscany (Di Cristofaro et al. 2018), may support the survival or resurgence of ancestral populations after the arrival of Bell Beakers, potentially accompanied by language replacement. More recent contacts of El Argar with Sardinia and Corsica, sharing related languages, may have allowed for the diffusion of common innovations among related cultures, even if the communities had separated much earlier. The analysis of modern mtDNA shows the typical variation of maternal haplogroups, although, interestingly, some modern subclades seem to coincide in their estimates with sampled Sardinian Bell Beaker mitogenomes (so e.g. HV0j, H3u2, K1a32, or U5b2b5), which points to the arrival of the culture as an inflection point in the genetic history of the island (Olivieri et al. 2017).

The arrival of J2a1b-M67(xM92)—a haplogroup associated with Anatolian Neolithic populations—in Sardinia, Corsica, Tuscany, and Provence (Di Cristofaro et al. 2018), may be related to Tyrsenian expansion, which has been related to the emergence of the Iolaei in the island (Ugas 2005), but also to more recent expansions of Greek or Roman settlers. Similarly, the appearance of J2a1-L26 lineages in eastern Iberia, and particularly J2a1d-M319 (found previously in Minoan samples), should probably be associated with Greek settlers, while the expansion of E1b1b1a1b1a-V13 (formed ca. 6100 BC, TMRCA ca. 2800 BC) in Sardinia and Iberia, as well as in Corsica, may be related to the Phoenician and Carthaginian occupations (Matisoo-

Smith et al. 2018), possibly related to the increased sub-Saharan admixture observed in Sardinia (Chiang et al. 2018).

VIII.4. Iberian EEBA province

VIII.4.1. Old and New Bell Beakers

The demographic or economic pressure of Yamna migrants must have been responsible for the events in Iberia before the arrival of East Bell Beakers, which brought about a reduction in the size of settlements and an increase in violence, signalled by changes in technology and organisation of metallurgy, concentration of wealth, proliferation of weapons, and displays of violence and individualised power, reflecting the synchronic economic and political transformations seen in western Europe (Blanco-González et al. 2018).

In the north, centre and west of the peninsula, the most common settlements are 'pit fields' (*campos de hoyos*), open settlements occupied temporarily or seasonally with varied structures used as silos to store grain, rubbish dumps, sites to place offerings, homes, graves, or dwellings. They were probably inhabited by dozens of people, and were probably highly autonomous in their production economy, evidenced by the tools found related to processing, storage, consumption of food, and production of pottery, stone, bone, and metal objects. Some hilltop settlements can also be seen, probably also non-permanent sites linked to seasonal exploitation of certain resources (Lull, Micó, Herrada, et al. 2013).

Their subsistence economy was based on stockbreeding, on an increasingly developed agriculture—with specialised flint working for preparation of sickle teeth—and increase in number of silos per settlement with greater storage capacity, in comparison with the Copper Age. Metallurgy also improved, with extensive extraction of ore in the centre and the north, not related to economic centres as in El Argar, but rather widely distributed locally among settlements. Pottery is dominated by plain vessels, continuing the East Bell Beaker *Begleitkeramik*, coexisting with local Bell Beaker developments (Lull, Micó, Herrada, et al. 2013).

While funerary customs do not show a clear break with the earlier collective burials, there is a trend towards reduction in size of the tombs and in the number of bodies they contained during the Chalcolithic. This tendency culminates in the practice of individual burials, especially in central and west Iberia, described as an evidence of social inequalities in these territories. Chalcolithic settlements of the south-west are abandoned, a sign of a drop in population and a change in social order, more radical and evident than in the central territories (Lull, Micó, Herrada, et al. 2013).

VIII.4.2. Meseta

In the northern Meseta, during the Bell Beaker phase (ca. 2500–1900 BC) a high degree of craftsmanship develops, with a standardised repertoire of pottery forms and decoration including incised (triangles), combed impressions, rare schematic representations, and burnished surfaces; flint for knapped blades; green stones for beads; and copper to smelt awls and flat axes. These distinctive items spread everywhere during the Bell Beaker expansion, elevated locations gain importance, sites decrease in size and are more distantly spaced, while burials in old megaliths coexist with isolated single burial pits and graves under tumuli with rich furnishings (Blanco-González et al. 2018).

Two subcultures appear in the northern Meseta: a south-western region, characterised by more labour-intensive tumuli, stone-walled and ditched sites, southern imports, and manufacture and distribution of local variscite beads; and the eastern region, featuring smaller tumuli, a lack of walled or ditched sites, and engagement in different exchange networks—including green talc beads, and characteristic pre-Beaker and Beaker pottery styles. Economic activity, rising since the Chalcolithic, peaked during this time (Blanco-González et al. 2018).

The Early Bronze appears in the north with the distinctive 'Parpantique group' in Soria (ca. 2100 BC), showing coarser pottery, with household wares predominating over fineware, bowls lacking careful burnished treatment, incised and figurative decorations disappearing, as flint becomes less common. Stone mining tools appear, as well as arsenical copper tools and new types of pottery, like carinated vessels, S-profile jars with flat bottoms and fingernail impressions on rims, and thumb-impressed rope design. Open-air sites predominated, with occupation of prominent hills (related to herding strategies) , but lowland pit sites continued, and some caves were also inhabited (Blanco-González et al. 2018).

In the southern Meseta ca. 2500–2000 BC, the Maritime style predominates in the initial stage, including undecorated Bell Beaker assemblages, and female burials have also been found. An abrupt change is visible particularly after ca. 2000 BC in the Tagus Valley, when agrarian landscapes became unsustainable and were transformed into diversified ones orientated to pastoralism, although a relative continuity in material culture and settlement patterns can be seen. Bronze co-smelting reached the Tagus basin ca. 1800 BC, probably from north-eastern Iberia, and exogamy dynamics are observed with immigrants from the Central System (Blanco-González et al. 2018).

A Protocogotas decorative style emerges ca. 1800/1700 BC, characterised by the application of motifs using incisions or impressions (ears of wheat, triangles) on the upper part of the vessels. Protocogotas evolves to Cogotas I ca. 1500 BC, featuring the use of geometrical motifs (garlands of concentric semicircles, wolf's teeth, rows of spikes or circles) executed by means of linear incision techniques, bouquique (dot and line decoration), 'sewn' decoration, and excision. Various vessels appear, with the emblematic pottery formed by dishes with the lower part of the body as a truncated cone shape with high carination, open platters and pots with prominent rim (Blanco-González et al. 2018).

Cogotas I pottery spreads across a large part of the peninsula, signalling the start of the Middle Bronze in different regions, coinciding with the last two centuries of the Argaric wold, although no significant archaeological change is perceived in these regions. In general, a shift of economic power is seen from the south-east to central and west Iberia with the demise of El Argar. From the Ebro to the Duero and upper Tagus regions, including the Atlantic coast, settlements continue to be divided into upland sites and 'pit fields' in the lowlands, with pits occasionally used as tombs for individual interment with few or no grave goods (Lull, Micó, Herrada, et al. 2013).

Before ca. 1300 BC, there seems to be no major differences in metallurgical production or any other economic aspect compared to the previous period, which suggests long-term stability. Settlements composed of a few dozen individuals, relatively high mobility, stockbreeding as the basic subsistence economy, with the relevance of agriculture and the population density being dependent on the geographical conditions (Lull, Micó, Herrada, et al. 2013).

After ca. 1300 BC there is an increase in exchange of products, particularly metal objects, connecting the Atlantic with the Mediterranean coast, suggesting a new gradual shift of economic power to the Mediterranean and the south, marking the beginning of the Late Bronze Age. In the Meseta, the Cogotas I style prevailed, with large hilltop settlements and small low-lying villages participating in the production and circulation of Atlantic bronzes. Certain central settlements seem to have dominated over surrounding territories (Lull, Micó, Herrada, et al. 2013).

VIII.4.3. Western Iberia

During the Chalcolithic (ca. 3300–2200 BC), south-west Iberia shows intense networks of contact and exchange, although there is great variability in terms of settlement and funerary rituals. Larger sites are occupied for centuries, while smaller sites seem to have a shorter life (few centuries or decades). Enclosed settlements featured round houses with stone foundations, within and outside of the walls, and evidence of metallurgical production. Distinctive ceramics, vessels with impressed acacia leaf designs, and plates with almond-shaped rim, as well as groundstone tools, grinding tools, flint blades and arrowheads, and copper items (Blanco-González et al. 2018).

The earliest Bell Beaker pottery appears ca. 2700 BC in fortified sties, of the International/Maritime, Palmela, and Incised styles. It is during this period when ditched enclosures made up of concentric rings of ditches and scattered pits, which had started ca. 3500 BC, reach their apogee, ca. 2500 BC, to disappear completely ca. 2250 BC. They showed evidence for productive activities (metallurgy), food consumption, depositional acts, and mortuary structures and rituals within the domestic space. The dead were housed collectively in *hypogea*, or in pits or reused caves and megaliths (Blanco-González et al. 2018).

The transition of the Late Chalcolithic to the Early Bronze Age (starting ca. 2250/2200) shows thus a clear discontinuity, a cultural collapse, with (Blanco-González et al. 2018):

- The end of ditch-digging and monumental negative earthworks, ca. 2250 BC.
- Monumental settlement architecture, typical of the Neolithic, disappears after ca. 2500 BC.
- Abandonment of sites, establishing new habitats, a process which had started ca. 2500 BC.
- Material culture shows an interruption in the pottery (plain pottery instead of incised wares), textiles (heavier loom weights), rarity of lithics, likely replaced by metal items.
- Iconoclastic attitude, probably related to a profound cosmogonic shift, with the disappearance of Chalcolithic figurative and geometric representations, such as engraved slate plaques, standardised astral, anthropomorphic, and zoomorphic items made in exotic materials.
- Shift from monumentalised collective burials to individualised interments in less visible tombs, beginning during the Beaker phase. Practices revolve thus around the singularisation of certain individuals in cists, with burial items associated with bodies, all in a more standardised way.

Bell Beaker graves are found in caves, *tholoi* and other megalithic tombs, showing an integration of the incoming ideology with the previous regional customs. Beaker objects found in cist burials belong to the Epi-Bell Beaker period, during the Early Bronze Age, during which individual graves were housed in separate cist burials, but were associated with objects typical of the Beaker period, such as Beaker vessels, copper daggers and wrist guards, as well as ceramics (like carinated vessels) found in the Middle Bronze Age. All this points to an archaising trend among Bell Beakers who settled in the region (Blanco-González et al. 2018).

During the Early Bronze Age (ca. 2200–1500 BC), there is thus a shift to a hybrid society which shows a semi-nomadic lifestyle, with less visible low-lying pit sites, and funerary practices involving inhumation in necropolis of cists, *covachos* and cairns, disconnected from settlements. Reuse of megaliths and natural caves has been interpreted as an appropriation of the past by these communities. The overall activity declines, showing probably a decrease in demographic density. Some hilltop settlements appear in the early 2nd millennium BC, possibly related to their more sedentary activity, such as metallurgy, and potentially under the eastern influence of El Argar settlers in the Guadalquivir River basin (Blanco-González et al. 2018).

The mining of copper and silver resources and their processing were probably the a key factor in the intensive occupation and control of the Sierra Morena Mountains during the EBA. The regional relevance of the industry is especially visible in the mines of central and eastern areas and during the Argaric Bronze Age, when the number of settlements increased compared to the previous period. Medium-sized settlements show evidence of the whole process of transforming mineral into metal, and their locations were most likely linked to territorial control, processing and distribution of the metal, and the spatial distribution and exploitation of the mines. Control over production and distribution was probably in the hands ofelites, which could have accentuated the social asymmetry seen in the so-called Alto Guadalquivir Argaric group, increasing the need for ornamental artefacts and weapons as a means of accumulating and displaying wealth and power (Arboledas-Martínez and Alarcón-García 2018).

In western Iberia, from the Low and Middle Tagus to the north, the Final Atlantic Bronze Age (from ca. 1500 BC) intensifies its contacts with the rest of the Atlantic and the British Isles, as evidenced by bronze weapons and tools, often gathered in hoards. Iron objects appear before the turn of the millennium (Blanco-González et al. 2018). The widespread anthropomorphic stelae and statue-menhirs of the west (Figure 55) may have been used as territorial markers, or formed part of funerary or commemorative practices linked to distinguished figures, maybe military leaders. They show the emergence of elite individuals who share the same symbols at a supraregional level, expanding from the lower Douro are to the south and south-east (Rodríguez-Corral 2018).

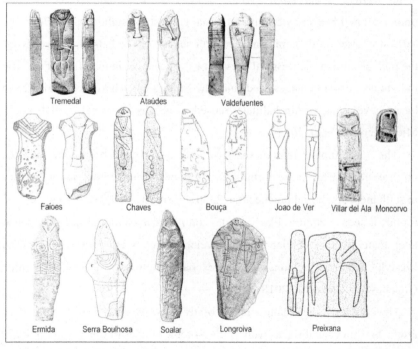

Figure 55. Stelae from the north-west Iberian group, after Bueno et al. 2005a. Image modified from Bueno Ramirez et al. (2011).

The lowest levels of human activity are reached ca. 1400 BC, increasing thereafter. Settlements in central and northern Portugal include hilltop sites between 0.05 and 1.5 ha, which reach their peak in the 10th c. BC, showing remains of intensive metallurgical production, with small communities and a subsistence economy based on agriculture, stockbreeding, acorn gathering, and limited hunting. This would give way to the Baiões-Vénat horizon at the end of the 9th to the mid–8th c. BC (Lull, Micó, Herrada, et al. 2013).

VIII.4.4. North Iberia

The prevalent decorative technique of Bell Beaker pottery in the Atlantic façade during the second half of the 3rd millennium was the shell impression using *Cerastoderma edule*, while from 2500 BC regional incised and impressed bell beakers are found in burial context throughout the region. The earliest nucleation dynamics in the north seem to have happened already by the mid–3rd millennium. Burial rites show the selective inhumation of specific individuals, often in places used since the Neolithic, such as rock-shelters and burial caves, pits within habitats, reused megaliths and small tumuli (Lull, Micó, Herrada, et al. 2013).

The northernmost regions (eastern Galicia, the Cantabrian strip, and the north-eastern sector to the north of the Ebro valley) underwent minor changes in settlement and burial practices ca. 2300 – 1900 BC, and no clear-cut cultural rupture is seen. Neolithic-like lifestyles continued, and cultural shifts happened later than in other Iberian areas, developing relatively sedentary agrarian lifestyles integrated in long-distance exchange networks since the Neolithic (Blanco-González et al. 2018).

Nevertheless, the change in decorative motifs and shapes on pottery artefacts from Cantabria, as well as the isotopic studies of diet and mobility in La Rioja, provide evidence for the movement of populations during the Late Chalcolithic and Bronze Age, with further smaller scale intra-regional movements found between the North Castilian plateau and the north, based—

among other data—on the presence of seashells in non-funerary contexts (Jones et al. 2019).

The Atlantic areas show a marked and statistically significant fall in human activity ca. 2200 BC, with a subsequent recovery ca. 1600 BC, which are matched by palaeoenvironmental proxies and a lack of known EBA sites. Asturias seems to have become the most dynamic area of northern Iberia, becoming an important metallurgical centre and trading nucleus for Iberian and Atlantic exchange, based on findings of weapons and metal goods, including mining tools. This exchange involved especially western Iberia, i.e. present-day Galicia and Portugal, while the western Pyrenées and Aquitania remained possibly isolated, based on the scarce findings from this period.

Three main mines show activity from the Bell Beaker period (ca. 2500 BC) up until ca. 1500 BC, with the mining complex of El Aramo representing one of the biggest subterranean prehistoric mining complexes in Western Europe, composed of an extensive system of galleries, pits, and wide excavations. The large-scale extraction activity from this mine (ca. 6700 tonnes extracted) can only be explained by a strong intra- and interregional demand for materials, and a shaft-hole axe from Bohuslän, Sweden (ca. 1600–1500 BC) may have originated in this mine (Reguera-Galan et al. 2018).

After a period of decline in international exchange coinciding with the exploitation of copper mines from Wales, there seems to be a poorly understood gradual change in material culture in the eastern Atlantic sector, dated around the mid–2nd millennium BC, and consisting of higher levels of agricultural production, settlement diversification, and increasing human pressure. These trends are different from the upper Ebro basin, which follows the cultural evolution of north-eastern Iberia (Lull, Micó, Herrada, et al. 2013).

viii.4. Lusitanians and Tartessians

The intrusion of steppe-related migrants represents a replacement of ca. 40% of the Chalcolithic ancestry, and near 100% of Chalcolithic male lineages in Iberia after ca. 2000 BC (Olalde et al. 2019). This replacement of old Iberian

Beakers by East Bell Beakers is seen in ancient samples almost overlapping in time (ca. 2500–2000 BC) from sites in the north, centre, south-east and south-west.

There is thus a clear population replacement marked by the arrival of Central European (Germany Beaker-like) ancestry in Iberia, with the highest values attested in the centre and north-west (around 65% to 90%), with lesser values and a wider range in the south-west (ca. 16% to 61%). The even more pronounced Y-chromosome turnover (ca. 100% of investigated Bronze Age haplogroups are R1b1a1b1a1a2-P312) point to a higher contribution of incoming males than females, also supported by a lower proportion of nonlocal ancestry on the X-chromosome, a paradigm that can be exemplified by a Bronze Age tomb from Castillejo del Bonete (ca. 1800 BC) containing a male with Steppe ancestry and a female with ancestry similar to Copper Age Iberians (Olalde et al. 2019).

The earliest Bell Beaker samples show no Steppe ancestry and predominantly haplogroup I2-M438 (at least six I2a1b1-M223 in the Meseta and the north, two I2a1a1-M26, and one I2a1a2-L161 in the south-west), as well as one G2-P287, one F-M89, and one H2-P96. Nevertheless, Chalcolithic samples from ca. 2500–2200 BC show the intrusion of Central European Bell Beaker ancestry in central Iberia (ca. 35–100%) and north-western Iberia (ca. 63–78%), with the earliest dated R1b1a1b1a1a2-P312 sample (with ca. 63% CEU BBC ancestry) found in El Hundido, in central Iberia (ca. 2410 BC), with at least six (probably eight) over twenty-three Chalcolithic samples showing Yamna lines.

Bronze Age samples from central Iberia show variable Steppe ancestry (ca. 34–70% CEU BBC), as do the slightly later samples from the north (ca. 41–60% CEU BBC), with an evident slight resurgence of Iberian Chalcolithic ancestry over the previous period, reflected also in the better fit of Iberian Chalcolithic samples with Steppe ancestry over CEU BBC, suggesting further local admixture events within Iberia. Most reported haplogroups are

R1b1a1b1a1a2-P312, fifteen samples out of sixteen, with one I2a1b1-M223 in the Meseta (ca. 1900 BC). Most reported subclades are under R1b1a1b1a1a2a-DF27, including three under SNP ZZ12[+], also found in the north-east. This is in contrast with the apparently higher variability of the previous period, where two R1b1a1b1a1a2b-U152 samples are reported, one from Madrid (ca. 2500–2000 BC), and another one from Burgos, under R1b1a1b1a1a2b1-L2 (Olalde et al. 2018; Olalde et al. 2019; Martiniano et al. 2017).

The expansion of early R1b1a1b1a1a2-P312 lineages with incoming Classical Bell Beakers, like R1b1a1b1a1a2b-U152 and R1b1a1b1a1a2a-DF27 subclades, confirms a late spread of R1b1a1b1a1a2a-DF27 subclades in Iberia, estimated with studies of modern populations to have happened ca. 2200 BC (Solé-Morata et al. 2017).

Interestingly, a male outlier from Camino de las Yeseras (ca. 2473 – 2030 BC) clusters with modern and ancient North Africans in the PCA, and like 3000 BC Moroccans (see *§iv.5. Late Afrasians*) can be well modelled as having ancestry from both Late Pleistocene North Africans and Early Neolithic Europeans. His haplogroup E1b1b1a-L539 (xE1b1b1a1-M78) and the different ancestry found in near settlements confirms a recent origin in North Africa, probably related to the presence of African ivory at Iberian sites. Another similar individual is found in the Bronze Age Loma del Puerco, in southern Iberia (ca. 1815 BC), which shows ancestry related to North Africans (ca. 25%), although none of these incursions had a genetic impact on Copper and Bronze Age Iberians (Olalde et al. 2019).

In the south-west, Bronze Age samples also show a highly variable penetrance of CEU BBC ancestry, even within the same site and chronological period, like the three samples from Monte da Cabida (ca. 2200–1700 BC), which shows a female with the least Steppe-related ancestry (ca. 16%) close to a female and a male of hg. R1b1a1b1a-L51 with higher values (ca. 35%). The eight reported lineages are from Yamna lines, all probably under R1b1a1b1a1a2-P312 (Olalde et al. 2019).

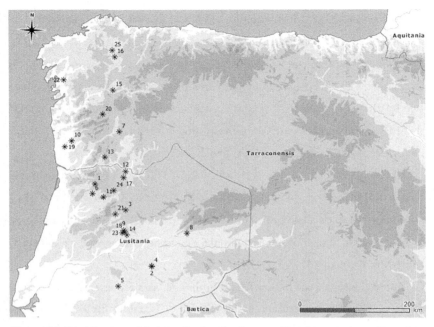

Figure 56. Distribution of Galaico-Lusitanian long and brief inscriptions. Data from Hesperia – Banco de datos de lenguas paleohispánicas, according to Vallejo (2013).

The only certain non-Celtic Indo-European language of Iberia is Lusitanian, which has been linked to a potential Galaico-Lusitanian group spread from the north-west to the central-south Iberian Peninsula, based on inscriptions, anthroponymy (Figure 56), and theonymy (Vallejo 2013). The expansion of proto-historical Lusitanian speakers may be clearly linked in archaeology to west Iberians spreading with anthropomorphic stelae from north-west Iberia during the Final Atlantic Bronze Age. There has been some discussion about the non-Celtic nature of the languages of Cantabri, Astures, Pellendones, Carpetani, and Vettones (Adrados 1998), which may be thus more or less closely associated with Lusitanian, too, as an ancestral Indo-European branch spread through the Meseta and west Iberia with Bell Beakers, before the arrival of Celts.

There are no samples from north-west Iberian Bronze Age or Iron Age groups, and it is unlikely that Lusitanian samples are ever fully assessed in genetics, due to their burial tradition of cremation. Nevertheless, Bell Beaker samples from the north-west show a radical intrusion of CEU BBC ancestry (up to 90%) and likely radical male lineage replacement, which was most likely continued until the expansion of Galaico-Lusitanian from that region to the south during the Bronze Age. Genetic isolation and thus continuity in north-western Iberia can also be inferred from the coarsest levels of genetic differentiation formed by modern Galician clusters close to the border with Portugal, representing half of the inferred clusters in all of Spain (Bycroft et al. 2018; Pimenta et al. 2019).

There is a comparatively lesser presence of R1b1a1b1a1a2a1-Z195 subclades—proper of north-central and north-east Iberians—in west Iberia, which be related to less marked Y-chromosome bottlenecks in general, and thus no episodes of radical male replacement after the Bell Beaker expansion. In particular, western Iberians show relatively high frequencies of R1b1a1b1a1a2a-DF27 (xR1b1a1b1a1a2a1-Z195) subclades (Solé-Morata et al. 2017), although the bottlenecks caused by the expansion of Celts and the Reconquista may have complicated the ancient picture (Bycroft et al. 2018).

While the position of Tartessian as Indo-European (Koch 2009) is highly doubted[24], there is some support for a borrowing of names from a "lost Indo-European language" over the course of long-term contacts (Mikhailova 2015). This is compatible with El Argar-related Proto-Iberian-speaking peoples occupying hilltop settlements and dominating over Indo-European-speaking peoples in south-west Iberian territories during the early 2nd millennium BC. Some of these territories would later form the Proto-Tartessian community, with close interactions between neighbouring Iberian- and Lusitanian-speaking peoples in south-west Iberia for centuries, before their historical attestation.

Sampled individuals attributed to the Tartessian culture from La Angorrilla in Seville (ca. 700–500 BC) show elevated Steppe-related ancestry (ca. 40–50%

---

[24] It was criticised extensively in a special section of Vol. 42 of The Journal of Indo-European Studies (No. 3 & 4, Fall/Winter 2014)

CEU BBC), with the best fit for a part of that increase (ca. 20%) showing a potential origin of the increase not related to the available Iberian BA samples, hence likely from outside Iberia, in line with the known arrival of Central European ancestry with Celts during the Urnfield period, and the likely presence of Celtic-speaking peoples neighbouring Tartessians.

VIII.5. Western EEBA province

VIII.5.1. Channel – North Sea

The Armorican Early Bronze age of north-western France is characterised by a hierarchical society, with classic groups of burial mounds similar to Wessex or Belgium. Settlements feature large houses, status symbols include daggers, halberds, and axes. Cremation cemeteries continue up to the Middle Bronze Age (Mordant 2013).

South of the IJssel, the Hilversum tradition develops, with close connections with the Channel – North Sea region, showing pottery with cord-decorated necks and very marked rim-profiles (ca. 1850–1600 BC), until this is replaced by Drakenstein pottery, ornamented with fingernail-impressed cordons. Cremation started already in the Bell Beaker period, and becomes dominant during the MBA. After 1600 BC, a regional Hoogkarspel style develops west of the Delta (Fokkens and Fontijn 2013).

Imported bronzes show a predominantly Atlantic origin. Deposits of weapons is common south of the Rhine, with swords preferentially deposited in major rivers and axes and spears in smaller bogs and streams in the near vicinity of settlements. This trend decreases drastically with the transition to the Early Iron Age, when deposition in Hallstatt chieftains' graves becomes more common (Fokkens and Fontijn 2013).

During the Middle Bronze Age, the Atlantic region shows the spread of the Deverel-Rimbury-type pottery. In the east, burial mounds become commonplace with the arrival of the Tumulus culture (pottery with excised decoration, pins, leg-rings), which spreads to the Paris Basin and the Loire Valley. Eventually, the Duffaits culture emerges from the Charente region to the Middle Loire, incorporating also Atlantic features (Mordant 2013).

In the 14th century BC, a clear east–west cultural divide is established, with the Atlantic world showing new areas of metalwork and rich bronze hoards on both sides of the Channel, evidencing the continuity of hierarchical societies. There is an increase in cremation in its funeral customs alongside more traditional burials. Rilled-ware pottery expands from the west to eastern France (Mordant 2013).

The maximum visibility of the western groups occurs ca. 1200–1000 BC with the Rhine-Switzerland-eastern France culture. The practice of cremation is established ca. 1300–1200 BC in the Paris Basin, reaching the Rhine ca. 1150–950 BC. The new period is characterised by cemeteries with highly contracted cists, and burial mounds reserved for important people, usually men, with rich hoards. Characterised by the systematic practice of cremation ('Urnfields') but also by fine incised and combed decorated pottery. This culture expands into the Rhône Valley and the Languedoc, where regional developments also continue local influences. The regions bordering the Channel continue the Channel – North Sea cultural complex until the appearance around the 9th century of smaller cultural groups and a more powerful Central France group (Mordant 2013).

VIII.5.2. British Isles

The initial Chalcolithic period (ca. 2500–2150 BC) shows the use of copper pre-dating the widespread adoption of tin–bronze. This use of copper was already present in northern France a millennium earlier, and its expansion is probably related to the arrival of Bell Beakers, supported by the synchronous appearance of Beaker pottery, stone wristguards, flint barbed and tanged arrowheads, copper daggers and gold basket ornaments. An exemplary sample comes from the Amesbury Archer (Figure 57), probably born in central Europe but buried in southern England with the earliest dated gold and copper objects in Great Britain, although older monuments also show Beaker pottery. Bell Beakers settle in south-west Ireland at least ca. 2400 BC (Roberts 2013).

The newcomers encountered the Neolithic custom of building circular or oval monuments of earth, timber, or stone, and pits with internal architectures and avenues in timber and stone emphasising the approach, and wooden palisades excluding external viewers, as exemplified in the Stonehenge monument, which has its parallels in central Europe. Burial mounds or barrows for Beaker burials in Britain, and megalithic wedge-tombs in western and northern Ireland were added to the funerary rites. These displayed striking objects in exotic materials (like gold, amber, and faience) show the influence of the Wessex culture on the whole British Isles. Local differences in burial types show an adaptation to ancient customs (Roberts 2013).

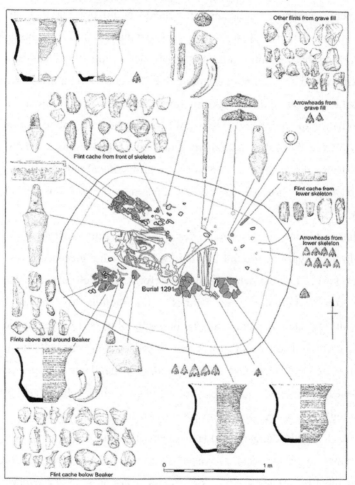

Figure 57. Plan of the burial of the Amesbury Archer with the position of the body and the artefacts, after Fitzpatrick (2011), 78, fig. 28.

Settlements show mainly short-term oval and circular structures formed by postholes and hearths, with subsistence economy pointing to a prevalence of cattle. This suggests the evolution to a mobile agropastoral economy—with adaptations of the different groups to the local environment—from the previous sedentary arable farming of wheat and barley. Navigation of waterways is evident from the similarity in architecture and artefacts between Britain and Ireland. During the subsequent whole Bronze Age period, the settlement evidence indicates dispersed population living in small communities, usually not larger than a few extended families (Roberts 2013).

Marking the transition to the EBA (ca. 2150–1600 BC), changes are seen in the increased circulation of copper in the 22nd and 21st centuries BC, topped by artefacts made of tin–bronzes in significant numbers. Following this, the accumulation of wealth and practice of hoarding begins, with exotic materials for jewellery (like amber, jet, faience and shells) found in increased quantities, and distributed over an ever-expanding area. A gradual population increase is inferred for the whole Bronze Age, compared to the previous period (Heyd 2013).

Flint and stone working flourishes at the same time as flint mines show a peak in activity, with ground and chipped axes, edge-ground knives, plano-convex knives and arrowheads, stone-perforated maceheads, axe–hammers, battle–axes, wristguards, whetstones, and moulds for metal objects. Goldworking also expands, as do dressing objects like jet spacer–plate necklaces, disk bead necklaces, V-perforated buttons and belt rings, amber spacer–plate necklaces, and faience beads and pendants. Copper mines of north-west Wales and south-west Ireland begin to be exploited using similar technology, as are tine ores from south-west England, to create the common flat axes, halberds, daggers, and later spears (Roberts 2013).

Cremation, which had coexisted with inhumation, becomes prevalent during the EBA. The placing of the dead overlaps with the everyday life, demonstrated by the extensive stone monuments constructed and reworked in Britan and Ireland. Funerary monuments include stone circles, standing stones, and ring–cairns, which are found in distinct layers also including settlements.

Hoards include bronze axes and halberds, which reveals a rapid expansion in the scale, diversity, and technique of craftsmanship in metal, ceramics, flint, stone, and exotic materials during the EBA (Roberts 2013).

During the MBA (ca. 1500 – 1150 BC), stone, flint, exotic organic and inorganic craftsmanship declines, as evidenced by a reduced quality, although they continue to be widely used. Metal tools, on the other hand, show more quantity and diversity, even though copper ore mining almost stops, which implies recycling and imports from the continent. There is a deliberate separation of copper and gold objects, and deposits can be seen: of shields in rivers and bogs; spears and swords in rivers, river valleys, and along the edges of wetlands; ornaments and tools in hoards in the landscape. Decorated and plain Barrel and Bucket urns become widespread in Britain and Ireland, coexisting with earlier forms and showing regional differences (Roberts 2013).

First a custom of building rectilinear field systems appears (especially to the south and east), probably related to intensification of farming economy, substituting previous communal efforts of building monuments, especially in river valleys, coastal lowlands, and the edges of wetlands. These fields needed the digging of ditches, erection of hedges and fences, building of gates, and placing of trackways. Flocks of sheep rather than herds of cattle become common, and the introduction of wells can be seen in agriculture, as well as a change in crop species (Yates 2007).

Only later is a widespread construction of circular settlements or roundhouses in timber or stone seen. Concentrations into villages is not common, and a pattern of abandonment and rebuilding of new settlements nearby can be seen, with offerings related to their foundation and abandonment. In England, cremation of the body and burial in flat cemeteries close to settlements is widespread, often accompanied only by pottery. In Ireland, cremation burials with Cordoned Urns continues, as does the construction of burial mounds or barrows until the 1st millennium BC. Nevertheless, deposition of cremated remains accompanied by plain coarse pottery vessels gradually increases (Roberts 2013).

The transition from MBA to LBA (ca. 1150 – 800/600 BC) is marked a reduction in upland settlements and an increase in settlements surrounded by banks, ditches, and wooden palisades in prominent places. This is possibly linked to colder temperatures and wetter conditions, in turn related to shortening of the growing season, increased consumption of dairy products (and decreased size and age ranges of sheep), and increased pressure on subsistence. Large accumulations of food consumption, animal management and craft production in middens is seen in southern Britain and south Wales during the early 1st millennium BC, overlapping with the peak intensity of bronze deposition throughout Britain and Ireland, which collapses 800 BC. New types of communal gathering-places emerge, such as middens of southern Britain, timber platforms, and the early hilltop enclosures of the north and west (Brück and Davies 2018).

VIII.5.3. Western and central Alps

The Rhône culture (ca. 2300/2200 BC) includes the Rhône Valley and part of the Massif Central, with its metallurgy and pottery reaching across eastern and central France and the Rhône corridor. Also included in western Bell Beaker groups are probably the Saône group from the Swiss and French Jura, and the Adlerberg group on the Upper Rhine. Its material culture recalls Late Copper Age assemblages, e.g. from Sion–Petit Chasseur I (of early Bell Beaker groups), including the first metal items such as decorated racket-head pins. Wetlands and lakeshores—offering open space, proximity of woodlands, agricultural soils, and aquatic resources, as well as defence and communication routes—remain the favourite locations for settlements on the Swiss Plateau and in the Alpine foothills. The economy shows innovations such as introduction of new cereals, and a grassland economy with intensified cattle breeding (della Casa 2013).

Supra-regional connections are evident from metal resources of the western Alps found in western regions—such as Armorican materials—during the late part of the Early Bronze Age, as well as from EBA *Überausstattungen* ('over-endowed graves') known across the continent, from Únětice to Wessex. Small burial mounds are the most common funerary ritual, but cists, caves, and megalithic monuments remain in use. Grave goods are also evidence of long-distance relations, to the ore-producing zones of the north-eastern Alps (Mordant 2013).

During the Middle Bronze Age (from ca. 1550 BC), metallurgy shows an increase in large-scale production, with technical innovations reaching areas like the Seine Valley, the Saône Valley, and the Middle Loire, at the heart of the new trading networks. With the arrival of the Tumulus culture, northern Alpine groups influence the development of local Rhodanian elements. Alpine settlements increase gradually, including sheltered camps and stone-built structures, with seasonal use of Alpine meadows in the context of an agropastoral economy. Possibly since the EBA, mining and production of Alpine copper is an important part of the economy, which increases in importance especially during the LBA and EIA (della Casa 2013).

There is abundant evidence for the use of 'sacred' natural places for ritual activities and depositions, especially flowing waters, lakes, and ponds, as well as mountain and pass regions. Alpine burnt-offering places are understood as an old, Bronze Age tradition which survives into the Iron Age, with the oldest findings showing calcined domestic animal bones and pottery. Gender subdivision is evident since the Copper Age, with female inhumations showing costume and ornament elements, and male inhumations featuring weapons, mainly daggers, in grave assemblages. Elite graves help support the existence of social structures during the MBA, and spatial clusters probably reflect kinship groups (della Casa 2013).

During the LBA, the Rhin-Suisse-France orientale group of the Urnfield culture develops, including the western Alps. Settlements increase in size, with quasi-proto-urban nature and complex structures, including defensive devices. Naturally defended sites such as promontories and hilltops are preferred for settlements in Alpine valleys and Prealps lowlands during the whole Bronze Age. The Inner Alps remained exposed to influences from the south, north and east. Urnfield swords, knives, bracelets, pins, and pottery are commonplace, as well as cremation burials, with regional variations in pottery and bronzes. Vertical social structures are marked by wealth of bronze objects, as well as sets of drinking vessels (della Casa 2013).

viii.5. Pre-Celts and Basques

viii.5.1. Pre-Celts

Most sampled British Neolithic individuals from Scotland, England, and Wales (ca. 3800–2500 BC), before the arrival of East Bell Beakers, form a close cluster, with their ancestry represented by NWAN (ca. 85%) and WHG (ca. 15%), except for three outliers with significantly more WHG ancestry. All Neolithic individuals show I2-M438 subclades, among them fourteen I2a1b-M436 subclades, at least five of them I2a1b1a1a1-L1195 (formed ca. 5100 BC, TMRCA ca. 3600 BC), and thirteen I2a1a2-M423, possibly all I2a1a2a-L161.

All British Bell Beakers, whether associated with Maritime or 'All-Over-Cord' Beaker pottery, show large amounts of Steppe ancestry, with strong similarities with central European Beaker-associated individuals, especially with those sampled from Oostwoud in the Netherlands, which supports the migration of Bell Beakers from a population close to the lower Rhine (see §viii.7. Germanic peoples). During the initial period (ca. 2450–2000 BC) ancestry proportions were highly variable, consistent with migrant communities just beginning to mix with the indigenous population, either before or after the arrival in the island (Olalde et al. 2018). Some samples with minimal British Neolithic ancestry further support a recent origin of the newcomers from continental Europe (Hoole et al. 2018).

There is a population turnover of ca. 90% of the local population, with Yamna lineages representing more than 90% of the haplogroups of individuals in Copper and Bronze Age Britain, and new mtDNA haplogroups such as I, R1a, and U4 being previously present among Bell Beakers from central Europe, but not among British Neolithic individuals. This supports the proposed considerable degree of mobility in Britain during this period, with little difference between male and female migration (Parker Pearson et al. 2016), rather than an exchange of female marriage partners (Brodie 2001) or inter-cultural contact consolidation (Vander Linden 2007), as previously proposed for the expansion of the culture.

A single source for most British Beakers is also supported by the Y-chromosome bottleneck of R1b1a1b1a1a2c-S461 lineages, whose presence among modern populations along the Atlantic façade possibly supports the original source of British Beakers near the lower Rhine, most likely south of the Rhine–Meuse–Scheldt delta. However, historical interactions of British populations with the Atlantic region may have introduced many of these subclades in the region at a later date. Most further reported subclades from the British Chalcolithic and Bronze Age are R1b1a1b1a1a2c1-L21[25] (TMRCA ca. 2200 BC), with only three specifically reported as R1b1a1b1a1a2-P312 (xR1b1a1b1a1a2c-S461), and one individual from the Roman period in England showing the rare subclade R1b1a1b1a1a2c1b-DF63 (Martiniano et al. 2016).

On the other hand, the investigation of Bell Beakers from Ireland suggests a potentially bimodal migration of East Bell Beaker migrants to the island, from both southern and northern European sources, with south-western individuals showing inflated levels of Neolithic ancestry relative to individualised burials from the north and east (Cassidy 2018). This is compatible with the migration of Bell Beakers from south-eastern France with increased Neolithic ancestry and mainly R1b1a1b1a1a2a-DF27 subclades, probably accompanying the Maritime style, while the rest of the Island would

---

[25] The Amesbury archer's reported hg. R1b1a1b1a1a-L151 may also be R1b1a1b1a1a2c-S461, an SNP call tentatively obtained with Yleaf from the petrous sample, from Wang et al. (2019) supplementary materials.

have been populated by migrants from Britain, mainly of R1b1a1b1a1a2c1-
L21 lineages and increased Steppe ancestry, as reflected in the Bronze Age
samples from the Rathlin Islands (Cassidy et al. 2016) and the reported genetic
continuity with modern populations (Gilbert et al. 2017).

Increased Steppe ancestry is found in the Netherlands (ca. 60%), similar to
some British groups (ca. 31-62%), most likely due to the admixture with
Corded Ware groups (see *§vii.1. Western and Eastern Uralians*), as reflected
also in the 'northern' shift in the PCA, with British Bell Beakers clustering
closer to Corded Ware samples than earlier central European groups. There is
higher Steppe ancestry (ca. 50%) from northern mainland sites, with samples
from the Haut-Rhin (ca. 2500–2200 BC) and Moselle (ca. 2430–2130 BC),
both of hg. R1b1a1b1a1a2-P312. Samples to the west of the Danube, from
Sion–Petit Chasseur (ca. 2500–2000 BC), show less Steppe ancestry (ca. 34%),
and both reported haplogroups are R1b1a1b-M269, including one R1b1a1b1a-
L51. The increased EEF ancestry in southern French and north Iberian samples
also support this interpretation of Steppe ancestry acquired in northern groups
through admixture (Olalde et al. 2018).

Samples from England evolve with an increase in Steppe ancestry: from ca.
50% in England and Wales Chalcolithic and England MBA, to ca. 66% in
Wales MBA, and ca. 56% in one LBA sample from England. On the other
hand, samples from Scotland show a steady decrease, from ca. 54% in the
Chalcolithic, to ca. 52% in the MBA, and ca. 46% in the LBA, suggesting
different gene flows (or genetic drift) affecting the different groups (Olalde et
al. 2018).

The controversial non-Indo-European substrate of Goidelic (Schrijver
2000, 2005) could be thus speculatively related to the previous intrusion of
Megalithic groups, or even to the migration of Bell Beakers from the southern
Atlantic façade, of elevated Neolithic ancestry. However, it could also mean
the survival of Neolithic vocabulary as substrate of the North-West Indo-
European dialects spoken by Bell Beaker groups migrating to Britain and

Ireland. Potential Vasconic substrate loanwords in Proto-Celtic (Matasović 2009), some traceable to North-West Indo-European, support their adoption before the arrival of Celts in the British Isles.

The few words of likely Indo-European and non-Celtic origin in Pritenic (Rhys 2015), the language of the Picts in Scotland, may reflect the Indo-European dialects brought by peoples of mainly R1b1a1b1a1a2c-S461 lineages across the Channel. Few useful phonetic data can be extracted from the fragmentary evidence, and it seems that the older Pictish inscriptions, dating to ca. AD 3rd–4th centuries (centuries earlier than previously thought), are composed essentially of non-alphabetic symbols, probably in reaction to contacts with Roman and Mediterranean cultures and scripts, and as a public form of display concerned with prestige and high-status identities and activities (Noble, Goldberg, and Hamilton 2018).

The peak of R1b1a1b1a1a2a-DF27 lineages among modern populations of the lower Rhine, close to the old Nordwestblock cultural region, may also hypothetically represent this lost Indo-European branch (or branches) of West Bell Beakers, of non-Celtic and non-Germanic nature (Kuhn, Hachmann, and Kossack 1986), although the evidence cited has been contested as Germanic, Celtic, or as of Old European or non-Indo-European substrate (Udolph 1994).

viii.5.1. Basques

Modern Basques, like other non-Vasconic-speaking modern Northern Spaniards and Southern French peoples from more isolated regions around the Pyrenees and the Atlantic façade, harbour increased NWAN-related ancestry, which links their language—like Iberian or Paleosardo (see *§vii.6. Basque-Iberians*)—to the resurgence of farming communities expanded from Anatolia (Gunther et al. 2015). Nevertheless, based on the modern Basque population as a proxy for the Vasconic-speaking Iron Age community, Pre-Basques to the north of the western Pyrenées before the Iron Age may have been different from neighbouring populations in their extra hunter-gatherer ancestry (Mathieson et al. 2015)[26].

It would be thus conceivable but highly controversial (Prósper 2013) to give credit to the nature of Proto-Basque as of Pre-Indo-European substratum (Forni 2013), or even as forming part of a Proto-Indo-European–Euskarian macro-family (Blevins 2018), beyond the known pre- and post-Roman Indo-European superstrata (Koch 2013). This could be nevertheless supported using genetic research by the presence of increased hunter-gatherer ancestry from the Villabruna cluster, including the presence of typical Villabruna-related R1b1b-V88 lineages in north-east Iberia and Sardinia since the Early Neolithic in the late 6th millennium BC (Haak et al. 2015) up to early Proto-Beakers in the late 3rd millennium BC (Olalde et al. 2018), continuing in Sardinia during the Bronze Age and Nuragic period (Marcus et al. 2019).

The modern population from historical Basque-speaking regions shows predominantly Yamna-derived lineages (ca. 90%), especially R1b1a1b1a1a2a-DF27 subclades, with its diversity suggesting a rather early infiltration of Bell Beaker lineages among the dwindling Chalcolithic-like population of the Atlantic façade to the north of the Pyrenees, as well as later Y-chromosome bottlenecks during their periods expansion.

Founder effects may have happened among Vasconic speakers during the Roman presence in Iberia, due to the Cantabrian Sea region's isolation from further Eurasian gene flows. Modern Basques show a close similarity with Celtiberian individuals from La Hoya in the modern Basque Country region (ca. 400–200 BC), who show high CEU BBC ancestry (ca. 53–70%), with the highest relative contribution of a 'foreign' central European source (ca. 35%) compared to other Iron Age samples from Iberia. This also which the likely arrival of Celtic-speaking peoples in northern Iberia during the Late Bronze Age, related to central European ancestry, hence possibly associated to the

---

[26] Remark made by Iosif Lazaridis on Twitter (2018).

introduction of the Urnfield tradition. The only reported haplogroup is I2a1a1a-M26 (Olalde et al. 2019).

Figure 58. Aquitani and neighbouring tribes around the Cantabrian Sea, as described by the Romans (ca. 1ˢᵗ c. BC). The Basque language likely expanded south and west of the Pyrenees into Indo-European-speaking territories during the Roman period. The term 'Vascones' only became applied to Basque-speaking tribes in medieval times. Map modified from image by Sémhur at Wikipedia.

This confirms that the expansion of a Proto-Basque-speaking community—isolated in the Atlantic Coast north of the Pyrenees, roughly coincident with the Roman province of Aquitania—into modern Basque-speaking territories south of the Pyrenees happened only during the Roman Iron Age, since Basque toponyms in the area are only attested from the Roman period on (Villar Liébana 2014).

One such bottleneck may be found in the recent expansion in north-central Iberia (north Meseta, Cantabrian region) of R1b1a1b1a1a2a1a-Z272 subclade R1b1a1b1a1a2a1a1a1-Z278 (formed ca. 2500 BC, TMRCA ca. 1200 BC), particularly its subclade R1b1a1b1a1a2a1a1a1a1-M153 (formed ca. 900 BC, TMRCA ca. 600 BC), almost exclusively present among modern Basques (Solé-Morata et al. 2017).

VIII.6. Central EEBA province

VIII.6.1. Danubian Early Bronze Age

The Danubian EBA complex, starting ca. 2200–2150 BC, comprises cultures from regions north of the Alps, along the upper and middle Danube corridor, from Switzerland to western Hungary, with most eastern groups having the Danube as a northern boundary. They showed continuity from the later phases (Begleitkeramik) of the East Bell Beaker group, most apparent in the jars/cups and bowls/plates and the changing details of pottery shapes and their decorations during their transitional stage. Multiple centres of gravity have led researchers to define regional groups: Singen and central Swiss, the Neckar group, Straubing, Linz, Unterwölbing, Leitha. Pitvaros/Maros, an exclave on the western bank of the Tisza river, possibly represents an early eastward migration at the beginning of the culture complex (Bertemes and Heyd 2015).

They formed a supra-regional interconnection, showed mainly gender-differentiated burials with individual inhumations in oval to slightly rectangular grave–pits, orientated north–south with varying depths, with side-crouched rite, men laid on their left side and heads towards the north, women on the right and head towards the south, and both genders facing east, probably towards the rising sun. Based on the many cemeteries and thousands of graves found, it seems that the Danube corridor was a demographic centre in Europe. Big cemeteries evidence the continuity of their use, e.g. Franzhausen I and II with ca. 500 years or 17 generations and around 1000 graves (Bertemes and Heyd 2015).

Danubian groups were distinguished by innovation and ideas: in their shared pottery and metal/bonework, metal processing technology, costume components, jewellery and personal adornments, weapons, and tools, apart from hoarding traditions. Sources for these innovations were drawn mainly from the south-east along the Danube river: pottery, weapons, jewellery, dress fittings, and the new dress code as a whole were drawn from the Carpathian

Basin and the Balkans. From the south, the Alps (and northern Italy beyond) were a model for halberds and dress pins, particularly the most popular form 'rudder-head' and 'roll-head' pins (Ruderkopf- and Rollenkopfnadeln). Other striking similarities in jewellery, dress fittings, burial customs, and pottery may be due to shared late Bell Beaker heritage. (Bertemes and Heyd 2015).

The Danube corridor became a hotspot for EBA Europe, connecting cultural norms and major copper ores, like those on the eastern Alps. Their settlements consisted of a few individual farmsteads featuring longhouses close to graveyards, which have an origin in Bell Beaker longhouses (like those known from Hungary, eastern France and the Netherlands). The basic village structure shows around five houses ca. 20–25 m long and 6-10 m wide, uniformly orientated (north–south), distributed over 2 ha, with postholes for their timber uprights. Later, the typical late European EBA fortified hilltop settlements and hoards with large quantities of metal appear, especially in the east (Bertemes and Heyd 2015).

Their burial rites and funeral equipments are rooted in the East Bell Beaker group—unlike e.g. the Adlerberg or Rhône groups in the west, which are based on a western European Bell Beaker substrate—and their pottery distinguished the Danubian EBA complex especially from Únětice, Nagyrév, and Polada. Unlike Únětice, who deliberately broke with gender distinction, they preserved the specific and strict bipolar gender position of the deceased along a north–south axis, which suggests that fundamental aspects of religious beliefs and concepts of the afterlife remained the same as in Bell Beakers. On the other hand, there is a clear discontinuity with Bell Beaker cemeteries in Danubian EBA, a trait shared with Únětice and Mierzanowice/Nitra (Bertemes and Heyd 2015).

Burial sites in Straubing and Unterwölbling, for example, had 30 to 70 graves, and lay close to settlements. Gender differentiation was strictly observed, and the way graves are fitted out shows a highly standardised composition. Women were orientated south–north, crouched, on their right side and facing east; men were orientated north–south, crouched, on their left side and also facing east. Bodies were placed in wooden coffins from hollowed-out tree trunks, linked with stones or stone slabs. Usual assemblages are richer furnishings than in neighbouring EBA cultures, with numerous objects made of sheet bronze (Jiráň, Salaš, and Krenn-Leeb 2013).

To the east, gender distinction is found up to the Wieselburg culture (also Gáta or Mosony culture), where bodies are buried in the crouched position, with women lying orientated south–west – north–east, on their right side and facing east, whereas men lie on their left side facing west. Graves are lined with stones, burials were made in tree–trunk coffins, and social status was accentuated by the provision of weapons, prestigious metal, glass, and amber objects, as well as by the number of pots (Jiráň, Salaš, and Krenn-Leeb 2013).

The most typical shape of Unterwölbling is the long-necked jug-like cups, with frequent decorative moulding running through them. Wieselburg pottery shows more moulding and incised decoration, and typical handles in the shape of hourglasses on jugs and amphorae. The Drassburg group, which coexists with Wieselburg and partially follows it at the end of the EBA, represents the north-west part of the Pannonian complex of Encrusted Pottery (Jiráň, Salaš, and Krenn-Leeb 2013).

The Pitvaros (Beba Veche/Óbéba–Pitvaros) culture was probably introduced by migrants from the south (northern Balkans), and spread to the lower Tisza Basin. It introduced the rite of gender-differentiated crouched inhumation with north–south orientation and rich goods to the area. Personal ornaments include objects made of copper or bronze, gold, tin, or faience (Marková and Ilon 2013).

The Maros (Periam/Perjámos-Szőreg, also Pécska, Mokrin or Maros/Mureş/Moriš) culture lived mostly on the same territory as the Pitvaros culture but it gave rise to its own settlements, suggesting a wave of migrants. Settlements were tells, with post-built houses with floor and hearth arranged in narrow lanes. Material culture evidences long-distance contacts, and burial rite consists of inhumations – with occasional cremation also found –, with bodies buried in crouched or sitting position (Marková and Ilon 2013). Social stratification with gender differences are especially marked in a late more standardised phase, with females on their right side and head towards the south, males on the left side with their head towards the north, both facing east towards the rising sun. Rich grave goods show women's dress with bronze or copper head ornaments, bone and faience beads, plain torcs and spiral bracelets. Men show weapons like daggers and axes as status symbols, while pottery is common in all graves (Teržan and Karavanić 2013).

The Danubian continuity with Bell Beaker traditions extended to the social and economic system, based on extended families with a common practice of exogamy, patrilineality, and first-born privileges to forge alliances with peer neighbours and inherit possessions and claims. Only gradually becomes the society more vertically stratified and horizontally complex in its transition to the European Bronze Age, while mixed farming system continues, land use intensifies, and settlements and cemeteries become bigger. Graveyards were probably shared by many farmsteads or villages, or both (Bertemes and Heyd 2015).

Most late Bell Beaker symbols of prestige, social status and power remain in place, and are still found in graves: copper tanged daggers (replaced with the triangular riveted dagger through technical innovations), conical V-perforated bone/antler buttons (shifting through technique and fashion to embossed copper tutuli), as well as arc-shaped bone or tusk pendants, copper awls, and metallic Noppenringe; sets of flint arrowheads and stone wrist-guards begin to lose their symbolic importance. The typical weaponry consisted eventually, in its most elaborated form, of the panoply of riveted triangular daggers, flanged axes, and halberds (Bertemes and Heyd 2015).

They formed exchange networks with other EBA cultures of the end of the 3rd millennium: the Rhône and Adlerberg groups (based on western Bell Beaker traditions) in the southwest to northwest; the Únětice Culture with its regional groups in the north and north-east; the early Mierzanowice and Veselé/Nitra groups (based on Epi-Corded Ware groups) in the northeast; the Nagyrév group in the east; and the Polada group in the south across the Alps. Other Epi-Corded Ware groups, such as Pot-Beaker and Riesenbecher groups; and Epi-Bell Beaker groups, such as the Veluwe group, were found farther to the north (Bertemes and Heyd 2015).

Unlike cultures north of the Danube, which underwent more technological and social innovations, Bertemes and Heyd (2015) believe that eastern Bell Beaker groups might have established a well performing economical and religious network along the Danube before 2200 BC, which had thus no incentive for radical changes.

VIII.6.2. Únětice period (EBA)

The Moravian Bell Beaker, with 1500 to 2000 sites, represents the greatest province of the East Bell Beaker group. Supraregional contacts of the group include the Moravian Corded Ware (a regional group of the Central European Corded Ware) and Makó/Kosihý–Čaka, as well as Somogyvár–Vinkovci and Early Nagyrév. Developments in common with the Moravian Corded Ware group pointed in the past to their parallel development into Proto-Únětice, but more recent assessments show that it was more precisely the CWC-related forerunners of the Makó/Kosihý–Čaka culture those who developed similar ewer shapes in parallel with Moravian Bell Beakers (Bertemes and Heyd 2002).

Similar to the Danubian Early Bronze Age, Proto-Únětice/Old Únětice is born ca. 2300/2200 BC as an intermediate phase between Bell Beaker and Early Bronze Age in the Moravian and Silesian region, and is the result of mainly early Bell Beaker culture plus few Corded Ware traditions plus innovations from the Carpathian basin. Distinct from Danubian EBA, however, is the relevance of Makó/Kosihý–Čaka (related to previous Corded Ware groups) in its foundation, which seems parallelled by the genesis of the Early Nagyrév culture, also influenced by early Bell Beaker in its origin (Bertemes and Heyd 2002).

Proto-Únětice shows developments in common with the South Danube region (Oggau-Wipfing horizon), and maintains close contacts with south German and Csepel late Bell Beakers, although it emerges as culturally disconnected from neighbouring Bell Beaker groups, a kind of cultural melting pot connecting different cultures and periods. This culture largely lacks metal, and a sudden expansion of Proto-Únětice is seen to the north-west into Bohemia and central Germany, and to the north in Silesia. Early pottery shows a limited range of shapes, including jugs, pots with horizontal handles, little amphorae, and bows of various shapes. These types evolve without much change into later stages of Únětice pottery, which tend to have perfectly smooth surfaces, often with a 'metallic' sheen, a preference shared with the Věteřov culture (Jiráň, Salaš, and Krenn-Leeb 2013).

The main difference between north and south of the Danube in this period (ca. 2200 BC) is reflected in the burial customs, with northern groups showing innovations probably due to the incorporation of cultural traits from central European cultures. Funerary rites of the Lower Austrian Únětice group are more likely to bury connected people together—including sororities, 'brothers-in-arms', and especially women and children—which can be interpreted as having a more personal quality, emphasising family relationships and emotive connections. On the other hand, individuals south of the Danube are almost always awarded individual graves, and categorisation as man or woman is central to the ritual, with personal relations fading into the background (Rebay-Salisbury 2019), which is reminiscent of the Yamna and classical Bell Beaker ritual.

The later stage of the Early Bronze Age is marked by the oldest classical Únětice bronze objects appearing in northern and central Germany and in the Polish Plains, still with Carpathian traits. The classical phase of Únětice is characterised by its distinctive pottery forms, and by the increase in grave goods made of copper alloy unusual for its higher tin content. Metal objects showing the specific Únětice style begin to be manufactured using local ore deposits from the Harz Mountains of the eastern Alps, to the south-west of the culture's region (Czebreszuk 2013).

A new core develops ca. 2000 BC, in the northern periphery of the classical Úněticean Cultural Circle (Northern European Lowlands, between the Elbe and the Oder rivers), which controls important trade routes and becomes the dominant cultural factor in a broadly understood central Europe, exerting a strong influence on the development of cultural groups of southern England (Wessex), southern Scandinavia (beginnings of the Nordic Circle), and in Iberia (including El Argar). Emulations or imports of Únětice daggers are found as far as Greece and Anatolia (Bertemes and Heyd 2002).

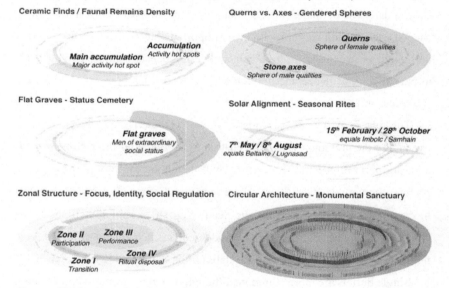

Figure 59. Layers of meaning of the Pömmelte enclosure as deduced from the archaeological record (design by André Spatzier). Image from Spatzier and Bertemes (2018).

The smooth transition seen from Bell Beakers (ca. 2300-2150) into Únětice (ca. 2200-2150 BC on) in the Pömmelte enclosure (Figure 59) is broken probably with this power shift (ca. 2050 BC), with the deconstruction of the enclosure and the definitive absence of Bell Beaker finds, although stone axes and 'formal' graves indicate the continuation of the spatial concepts until the 20th–19th c. BC. New features are added to it, with sporadic re-use until is abandonment probably ca. 1600-1500 BC. The overall structure of the enclosure, divided into three distinct layers divided by a semi-translucent post border (zone I) and a wooden wall (zones II-III) facilitated the experience of entering and leaving the monument as reflecting the three stages of 'rites of passage' (separation, liminality, and incorporation). This sanctuary reflected thus the *Weltanschauung* of the people who built and used it (Spatzier and Bertemes 2018).

This Northern Únětice group is characterised by the unequal distribution of the right to burial, granted mainly to members of the upper class, which suggests a greater social stratification in the north than in the south. They also show a daily use of amber objects, including large quantities of stunning disc-shaped artefacts and kurgans with many imported objects, gold, complex wood and stone constructions. To the south, amber products are represented by beads as part of composite necklaces, frequently with coiled copper–wire ornaments (Czebreszuk 2013).

The classical Únětice standard shows cemeteries on level ground, expanding the previous early EBA custom of Moravia, northern Bohemia and adjacent parts of Austria, contrasting with neighbouring groups which used preferently mounds, even though the arrangement of the pit suggests an effort to create an insulated space for the dead, with sides (and sometimes floor) walled with stones, and the use of wooden coffins. Chambers of tombs were hollow, covered with beams or stone slabs (Jiráň, Salaš, and Krenn-Leeb 2013).

Single burials are more common, although two, three or more bodies could be buried, either simultaneously or subsequently. The body was buried in clothing, placed lying on its right side in a crouched position, or supine and with legs turned sideways, orientated south–north irrespective of the gender. Grave assemblages included mainly pottery, but also personal ornaments, and sometimes weapons (daggers, axes, and axe–hammers); certain individuals showed prestige artefacts (Jiráň, Salaš, and Krenn-Leeb 2013).

Burial structures and grave goods reflect a strictly hierarchical society from as early as 2000 BC. At the top of the hierarchy are the 'princely graves' (such as those of Leubingen and Helmsdorf, or comparable tumuli at Łęki Małe), which feature bodies in a supine position, in contrast to the usual crouched burials. Standard assemblages include mainly gold jewellery (hair-rings, pins, a bracelet), but also, especially in later burials, some bronze or golden weapons (daggers, halberds as a pan-European weapon, axes). Social stratification explains the difference between princely graves and the generally modestly furnished flat graves common in Únětice, while their concentration around copper deposits and potential trade routes point to the origin of their power (Jockenhövel 2013).

A particularly high-level burial was found at Bornhöck, with a mound ca. 20 m in height and 90 m in diameter (ca. 65 m in the EBA, enlarged in later periods), with a 18m-diameter stone core (similar to princely graves) of boulders surrounding a tent-like chamber constructed of oak boards. Hoards in the surrounding region yielded 150 kg of bronze, and more than 1 kg of gold, dating to ca. 1950–1650 BC, which imply that this was a centre of power over several centuries, probably until ca. 1600–1550 BC. Its longevity and size suggest that this ruling class was at the top of the social pyramid, representing a kind of king among the elite. The lack of fortifications in the region further suggests the presence of a well-organised, professional army that could keep peace both internally and externally (Meller 2017).

Hoarded weapons near princely graves probably represented actual 'soldiers' and 'military units' garrisoned in what has been called a "men's house". The death of the prince would have then caused the groups of soldiers to deposit the weapons as a sacrifice in front of their ritual building. The number of each type of weapon may reflect systems of military order, whereby 30 axes or soldiers would have been led by a halberd-bearer; 60 soldiers would have been under the command of a dagger-bearer; and the largest combat unit of 120 soldiers would have been led by a double axe-bearer (Meller 2017).

Above-ground houses with upright posts predominate in settlements. The most striking feature of houses is their length, commonly around 20 m in length and 7 m in width, with the longest one found in Březno, Bohemia, measuring 32 m (Pleinerová 1992). Finds of mass deposits of human remains in pits is common at the edge of settlements, where manufacturing and storage areas were located. This custom continues into the Tumulus culture and the Urnfield period (Jockenhövel 2013).

The Únětice culture has been cited as a pan-European cultural phenomenon, whose influence covered large areas due to intensive exchange (Pokutta 2013), with Únětice pottery and bronze artefacts found from Ireland to Scandinavia, the Italian Peninsula, and the Balkans. It was only after 2000 BC that large-scale mining operations and production which required specialised metallurgical and organisational know-how began in a few centres, and they reached distant regions as far as Northern Scandinavia. And only from 1750/1700 BC began the actual pan-European tradition of metal work until its consolidation ca. 1600 BC, with different regions in Europe producing their own products, most specially the cultures of the Carpathian basin (Kristiansen and Larsson 2005).

The contacts of Únětice with Carpathian territories are constant, e.g. in the Únětice–Nitra and Únětice–Hatva horizons, where settlement microregions and relationships are difficult to assess. Únětice elites controlled trade routes from the Baltic Sea shores to Aegean Sea artisans. Úněticean daggers are found all over Europe and in Anatolia, and the nature of weapons and metal work suggest a chronic state of warfare and the emergence of a warrior class until its demise. The downfall of the structures of the Únětice culture began probably prior to 1700 BC, and is associated with the culture-making role being taken over in Central Europe by the Füzesabony culture (of rather Aegean than Central European character); with the conditions allowing the emergence of the Tumulus circle from the Danubian region; and with the expansion of the Trzciniec culture into occupied Mierzanowice areas that gave way to its classic phase (Bertemes and Heyd 2002).

Before the eventual collapse of the Únětice culture (ca. 1600 BC), amber was contained within its territory and that of its trading partners in the Alpine region. After its internal system broke down, first amber disappeared from Bohemia, and appeared in the Mad'arovce–Věteřov cultural complex of the Carpathian Basin instead; at the same time, amber suddenly began to arrive in distant regions, including western Germany, Italy, or Mycenaean Greece. The development of the Nordic Bronze Age—largely reliant on unlimited supply of copper from the south via Central Europe—also occurred after the collapse of Únětice (Meller 2017).

At the end of the Únětice culture, during the transition to the Middle Bronze Age, fortifications or small hill forts emerge, showing strong connections to the Middle Danube area. This connection is also seen in the increase in the range of metalwork, with new artefacts such as knives, sickles, razors, tweezers, as well as ornamentation and production techniques (clay-core casting, recasting). The shape of these artefacts is clearly linked to the Middle Danube and the Carpathian basin (Jiráň, Salaš, and Krenn-Leeb 2013).

The Nebra 'Sky Disc' (Figure 60) is traditionally associated with Únětice, given the use that had been given to it—and the many reworked objects—for generations before being interred, with grave materials found around the disc dated ca. 1600–1560 BC. Its location near Sögel–Wohlde materials suggest the (at least partial) replacement of the particular religious worldview represented by the disc with the arrival of Tumulus and Sögel–Wohlde cultures to the region. It depicts astral symbols (sun, moon, stars), a boat (?) and two 'horizon arcs, being the oldest concrete representation of the heavens, and a kind of calendar – also presumed for later gold 'hats' during the MBA (Jockenhövel 2013).

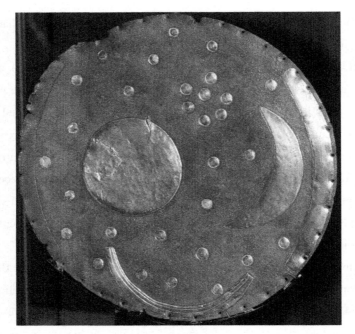

Figure 60. The Nebra Ski disk, from Mittelberg. Image from Wikipedia.

VIII.6.3. Tumulus period (MBA)

At the end of the Únětice period, during the transition to the Middle Bronze Age, fortifications or small hill forts emerge, showing strong connections to the Middle Danube area. This connection is also seen in the increase in the range of metalwork, with new artefacts such as knives, sickles, razors, tweezers, as well as ornamentation and production techniques (clay-core casting, recasting). The shape of these artefacts is clearly linked to the Middle Danube and the Carpathian basin (Jiráň, Salaš, and Krenn-Leeb 2013).

Amber beads, characteristic of southern Únětice groups, become the main amber product in the Middle Bronze Age until the Hallstatt period, when they become especially widespread, further supporting the cultural shift from a northern lowland to a southern, Middle Danube centre of influence. Hoards of bronze objects become common throughout the Bronze Age probably due to the pan-European influence of the Tumulus culture (Czebreszuk 2013).

The appearance of the Tumulus culture (ca. 1600 BC) marks the beginning of the MBA in central Europe. The new burial rite features inhumations beneath large roundish-oval mounds, about 1–2 m high, most often made of heaped rocks. Kurgans were grouped together in cemeteries that range in size from fairly small to quite large, with up to dozens of burials. Rich graves accompany burial mounds, which are built of soil, sand, turf, stone, or a combination of these materials, and are often bound by a stone setting, a ring ditch, or rings of wooden posts in the lower Rhine and the Low Lands. Grave goods reveal only slight social ranking, and a largely egalitarian or homogenous society can be inferred (Jockenhövel 2013).

Single burials predominate initially, with each mound belonging to a small family group. The body is usually buried prone and orientated north–south or east–west, in graves often protected by stones or burial chambers with wooden fittings. Assemblages included weapons (dagger, sword) and ornaments (tools, gold spirals, less often razors, pins) for men, and rich dress decoration, ornaments, necklaces, and pairs of pins for women, with amber ornaments (spacer plates) being very popular, more than in Nordic Bronze Age graves. The central burial is eventually joined by additional burials, usually on higher levels in the mound, sometimes with flat graves between the mounds. Cremations begin and increase during the MBA (Jockenhövel 2013).

The Tumulus tradition is presented as a warrior society which expanded with new chiefdoms eastward into the Carpathian Basin (up to the river Tisza), and northward into Polish and central European and Únětice territories, with dispersed settlements centred on fortified structures. Innovations spread quickly during this time, including weapons—swords (from influences of the Danube region), spears (socketed spearheads), and small axes (flanged axes) —and tools—two-edged razors, tweezers, knives, and sickles. Horses become particularly significant as a transport animal, for wagons and battle chariots, evidenced by bridle or cheek-pieces made from antler and bone (Jockenhövel 2013). Regional groups are distinguished based on metal fittings worn on their clothing, with a basic difference seen e.g. between groups south of the Mittelgebirge and the Lüneburg groups to the north (with features of the Nordic Bronze Age), and the western groups in the lower Rhine, closer to the Low Lands.

Grave goods reveal only slight social ranking, and a largely egalitarian or homogenous society can be inferred. In the subsequent period of crisis, it developed into bands of raiders and mercenaries, and took control of peasant societies, as happened in several regions during the Urnfield and La Tène periods, and similar to the society of mercenaries and warring city states in the Celtic period. This warring state is coupled with exogamous and endogamous strategies, and variable distances of marriage exchanges to maintain alliances, the so-called *fremde Frauen* phenomenon (Kristiansen 2000).

Settlements consisted probably of a few houses or just a single farmstead, with hill forts seen at the beginning and end of the period. The economy probably relied on regional transhumance, as well as mining of local copper (unproven) and salt production. This is therefore a time of settlement expansion into fertile lowlands and productive loess soils—characteristic of an agropastoralist society—together with defensive higher areas and hill sites. This expansion coincides with the wide settlement of the Alps and the beginning of a system similar to mountain pasture economy, as well as Alpine copper mining in the Inn Valley in Austria (Jockenhövel 2013).

Pottery is represented by small amphorae, with or without a foot, footed bowls, and small jugs. The Tumulus tradition shows preference for ornament, whether incised or plastic, in contrast to the smooth pottery typical of the Únětice period. The main ornament types are triangles, ladder-like bands, fig tree-like ornaments, and concentric or multiple circles. In the later period of the culture, the preference was again smooth surfaces and knobs (outlined with circular or horseshoe-shaped grooves), coexisting with various kinds of plastic protrusions (Jiráň, Salaš, and Krenn-Leeb 2013).

During the MBA, the north Alpine forelands show a tradition related to the Tumulus culture, visible in grave assemblages displaying pins with perforated shaft and spiral sheet ornaments. This influence on the region persists into the LBA, with a noticeable increase of bronze objects in hoards and graves, found also in northern Italy and the Ticino. The strongest affinities in south Alpine valleys is found at the end of the LBA, with the Canegrate group of the Po plain, and the subsequent Protogolasecca facies, with typical carinated, grooved, and smoothed black ware and the first bow fibulae (della Casa 2013).

In the south-east, the Maďarovce–Věteřov–Böheimkirchen cultural complex (Slovakia, Moravia, and Austria) shows an unbroken evolution from the Únětice culture. It features open settlements on level ground, frequent fortified settlements, and sporadic tells. A new range of ornament forms appears along with a new bronze implement (the sickle) and weapons (socketed spearheads and short swords). Casting technology with tin–bronze shows that the ores used were from the eastern Alps. Inhumation is the main funerary rite, with tumuli and cremation burials seen at the end. Towards the end of the period, the culture participated in long-distance exchange networks, with many findings belonging to North Pannonian and Ottomány cultures, evidence of its nature as a north–south intermediary in amber trade (from Lesser Poland to the Iron Gates), and an east–west trade network evidenced by *Brotlaibidole* ('loaf-of-bread' idols). The culture disappeared at the time of increasing exchange and mobility, replaced by the Urnfield culture (Marková and Ilon 2013).

The European world ca. 1450–1100 BC has been compared to the Viking Age, with population pressure and lack of land for young sons with no inheritance leading to war-bands that engage in seasonal raiding, trading, and piracy. This was followed up by more massive colonising ventures and migrations, and a political economy based on a chiefdom form of society where free farmers were the dominant class, with commoners and slaves as dependent groups (Heyd 2007; Kristiansen 2016).

At the end of this period, ca. 1200 BC, a great battle seems to have happened in the Tollense valley in north-eastern Germany, at the confluence between Nordic, Tumulus, and Lusatian cultures (see *§viii.8. Balto-Slavs*). It is estimated that more than 4,000 warriors took part, based on the hundred and thirty bodies and five horses found in Tollense riverbank, and the likely hundreds more which remain unexcavated, accounting for one in five participants killed and left on the battlefield. Body armour, shields, helmet, and corselet used may have needed training and specialised groups of warriors, with their organisation being a display of military force (Jantzen et al. 2017).

According to Kristiansen (Curry 2016), this battle is therefore unlike any other known conflict of this period north of the Alps – circumscribed to raids by small groups of young men –, and may have heralded a radical change in the north, from individual farmsteads and a low population density to heavily fortified settlements. This period is coincident with the time of the mythical battle of Troy, with the collapse of the Mycenaean civilisation, and with the raids of Sea People in Egypt and the collapse of the Hittites.

VIII.6.4. Urnfield

The Urnfield culture (ca. 1300–750 BC) marks the beginning of the LBA, and shows the increasing acceptance of cremation, already present during the MBA, which is initially variable in its ritual burial. The gradual disappearance of burial mounds and inhumation represents probably a change in religious beliefs, based on social status and identity, burial rites, and a new range of symbols (water birds). The dead were burnt on a pyre, and remains of their bones and ashes were picked out, scattered in graves, or interred in clay pots (Jockenhövel 2013).

The earliest hill forts lie in the south-eastern Urnfield group. The Piliny culture represents the earliest Urnfield culture in central Europe, if we ignore earlier cremation burials from the Vatya and Hatvan cultures. The Piliny tradition survived the expansion of the Tumulus culture as a continuation into the EBA of the Ottomány and Hatvan cultures in the Pannonian Basin. There are open-land and high-altitude settlements surrounded by ditches and ramparts, with large settlement agglomerations forming in both upland and lowland sites, and serving apparently as administrative and economic centres. Notable are its swords of Riegsee-Ragály type with elaborated ornamented hilts and pommels, also appearing to the north in Lusatian areas (Marková and Ilon 2013).

The ritual becomes homogenised ca. 1100 BC (Hallstatt A2) with the urn burial in southern Germany. The urn is placed in the grave together with other clay vessels (Figure 61). Most graves are of adult men, described as chieftains, warrior elites equipped with swords (both flange-hilted and solid-hilted), spears, and armour (helmet, breastplate, greave, shield). The wealthiest ones contain larger weapons (swords and spearheads), bronze drinking vessels, wagon parts, or high-quality bronze and gold ornaments. Female graves show rich ornaments and dress fittings, and are generally less richly furnished. The size of the graves and urns reflect the age and sex differences. Hundreds of hoards show the continuity of this tradition from the Tumulus culture to the Urnfield culture (Jockenhövel 2013).

Figure 61. Typical burial of cremation urn, by José Manuel Benito Álvarez.

Urns contain not just burnt human bones, but also burnt animal bones. While personal ornaments passed through the fire of the pyre, tools—knives and razors—and other bronze goods were added to the bodily remains after cremation. The first metal vessels and armour (helmets, corslets, greaves) date from this period, suggesting a peak in the production and use of bronze objects. The sun-bird-boat (*Sonnenvogelbark*) identified on sword grips, greaves, diadems, belt-plates, and bronze vessels, is a prevalent religious motif that expands into the Nordic Bronze Age (Jiráň, Salaš, and Krenn-Leeb 2013).

The emergence of the Urnfield culture is thus associated with the rise of a new warrior elite, and the formation of new farming settlements and their urnfields. In some areas there is continuity from Tumulus to Urnfield culture, with narrowing and concentration of settlements on the fertile soils and along the river valleys, with proof of a very dense settlement and wide-ranging migrations. Above-ground post-built houses remain common during the MBA and LBA, orientated north–south, and in this period they are usually smaller, although sizes are variable (Jockenhövel 2013).

Settlements are larger, with villages of ca. 10–20 ha, but not very intensively occupied. Hearths appear outside the houses, probably shared by several families. Most settlements show no protection, although some evidence of fences suggests they were used to divide settlements in enclosed compounds. In the FBA, typical settlements took the form of independent farmsteads (Jiráň, Salaš, and Krenn-Leeb 2013).

The LBA shows therefore a great degree of standardisation following the cultural divisions of the MBA, with many metal forms (weapons and tools) distributed across large areas. The warrior now has a spear for throwing or thrusting at his side, with spear shafts made of ash, and arrows with specially shaped heads used as projectiles or for hunting. The new swords with leaf-shaped blades are used to cut or slash, while earlier blades were used as thrusting weapons (Jockenhövel 2013).

Pottery include biconical vessels, amphorae, storage vessels, mugs, jugs, bowls, cups, and beakers.   Regional variations in shapes, typology and ornamentation of pottery allow for the division into local groups within the largely homogeneous Urnfield tradition (Jockenhövel 2013):

- Alpine groups to the south: north-eastern Bavarian, Lower Main–Swabian, north-western Transdanubian.

- Central or Bohemian groups: from west to east Rhenish-Swiss, Unstrut, Milavce, Knovíz, and Suciu de Sus.

- Lower Rhine groups to the west in close contact with the Low Countries: Lower Hessian, North Netherlands–Westphalian, North-West group in the Rhine Delta.

- Middle Danube groups to the east: Velatice–Baierdorf, Čaka, Gáva, Piliny, Kyjatice, and Makó cultures.

- The closely related Lusatian fringe group to the north-east is also distinguished by other features (see §VIII.8. Eastern EEBA province).

Typical of the LBA is thus the reappearance of heavily fortified settlements (which were common in the EBA in the Middle Danube culture), those in the east belonging mostly to the early and middle phase of the Urnfield period, and those in the west to the late phase, which may suggest the regions of increased external conflict during each period. Massive ramparts were constructed using a variety of techniques, depending on the terrain and the specific demands of the site, and were frequently accompanied by deep ditches. Fortified settlements were often divided into subareas according to their economic or social purpose, indicating a variety of functions and occasionally depicting a specialisation of the site, from power and interregional trade centres to ritual sites (Jiráň, Salaš, and Krenn-Leeb 2013).

In the Alpine region, settlements in exposed locations are often constructed close to sites of mineral extraction. The overall settlement structure reflects that they were tied to a system that provided for processing and transportation of raw materials, and for interregional exchange. At the end of the LBA, a particular form of settlement begins in southern Bavaria, with a single farmstead inside a rectangular system of palisades and ditches, the forerunners of the leader's compound (*Herrenhof*), a popular Iron Age settlement form (Jockenhövel 2013).

At the end of the period, Pre-Scythian (Cimmerian) influences are seen in the east up to the Hungarian steppe belt, displacing Urnfield and Lusatian groups to the west and north. Changes are seen in inhumation graves, with remains of horse harness in bronze and iron, bone plates with typical ornamentation, and cattle and sheep bones. Increasing influence is felt in metal production, warfare, horse harness, animal breeding, religion, and long-distance trade. West of the Tisza, hoards of Románd type show this influence, before being eventually replaced by the eastern provinces of the Hallstatt culture (Marková and Ilon 2013).

VIII.6.5. Hallstatt – La Tène

From the early Urnfield culture expanded the Hallstatt culture (ca. 1200–450 BC). During the first period (ca. 1200–800 BC), there are several regional cultures under the Hallstatt sphere of influence, with differences appearing in funerary rite and settlement. Cremation is the dominant rite, with ashes and calcined bone, small vessels, and personal items placed into large biconical urns before burial in (occasionally vast) Urnfield cemeteries. Settlements included post-built structures within stockade and fortified compounds, with fortifications and wooden palisades increasingly used (Malin-Boyce 2004).

The true Hallstatt Iron Age (ca. 800–450 BC) is characterised as a period of extraordinary cultural flourishing everywhere in continental Celtic Europe, with elaborate burials including rich assemblages, often called chiefly or princely graves, and also hill fort settlements. Tombs and enclosed fortified hilltops signal the transformation of social organisation to a political economy that controlled the movement of luxury goods. Distribution of goods such as Massiliot amphorae that contained wine shows that western and eastern Hallstatt were included in the Mediterranean trading and gift exchange. The site of Halllstatt is positioned between the broadly defined eastern and western Hallstatt traditions, which shows influences from different neighbouring regions and their distribution networks, such as salt mining, Baltic amber, African ivory, Slovenian glass, Hungarian battle–axes, Venetian knives and brooches, and Etruscan drinking paraphernalia (Malin-Boyce 2004).

The Hallstatt culture represents a significant population growth continuing a Late Bronze Age trend, with networks of microregions or stable rural communities (composed of multiple villages) forming in many regions, particulary in the east. It continues in part the previous amber route from the Gdańsk area, although from the Moravian Gate it extended now to the eastern Alps and the Caput Adria, finishing in central Italy, which is supported by the synchronic finds of house–urns and face–urns in the Gdańsk area and in Italy (Czebreszuk 2013). European wagon graves – with a direct origin probably in the Carpathian basin – peak during the Hallstatt and La Tène periods (Boroffka 2013).

The later expansion of La Tène culture (ca. 480–15 BC) from certain core Hallstatt regions—valleys of Marne and Moselle and neighbouring Rhineland in the west, and a Moravian zone in the east—has been linked to the spread of Common Celtic languages, as described in classical sources. The transformation of late Hallstatt to La Tène is associated with changes in burial rite, from large tumuli to flat inhumation graves, although aspects of the tumulus burial tradition continued in parts of the Alpine and surrounding regions. This period is coincident with the Golasecca material culture in northern Italy, and with the appearance of the 'early style', of Etruscan influences, with the compass becoming a design tool for bronze vessels, ornamental metal disks, and even ceramic vessels (Malin-Boyce 2004).

Most elevated and fortified settlements were abandoned, and the apparent centres of power collapsed, at the same time as rich burials continued, showing a shift of power northward to the Hunsrück-Eifel region along the Moselle River. Settlements and burials become thus smaller than in the previous period, suggesting a more dispersed population and decentralised social and political power. The migration or expansion of Celtic peoples is usually associated with the depopulation ca. 400 BC of Marne, Champagne, Bohemia, and possibly Bavaria, signalled by a decrease in warrior graves and adult male burials in general, with less weapons in the remaining graves, and a different ceramic burial assemblage. During this period, less labour-intensive internment begins as the dominant rite, flat inhumation without grave markers (Malin-Boyce 2004).

Figure 62. Reconstruction of a late La Tène period (2nd/1st century BC) settlement in Havranok, Slovakia. Photo by Marek Novotnak.

Middle La Tène (ca. 280–125 BC) sees the appearance of oppida, proto-urban settlements signalling a consolidation of power and reorganisation of the social and economic structure of Celtic societies. Migration and expansion, disruption and settlement are all probably part of this period, with inhumation burials disappearing as cremation fully replacing it. Possibly, the impact of agglomerated settlements caused this shift to the disposal of the dead, which affected also the social and political elite. The Graeco-Italic 'vegetal style' (appearing ca. 320 BC), including stylised palmettes and lotus patterns becomes the main motif in bowls, helmets and scabbards. Late La Tène (ca. 125–15 BC) is linked to the rise of the Roman colonial expansion and its impact on neighbouring population. This period is characterised by the abandonment of the oppida in the west (ca. 80–40 BC), and later – coinciding with the Germanic expansions – in east-central Europe (Figure 62).

viii.6. Celts

Clear patterns of patrilocality and female exogamy have been found in the Upper Danube, apart from a continuing kinship relation in the transition of the Chalcolithic to the Bronze Age. There is evidence of continuing traditions from the Bell Beaker cultures to Early Bronze Age cultures in the region, with female mobility as a force for regional and supraregional communication and exchange (Knipper et al. 2017).

There is a variable contribution of Steppe ancestry in early Bell Beaker samples (ca. 2500–2000 BC), consistent with a period of constant migrations: Bavaria shows a decrease in Steppe ancestry (ca. 44%), including samples from the Lech Valley (ca. 52%), compared to previous Corded Ware groups (ca 65%) (Mittnik, Massy, et al. 2018); similarly, central European samples near the Rhine (ca. 51%) and from Esperstedt in Saxony-Anhalt (ca. 48%) show a decrease compared to previous samples from the area (ca. 71%), whereas in Bohemia Bell Beakers represent a slight increase (ca. 45%) over the previous late Corded Ware groups (ca. 40%), possibly due to the closeness of this territory with the East Bell Beaker homeland, and to the previous resurgence of Neolithic ancestry in the area (Olalde et al. 2018).

Almost 100% Y-DNA haplogroups among the approximately fifty reported (of more than a hundred samples from central Europe) belong to Yamna R1b1a1b1-L23 lineages, safe for one G2a2a1a2a1a-L166 subclade from Augsburg (ca. 2350 BC), representing an almost full replacement of male lines among buried individuals, although the later resurgence of Neolithic lineages in the area suggests the survival of groups absent from the archaeological record. Twenty-eight samples are of R1b1a1b1a1a2b-U152 lineages, among them R1b1a1b1a1a2b1-L2 subclade is reported for twenty individuals from Bohemia and six from Bavaria. Apart from these, there is a sample of hg.

R1b1a1b1a1a2-P312 (ZZ11+, DF27 equivalent) from Quedlinburg, and another possibly of hg. R1b1a1b1a1a1-U106[27] from Radovesice, supporting the initial variability of expanding groups before subsequent Y-chromosome bottlenecks.

Later samples from the Maros culture, from Szöreg (ca. 2100–1600 BC), show an ancestry in common with Carpathian Bell Beakers and cultures derived from an admixture with Yamna settlers. Interestingly, one sample clusters close to the available Early Celtic group formed by Celtiberians (likely of Urnfield origin) and Hallstatt samples, with the other two Maros samples appearing within the range of Hungarian EBA and later Roman samples, suggesting that the Danubian EBA represented at least part of the common population that spoke Italo-Celtic. One individual is of hg. G2a2a1a2a-Z6488, a haplogroup also found in a previous central European Bell Beaker, in the Vučedol Tell, and earlier in Ötzi the Iceman (Allentoft et al. 2015).

The pan-European nature of Únětice makes it the best candidate for a late community connecting a *continuum* of already separated dialects: Pre-Celtic near the lower Danube, Pre-Italic south of the Alps, Pre-Germanic to the north around Scandinavia, and Pre-Balto-Slavic to the east, probably represented in this period by either the North-Eastern EBA province or Mierzanowice-Nitra. Particularly strong may have been the connection between Pre-Germanic and Pre-Balto-Slavic with the shift to a northern centre of gravity represented by the Classical Únětice stage, and the emergence of Trzciniec potentially allowing for the spread of certain innovations and vocabulary (Kortlandt 2016), although an earlier link through the Northern European Plains with the spread of R1b1a1b1a1a1-U106 lineages may offer a better explanation for the shared

---

[27] Originally reported as R1b1a1b-M269, also assigned to this haplogroup with Yleaf in (Wang et al. 2019) supplementary materials. Further subclade R1b1a1a2a1a1c2b2-Z9 reported by Richard Rocca. Nevertheless, Alex Williamson reports this SNP call as potentially the result of deamination, and bad coverage cannot help distinguish even within the R1b1a1b1a1a2-P312 or R1b1a1b1a1a1-U106 trees.

substrate (see *§vii.1. Western and Eastern Uralians* and *§viii.7. Germanic peoples*).

Thought to have evolved from the admixture of Bell Beakers with late Corded Ware groups, Únětice shows similar Steppe ancestry in samples from Saxony-Anhalt (ca. 54%) and Bohemia (ca. 50%), consistent with a common origin in the south-east and some degree of demic diffusion to the north into early Bell Beaker groups and other indigenous groups derived from late Corded Ware. There is at least a partial resurge of hunter-gatherer ancestry in Únětice, although only a slightly lesser genetic affinity to Yamna than in Bell Beaker groups (Haak et al. 2015). A resurgence of the previous male lines is observed directly from one of the oldest individuals attributed to Proto-Únětice groups, one Łęki Małe (ca. 2300–2050 BC), of hg. R1a1a1-M417 (Allentoft et al. 2015); three from Czech Proto-Únětice or Old Únětice from Moravská Nová Ves (ca. 2300–1900 BC), two of hg. R1-M173, one of hg. G2a2a1a-PF3177; and among those of Únětice proper, of typical Neolithic I2-M438 and Yamna R1b1a1b1-L23 lineages:

Central European samples (ca. 2140–1940 BC) include one I2-M438 from Eulau, one I2a1b2-Y10705 and one I2a2-L596 from Esperstedt (Mathieson et al. 2015; Haak et al. 2015); samples from Bohemia (ca. 2200–1700 BC) include one I2a1a-P37.2, and one I2a2a-S6635, apart from three of hg. R1-M173, one of them of hg. R1b1a1b1a1a1-U106 (subclade R1b1a1b1a1a1c1a-S497, formed ca. 2200 BC, TMRCA ca. 2200 BC), and another of hg. R1b1a1b1a1a2-P312 (Olalde et al. 2018).

This resurgence of Neolithic I2-M438 and typical CWC R1a1a1-M417 haplogroups is probably related to the loss of internal coherence among Bell Beaker groups, suggested by the emergence of Proto-Únětice as an amalgam of Bell Beaker and local traditions. This interpretation is supported by similar resurgence events of local haplogroups, e.g. of I2-M438 in late Corded Ware groups from the central European areas, as the CWC grip weakened against the expansion of Yamna and Bell Beakers, and the centre of gravity shifted to

the east (see *§vii.1. Western and Eastern Uralians*); as well as in late Bell
Beaker groups from the Carpathian Basin (see *§viii.10. Carpathian Bell
Beakers*).

On the periphery of the Únĕtice territory, a sample from Untermeitingen
(ca. 1600 BC) shows hg. R1b1a1b1a1a-L151 (xR1b1a1b1a1a2-P312), before
the shift of power that accompanied the emergence of the Tumulus culture
from Upper Danube groups (Allentoft et al. 2015). Samples from the Lech
Valley show continued patrilocality, in spite of the steady increase in Neolithic
ancestry, with Steppe ancestry dropping from ca. 42% during the Bell Beaker
period to ca. 38% during the EBA, and to ca. 26% during the MBA (Mittnik,
Massy, et al. 2018).

Scarce samples from the Urnfield culture, all from a north-eastern territory
in modern Saxony, near groups of the Lusatian culture, show a mixture of
lineages, suggesting continuity with earlier Únĕtice groups of the area: a
sample from Halberstadt (ca. 1085 BC) shows hg. R1a1a1b1a2-Z280 (Lipson
et al. 2017), and among the reported haplogroups from the Lichtenstein cave
(ca. 1000 BC) there are eight I2a1b2a-L38, one R1b-M343, and two possibly
R1a1-M459[28] (Schilz 2006).

The Hallstatt culture has been traditionally associated with the Proto-Celtic
expansion (Chadwick 1970). Two inhumated individuals of the Hallstatt
culture from Lovosice, Bohemia (ca. 840–690 BC), hypothesised to
correspond to immigrant nobility among cremated individuals, cluster among
central European populations, but apparently with some Scythian-like
contributions, proper of Balkan populations to the east (de Barros Damgaard,
Marchi, et al. 2018). One of them is of hg. R1b1a1b1a1a2b-U152[+], while
another sample from Mitterkirchen (ca. 700 BC) shows hg. G2a2b2a1b-L497
(Kiesslich et al. 2004), which supports the origin of Urnfield and especially
Hallstatt among southern groups of central Europe.

---

[28] Haplogroup R reported respectively as Ri and Ri?

The Mainz research project of bio-archaeometric identification of mobility has not proven to date a mass migration of Celtic peoples in central Europe ca. 4th–3rd centuries BC, i.e. precisely in a period where textual evidence informs of large migratory movements (Scheeres 2014). La Tène material culture points to far-reaching interregional contacts and cultural transfers (Burmeister 2016), which may suggest that the sociocultural phenomenon associated with the expansion of La Tène culture (and Common Celtic-speaking peoples) is different from previous expansions, and closer to later ones, based on alliances and confederation-like multi-ethnic groups.

Nevertheless, the arrival of Celts in Iberia was likely marked by the increase in Steppe-related ancestry in all sampled Iron Age populations. The best fits for the source population vary between groups, but for Celtiberians from La Hoya in the modern Basque Country region (ca. 400–200 BC), showing the highest relative contribution of a 'foreign' source (ca. 35%), it is likely a central European source, and Pre-Iberian and Iberian samples from the north-east show up to 98% of CEU BBC-related ancestry (Olalde et al. 2019). In the British Isles, this expansion probably corresponds to an 'eastern' shift observed in the PCA of Roman Iron Age samples (ca. AD 250) from England (Martiniano et al. 2016) compared to previous Chalcolithic and Bronze Age ones (Olalde et al. 2018). At least in Iberia, this admixture is estimated to have occurred likely corresponding with the arrival of the Urnfield tradition.

This arrival of Celts was most likely related to the spread of, among others, late R1b1a1b1a1a2b-U152 and R1b1a1b1a1a2a-DF27 lineages—shared with central European or northern Italian populations—into Iron Age Britain and Iberia, possibly associated with the expansion of variants involved in lactase persistence and skin depigmentation, in spite of the described general genetic continuity between EBA and modern populations in Ireland and Great Britain (Cassidy 2018). The only reported haplogroup among three sampled Celtiberians is I2a1a1a-M26.

It is unclear which precise R1b1a1b1a1a2b-U152 subclades may correspond to the expansion of Celts and which ones to Roman peoples, without ancient DNA samples. In fact, I2a1b1a1a-M284 lineages concentrated in Great Britain (with mutational divergence suggesting its foundation ca. 300 BC) provide "some tentative evidence of ancient flow with eastern areas that could support the idea that the La Tène culture was accompanied by some migration" (McEvoy and Bradley 2010).

Similarly, the spread of R1b1a1b1a1a2a1b1a1-M167/SRY2627 (TMRCA ca. 1500 BC), with subclades Z202 and Z206 peaking in modern eastern Iberian populations (Solé-Morata et al. 2017), but also found widespread in France and southern Germany, may represent the expansion of Celtic peoples with these lineages, originally probably associated with the Urnfield or Mailhacien cultures in northern Iberia.

Later samples from north-east Iberian Iron Age, from the Greek colony of Emporion (ca. 500–100 BC), show at least one haplogroup R1b1a1b1a1a2a1b2-L165 (formed ca. 2500 BC, TMRCA ca. 2200 BC), subclade of R1b1a1b1a1a2a1b-S228, from which R1b1a1b1a1a2a1b1a1-M167 ultimately derives; and R1b1a1b1a1a2b1-L2[+], a subclade of R1b1a1b1a1a2b-U152 (Olalde et al. 2019). Both attest to an earlier presence in Iberia than the Roman invasion, and thus support their potential arrival with incoming Celts, if not from earlier migrations.

VIII.7. Northern EEBA province

VIII.7.1. Rhenish / Dutch groups

The clearest prehistorical natural division in the region is marked by the wide river areas of the Rhine, Meuse and Ijssel, constituting a permanent border between a Nordic network to the north and east, and an Atlantic network to the south and west. In the early Neolithic, loess soils were inhabited by farmers of the Linearbandkeramik culture and related groups, while the delta was occupied by farmer-hunter-fishers of the Swifterbant culture, and later the late Vlaardingen culture. The Single Grave culture was widely distributed as successor to the Funnel Beaker culture, and its barrows are seen from ca. 2900 BC onwards, replacing the earlier megalithic tradition. Until 2500 BC, the Stein group dominated the areas of the Meuse region down to the Belgian border (Fokkens and Fontijn 2013).

Shortly after 2500 BC the first Bell Beaker traits appeared in the north, possibly through the south-western German province along the Rhine, with influence under the early Mittelelbe–Saale province—closely related, like the Danubian EBA and North Italian province, to the early expanding East Bell Beaker group—with a core development in the Lower Rhine / Low Lands area. The earliest use of metal in the region date to the late phase of the Bell Beaker culture (ca. 2300–2000 BC), with evidence of local metalworking replacing stone as the dominant material for the production of axes (Fokkens and Fontijn 2013).

The Rhenish / Dutch Bell Beaker province, although not part of the East Bell Beaker core, had an important role as transmitter of impulses for the north, similar to the role that the North Italian core had for the south. Although Bell Beakers and their immediate cultural successor EBA Barbed Wire Beaker groups appear as a coherent tradition, this homogeneity is only apparent from similarities in building monumental barrows (lasting until ca. 1400 BC), and by the common developments, like the addition of tin–bronzes to metalworking ca. 2000–1800 BC, in common with adjacent western Germany and northern France. Traditional cultural divisions marked by geography probably persisted, though (Fokkens and Fontijn 2013).

The Riesenbecher group appears between the lower Rhine and the Elbe, with their twisted cord-decorated pottery (*Wickelschnurkeramik*), in the transition to the Middle Bronze Age. The region shows leaf-shaped flint daggers, like those of the Nordic Bronze Age, and imports from other neighbouring regions, and especially from the British Isles, which puts the lower Rhine region together with the Low Lands as intermediaries between Atlantic and central European traditions (Fokkens and Fontijn 2013).

At the end of the EBA (ca. 1850 BC), this division becomes evident in archaeology again: north and east of the rivers Ijssel and Vecht, the Elp tradition shows plain, undecorated pottery tempered with broken quartz. Longhouses, typical of the lowlands and Scandinavia since the Late Neolithic, must have gradually increased during the EBA, and are dominant since ca. 1500 BC over a much larger area in north-west Europe (in low-lying areas).

This house type was probably related to the expansion of mixed farming combined with cattle-stalling and collecting of manure, and may have inhabited by extended families. Settlements appear to be formed by one or two farmsteads, and repeated use of settlements and periods of abandonment can be seen. Outbuildings probably show granaries, and circular ditches and pit circles probably functioned as grain-storage facilities, similar to low-lying areas of Denmark. In north-west Germany, the typical settlement consisted of a long *Wohnstallhaus* (house-and-barn) with small ancillary buildings, protected by simple fences. They represent largely self-sufficient farmsteads, with five to eight families, which lasted maximum three or four generations. No fortified settlements are found in the area (Fokkens and Fontijn 2013).

The subsistence economy includes stock rearing and arable farming, with the system of 'Celtic' fields being developed from the MBA, and probably reaching full development during the LBA, although probably only during the Iron Age were large continuous fields present around farms. Wide banks around the fields have been explained as evidence of mixing depleted topsoil from the fields approximately every five years with dung from stables, and then bringing the enriched soil back onto the field. Bronze production increases during this period, with axes, spearheads, arrowheads, knives and ornaments locally made, while flint remained in use (Fokkens and Fontijn 2013).

The tradition during the Bronze Age (until ca. 1200 BC) is inhumation, with dead laid out stretched on their back, sometimes accompanied by grave gifts, rarely bronzes and pottery. Bronze Age barrows are more modest than those of the Nordic Bronze Age (ca. 15 m) —their size not representing the status of the dead—and they are occasionally surrounded by wooden posts. Chieftain burials show a set of weapons and standardised tools, and may represent an idealised way to bury important ancestors, with barrows often built on older ones. Imports from the Atlantic region show maritime connections linking the Channel coasts to north German and Danish areas. Occasional Nordic imports also support these trade connections. Atlantic and continental contacts shift during the Middle and Late Bronze Age, probably representing shifts in the main centres of trade (Fokkens and Fontijn 2013).

After 1200 BC, Urnfield pottery appears in the Ems group north and east of the Ijssel, while the southern regions are under the influence of the Lower Rhine Urnfield culture, in contact with the Rhin–Suisse–France Oriental tradition and their marked forms and incised decoration. Cremation becomes the dominant treatment of the dead, and urnfields develop first with monumental barrows on the same spots (which points to long traditions of intermittent use), with pottery featuring prominently in cemeteries. After 1000 BC all urnfield barrows show the same form, small barrows surrounded by a shallow ditch and a causeway in the south-east (Fokkens and Fontijn 2013).

During the Late Bronze Age (1000–800 BC), the longhouse disappears, and a new, smaller type dominates during the Early Iron Age, possibly connected to a change in social structure into single family groups, also seen in the transition from barrows to urnfields. More people are buried visibly in this period. Based on the small number of families represented in urnfields, communities probably consisted usually of three or four farmsteads (Fokkens and Fontijn 2013).

VIII.7.2. Nordic Late Neolithic

In Scandinavia, farming communities had already abandoned their subsistence strategy for the development of transhumance (Jensen 2003). With the latest Middle Neolithic phase (ca. 2800–2400 BC), Corded Ware/Battle Axe groups appear in Norway, but the extent of their influence is unclear, and seems constrained to some limited "islands" or groups in the east, probably interacting with late Funnel Beaker and hunter-gatherer groups (Prescott 2012).

The Corded Ware migration was the result of small-scale immigration, which brought about changes in subsistence economy in the new small settlement patches mainly concentrated in southern Scandinavia. The arrival of Corded Ware settlers did not represent a significant change from older traditions, with migrants having a more pronounced terrestrial bearing, targeting pastures and hunting grounds rather than waterways. They did not trigger any substantial regional change (Prescott, Sand-Eriksen, and Austvoll 2018).

A migration of Bell Beaker groups to Jutland during the mid–3rd millennium BC seems to have brought skills in mining and sailing, introducing mass production of flint daggers, as well as the first metal daggers (an imitation of copper and bronze prototypes). This Dagger Period of the Late Nordic Neolithic also represents the introduction of a more ranked social organisation, and a new ideology, with a farm institution (longhouses and fields), and an economy based on agropastoralism, integrating the diverse previous cultural traditions into a single south Scandinavian cultural sphere (Kristiansen 2009).

Bell Beaker settlers, probably from northern Jutland, migrated thus to western Scandinavia, evidenced by the appearance of bifacial tanged–and–barbed points ("Bell Beaker points") in the early Bell Beaker period ca. 2400 BC. Their coastal distribution in northern Scandinavia and limited inland expansion underscores the maritime nature of the initial Bell Beaker expansion. The new settlers were probably attracted by hunting products, political power, pastures, and most especially metals (Prescott, Sand-Eriksen, and Austvoll 2018).

A massive transfer of knowledge, institutions and practices—accompanied by a massive movement of peoples—happened thus ca. 2400–2350 BC in the coasts of northern Scandinavia, with some of the first migrants probably disembarking at or near the harbour discovered in Slettabø. Southern immigrants occupied environments similar to their territories in Jutland. Metal prospecting would explain the initial exploration along the western coast and the fjords, reaching as far north as Mjeltehaugen, possibly as 'scouts' (Anthony 1990). These prospectors eventually established permanent settlements on the coast, and long-term links with neighbouring indigenous groups, opening thus new territories, and having a significant transformative impact during the following generations by controlling the maritime network (Prescott, Sand-Eriksen, and Austvoll 2018). They eventually established a new coastal elite (Sand-Eriksen 2017).

The rapid adaptation of new practices to such hostile environments indicate the active participation of people with long traditions in the region. Such migratory movements "were probably related to the inherently expansive pastoral ideology, bolstered by a male warrior ideal, wanderlust, ideologically encouraged travelling/knowledge seeking, but also resource prospecting in a world rapidly embracing metallurgy and trade in exotica" (Prescott 2012).

A long transition follows the arrival of Bell Beakers, from around 2200 BC to 1700–1600 BC, which continues in part Late Neolithic traditions—such as longhouses, flintwork, metalwork and burial rites—and incorporates them to the new culture (Figure 63). The Dagger Period integrated the diverse cultural traditions of the previous period into a single south Scandinavian cultural sphere under the influence of Bell Beakers (Prescott 2009), which suggests the

formation of "a shared Nordic language based upon the frequent interaction
that followed from the distribution of flint daggers" (Kristiansen 2009).

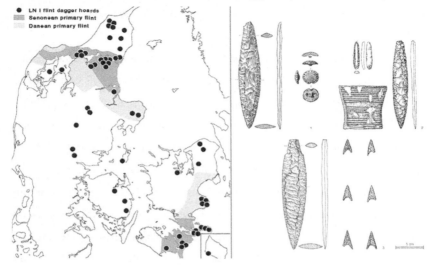

*Figure 63. Left: Hoards of type 1 flint daggers and sources of flint, coinciding with the
concentration of Beaker material in northern Jutland (Prescott 2009). Right: Beaker
burials from northern Jutland including type I flint daggers. Images from (Vandkilde
2005).*

This regional continuity is seen in the thousands of flint daggers (hence the
'Dagger Period'), while the European connection is evident from metal finds,
particularly flat axes and flanged axes, first imported from central and western
Europe (Anglo-Irish axes), but gradually increasing in native forms with a
different craft tradition; metal supply was dependent on central European ores;
and rich metal hoards show close contact zones between the Únětice culture of
central Germany and the EBA in Mecklenburg. (Jockenhövel 2013).

Such a direct strong cultural connection was possible thanks to
communications through the strait of Skagerrak between northern Jutland and
southern Norway. This, and the superior attractiveness of the Bell Beaker
culture—apart from its military expansiveness—provided the necessary
unifying conditions and infrastructure for the expansion and linguistic
unification of Scandinavia quickly during the following Late Neolithic and
early Bronze Age period (Prescott 2012).

To a certain extent, taking the example mentioned by Prescott (2012), the previous Corded Ware and the following Bell Beaker cultures could be compared with explorations of Sparta and Athens: Sparta and Corded Ware represent terrestrial brutal force, while Athens and Bell Beaker represent maritime mobility and trade, and an appealing ideology.

VIII.7.3. Northern EBA – MBA

During the Bronze Age, at least two social spheres can be described in Scandinavia: one of agriculture and husbandry related to the inland; and one of maritime nature, forming a decentralised social organisation led by warriors focused on seaborne transport, trade, and raids, related to the sea and the coastal rocks (as well as to rock art, barrows, and burial cairns). Unlike in the previous Neolithic period, certain parts of the elite invested in the maritime forces of production and controlling long-distance trade, establishing chiefdoms from coastal settlements close to agropastoral production areas (Earle et al. 2015; Ling, Cornell, and Kristiansen 2017; Prøsch-Danielsen, Prescott , and Holst 2018).

Geography defines long-lasting cultural divisions: southern Scandinavia (Jutland and southern and western Swedish coasts) shows best conditions for agriculture; central parts of Sweden and southern Norway (as far north as Trondheim) show arable zones along the sea and near Swedish lakes, but with pine forest dominant to the north; the north and the inland mountain zone shows limited potential for agriculture, and thus continuing Mesolithic economy with hunting and fishing as main components (Thrane 2013).

Southern Scandinavia, with its participation in the larger European network of bronze exchange, may have acted as the periphery of European Bronze Age societies. A more complex distinction may be more precisely made on a regional scale between southern, central and northern Scandinavia, with centre–periphery relationships based on the dynamics of regional cycles of production and alliances. Rock carvings define a common culture concentrated especially in western Sweden and south Norway, and help at the same time determine influence zones. A northern Neolithic tradition of hunters shows big game and fish motifs, located on rocks in the north and along inland rivers; a farmers' or southern tradition is mainly represented by ship depictions, but cattle and other domestic motifs also occur (Thrane 2013).

The longhouse, which continues a Neolithic tradition as two-aisled, changes to a three-aisled structure, an innovation that connected the region with the south and the western Baltic. The orientation is nearly always west–east, with entrance on the long side, and living quarters in the west. In central Scandinavia and the northern coasts, small huts—resulting from seasonal settlements—are also seen. Subsistence economy included cereal cultivation (mainly barley, also emmer and spelt), cattle and sheep herding, with farms described as mobile, evidenced by shifting settlements over small territories (Thrane 2013).

Hemispherical burial mounds predominate as funerary rituals, with turves in the south and cairns formed of boulders in the north. Both tend to form lines along land routes and coasts, with clusters indicating centres of population (Johansen, Laursen, and Holst 2004). Initially conceived for single burials, barrows could be subsequently enlarged to accommodate more burials. Their relative number (a hundred thousand mounds in the south, thirty thousand cairns in the north) may give an approximate idea of the relative population density of those who shared a similar culture (Thrane 2013).

Burials show wooden coffins, with the body extended on its back, head to the west (changing in the MBA to a north–south orientation). Pottery shows scarce decoration and continuity with Late Neolithic *Kummerkeramik*. Tumulus and Lusatian pottery influences local pottery with new types—small amphorae with two small handles—and a smoother appearance (Thrane 2013).

At the beginning of the central European MBA (ca. 1450 BC), tin–bronze becomes established initially marked by widely distributed flanged axes, early spearheads, and pins with perforated spherical head, from south German and Swiss culture areas. Influences from central Europe are seen in all Bronze Age stages: early in Apa-type swords, the first spearheads, and the spiral ornamentation, together with local forms. Bronzes were often cast with little reforging. Some assemblages are reminiscent of Mycenaean, Near Eastern, and Egyptian models, with findings of Baltic amber in the eastern Mediterranean pointing to indirect connections with the region via land or sea (Jockenhövel 2013).

Swords become the emblem of the Bronze Age, and are especially numerous in south Scandinavia. Imported Apa-type swords from south-east and central Europe reach as far as Uppland (eastern Sweden). To the south, in north Germany, short swords of the Sögel–Wohlde culture (ca. 1450–1100 BC), apparent heir of the earliest Nordic Bronze Age in southern Jutland, are found in the eastern lowlands, from the Rhine in the west to the Elbe in the east, and to Jutland to the north. It features inhumations in large burial mounds—unlike the contemporaneous Tumulus culture of central Europe—with male-only stone cist graves (Jockenhövel 2013). In the north, the Valsømagle long sword represents the start of solid-hilted swords in few regional workshops. Octogonal-hilted and flage-hilted swords of the type of the Tumulus culture are also imported. Spearheads are also characteristic of the whole Nordic BA, as are different axe types. Flintwork remains in sue but gradually decreases in quality (Thrane 2013).

Southern groups can be identified by specific weapon combinations: the West Holstein group (sword, spearhead), the Segeberg group (sword, plastave, like the Stade group), and the West Mecklenburg group (sword, palstave, dagger). In central Scandinavia, groups are defined by local environment, such as the segmented fjord landscapes of Norway, along the big rivers and lakes of Sweden, inland and coastal settlements of Sweden. Male burials show an emphasis on fighting, and settlements are isolated farmsteads—formed by house–and–barn buildings, and a byre provided for cattle—near the burial mounds. Hence chiefs and warriors represented a prosperous rural community.

Population density seems to have been limited, and settlements unstable, compared to other European regions (Jockenhövel 2013).

Figure 64. The gilded side of the Trundholm sun chariot, possibly of Danubian influence because of its early date (ca. 1400 BC). Image modified from original of Nationalmusset at <http://samlinger.natmus.dk/DO/2613>.

Mounds may contain several graves, often a man and a woman placed together, and possibly successively showing a distinction between generations. Graves are identified by their goods: short swords or daggers, flanged axes, heart-shaped flint arrowheads, pins, and occasionally small spiral-shaped gold rings. The mound can thus be viewed as a family burial site of an egalitarian society, belonging to an agriculturally-orientated single farm (Jockenhövel 2013). Annual imports of metal in the region—that began during the EBA—require regular and well-organised long-distance trade expeditions. Similarly, woollen textiles, whether finished or semi-finished, were also imported, with a market of Baltic amber (as found in Iberia, especially concentrated in Catalonia) cited as one potential north–south trade network established that justifies the presence of Iberian metals in Scandinavia from at least ca. 1200 BC (Radivojević et al. 2018).

During the late phase of the Central European MBA, other regions are incorporated into the Nordic BA, especially Mecklenburg–Vorpommern, in an expansion that remains unclear in archaeological terms, with the first imports from the Danube–Moravia–Bohemia region appearing and giving rise to local imitations (Figure 64). The new central European religious movement reaches the north, bringing cauldron–wagons, bird symbolism, and a change from inhumation to cremation (which becomes the only burial rite in the LBA). Cemeteries contain up to several hundred urn burials (urnfields), as in central Europe (Jockenhövel 2013).

VIII.7.4. Nordic LBA

The Nordic LBA (from ca. 1100 BC) brings thus pots used as containers for cremated remains more often than before, but without reaching the variety of central Europe or the Lusatian culture. The region north of the Mittelgebirge zone, between the lower Rhine and the Saale and Elbe, which already showed pottery and bronzes with less differentiation during the Urnfield period, become increasingly influenced by the later Nordic Bronze Age from around 1000 BC (Jockenhövel 2013).

Cultural and political influences characteristic of the north—single-bladed razor-knives, often with boat decoration, tweezers, brooches, and cast bronze bowls—are spread in burials and hoards across the European lowlands from the Rhine to Pomerania, with certain richly equipped graves among the common modest graves showing a social evolution similar to contemporaneous central European trends. The Urnfield *Vogelsonnenbark* (bird-sun-boat) is copied from imported bronze vessels (Thrane 2013).

Graves become smaller because of the cremation rite, and large artefacts are no longer found in assemblages. During this period, urns take over as containers of the dead, although stone cists and cremation pits are also found. Most cremation burials do not show metal objects. The decline in swords used as grave goods coincides with a more limited import of swords from the Urnfield culture, and a development of local types with kidney and horned pommels, and a monotype with reinforced tip. Socketed axes dominate during the whole LBA, in increasingly small versions (Thrane 2013).

In the early phase (ca. 900–700 BC), cross-regional communication becomes evident between the Danube region and the Elbe and Oder, with cultural links reaching as far as the Pyrenées. Herzsprung-type round shields appear probably first as wooden shields in Ireland, and then expand as leather or bronze shields to the Nordic Bronze Age and up to the eastern Mediterranean (Thrane 2013).

VIII.7.5. Pre-Roman Iron Age

The transition to the Iron Age shows continuity (e.g. longhouses and hoard deposition) with new Hallstatt elements (such as new types of pin, razors, and absence of native weapons) marking a break with the previous period. The appearance of the Jastorf culture (ca. 600–550 BC) east of the Rhine signals the end of the Bronze Age in the region. It contrasts in material culture, especially metal ornaments and pottery, with the La Tène style to the south and west, and shows the clearest connection to Germanic tribes mentioned in ancient sources during the first century BC (Jockenhövel 2013).

The Pre-Roman Iron Age in Scandinavia spans the period ca. 500–1 BC, when bronze was replaced by iron in most tools and weapons. While the technology was introduced from central Europe, iron ores were readily available as raw materials in Scandinavian territory, and efficient techniques were developed to extract serviceable iron from the many impurities contained in local sources. The society was organised by ranks, and neck rings were a marker of elite status. Bog offerings continue during this period, while human sacrifice becomes widespread only from ca. 1st century BC (Perdikaris 2004).

The Pre-Roman Iron Age is considered a regression period, with continuity in settlement patterns—with site types correlated with soil types—but materials evidencing a decline in the population, possibly due in part to a wetter and colder climate that caused deciduous trees to disappear and glaciers to re-form on high grounds. This trend lasted 260 years, starting ca. 600 BC, with further fluctuations seen ca. 300 BC and then close to 1 AD. This affected farming, with woodlands expanding at the expense of pastures and arable land, possibly also due to a concentration of settlements in permanent farms and villages. In Jutland, longhouses become much smaller, with room for one family household, but many clustering together to form villages (Perdikaris 2004).

During the period ca. 200 BC – AD 200, a generally warm, dry climate was favourable for cereal cultivation, which marked the development of the agricultural landscape (with coexisting intensive and extensive strategies), and also the economic and social landscape. 'Mobile villages' point to the formation of so-called Celtic fields—in common with central Europe—and evidence of fences from ca. 300 BC, to protect villages and cattle, eventually surrounding each farmstead or building complex. Economic activities included cattle breeding, crop raising, and some blacksmithing, pottery making, weaving, and spinning (Perdikaris 2004).

During the 3rd to mid–2nd c. BC, the last enclaves of the Lusatian culture and mainstream Pomeranian culture disappeared under cultural influences in their western territories. Along the Oder river, Pomeranian societies were replaced by so-called *Pit Grave* groups under the influence of expanding Proto-Germanic Jastorf culture, probably from migrations from its cradle in Jutland and northern Germany. The Przeworsk culture emerged in central Poland (see *§VIII.8.5. Pomeranian and West Baltic Kurgans culture*), while the strongest impact was seen in the north, where the Oksywie culture formed in the lower Vistula region. Women and men were buried according to distinct rites. Cremated female bones were put in simple pits, males were buried in urns. Stone covers or standing stelae are characteristic of these graves. This culture gave rise eventually to the Wielbark culture, identified with the Goths (Perdikaris 2004).

viii.7. Germanic peoples

The Bell Beaker period is the only reasonable candidate for the spread and final entrenchment of a common Indo-European language throughout Scandinavia, and particularly Norway (Prescott and Walderhaug 1995). The best candidate for an original homeland of the Pre-Germanic dialect of North-West Indo-European migrating into Scandinavia is the Beaker culture of the Low Countries and the western part of the Northern European Plain (Kristiansen 2009). Samples of Bell Beakers and Barbed Wire Beakers from Oostwoud in the Netherlands (ca. 2500–1900 BC) show elevated Steppe ancestry (ca. 58%) and R1b1a1b1a1a2-P312 lineages, compatible with the admixture of Yamna lineages with local Corded Ware peoples.

Dutch–German lowland areas share cultural roots with the southern Scandinavian area (Butler, Arnoldussen, and Steegstra 2011/2012), which predate technological and economic exchanges between Urnfield and Northern Bronze Age Scandinavia (Kristiansen and Suchowska-Ducke 2015). Samples of the Bronze Age Elp culture from Oostwoud (ca. 1900–1600 BC) show Steppe ancestry (ca. 51%), and hg. R1b1a1b1a1a1-U106, which is consistent with the apparent Y-chromosome bottleneck of Scandinavian Bell Beakers, and thus with the development of a Pre-Germanic community first around Jutland.

Nordic Middle Neolithic samples include an individual from Kyndelöse (ca. 2900–2500 BC), of hg. R1a1a1b1a3a-Z284, subclade R1a1a1b1a3a2a1-Z281/CTS2243[+] (Allentoft et al. 2015), and a Late Neolithic sample from Ölsund, central-east Sweden (ca. 2600–2150 BC) shows hg R1a1a1b-Z645 (Mittnik, Wang, et al. 2018), both lineages related to Corded Ware settlers. A replacement of male lines is observed already during the Dagger Period, with two samples reported from Skåne, one from Lilla Bedinge (ca. 2150 BC) of hg. R1b1a1b1a1a1-U106[+], typical of incoming Bell Beakers, and another from Abbekås (ca. 1900 BC) of hg. I1-M253, proper of Neolithic Scandinavia. Dubious is the subclade of a sample from Marbjerg, Denmark (ca. 2080 BC), of hg. R1-M173 (Allentoft et al. 2015), although—based on later samples— probably also R1b1a1b1a1a1-U106.

There is continuity in southern Scandinavia during the Bronze Age (ca. 1500–1100 BC), with three samples from Skåne showing hg. I-M170 (probably all I1-M253), and one from Denmark showing hg. R1b1a1b-M269 (xR1b1a1b1a1a2-P312), i.e. likely R1b1a1b1a1a1-U106 (Allentoft et al. 2015). An LBA sample from Trundholm also shows hg. R1b1a1b1a1a-L151, clustering closer to central European BA compared to the previous samples from Scandinavia, which clustered between central European Corded Ware and Bell Beaker samples (Mittnik, Wang, et al. 2018).

These scarce samples probably reflect thus the expansion of Pre-Germanic-speaking R1b1a1b1a1a1-U106 lineages from the Northern European Lowlands into southern Scandinavia, replacing previous Corded Ware/Battle Axe R1a1a1b1a3a-Z284 lineages in Jutland and the northern Scandinavian coastal areas around the Skagerrak strait, or displacing them to the inland. The close interaction of the newcomers with the Battle Axe culture in Scandinavia (characterised by the Y-chromosome bottleneck of R1a1a1b1a3a-Z284 lineages), connected with the eastern Baltic (see *§viii.16. Saami and Baltic Finns*), is evidenced by the evolution of a North-West Indo-European-like Pre-Germanic phonology to a Proto-Germanic stage with strong phonetic Uralisms, which is compatible with long-term Finno-Samic–Germanic bilingualism and with Finno-Samic bilingual speakers eventually becoming monolingual speakers of Germanic (Kallio 2001; Schrijver 2014).

Haplogroup I1-M253 was reported previously only in a hunter-gatherer (ca. 7000 BC) from Gotland (Günther et al. 2017), and it is not clear the extent of its expansion when migrants occupied Scandinavia, first with the Corded Ware culture, and later with the Bell Beaker culture. TRB and Pitted Ware (PWC) cultures coexisted ca. 3300–2800 BC in Gotland (Fraser, Sanchez-Quinto, et al. 2018), while CWC migrated into the PWC area around 2800 BC, and both CWC and PWC lasted until their replacement by the Late Neolithic ca. 2300

BC (Vanhanen et al. 2019). A replacement of ca. 50% mtDNA haplogroups by steppe lineages during the EBA (ca. 1700–1100 BC) has been reported (Fraser, Sjödin, et al. 2018). Both facts suggest that I1-M253 lineages had a strong presence in southern Sweden at least before the arrival of Bell Beakers, and thrived once integrated into the new emerging Scandinavian Late Neolithic social structure, probably spreading to Jutland through the Kattegat sea area already mixed in different tribes with R1b1a1b1a1a1-U106 lineages, before the migration period.

During the migration period, the Baiuvarii, Alamannic peoples who settled in modern-day Bavaria, show in two sampled sites (AD 460–530) that men resembled closely modern northern and central Europeans, whereas women exhibited a high genetic heterogeneity, including signals of genetic ancestry ranging from Europe to East Asia, among them women with artificial skull deformations, whose genetic ancestry suggests an origin in south-eastern Europe (Veeramah et al. 2018). The Y-chromosome haplogroup reported for six individuals is R1b1a1b1a1a1-U106[+], including two R1b1a1b1a1a1c1-S264[+] subclades (formed ca. 2700 BC, TMRCA ca. 2200 BC), which suggests an overwhelming majority of R1b1a1b1a1a1-U106 subclades among the Alemanni.

Longobard migrants from Szólád (AD 412–604) and from the Longobard Kingdom in Collegno (AD 580–630) also show typical northern/central European ancestry (Amorim et al. 2018), compatible with their described origin in southern Scandinavia. Among reported haplogroups clearly associated with Scandinavia, there are two I1a3-Z63 (formed ca. 2600 BC, TMRCA ca. 2500 BC), one I1a1b1-L22 (formed ca. 2000 BC, TMRCA ca. 1800 BC), one R1a1a1b1a3a-Z284, and five R1b1a1b1a1a1-U106, one of them R1b1a1b1a1a1b-Z19 (TMRCA ca. 1600 BC) and the other four R1b1a1b1a1a1c-S263 (TMRCA ca. 2700 BC), including one R1b1a1b1a1a1c2b2a1b1a-Z8 (formed ca. 1800 BC, TMRCA ca. 1000 BC), and another R1b1a1b1a1a1c2b2a1b1a1-Z11 (formed ca. 1400 BC, TMRCA ca. 1400 BC).

Wielbark culture cemeteries east (Kowalewko) and west (Masłomęcz) of the Vistula have been reported as showing changes consistent with migrations during the 3rd–6th centuries AD, in terms of mtDNA (Stolarek et al. 2018), and in terms of their small genetic distance with Jutland Iron Age individuals, supporting the arrival of Goths from Scandinavia. The presence of varied haplogroups, including one I1a3a1a1-Y6626, one I2a1b1a2b1-L801, and two G2a2b-L30, compared to the uniform genetic structure of West Germanic tribes, supports the multi-ethnic nature of the East Germanic expansion (Stolarek et al. 2019).

In the north Pontic steppe, the transition from Scythian domination to the Chernyakhiv culture (ca. 200 BC – AD 300) shows a clear genetic shift to Bronze Age / Iron Age Europeans, lacking the Altaian component entirely and showing an increase in Near Eastern ancestry, which is compatible with the Ostrogothic origin of the culture. Its multi-ethnic mix may be seen in the wide cluster formed by the three reported females (ca. AD 250–550), which cluster among eastern Europeans, central Europeans, and south-eastern Europeans respectively, showing a 'central European' shift relative to the wide cluster formed by western Scythians (Järve et al. 2019).

In Iberia, samples from the Visigothic site of Pla de l'Horta in the north-east (ca. AD 500–600) are shifted to the northern and central Europe, bringing Asian mtDNA C4a1a also found in Early Medieval Bavaria. Haplogroups related to the arrival of Visigoths likely include one I-M170, R1b1a1b1a1a-L151, and a later R1b1a1b1a1a1c1a-U106 sample of a Christian interred in Sant Julià de Ramis (around the 9th c.), likely a remnant of the previous incursion. Interestingly, one sample is of E1b1b1a1b1-L618 lineage, a haplogroup also found in one Scythian from Glinoe, in a Longobard sample from Szólád, and later among early Slavs (see *§viii.8. Balto-Slavs*), and subclade E1b1b1a1b1a-L540 is found in two medieval samples from south-east Iberia (ca. AD 1000–1300). Another Visigoth is of hg. J2a1-PF4610, whose origin is difficut to classify as Mediterranean or East Germanic without further subclades (Olalde et al. 2019).

Vikings from Iceland (AD 10th–11th century) and later Icelandic individuals show six samples of hg. R1a1a1b1a3a-Z284, one of them R1a1a1b1a3a2-Z287 (formed ca. 2300 BC, TMRCA ca. 2100 BC), three of hg. R1a1a1b1a3a1-L448 (formed ca. 1200 BC, TMRCA ca 800 BC), one of which shows R1a1a1b1a3a1a-CTS4179 (TMRCA ca. 300 BC); six samples of hg. I1-M253, one of them I1b-Z131 (formed ca. 2400 BC, TMRCA ca. 2000 BC), two I1a1b1-L22, one I1a2a1a-Z62 (formed ca. 2300 BC, TMRCA ca. 2300 BC); and nine samples of hg. R1b1a1b1a-L51, at least one of them R1b1a1b1a1a1b-Z19, three unclear, and five of hg. R1b1a1b1a1a2-P312, one showing the rare subclade R1b1a1b1a1a2d-L238 (TMRCA ca. 2500 BC), found mainly among modern Scandinavian peoples, and four R1b1a1b1a1a2c1-L21, with an ancestry close to modern Welsh peoples, probably related to slaves imported from Britain (Ebenesersdóttir et al. 2018).

Late Vikings from the town of Sigtuna, in east–central Sweden (AD 10th–12th century), show varied Y-chromosome haplogroups and high genetic diversity, compatible with the intense international contacts and the Christian character of the culture (Krzewińska, Kjellström, et al. 2018). This particular sampling also shows the first haplogroup N1a1a1a1a-L392 in Sweden, found in an individual of local origin based on strontium isotope analysis and genetic structure, hence probably an integrated Proto-Germanic lineage related to earlier migrations of Iron Age Akozino warior-traders (see *§VIII.15.3. Ananyino and Akozino* and *§viii.16.2. Baltic Finns*).

While it is clear that the Y-chromosome bottleneck of R1b1a1b1a1a1-U106 lineages in northern Europe—and thus their successful expansion with certain clans into Scandinavia—is responsible for the creation of a Pre-Germanic community at the turn of the 2nd–1st millennium BC, it is unclear where exactly the Proto-Germanic community expanded from: i.e. whether it was a recent expansion of certain tribes over the whole Nordic Bronze Age territory (unifying their language before the Iron Age), or their evolution can be described as one of divergence and convergence trends between related dialects, similar to the history of the Modern German language.

Figure 65. Distribution map of 'Wedel' toponyms in Europe. This is one of the traditional reasons adduced to propose an expansion from Jutland to the south. This must be rejected, though, because of its younger distribution north of the Elbe, which supports a south–north expansion direction. Modified from Karte 71 in Udolph (1994).

The Jastorf culture can be directly connected to previous groups of southern Jutland and Northern European Lowlands, and its expansion to the spread of Germanic groups, but it is unclear to what extent this influence reached northern Scandinavia, which speaks in favour of at least some degree of long-term convergence of closely related dialects in north Scandinavia. Nevertheless, onomastic data points to the Northern European Plains between the Weser and the Oder (particularly the Weser–Elbe interfluve) as the most likely Common Germanic homeland (Figure 65), with Scandinavia as a region of late expansion with a clear non-Indo-European substrate (Udolph 1994; Kuhn, Hachmann, and Kossack 1986), which is consistent with the traditional description of Fennoscandia as Uralic-speaking (Dolukhanov 1989; Wiik 1997; Künnap 1997; Schrijver 2014).

The available data from the Barbarian invasions suggest an overwhelming majority of R1b1a1b1a1a1-U106 subclades among Elbe Germanic tribes, like the Alemanni, and probably even more so among Weser–Rhine Germanic tribes, like the Franks, based on modern populations from the western Germanic-speaking areas. North Sea Germanic tribes, like Longobards, were possibly more admixed with I1-M253 lineages in Jutland, although the mixture of Longobards with Goths incoming from the east makes the original situation less clear. North Germanic tribes, based on data from Vikings, show I1-M253 and also R1a1a1b1a3a-Z284 lineages, apart from R1b1a1b1a1a1-U106, which is probably to be expected among East Germanic tribes, too, deemed to have migrated from northern Scandinavian territories.

The association of West Germanic tribes with hg. R1b1a1b1a1a1-U106 is further supported by samples during and after the medieval *Ostsiedlung*, showing a west–east cline of R1b1a1b1a1a1-U106 (including also I1-M253) vs. R1a1a1b-Z645 (xR1a1a1b1a3a-Z284) compatible with the Germanisation of Slavs to the east of the Elbe. Although modern population samples from eastern Europe are difficult to assess without genealogical information, due to the expulsion of Germans after World War II, medieval samples from Podlažice (ca. 1180 AD) in Bohemia, as well as Nicolaus Copernicus' family origin from Koperniki near Nysa in Silesia before the 14th century (Bogdanowicz et al. 2009), seem to support the expansion of R1b1a1b1a1a1-U106 lineages associated with German settlers of the Holy Roman Empire east of the Elbe.

VIII.8. Eastern EEBA province

VIII.8.1. Mierzanowice–Nitra

The East Early Bronze Age refers specifically to the Chłopice–Veselé and Mierzanowice cultures, spanning from north-east Moravia to Lesser Poland. It represents the south-eastern periphery of the Bell Beaker culture, and is characterised by vessels and ceramic technique, including cord decoration: horizontal bands on the upper part in Proto-Mierzanowice (ca. 2350/2300–2200 BC) and with supplementary bands in the bottom half in Early Mierzanowice (ca. 2200–2050 BC). Nitra appears later, after ca. 2050 BC, with the classic phase of Mierzanowice (during its eastward expansion), probably as part of the Chłopice–Veselé culture (coincident with Proto- and Early Mierzanowice) under Únětice influence (Bertemes and Heyd 2002).

The Epi-Corded Ware Chłopice–Veselé culture represents a southern expansion of late Corded Ware groups, from Lesser Poland into the Carpathian Mountains, where they formed a border culture with influences from Pannonian cultures. The appearance of Bell Beaker communities of Silesia (ca. 2350 BC) occurred simultaneously with the transformation of the Chłopice–Veselé culture, with Bell Beaker cultural patterns influencing its transition from late CWC, evidenced by mixed materials found in Upper Silesian settlements ca. 2300–2200 BC (Furmanek et al. 2015).

Chłopice–Veselé shows flat inhumation graves with funerary ritual inherited from the Corded Ware culture and cord ornamentation, as well as copper–wire artefacts and willow–leaf ornaments, proper of the eastern regions. Bell Beaker materials disappear from Upper Silesia ca. 2150 BC. Another part of the Epi-Corded Ware complex is the Košťany culture in the north-eastern Carpathians, known from inhumation graves in flat cemeteries and similar material culture (Furmanek et al. 2015).

Proto-Mierzanowice appears with the arrival of Bell Beakers in the west part of Lesser Poland (ca. 2400–2300 BC), possibly representing an infiltration of groups rather than a massive migration. In the Proto-Mierzanowice phase, only scattered graves and short-lived settlements are found, and their distribution pattern is similar to the previous Corded Ware settlements. These small groups were very mobile, with traces found from Moravia to Volhynia. One of the important signs of change associated with BBC in this period is the position of the deceased—inverted with respect to the characteristic Corded Ware tradition—and the nature of the deposited grave goods (Bertemes and Heyd 2002).

The early phase lasts probably no more than three generations, with dynamic internal processes of indeterminate nature resulting in a stabilisation of the settlement, the establishment of large permanent settlements (like those at Mierzanowice and Iwanowice), sudden demographic development and accompanying changes in economy (animal husbandry replaced by agriculture) and society (dominant family groups replaced by local or village groups). This evolution period ca. 2300–2200 BC is coincident with the increasing advantage gained by the Únětice cultural model to the west (Włodarczak 2017), which may have triggered this reaction (Bertemes and Heyd 2002).

An adaptation to Corded Ware ideas is seen in the following period (ca. 2200–2050 BC), represented by a 'weak' acculturation and evolution of a local ethnic identity, marked by the increasing frequency in cord ornaments and the growing elaboration of decorative motifs made with the technique of cord impressions. The Mierzanowice culture gradually cut its contacts with the west, and after ca. 2000 BC the upper Oder and Vistula rivers became a real cultural barrier among Mierzanowice (to the south), Únětice (to the west), and the developing Trzciniec culture (to the north).

Similar to the Proto-Únětice evolution, Mierzanowice does not follow Corded Ware cultural traits directly during this development (like the usually proposed Kraków–Sandomierz Corded Ware group of Lesser Poland), but rather Epi-Corded Ware cultures from the Carpathian Basin over a Bell Beaker culture (Figure 66): in the stable network of large and long-lasting head settlements, the consistency in observing strict rules of funerary rites, and organisation based on sex. Such Epi-Corded Ware groups of south-east Europe include north-western Makó/Kosihý–Čaka; south-eastern Ljubljana; central Early Nagýrev, Pitvaros(–Maros); north-eastern Ada; central and southern Transdanubian Somogyvár–Vinkovci, Vučedol; southern Balkans Belotić–Bela Crkva (Włodarczak 2017).

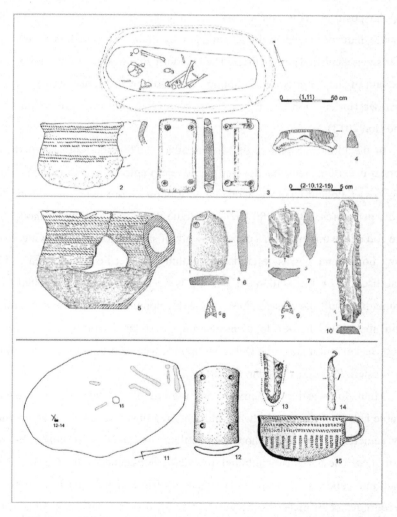

Figure 66. Grave of the Mierzanowice culture with wristguards. Modified from Jarosz et al. (2011).

The Nitra culture was also formed under the influence of Chłopice–Veselé, Makó/Kosihý–Čaka, and Bell Beaker cultures, although the gradual decrease of elements of eastern origin—such as copper willow–leaf ornaments, chipped stone in the form of shouldered points, and aspect s of funeral rite—suggest a greater western EBA influence of the culture. Bodies are in the crouched bipolar position, with a basic east–west orientation. Grave pits and pot-built houses indicate social ranking, with graves of hunters, medicine men and craftsmen identified among them. The Únětice culture expands coinciding with the end of the Nitra culture, although the tradition of bipolar west–east and east–west orientation usually survives in graves of Nitra tradition (Marková and Ilon 2013).

In the three late phases of Mierzanowice (2200–1600 BC), settlements appear in certain areas that develop stable microregional structures, centred on the Lesser Poland territory, while some groups—more numerous during the older period (ca. 2300–2200 BC)—continue the mobile settlement model. At the end of the millennium, a dense network of small settlements (having just a few homesteads) was established within the fertile loess areas. The stabilisation of the settlement pattern is seen especially after 2000 BC, coinciding with the classic phase of the development of the Únětice culture; until that point, the development of groups correlated with the late phase of Bell Beaker culture, e.g. the Dobre group in Kuyavia, or the Lower Oder group in Western Pomorze (Włodarczak 2017).

Main, long-lasting settlements and regions of constant occupation with stable households appear, always in higher regions, and always accompanied by cemeteries, alongside short-term settlements linked to certain economic activities. The burial rite, although remaining entrenched in the Corded Ware tradition and symbolism—like gender-differentiated burials with a predominance of males—shows a reaction against the previous beliefs in the avoidance of kurgan building and the use of communal graves. The position of the lower limbs was clearly less flexed, and at the same time more bodies appeared in a lateral position, which led to the crystallisation of a new tradition (as in cemeteries of the Strzyżów culture) of dead interred in a slightly flexed or extended position (Włodarczak 2017).

The social structure is based on the family unit, which inhabits a farmstead. Multiple farmsteads and a cemetery form a village, and a settlement microregion is formed by various local groups. Economic autarchy and cultural homogeneity of local groups point to their ethnic unity, but only in the latest stage would a common language be needed, because of the intense exchange contacts. Due to the homogeneity in decoration, female exogamy was probably restricted to the own culture. In the three earlier phases, Mierzanowice was a fully egalitarian society, but there was gender-based asymmetry (as in the previous Neolithic and Corded Ware cultures of the region), and also some interest in imitating prestige goods of western cultural centres, from local raw materials (Kadrow 2007).

Microregions had an area of few to 10 km^2, and some of them existed for the whole timespan of the culture. Agriculture played an important role in its subsistence economy, as did pastures at some distance of the settlements, for relatively big herds of cattle and sheep. Each settlement had 5–20 farmsteads, each with at least 200 m^2 and probably multiple buildings, including a cellar. Most settlements had less than 150–200 inhabitants, with only a few (like Mierzanowice and Wojciechowice) having more (Kadrow 2007).

Interestingly, microregions of western Lesser Poland (including the Iwanowice settlement), the Sandomierz-Opatów Upland, and the Upper Bug, appear to have suffered ca. 2050 BC a conflict and disruption of the moral order, with 'a return to the roots', reflected in the abandonment of cord ornamentation on ceramic vessels, and in the predominance of undecorated pots with knobs on their necks or rims. Similar forms were used at the beginning of the Mierzanowice culture, and also in Bell Beaker settlements over vast areas in Europe, e.g. in late groups from nearby Moravia. This process has been described as a likely rebellion whose leader would have acquired certain features of a traditionalistic ruler, invoking the 'sanctioned' Bell Beaker tradition, in order to assume power more securely, a power structure that could be maintained until ca. 1850/1800 BC (Kadrow 2017).

Before 1900 BC, there is no proof of long-distance exchange, with mostly local raw materials. The circulation of imports begins in the latest phase, and includes stone sickles, faience pearls, and rarely metal objects, at the same time as foreign influence is noticed in the local pottery production. Until then, all microregions had shown a great unity in style and typology, in spite of specific local elements. A ranked society appears in this latest phase marked by rich graves, signalling the elevated social position of some males and females, and putting an end of the gender-asymmetry (Kadrow 2007).

In the earliest phase, there were two main regions: a western one, with corded and incision ornamentation, and an eastern one, with only corded decoration. In the classic phase, the Nitra group/culture appeared in the south-west, and the Strzyżów culture in the north-east. While violence from close combat with axe–hammers is evidenced in human remains, the use of archery and related war culture proper of Bell Beaker and Únětice peoples also continue in these groups (Kaňáková, Bátora, and Nosek 2019). In the latest phase, the Mierzanowice style—initially appearing on mugs, jugs, and amphorae, and later on jars—was fragmented into four distinct local groups based on their different regional styles: Giebułtów, Szarbia, Pleszów, and Samborzec groups (Kadrow 2007).

VIII.8.2. North-Eastern province – Iwno

Before 2500 BC, the Single Grave culture had reached from Jutland to Mecklenburg and to the Polish Lowlands, through a stable network of long-range contacts that had been created in the Corded Ware A-horizon, and which followed previous similar routes of Mesolithic and Neolithic expansions, facilitated by the geographical low plains connecting the coastlines of the North Sea and the Baltic Sea. Within that framework, the Northern European Plain was connected from Dutch Beakers in the west to Jutland and to the

Polish Lowlands in the east, creating a distinct north group in the pan-European Bell Beaker network. Bell Beakers from Jutland and north-eastern Germany were the source of Pomeranian and Kuyavian Bell Beakers (Czebreszuk 2013).

The special character that distinguish them is that Bell Beaker traits are found chiefly in domestic contexts, and to a much lesser extent in burials, which manifests as secondary burials in older communal graves. Pottery shows a specific ornamentation, initially using a knurling technique for patterns, (including cord impressions or incisions), then evolving from slender beakers to shorter and squattier vases (using mainly the incision technique), and eventually developing in the latest stage barbed wire ornament, in the south-west Baltic (Czebreszuk and Szmyt 2011).

From 2400 BC, a change in the Polish Lowlands is seen with domestic sites showing signs of stabilisation towards a network of permanent territorial communities, as the result of a new system of social organisation. Larger encampments change into settlements, with occasional buildings for economic and sometimes domestic purposes, culminating in the Bronze Age. Economically, it would mean a decreased or modified role of animal husbandry (from nomadic to semi-nomadic, then to sedentary), as well as a shift to dependence on the 'politics' and local natural environment in respect to stable, farming communities, with a social system still marked by social differentiation (Czebreszuk and Szmyt 2011).

Cereal cultivation appears abundantly only after 2400 BC, first recorded in Kornice, the first Bell Beaker settlement in southern Poland, with settlements in Lesser Poland showing an increasingly important role of cultivation dated to the final Eneolithic or beginnings of the Bronze Age (Kośko 1979).

In contrast to the previous Corded Ware package, the Bell Beaker package in the Polish Plains and the south-west Baltic is recorded (from ca. 2500–2400 BC) mainly in materials from settlements and encampments, less often in funeral complexes, and is superimposed to the earlier elements without replacing them, such as ornamentation with typical Bell Beaker patterns (of fundamental significance is the bell beaker with zone and metopic-zone ornamentation, made with knurl technique or engraved), as well as stone archer's wrist guards and dagger (Czebreszuk and Szmyt 2011). The main features of this north-eastern Bell Beaker border region are thus:

- Genuine Bell Beakers.
- Zone-metope decoration.
- Application of comb–stamp decoration technique.
- Zonal decoration in general.
- Wristguards.
- Bifacial flint daggers (along with copper daggers).
- A variety of small finds, such as the V-shaped buttons.

The south-eastern Baltic centre was included in the new interregional network of exchange, with amber products becoming a widespread feature of Bell Beaker graves overall in Europe, one of the determinants of the Bell Beaker package in different regions. It can be assumed that communities living in the southern shores of the Gdańsk Bay were the main producers and distributors of amber ornaments from the turn of the 4th-3rd millennium BC until the Early Bronze Age (Włodarczak 2017).

In its western area, the eastern Bell Beaker province paved the way ca. 2300/2250 BC for the earliest traces of the Únětice culture (in its Proto-Únětice phase), in Silesia, and later in the Polish Lowlands and in the Lower Oder. The latest dates of bell beakers ca. 1800 BC are characteristic of the Iwno culture, a "syncretistic culture" where the original traits had become increasingly transformed under the influence of the Únětice culture, in a region on the route between the Únětice and the rich amber deposits on the Gulf of Gdańsk.

In the final phase of the Final Eneolithic, in north-eastern Poland, Kuyavia and Greater Poland—at the settlements of Iwno and Masuria cultures—pig rearing regained importance, which had been lost with the arrival of Corded Ware settlers (Włodarczak 2017). Since the EBA, cattle were the chief livestock, whereas pig and sheep–goats were of secondary importance, and of comparable quantity until the Late Bronze Age/Hallstatt period (Włodarczak 2017).

In the eastern area of the Polish Lowlands and Greater Poland, the late Bell Beaker stage, in combination with local post-Corded Ware and Neman groups, marked the inception of a sequence of changes that led to the so-called Trzciniec horizon, from the Warta drainage as far as the middle Dnieper (Czebreszuk and Szmyt 2012). This culture may be also related to the adoption or imitation of Bell Beaker in marginal influence zones, such as the isolated finds of comb–stamp decoration or flint daggers in the eastern Baltic, Finland and Belarus (Włodarczak 2017).

The littoral zone from the Oder delta to the Vistula delta kept a particular character, distinct from the EBA and MBA cultures developing in the area related to central Europe, because of the diverse ecological niche of the coastline and the abundant deposits of amber, a commodity in Europe during the Bronze Age. It shows stable settlements and an extensive network of cultural exchanges from the Baltic shore to the North Sea in the west, with one stable seaway connecting the lower Vistula region, Pomerania, and Mecklenburg with Jutland, and further away with the North Sea, the British Isles and Atlantic Europe (Czebreszuk 2013).

At least in the Polish Lowlands, GAC groups coexisted ca. 2400–2200 BC with little cultural interaction with Bell Beakers, which suggests a significant cultural barrier between both groups. Later, clear cooperation is seen between Bell Beaker and Únětice, while isolation of GAC groups continued, despite the absence of geographical barriers among these cultures (Włodarczak 2017).

The BBC concentration of Silesia (giving rise to proto-Únětice) was more closely connected to the Bohemian Basin, and the Lesser Poland enclave more closely connected to Moravia, both communities being therefore part of the core East Bell Beaker migration, contrasting with the northern Bell Beaker groups of the Polish Lowlands, which mixed with groups heir of the Single

Grave group of the CWC to form eventually the Trzciniec horizon
(Włodarczak 2017).

VIII.8.3. Trzciniec

During the EBA, para-Neolithic societies still survived in north-eastern
Poland, with pottery showing contacts with north-eastern Bell Beakers, but
their way of life depending on gathering and fishing, with agriculture
representing only a small part of their subsistence economy. After ca. 2000 BC,
the Trzciniec culture continued Bell Beaker traditions of the North-Eastern
BBC province (Czebreszuk 2001), and began to spread from the west (Kuyavia
and Great Poland), to the east (Masovia, Podolia, Volhynia), incorporating
these para-Neolithic groups, where it eventually developed into its distinct
archaeological form east of the Vistula. It expanded later—during its classic
phase—to the south, into Lesser Poland.

Pottery in Pomerania, Masuria and Masovia followed a different course
from those to the west and south, with less stability and inferior craftsmanship.
The most characteristic trait of the culture is the pottery of the Riesenbecher
type, featuring a small bottom and S-shaped profile. This specific type may
have had its origin during the decline of the Neolithic, with sinuous-profile
pots decorated with the so-called barbed wire ornament, also known as the
ornament of "a cord wound around a flint flake" (a decorative strip running
from the neck of the pot across the body), which connected together the vast
territories of the Northern European Plain, from England to the mouth of the
Rhine, northern Germany, Denmark, and well into east Europe (Kadrow 1998).

The first similar Riesenbecher types are found in Únětice on the lower Elbe,
and in the late Bell Beaker (or Barbed Wire Beaker) groups of north-west
Germany and Jutland, and from Iwno centres (with many significant
ornamentation patterns), which points to its expansion through the Northern
Lowlands during the Early Bronze Age. The Trzciniec pot prototypes appeared
in the Kuyavia region rather early (before 2300 BC), accompanied by the
kurling technique, which connects it with the Bell Beaker tradition. Its

expansion with migrants is evidenced by their appearance in Lesser Poland ca. 1900 BC, expanding then to the south, into the Carpathians and Ukraine (Figure 67) in the mid–2nd millennium BC (Czebreszuk 1998).

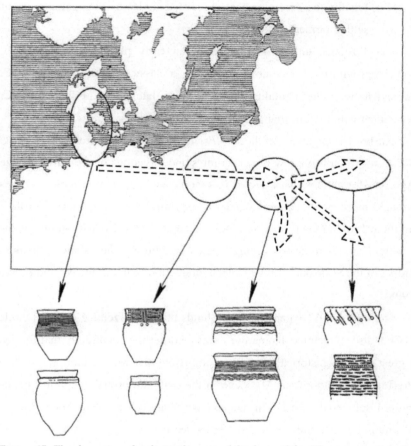

Figure 67. The dynamics of stylistic changes of the form of the "Trzciniec pot" in the lowland regions of Central Europe, and spreading routes of the Trzciniec package in Central Europe. Modified from Czebreszuk (1998).

The emergence of Trzciniec in Mierzanowice territory has been described by Jacek Górski and Sławomir Kadrow as follows (Czebreszuk 1998):

1.   Migration of "Trzciniec" population from the Lowlands.

2.   Initially the migrants occupy in the south only those ecological niches which they know from the Lowlands, i.e. the sandy oecumene.

3. The migrants come into contact with local settled farmers,
    represented by the Mierzanowice culture, which was then in a crisis;
    they adopt traits that will enable them to exploit loess niches.
4. Finally, the Trzciniec package is shared also by the communities of
    settled farmers of loess areas.

The Trzciniec culture is divided in an early phase (2000–1600 BC,
coincident with the Mierzanowice culture), a classic phase (1600–1400 BC,
coincident with the Tumulus culture), and a late phase (1400–1200 BC,
coincident with the Lusatian culture).

The borderland nature of the *stabilised* Trzciniec culture from ca. 1900 BC
makes it difficult to know the exact rates and directions of the Early Bronze
Age transformations that affected its emergence. Apparently, these societies
adopted more stable cultural standards only after their migration from their
northern lowland enclave, when they encountered the EBA traditions of the
Circum-Carpathian zone. Among 'eastern' traditions, they show cremation,
proper of the Sofievka–Middle Dnieper cremation centre (Klochko and Kośko
1998).

The traditional "expansive" view holds that the Trzciniec Cultural circle
(TCC), also "Trzciniec–Komarów", was a borderline community that formed
a great cultural–historical province, comprising different cultural groups like
Pre-Lusatian in the west, Abashevo in the east, and probably cultures of the
eastern Baltic to the north. This would have been a 'phenomenon' or a 'process
of cultural integration' (under a "Trzciniec package") of a society centred
around the potential deposits of copper in Volhynia, and located among three
large culture-making Early Bronze Age centres: Únětice–South German
(related to Pre-Lusatian), Carpathian–Danube (related to the Multi-Cordoned
Ware or Babino culture in the borderland), and Volga–Ural (related to
Abashevo and Srubna cultures). This phenomenon would have been made up
of different relatively highly autonomous groups, connecting the Carpathians
to the Balkans, Anatolia and the Mediterranean. This wide TCC community

would have developed into the Noua–Sabatinovka and eastern Trzciniec in the west, and Late Srubna and Sosnytsa in the east (Klochko and Kośko 1998).

Nevertheless, the Trzciniec culture proper (ca. 1700–1200 BC) formed its core area apparently on the drainages of the Lower and Middle Vistula, the Neman, and the Upper Pripyat, and in the taiga in the western part of the Dnieper's drainage, and expanded to the south-west and south, generating the loess groups and the Komarow culture. This area was apparently inhabited by sub-Neolithic forest or East European groups, characterised by Comb-like and Stroked Pottery culture represented by Linin-type pottery. A high density of settlement sites on the lowlands may indicate that the main reason for the population movement to the south was the increasing overpopulation of areas of poor soil between the middle Vistula, the Upper Pripyat and the Middle Neman rivers, and a resultant ecological crisis (Makarowicz 2010).

The Trzciniec culture connected the amber trade between the Baltic coast and the Carpathian Basin. The first amber route (first half of the 2nd millennium BC) ran from the Bay of Gdańsk through Kuyavia, Great Poland, Silesia, and the Carpathian Mountains through the Moravian gate, connecting with representatives of the Ottomány-Füzesabony and Mad'arovce cultures, as well as (slightly later) Piliny, Suciu de Sus, as well as Middle Danubian and Carpathian groups of the Tumulus culture. This route was further connected to the Adriatic and to the Peloponnese (Czebreszuk 2013).

A significant permeation of artefacts of southern features is observed in this area, starting only with the emergence of the Trzciniec culture. While many non-ceramic objects may be attributed to imports, due to the formation of local elites in western Lesser Poland acting as intermediaries, the imitation of vessels points to an admixture of population with that of Krakow and the Carpathian zone (and to the south), which has been suggested as the product of exogamy from around 1650/1600 BC (Górski 2012).

These increased population movements happened at roughly the same time as other European expansions, namely the Nordic culture in western Pomerania (after ca. 1700 BC), and the Tumulus culture in Lower Silesia and Lesser Poland, probably after ca. 1600 BC, both maintaining strong cultural contacts and remaining part of a unitary cultural sphere that included kurgans and hoards of metal objects (Czebreszuk 2013).

Kurgans were only one among a great variety of elements of the burial rite found in different Trzciniec communities. A common misconception is that Trzciniec *continues* the Corded Ware tradition of building kurgans over graves, because Bell Beaker and Corded Ware cultural patterns can be seen e.g. in Mazovia and in north-eastern Poland as late as the 2nd millennium BC (Włodarczak 2017). However, the appearance of a general burial rite including barrows took place only in the classic phase (ca. 1800 BC at the earliest), in the upland belt of its central and eastern European territory, between the Upper Vistula and the Upper Dniester, and on the Podolia and Volhynia uplands.

Before this period, there was a clear decline in the number of settlement sites, both in the upland and in the lowland zones, and small-sized, short-term 'campsites' in the valleys of large rivers seem to represent most settlements, evidencing a mobile economy with a pastoral or nomadic way of life since ca. 2200 BC. Only at the beginning of the 2nd millennium appear the first (rare) kurgans in the Strzyżów culture, which usually continues flat necropolis similar to the late-stage Mierzanowice tradition. These first kurgans have a different form than earlier ones, with ca. 12 m in diameter, and ca. 1.5 m. in height, containing as many as four individual graves, arranged as three graves surrounding one in the centre. This suggests a custom of honouring some people with a special type of burial that required a substantial effort in the erection of a mound (Włodarczak 2017).

There is, therefore, a gap of 200–400 years between the complete demise of late Corded Ware groups and the emergence of early Trzciniec societies in the area, and still more until their appearance in the eastern Komarow territory, so no direct borrowing or *continuation* was possible (Czebreszuk 1998; Włodarczak 2017). It is thus more likely that they adopted the tradition from autochthonous groups at the core of the culture's origin in Lesser Poland (such as Strzyżów), or from contacts with neighbouring western Bronze Age communities during their origin and expansion, such as late Bell Beaker, Únětice, Iwno, or even expanding Nordic and Tumulus cultures.

During the first half of the 2nd millennium BC, a further transition in burial customs is seen, to a less contracted burial position. A change of the Corded Ware (and 'reversed' Bell Beaker) tradition in body positioning is seen, with bodies placed supine with the legs slightly flexed. Strzyżów also continues the Kraków–Sandomierz group tradition of egalitarian necropolis (Włodarczak 2017).

A compelling argument against this adoption from neighbouring cultures is the lack of interest of the immediate predecessor of Trzciniec in the region, the Mierzanowice culture (which they replaced), in raising mounds. On the other hand, Mierzanowice was an egalitarian society organised along territorial patterns, living in large settlements and using communal cemeteries, whereas Trzciniec communities were organised in kinship groups or lineages and mobile settlements, which may have favoured the adoption of this single grave symbolism, with functions related to the identity, integrity, funerary rites, and spatial behaviour of human groups. Especially important was then the role of grave fields as stable points for the new microregional structures, in contrast to the settlements of the previous period (Makarowicz 2010).

It has been suggested that Trzciniec colonisers adopted the custom of raising barrows—usually bigger than those of the Corded Ware culture, and on the highest elevations of any given area—by imitating those seen in the landscape, as the material embodiment of a new foundation myth. This would have allowed the newcomers to take root in the new environment, among Mierzanowice populations organised in territorial communities, in an attempt to incorporate the "pre-Mierzanowice past" by legitimising their own claims to the occupied territories (Makarowicz 2010).

The colonisers would have thus won arguments sanctioned by tradition, which carried more weight with illiterate societies, while possibly Mierzanowice peoples had not raised barrows precisely to distinguish themselves from the previous Corded Ware communities. The fact that barrows were built in linear arrangements on deforested watershed hilltops may indicate communication trails following watersheds, conducive to the movement of people, animals, goods, and possibly wagons (Makarowicz 2010).

Trzciniec settlements were often inhabited by a single family, and settlers of a microregion—using common lands for burials—were probably related by kinship and organised into clans. Subsistence strategies depended upon the specific territory, and the later phase shows also metallurgy with its own style, in contrast to previous periods of scarce imports from the west (Tumulus culture) or the south (Kadrow 2007).

Eventually, the different autonomous regions of the Central European Plain or the eastern European taiga adapted to different technical, utility and ideological patterns generated by elitist societies of the south, as well as to the expanding groups from the west and east, and the so-called Trzciniec Cultural circle gradually disappeared ca. 1300–1200 BC (Klochko and Kośko 1998).

VIII.8.4. Lusatian culture

The Proto-Lusatian culture emerges as a fringe group of the central European Urnfield culture, acquiring cultural independence at the start of the LBA (ca. 1400 BC), and showing a period of uninterrupted prosperity lasting for almost a thousand years. It spans the great river systems from the Elbe, Oder, and Vistula, and acts as a mediator between south and north. Different regional groups show influences from their neighbours, but there is a strong ideological or political structure that unifies them (Jockenhövel 2013).

The Pre-Lusatian period (ca. 1700–1400 BC) represents an evolution of Únĕticean groups originally located between the Elbe and Oder basins, under the strong influence of the Tumulus culture. The area around Bruszczewo, from the Bruszczewo-Łęki Małe group (ca. 2100–1600 BC), may serve as an example of the various local disasters that could have led to this cultural division in eastern Europe: steady and intensive occupation of the land caused the depletion of trees; farming and cattle grazing which led to the degradation of the top humus layer and intensified erosion; changes in water composition including algae, eggs of human and animal parasites, and coprophilous fungi. It is very likely that the destruction of the environment ended with the demise of the group and the abandonment of the Bruszczewo settlement (Czebreszuk 2013).

Nevertheless, continuity is seen in pottery and cemeteries from the oldest period, supporting the long-term stability of the Lusatian culture in the western region. So, for example, the Kietrz cemetery, featuring approximately four thousand excavated graves in Upper Silesia, is among the largest in the entire Urnfield zone, and was used continuously from the Tumulus period up to the later stages of La Tène. Similarly, the high technological standard and specific ornamentation of knobbed ware—with knobs applied to the surface or shaped as protrusions from inside the body of the vessel—emerges during the late Tumulus and early Lusatian period. Similarities to the Eastern EBA province include the Lusatian pottery, greatly divergent from western technological standards and stylistic patterns (Czebreszuk 2013).

The western Lusatian group, between the Elbe and the Oder, can be divided into subgroups—Saale Mouth, Unstrut, and Elmsdorf or Elb–Havel groups— based on differences in burial features, pot styles and costume habits, potentially showing impediments to the spread of material culture. Urnfield groups in contact with Lusatian groups include the Middle Danubian group and the Knovíz culture to the south (in the Upper Danube) which belonged to the sphere of influence of southern Urnfield territory; whereas the Lusatian tradition belonged to the cultural orbit of northern Urnfield groups (Jiráň, Salaš, and Krenn-Leeb 2013).

During the MBA, the Lusatian tradition expanded (ca. 1400/300–500 BC) to the south-east into territories of the late Věteřov culture (heir of Únětice in

Moravia and Bohemia) forming the Moravian group. It also spread to the east into territories of previous Trzciniec culture, with a more complex expansion: in Lesser Poland, a gradual migration from Silesia is seen from ca. 1300 BC, breaking the traditional cultural barrier between the Upper Oder and Upper Vistula. In north-eastern Poland, the expansion of the culture differed from the more standard groups of Lower Silesia, Great Poland, Kuyavia, and Lesser Poland; whereas bronze objects are more abundant, population density is lower. In south-eastern Poland, the Tarnobrzeg group constituted a distinct cultural sphere, with influences from Carpathian Ruthenia to the south and the steppes to the east (Czebreszuk 2013).

The Lusatian tradition features typically large urnfields, containing thousands of graves, occupied over many generations. In contrast to Knovíz and the Middle Danubian Urnfield, where inhumation is occasionally seen, in Lusatian and Silesia–Platěnice cultures cremation is universal, and vessels are especially numerous in burial assemblages. Grave goods comprise almost exclusively large numbers of pots, with few and small metal objects. There are no graves with weapons and rich ornaments, except for the Elbe–Saale region, which functions as corridor between the Danube and the western Baltic, so the social hierarchy remains obscure (Jockenhövel 2013).

Pottery shows strong similarities in shape, typology, and ornamentation with the Urnfield culture, but differences in the evolutionary pattern can be observed, also internally among regions (Jiráň, Salaš, and Krenn-Leeb 2013):

- Initially they used decorative plastic knobs outlined with channels or grooves (heir of Tumulus culture traditions, see *§VIII.6.3. Tumulus period (MBA)*).

- In later periods, it shows continuous vertical striation, and later still these are broken into 'bundles'. There is a clear division of cooking ware and table ware, with a high technological level. In terms of shape, vessels evolve from sharply contoured forms toward soft, flowing profiles and a reduction in the height of certain forms. The great variety of pot types include zoomorphic and miniature vessels, rattles, and shoe-shaped containers.

- During the FBA, the Silesian phase of Lusatian and the Silesia–Platěnice culture show vessels with well-smoothed surfaces and finely polished or graphited, as well as richly ornamented rattles and so-called drinking horns.

The Lusatian culture brought the stabilisation of settlement, with societies inhabiting particular microregions permanently. A dense network of fortified settlements appeared, as in central Europe, preferentially on high ground and hilly terrain, on marshlands and islands, apparently avoiding flat open country. Settlements concentrated on brown soils and their variants, and provided probably a safe haven to guard communication routes and important microregions. In the FBA, settlements moved to chernozems, which had a steppe character during this warmer and drier period, and were thus more suitable for stockbreeding, the main activity of the culture (Marková and Ilon 2013).

Fortifications likely represented for the surrounding microregions the centres of political, social, economic and religious life of the local community, with special emphasis on metallurgy, where bronzeworkers enjoyed high standing. They were probably adjacent to unfortified agrarian settlements that belonged to their sphere of influence. Unlike in the neighbouring Urnfield culture, where fortified settlements are limited to certain regions (adjacent to different cultures) and early periods, Lusatian forts continue into the earlier Iron Age, with many being built during this period. (Jockenhövel 2013).

A possible origin of its characteristic fortified settlements—potentially in common with the Urnfield culture—can be found during the early 2nd millennium BC in Bruszczewo in Great Poland, and in the Carpathian foreland strongholds of the Ottomány-Füzesabony culture. The regions of Kuyavia and Greater Poland show a complex of fortified settlements (Figure 68)—formed by compact groups of a dozen rows of houses, each row containing a dozen houses—while Silesia shows some isolated fortified settlements (Czebreszuk 2013), all probably pointing to a western fortified zone in the border regions with Nordic and Urnfield cultures. After a formative phase, the Lusatian culture shows an increase in settlement density and in production of bronzes.

Figure 68. Reconstructed gate and wall of Lusatian settlement from Biskupin. Photo by Fazer.

The Lusatian culture came to an end ca. 500–400 BC, coinciding with an increase in fortified settlements suggesting intertribal conflict, probably because of worsening climatic conditions, soil erosion, indigenous and exogenous factors, and the emergence of iron technology. After 800 BC, traces of the Hallstatt culture are felt in the west, mainly in Lower Silesia, but also scattered from Greater Poland to Kuyavia. From the east, expanding Scythians or other mounted nomads, whose evidence is found as far away as the Oder, also contributed to the Lusatian culture's demise (Jockenhövel 2013).

VIII.8.5. Pomeranian and West Baltic Kurgans culture

In the Baltic region, low population density at the turn of the $2^{nd}/1^{st}$ millennium BC changes after ca. 900 BC, evidenced by the substantial deforestation that happened over the next 500 years, and by the new necropolises and settlements, as well as numerous hoards, associated with the Pomeranian culture in its Władysławowo phase. Settlements appear in previously uninhabited territories, such as the coastal areas in Kashubia and the Gdańsk Bay, and a dense network of new villages and burial grounds grow in microregions, located at the edges of river and lake valleys, usually on level sections of slopes, but also on hilltops. Settlements feature a dense layout of structures, suggesting an intensification of food production, especially concentrated in several clusters. The majority of dwellings were, similar to Lusatian, aboveground structures with a log-frame construction, attesting a certain degree of carpentry skill (Dzięgielewski 2017).

The oecumene appears to have gradually expanded from the Oder to the east during the Warzenko and Siemirowice phases (ca. 1300–900 BC), concentrating on the upland and strips of land along the Baltic coast and the Gdańsk Bay, with severe deforestation starting only at the end of this phase. In the Władysławowo phase (ca. 900–600 BC) there is a a settlement expansion towards the coast, especially the Gdańsk Bay, and into the great river valleys, with strong internal colonisation of moraine uplands, with development of exchange relationships and long-range trade routes and bronze metallurgy (Dzięgielewski 2017).

A metallurgical centre in the lower Vistula basin produced many original forms, despite remaining under the influence of bronze-casting workshops of the Nordic circle. Imports from the north are common, while less numerous artefacts from south-central Europe are also found, with Rhine or western European findings being the least numerous. Intense contacts with Baltic cultures continues from the Bronze Age, at the same time as the western Baltic area becomes increasingly homogeneous in style of pottery and bronze metallurgy. Regions around the Baltic sea constituted a kind of communicative community, but symbols and imagery demonstrate they remained different worlds: the Nordic world, with motif of boats in bronze decoration and on rock carvings, and the Pomeranian world, with Urnfield ornitomorphic motifs (Dzięgielewski 2017).

Fortified settlements appear usually marking micro- and mesoregional clusters, without a clear defensive role, given their location outside of densely populated areas and far from the borders of the culture. They reflected thus the emergence of social differentiation, signalling the start of a strictly kinship-based chiefdom system in the area. There are no 'centres' of regional power similar to those of southern Scandinavia, though. Burial practices in certain regions also point to limited practices of polygyny and extended exogamy (sign of increasing social stratification), probably continuing from the Bronze Age Lusatian culture based on indirect data such as votive hoards. This could have eventually led to increased mobility of young males without prospects, especially in the later, Karczemki phase, which justifies in part the culture's progressive colonisation of the northern area and eventual expansion to the south, possibly also triggered by the desire to control trade routes, like those developed by the Pomeranian amber exports, e.g. along the Vistula and Warta rivers (Dzięgielewski 2017).

The old tumulus necropolises disappear ca. 1000–900 BC, and 'flat' burial ground emerge ca. 900 BC at the earliest, most of them appearing only after ca. 800/750 BC. Nevertheless, 'Tumulus' communities appear to have been at the foundation of the demographic growth observable during the Władysławowo phase. Flat graves included some construction elements (cobbles and linings), and contained rectangular or polygonal stone cists, each containing one, two, or rarely several units. Deposited vessels found in funerary and settlement contexts were all produced in accordance with the 'Urnfield canon', and included middle-sized pots or, less frequently, large pots with two handles or vases with a round body and a narrowing neck used as urns (Dzięgielewski 2017).

The Karczemki phase of the Pomeranian culture (ca. 650–400 BC) represents the latest expansion phase, and the eventual change to alternative economic strategies, such as transhumance based on sheep–goat herds and cattle, because of dwindling resources. There is a decrease in the number of large agricultural settlements, and settlements became smaller and more scattered, with the establishment of small, clan cemeteries. Amber trade probably allowed for certain groups to survive, leading to concentration of assets in some regions, and to the increase polygyny and thus the chance for the reproductive success of some clans (Dzięgielewski 2017).

Culturally, this phase is characterised by the presence of Hallstatt-style items alongside local forms of pottery and ornaments. Remarkable is the sudden appearance of face urns only in funerary contexts, geographically limited to the west, and with a likely origin in simpler Władysławowo phase depictions, with similar anthropomorphic models of urn decoration found in Jutland and Germany by the end of the 2nd millennium BC, and in Etruscan Canopic jars in Italy. Pomeranian culture expanded to the south ca. 500–400 BC, to almost all regions of the Polish Lowland, during a period corresponding to the La Tène period north of the Alps (Dzięgielewski 2017).

At the same time as the Pomeranian culture retreated and expanded east and south following the expansion of the Jastorf and Hallstatt/La Tène cultures, the West Baltic culture of cairns (ca. 650–150 BC) also expanded in the east, evolving from the previous Lusatian culture. Further complex population movements were caused by the pressure from Germanic migrations to the south and east from Scandinavia and the German lowlands, represented by Oksywie (2nd c. BC – 1st c. AD) and later Wielbark (1st c. AD – 4th c. AD) cultures in eastern Pomerania.

The Przeworsk culture (3rd c. BC – 5th c. AD) shows continuity in its roots with the preceding Pomeranian culture, but its extension north from the Vistula to the Oder, and south toward the middle Danube from the Dniester to the Tisza valley was accompanied by significant influences from La Tène and Jastorf cultures. The subsequent absorption into the Wielbark culture—related to the East Germanic expansion—makes its precise ethnolinguistic association difficult, and it is sometimes viewed as an amalgam of a series of localised cultures (Mallory and Adams 1997), although it was likely an East Germanic-dominated culture.

East of the main Przeworsk zone was the Zarubinets culture (3rd c. BC – 2st c. AD), traditionally considered a part of the Przeworsk complex (Mallory and Adams 1997), located between the upper and middle Dnieper and Pripyat rivers. Early Slavic hydronyms are found in the area, and the prototypical examples of Prague-type pottery later originated there (Curta 2001). It is therefore the most likely culture to be identified as ancestral to Proto-Slavic (Kobyliński 2005).

Zarubinets came to an end with the migration of its population, linked to the increasingly arid climate. By the AD 3rd century, western parts of Zarubinets had been integrated into the Wielbark culture, and some Zarubinets groups had moved southward into river valleys, moving closer to Sarmatian and Thracian-Celtic groups of the Don region, forming the Chernoles culture. Central late Zarubinets sites gradually turned into the Kyiv culture (ca. 3rd-5th c.), widely considered the first identifiable Slavic archaeological culture, from which the Prague–Korchak culture—traditionally identified with the expansion of Common Slavic (Mallory and Adams 1997)—descended about the 5th c.

viii.8. Balto-Slavs

Sampled Bell Beakers of the Silesian group (ca. 2450–2050 BC) show a mean of ca. 43% Steppe ancestry: two samples from Kornice, one of hg. R1b1a1b-M269; one from Jordanów Śląski, of hg. R1b1a1b1a1a2b-U152; one from Żerniki Wielkie; and one of Strachów. Three Bell Beakers of the Vistula group from Samborzec (ca. 2450–2150 BC) have ca. 46% Steppe ancestry, all showing hg. R1b1a1b-M269, one of them R1b1a1b1a1a-L151, and one R1b1a1b1b-Z2103 subclade (Olalde et al. 2018). The influence of Mierzanowice–Nitra (with strong Carpathian influence) in the later formation of Trzciniec and Lusatian groups may justify the existence of stronger Balkan-related influences in Proto-Balto-Slavic compared to other North-West Indo-European dialects (see *§viii.11. Thracians and Albanians*). The presence of hg. R1b1a1b1b-Z2103 in the area before the emergence of the likely Proto-Balto-Slavic community further attests to such interaction around the Carpathians.

This period of dominance of R1b1a1b-M269 lineages with Bell Beakers was partially interrupted by the resurgence of previous lineages and Steppe ancestry (ca. 57%) during the Bronze Age in Upper Silesia (ca. 2290–2040 BC), in the previous area of the Bell Beaker Silesian groups: one sample from Dzielnica, of hg. R1a1a-M198, corresponds to the cultural transformation from Bell Beaker into the Chłopice–Veselé culture; one sample of the Chłopice–Veselé culture from Racibórz-Stara Wieś, near Kornice, of hg. R1b1a1b1a-L51; and a female from Iwiny (Olalde et al. 2018).

An EBA sample from Gustorzyn in the Kuyavian area (ca. 2015–1775 BC), belonging to the Iwno or Proto-Trzciniec stage, clusters closely with previous late Corded Ware samples from the area (Fernandes et al. 2018), and shows haplogroup R1a1a1b1a2-Z280, subclade R1a1a1b1a2c-S24902[+] (formed ca. 2600 BC, TMRCA ca. 2400 BC). The wide distribution of this subclade from west to east Europe points to its expansion earlier with Corded Ware groups, as suggested by its early split.

Samples from the Turlojiškė complex in south-west Lithuania, tentatively attributed to the late Trzciniec culture (common range ca. 1200–500 BC), show admixture of Baltic Late Neolithic population with WHG and Baltic hunter-gatherers, clustering closely to Latvian samples from Kivutkalns and to modern Lithuanians and Estonians, slightly to the north of modern eastern Europeans (Mittnik, Wang, et al. 2018). Samples include three of hg. R1a1a1b-Z645, including one subclade of hg. R1a1a1b1a2a-Z92 (YP617+)[+] (formed ca. 1400 BC, TMRCA ca. 1400 BC). The distribution of R1a1a1b1a2a-Z92 (formed ca. 2600 BC, TMRCA ca. 2500 BC) mainly among modern Fennoscandian peoples and northern Russians, and the ancient cluster formed with other Baltic peoples, points to the relationship of this haplogroup with the eastern Baltic rather than with the Trzciniec culture (Suppl. Graph. 11).

Since both territories of the Trzciniec culture sampled lie each at one edge of its east–west territory, and no sample can be clearly attributed to the culture (one is too early, the other too late), the overall genetic picture of the culture remains unclear. However, the presence of one clear outlier in Baltic Bronze Age samples from Turlojiškė (ca. 1075 BC) supports the close contacts of this area with central Europe, most likely facilitated by the Trzciniec culture, which can then be classified as genetically central European rather than Baltic-like, consistent with its cultural influences. These and later interactions with peoples of the Battle Axe culture reveal the origin of long-term Balto-Slavic–Finno-Permic contacts (Koivulehto 2006; Kallio 2008), including the likely evolution of North-West Indo-European-like Pre-Balto-Slavic phonology derived from Finno-Permic bilingual speakers becoming eventually Balto-Slavic speakers.

It is therefore likely that the central European-like ancestry of Iwno–Trzciniec became even more western European with the expansion of the Lusatian culture, under the influence of the Tumulus and Urnfield cultures. Even though there is no sampling of the Lusatian culture yet, the Urnfield samples from the Lichtenstein Cave in Saxony-Anhalt (ca. 1000– 00 BC) lie close to the culture's border, and they show a mixed society including probably ten individuals of hg. I2a1b2-L621, one R1a1a1b-Z645, and one R1b1a1b1a-L23 (Schilz 2006; Lipson et al. 2017), as is expected from a developing Balto-Slavic community in the east, based on findings among early Slavs (see below).

Chemical traces suggest that warriors from Tollense (see *§VIII.6.3. Tumulus period (MBA)*) close to the Lusatian culture territory, came from far away, with only a few showing values typical of the northern European plain. While the majority of sampled individuals fall within the variation of contemporary northern central European, but slightly shifted to EHG populations, there are some outliers closer to Neolithic LBK and modern Basques (Suppl. Graph. 12), suggesting that central and western European

EBA cultures were still at that time closely interconnected (Sell 2017). The renewed contacts of the Late Bronze age between the British Isles, Iberia, Sardinia, and Scandinavia, apparent in the pan-European warrior symbolism—such as bi-horned warriors and their presence in rock art panels—likely relied on close and direct human interaction (Melheim et al. 2018), continuing thus the connections created during the Bell Beaker expansion a thousand years earlier.

The east-central European origin of Balto-Slavic peoples during the Bronze Age seems thus to be supported by the findings of the Tollense valley, where most sampled warriors cluster closely to modern northern-central Europeans, including East Germans, Austrians, and West Slavic populations (Sell 2017). The prehistorical regions of interaction formed by Únětice–Mierzanowice, Tumulus–Trzciniec, and Urnfield–Lusatian cultures are thus the best candidates for the ancestral Balto-Slavic community, as is the partial continuity in lineages under I2a1b2-L621 and R1a1a1b1a1a-M458 in early Slavs.

The nature of Balto-Slavic peoples as stemming from an east-central European population, initially not related to Corded Ware-related ancestry, is more clearly seen in the genetic shift from the Corded Ware population—originally linked to Uralic-speaking peoples (see *§vii.1. Western and Eastern Uralians*)—towards a central European cluster in the late Trzciniec outlier and early Slavs (see below), continued today in modern West Slavs.

This cluster is also close to the only available samples from ancient east-central Europe: a late Corded Ware/Proto-Únětice sample and the two Iwno/Proto-Trzciniec samples. The multiple documented migrations of steppe-related peoples to the west (see *§viii.19. Iranians*), and the hypothesised alternative origin of the Slavic expansion near the north Pontic area should have shifted early Slavs genetically from a Corded Ware cluster to the east, and not—as these ancient samples and Modern Slavs show—to the west.

This east-central European origin stemming ultimately from the Bell Beaker expansion is also supported by the sizeable presence of varied

R1b1a1b1-L23 subclades (ca. 10-30%) in Slavs of east-central Europe and among Balts (Semino 2000; Luca et al. 2007; Rębała et al. 2012; Kushniarevich et al. 2015), in contrast to the bottlenecks seen in some East Slavic (under typically Finno-Ugric R1a1a1b1a2a-Z92 subclades) and South Slavic groups (under typically Balkan subclades). The simplistic attribution of these varied R1b1a1b1-L23 lineages to recently acculturated "Germanic" or "Celtic" peoples must be, therefore, rejected.

viii.8.1. Balts

There is a great degree of genetic continuity in modern Baltic-speaking peoples with the Bronze Age population of the area (Mittnik, Wang, et al. 2018), which suggests either an infiltration of peoples of Lusatian origin in the Pomeranian and related West-Baltic culture of cairns and admixture with locals, or rather an earlier infiltration through the Trzciniec culture, as evidenced by the Bronze Age outlier. In fact, we could tentatively identify the infiltration of Proto-East Baltic peoples among Baltic populations—hence retaining mainly their 'eastern' male R1a1a1b1a2-Z280 lines—with late Trzciniec, and a slightly later arrival of Proto-West Baltic peoples with the West-Baltic culture of cairns and possibly more R1a1a1b1a1a-M458 lineages, which would fit their ancestral split.

Before the migration period, Baltic peoples probably bordered Finno-Permic tribes around the Upper Daugava and the Upper Dnieper, even though studied hydronyms show that Finno-Permic names reached the Lower Daugava, too (Ojārs 2014). The Late Dyakovo culture (ca. AD 3rd–7th c.) and the Long Barrow culture (ca. AD 5th–10th c.) probably represent the continuation of the previous Dnieper–Dvina culture as West Uralic in nature[29],

---

[29] According to Kallio (2015): "(...) the substrate toponyms tell us more about the extinct Uralic languages spoken further in the north in the Northern Dvina region where the Slavicization took place so recently during the third quarter of the second millennium AD that its Uralic substrate toponyms are much easier to identify. In addition to later Finnic strata, there also seems to have been an earlier stratum having close ties to Saami, even though it most likely represented another separate branch of Finno-Mordvin (Saarikivi 2004b, 2007a; Helimski 2006)."

the proto-historical Chudes (Figure 69), at the same time as the Scratched Surface Ceramics typical of Baltic countries influenced the western areas, likely representing incoming Eastern Balts. The Long Barrow culture was also influenced in a later period by East Slavs from the south (Rahkonen 2011).

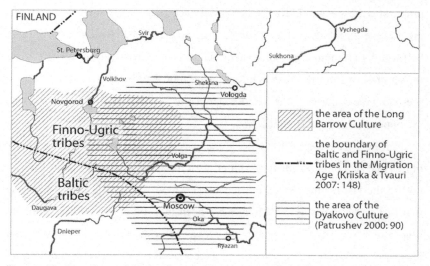

Figure 69. Boundary of Finno-Permic and Baltic tribes in the Age of Migrations according to Kriiska & Tvauri (2007:148). Image modified from Rahkonen (2011).

The Kolochin material culture was a transformation of the old Kyiv culture (Kobyliński 2005), but evidence of Baltic river names in the region has made some propose an original Baltic occupation (Mallory and Adams 1997) before the East Slavic migration. Indeed, Baltic peoples have been found to be genetically the closest to East Slavs (Kushniarevich et al. 2015), which is compatible with Baltic- and Finno-Permic speaking peoples undergoing a cultural assimilation ('Slavicisation') with the East Slavic expansion, evidenced by a stronger influence of Finno-Permic on Slavic than on Proto-East Baltic or Proto-West Baltic. A precise analysis of a temporal transect of Finno-Ugric and Baltic populations would be necessary to discern which R1a1a1b-Z645 (and N1a1a1a1a-L392) subclades may have been associated with which migrations and expansions in north-eastern Europe.

viii.9.2. Slavs

The division of historical Slavic tribes in territories and cultures of the AD 5th–7th centuries remains a hotly debated topic (Curta 2001), and the adoption or introduction of Slavic in east-central and eastern Europe is impossible to pinpoint with precision, despite commonly accepted views such as the link to the Prague-Korchak culture (Suppl. Fig. 16). Nevertheless, this culture is believed by German archaeologists to have come to east-central Europe from the south, not from the east, while archaeological influences seen in the east seem to have come from the Middle Danube to the Middle Dnieper, and not in the opposite direction (Curta 2019).

For the expansion of Slavonic, some have proposed the model of a *koiné*, others that of a *lingua franca*, the latter most likely used within the Avar polity during the last century of its existence. The most acceptable model today is that Proto-Slavic movements may have been initially triggered by Germanic migrations (see *§viii.7. Germanic peoples*), spreading thus from a tiny region close to the West Baltic (based on its connection with Baltic languages). Common Slavic must have spread closer to the Carpathians in the second half of the first millennium, with the first unequivocal historic attestations appearing around the Middle Danube (Curta 2019).

Early Slavic is known to have spread differently in the different regions: the sparsely populated area in the north-west was probably subjected to migration; the east shows mainly assimilation and language shift among Finno-Ugric groups; and the south-east might show a more complex scenario, involving both phenomena, migration and language shift (Lindstedt and Salmela 2019).

Two females of the Avar culture in Szólád (AD 540–640) are genetically similar to modern eastern Europeans: one clusters between modern Russians, Ukrainians and Latvians (consistent with the contacts of Avars in their migrations through eastern Europe), and one closer to Poles (consistent with the admixture of Slavs, of a more western cluster); both suggest thus a rapid population turnover after the Migration Period (Amorim et al. 2018). Two Early West Slavic females from Bohemia (ca. AD 600–900) cluster with modern Czechs, western Poles, and eastern Germans, suggesting a great degree of continuity among West Slavic populations since the Middle Ages (Allentoft et al. 2015).

The complex nature of early Slavonic ethnicity is also reflected in the varied haplogroups among early Slavs: Two West Slavs from Niemcza, Silesia (AD 900–1000) show hg. I2a1b2-L621 and J2a1a-L26; one from Markowice, Greater Poland (AD 1000–1200) shows hg. I1a2a2a5-Y5384 (Stolarek et al. 2018)[30]; two from Usedom, in Mecklenburg-Vorpommern (AD 1200), show hg. R1a1a1b1a1a-M458 and E1b1b-M215 (Freder 2010), and another one from Hrádek nad Nisou, in Northern Bohemia (ca. AD 1330), also shows E1b1b-M215 (Vanek et al. 2015). An early East Slavic individual from Sunghir (ca. AD 1100-1200), probably from the Vladimir-Suzdalian Rus', shows hg. I2a1a2b1a1-CTS10228[+] (formed ca. 3100 BC, TMRCA ca. 1800 BC), while the paternal lineage of Yaroslav Osmomysl, the Prince of Halych, has been reported to be E1b1b1a1b1a-V13.

The high variability in haplogroups, and the common finding of I2a1b2-L621 (likely I2a1a2b1a1-CTS10228) and E1b1b-M215 (likely E1b1b1a1b1a-V13) lineages in independent early Slavic samplings, apart from the prevalence of I2a1a2b1a1-CTS10228 among modern South Slavs, and their sizeable presence among West Slavs, supports that the current distribution of R1a1a1b1a-Z282 lineages in Slavic populations is mainly the product of recent bottlenecks. Individuals of hg. E1b1b1a1b1a-V13 and I2a1b2-L621 among Hungarian Conquerors and Early Hungarians (see below *§viii.17.1. Ugrians*) support that these were originally paternal lines associated with early Slavs from the Carpathian Basin.

---

[30] Two more samples from Poland are reported as E1b1-M215 and R1a-M420, although the precise subclades and sites are unknown, and they could be related either to East Germanic or to West Slavic peoples.

The shared E1b1b1a1b1a-V13 lineages from the West Baltic to the Balkans during the Iron Age (see below *§viii.11. Thracians and Albanians*) would support an origin of the expansion around the Carpathians. The prevalence of this subclade among Rusyns (ca. 35%)—East Slavs from the Carpathians not associated with the Kievan Rus' expansion—coupled with studies of Slavic toponymy (Figure 70), place the East Slavic homeland white accurately north of the Carpathians (Udolph 1997, 2016).

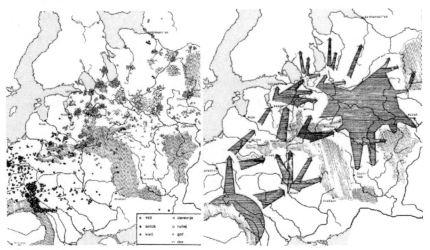

Figure 70. Left: map of older and younger East Slavic names. Right:Conversion of data to expansion of East Slavic settlements. Image from Udolph (2016).

An individual of European admixture of the Golden Horde Mongol State, from Karasuyr, Kazakhstan (AD mid–13th c.)—buried together with a high status individual of East Asian ancestry and hg. C2-M217, both with buddhist customs (de Barros Damgaard, Marchi, et al. 2018)—clusters close to Baltic Bronze Age and Iron Age samples (see below *§viii.16. Saami and Baltic Finns*). His haplogroup, R1a1a1b1a2a1a1a1-YP575 (formed ca. AD 250, TMRCA ca. AD 250), a subclade of hg. R1a1a1b1a2a-Z92, is also related to ancient north-eastern Europeans, and is present in modern populations from Fennoscandia and Eastern Europe.

This individual was probably related to early East Slavs from the region, hence a paternal line corresponding to acculturated Baltic Finns or Volga Finns, since it is generally accepted that Russians assimilated many Finno-Ugric groups of East Europe before the Slavonic migration to the area. Alternatively, he may have been himself the product of the eastern European slave trade that connected eastern Europe with Fennoscandia (Korpela 2019), although the features of the burial do not seem proper of a recent slave. Both interpretations may explain the high Finno-Ugrian admixture found in the modern East Slavic populations, reflected in their *eastern* cluster in the PCA and in their prevalent R1a1a1b1a2a-Z92 subclades, which further supports the origin of early Slavs to the west. This Finno-Ugric origin of East Slavs, especially among the Kievan Rus', is also supported in whole genomic studies of modern Russians (Zhernakova, Evsyukov, et al. 2019; Zhernakova, Brukhin, et al. 2019).

The expansion of the Penkov culture in the Danube has been related to the expansion of South Slavic, although it was a culture most likely related to steppe nomads. Confusing accounts of the Byzantine Empire of the raids and migrations of a federation of tribes (the Antes and the Sklavenes) in their frontiers give a general idea of the complex interaction of different groups in the Balkans (Curta 2001, 2019). The prevalent distribution of hg. I2a1b2-L621 among modern South Slavic populations (Kushniarevich et al. 2015) suggests a relevant role of Slavic migrations to the area, apart from recent bottlenecks.

The western Baltic and eastern European peaks in the modern distribution of R1a1a1b1a1a-M458 lineages (Underhill et al. 2015), especially R1a1a1b1a1a1-Y2604 (formed ca. 2700 BC, TMRCA ca. 2500 BC) with its main subclades R1a1a1b1a1a1c-CTS11962 (TMRCA ca. 1100 BC) and especially R1a1a1b1a1a1a-L260 (TMRCA ca. 500 BC), support west–east migrations of this lineage coinciding with the Late Bronze / Iron Age, potentially associated (at least in part) with Balto-Slavic movements. On the other hand, subclades R1a1a1b1a1a1a1-YP256 (TMRCA ca. 200 BC) and R1a1a1b1a1a1a2-YP1337 (TMRCA ca. AD 450 BC) could be linked to Proto-Slavic migrations under these lineages during the Iron Age / Early Middle Ages (Horváth 2014). This is also suggested by the presence of rare

R1a1a1b1a1a-M458 subclades in modern Poles, and by the lack of this haplogroup to date in sampled north-eastern European (i.e. Finno-Ugric) and steppe (i.e. Indo-Iranian) peoples, contrasting with R1a1a1b1a2-Z280 lineages, which are found widespread in eastern Europe and Asia.

Certain R1a1a1b1a2-Z280 (xR1a1a1b1a2a-Z92) subclades have been proposed to be involved in early Slavic expansions; for example, R1a1a1b1a2b3a-CTS3402 (formed ca. 2200 BC, TMRCA ca. 2200 BC) is prevalent among R1a1a1b1a-Z282 subclades in modern Slovenians (Maisano Delser et al. 2018), and other subclades are also found among modern West, South, and East Slavic populations, as well as some modern central European peoples.

However, the widespread presence of R1a1a1b1a2b-CTS1211 and shared haplotypes in modern Finno-Ugrians on both sides of the Urals—including its presence among Hungarian Conquerors (see below *§viii.17.1. Ugrians*)— suggest that this haplogroup was originally a Finno-Ugric paternal line, and many modern (especially East) Slavic R1a1a1b1a2b-CTS1211 lines are from recently acculturated Finno-Ugric populations in the past 1,000 years. Nevertheless, some early subclades seem to have formed part of ancient east-central European populations, likely including Proto-Baltic and Proto-Slavic peoples close to the Baltic, before their expansions to the east and south, respectively.

VIII.9. Adriatic province

VIII.9.1. Cetina

Proto-Cetina/Cetina, in the southern Balkans, appears as a Bell Beaker periphery connecting the West Adriatic coast with the East Adriatic area ca. 2400–2300 BC, under the influence of Central Mediterranean Bell Beakers, whose heartlands are on one hand northern Italy and Tuscany, and on the other hand Sardinia and western Sicily (Heyd 2007).

Wristguards are present in higher quantity than in northern Italy or the Csepel group, and known from the published sites both in some numbers and as single finds, in settlements as in graves. There are also triangular riveted daggers, apart from gold jewellery in a rich grave inventory in Nin–Privlaka. There are many undecorated bowls, jugs, and cups, proper of the Begleitkeramik of the Middle Bell Beaker period, instead of Bell Beakers, of which only two beaker derivates are found, created in contact with the Adriatic variant of Vučedol (Heyd 2007).

Tumuli of several meters in diameter, primarily of stone, can have a kerb of large stones. They contain usually a rectangular cist grave made of stone slabs, with a stone-covering slab. A single person buried in a contracted position on the left or right side is the standard. Cremation is mixed with inhumation, showing local differences in the burial ritual. Tumuli with no remains are common, probably representing cenotaphs (Teržan and Karavanić 2013).

Cetina is therefore a syncretistic culture developed probably in combination with local cultures by migrating Bell Beakers, likely from a region near the Adriatic island of Palagruža, where Bell Beaker elements are predominant: wristguards, comb–stamp decorated pottery sherds with Bell Beaker decoration, and flint-inventory with characteristic arrowheads typical of Mediterranean Bell Beakers (Heyd 2007). Characteristic settlements, especially in the western Balkan hinterland, suggest that Cetina settlers were nomadic herders.

The twenty-five Cetina sites comprise the whole northern and western Adriatic shore, stretching from Trieste in the north to the 'heel' of southern Apulia, with concentrations around the Daunia peninsula and the Apulian plain, with related pottery in the Corazzo–Zungri settlement showing extension towards Calabria and further inland, including also a northern site in the province of Trento. Its influence is thus felt along the Adriatic from Istria and the karst hinterland of Trieste to the Peloponnnese and the southern Apennines, but also to the western Balkan hinterland, where no settlements (other than cave shelters) are known (Heyd 2007).

Chronologically, it seems that first maritime beakers appear ca. 2500 BC or shortly after that in south and south-east Italy, impacting native cultures like the Laterza–Cellino San Marco culture. After that, Italian Cetina appears ca. 2500–2300 BC, under the most recent Bell Beaker influence with the stamp and puncture decorated vessels preceding the classic (East Adriatic) Cetina phase (Figure 71) and its typical framed decoration that appeared later (Heyd 2007).

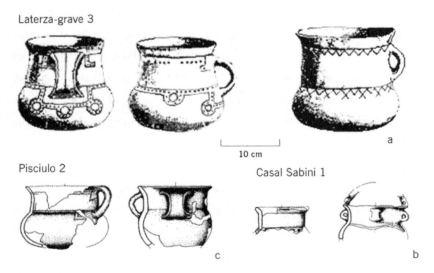

Figure 71. Cetina-type pottery from Apulian sites. Image modified from Pacciarelli, Scarano, and Crispino (2015).

VIII.9.2. Castellieri

The term Cultura dei castellieri or Kašteljerska kultura is used to define the Bronze Age culture with characteristic settlements particularly prevalent in the northern and north-eastern Adriatic region. The culture features *castellieri-gradine*, settlements in strategic positions that could be easily defended—like prominent hills, edges of high plateaus, tongue-shaped promontories on valleys—fortified with dry-stone ramparts adapted to the terrain, either surrounding the settlement or built on the more accessible places (Mihovilić 2013).

It features a well-organised society with knowledge of building methods. Settlements located on tops of hills or other selected sites were levelled, with stone being broken and extracted. Plans show a proto-urban organisation, with the larger settlements featuring a separated fortified citadel or acropolis containing large structures, covered doorways, narrow passageways, etc. Labyrinthine entrances became with time an additional way to secure the settlements, as was the additional earthwork with sharp upright stones found some 10 m in front of the rampart circuit in certain settlements (Mihovilić 2013).

Findings in central areas confirm they were inhabited by a ruling elite, supporting the existence of a stratified society. All areas surrounded by ramparts—which ranged from 2/3 to 10 m in width, and from 3 to 6/10 m in height—were intensively settled. Apparently, houses had rectangular, 1m-high stone foundations often carved into the level bedrock, complemented with a wooden superstructure. Cavities hollowed out from the bedrock may have served to collect rainwater from house roofs, which would have been necessary since the Adriatic has a problem of water supply (Mihovilić 2013).

Castellieri appear to have formed centres of specific surrounding microregions, potentially specialised and forming alliances with others. Near the castellieri, short-lived settlements are known from caves and rock-shelters, and the importance of cattle-breeding supports its potential link to the main settlements. Grinding stones confirm the importance of agriculture, and vine-growing areas are also found. Long-range trade contacts are evidenced by loaf–of–bread idols (particularly important in the Lower Danube, Moravia, and northern Italy), amber beads (typical of southern Únětice and Tumulus), and finds of bronze weapons of south-eastern (Aegean) and north-western (Rhône, Italian) origins (Mihovilić 2013).

Inhumations in stone cists covered with stone tumuli or in small cemeteries beside the main entrance are the standard from the EBA on. The fortified settlement at Monkodonja, characteristic of the culture, shows two peculiar tombs integrated into the monumental labyrinth-like main entrance, containing rectangular stone cist graves. They represented probably special burials of selected members of the local elite, with cult of the forefathers (Teržan and Karavanić 2013). The emergence of cremation marks a crisis during the Urnfield period, with abandonment of some settlements and a new wave of castellieri being established, at the same time as Proto-Villanovan and Late Helladic IIIC findings appear in its material culture.

The Posušje or Dinaric culture of the Dalmatian hinterland lasted from the EBA to the MBA, and features small hill forts of a mean 50–100 m^2, elevated settlements fortified with powerful walls, in some cases including bastions, made in the dry-stone technique. Larger settlements (ca. 150 m^2) have an interior with additional walls, showing a complete fortification with an acropolis. Posušje hill forts shows parallels with the Castellieri culture, and its sedentary farmers (primarily agriculturalists) coexisted with the Cetina culture of nomadic herders in the same geographical area. In the Adriatic and its hinterland, inhumation is the main rite, although in some places cremation was also used (Teržan and Karavanić 2013).

In the Late Bronze Age (ca. 1200–800 BC) human occupation in the valleys (*polja*) of the Dinaric Alps in Croatia, like Gacka to the north and Ličko to the south, show a change from ephemeral sites to increased burial activity, including inhumations under earthen and stone tumuli, and the emergence of hill forts, which proliferate near mountain passes and river access points, suggesting their need for defence and control of resources. The largest hill forts in each valley acted as a centralising force for smaller forts and settlements nearby (Zavodny et al. 2018).

The end of the Bronze Age marks a dramatic change in regional burial practices to large communal necropolises close to hill forts, with the appearance of Baltic amber in graves highlighting changing sociopolitical and economic forces, including the participation in interregional trade networks, marking the start of an integrative regional culture known as the Iapodians, who existed until the Roman conquest (ca. 35 BC). This period marks a trend towards intensified and expanded animal management practices, with cattle and sheep–goat herds becoming larger and more numerous, necessitating non-local pastures, which were found in the hillsides around valleys or into even higher mountain areas, in order to preserve valley bottoms for agriculture (Zavodny et al. 2018).

VIII.9.3. Vatina

The continental areas of the western Balkan Peninsula south of the Pannonian basin and west of the Dinaric mountain range form part of an extensive ore-bearing region, probably exploited throughout the Copper and Bronze Ages. The Somogyvár–Vinkovci culture dominated to the north, as a transitional cultural phenomenon related to traditions of the preceding Vučedol culture. Settlements were usually located on elevated positions near waterways, including artificial heights like tells, usually without fortifications. Houses were rectangular, above-ground, single-roomed constructions built with load-bearing wooden beams. Dug-in structures were also common, potentially as cellars or storage pits. Subsistence economy was based on stockbreeding, mostly cattle, but also pigs and small animals, and a mainly sedentary way of life can be assumed (Teržan and Karavanić 2013).

The Vatina culture (ca. 2100–1600/1500 BC) represents a significant cultural shift in the whole region. It is represented by few large fortified 'central' settlements dominating over microregions. This contrasts with previous periods, where large numbers of smaller, mostly unfortified hamlets predominated. Settlements were surrounded by a defensive ditch and earthen bank with palisade, with some kind of 'suburb' or outlying settlement outside the defences. The fortified area showed a proto-urban organisation, with standardised rectangular houses arranged along narrow streets, with some broader ones representing the main corridors. The house interior fittings showed a high level of living style. Up to one thousand people could inhabit the whole settlement area (Teržan and Karavanić 2013).

In the mountainous parts, in the middle of ore-bearing areas, contacts and synthesis are seen between the Mediterranean and areas of Carpathian–Danubian cultures, forming the so-called 'transitional zone' between Pannonia and the Adriatic. Small, elevated settlements or hill forts with natural defences are prevalent from 2000–1600 BC, with high population density and a clear sociopolitical connection with Vatina, reflected in the proto-urban organisation and layout of settlements. Traces of metallurgical activity are found in these settlements (Teržan and Karavanić 2013).

During the MBA, smaller unfortified settlements replace the previous large Vatina settlements, mainly along the edges of the plateau and on lower-lying terraces, at roughly equal distances from one another, mainly small hamlets with 2–6 buildings up to 50 m from one another, indicating individual farms. This new economic base and spatial utilisation suggests an organised colonisation of the area, possibly with a hiatus from the previous Vatina culture (Teržan and Karavanić 2013).

Cremation burials were prevalent, as in many groups in Pannonia and the western Balkans, but there were also individual inhumations featuring weapons (swords and battle–axes) already during the EBA, without a direct relationship to the Tumulus culture, which suggest some sort of convergence phenomenon. This trend is later kept in the cultures succeeding Vatina, and spreads into more southern groups like Donja Brnjica–Gornja Stražava group (Teržan and Karavanić 2013).

During the classic Urnfield period, new groups featuring large flat urnfields with hundreds of graves settle the central Danube basin up to the south in modern Slovenia, showing strict gender differentiation and social stratification. In central and eastern Serbia, the surviving groups succeeding the Vatina culture during the LBA show tumuli as the standard burial ritual, but cremation is also common. Material culture points to strong contacts with Glasinac, but also with Danubian, other western Balkan, and Aegean cultural spheres (Teržan and Karavanić 2013).

VIII.9.4. Glasinac and Paraćin

The Glasinac culture evolves from Vatina in modern central Bosnia and western Serbia, and continues into the Early Iron Age. This regional variant shows mainly earthen tumuli of ca. 8–12 m diameter found in large groups. Mounds contain usually several graves with pebbles on the base, lined and covered with stones, with the dead in an extended or slightly contracted position, but there are also cases of cremation. The erection of mounds suggest the use for family burials for one or two generations, and together with rich assemblages they evidence social stratification and cult of the warrior (Teržan and Karavanić 2013).

Further to the south, the Paraćin group (along the course of the Morava) and the Donja Brnjica–Gornja Stražava group to the south and west of Paraćin show mainly cremation and urn burials coexisting with inhumation, with a complex burial rite featuring special constructions of stone slabs and circuits of stones, and grave pits lined and covered with stones suggesting graves or clusters of graves under small tumuli.

Weaponry and prestige goods in inhumations suggest that they were representatives of the social elite, possibly of foreign origin. Tumuli are the dominant form of grave monument, with no or scarce grave goods, and warrior cult manifested through weaponry in assemblages. Apart from local differences (such as the body position), the burial rite shows a tradition rooted in the Cetina culture. Nevertheless, some MBA groups in the Adriatic hinterlands show collective or double burials with specific rituals that probably reflect some degree of isolation of different communities (Teržan and Karavanić 2013).

To the west of the Middle Danube, the Virovitica culture replaced the *Litzenkeramik* group of Somogyvár–Vinkovci, and expanded further to the south, with numerous settlements located in plains on low elevations near waterways, sometimes with defensive ditches fortified with a palisade. Houses were single-roomed buildings joined in small, dense groups around a courtyard area that contained several hearths or ovens, probably representing farming settlements (Teržan and Karavanić 2013).

The LBA marks another change in settlement pattern, with a large number of MBA settlements abandoned. The Kalakača–Bosut horizon shows the emergence of settlements arranged in groups of several small rectangular buildings representing individual farming households. Basarabi-type pottery appears from the eastern Balkans, and the synchronic radical reduction of settlements—with the survival or emergence of a few on fortified positions—supports an invasion of nomadic horsemen from the eastern steppes (Teržan and Karavanić 2013).

West of the Danube, an increase in occupation is seen during the Urnfield period in the lowlands along watercourses, coinciding with an increase in metallurgical production and extensive trade, probably led by specialised craftsmen and travelling prospectors. Two main types of settlements can be distinguished: open or scattered settlements without defensive systems, probably individual farmsteads; and fortified, central settlements with proto-urban features, especially after ca. 1000 BC, located primarily on elevated outcrops or high river terraces. These lasted until the Iron Age, when new fortified settlements, hill forts, formed at elevated spots, leading to a new territorial organisation (Teržan and Karavanić 2013).

viii.9. Messapians and Illyrians

It remains unclear if Messapic expanded with Bell Beakers migrating through the Italian Peninsula, or rather southward through the eastern Adriatic coast. Based on the connections of the Cetina culture with Bell Beakers from the Italian Peninsula, and the potential nature of Messapian as a North-West Indo-European dialect, it seems more likely that Proto-Messapic speakers expanded first southward from the Alps into mainland areas east of the Appennines, and were later replaced and displaced to the south-eastern corner with migrations of Italic peoples.

Two individuals from Early/Middle Bronze Age from Veliki Vanik in Split-Dalmatia (ca. 1630–1510 BC) include one of hg. J2b2a-M241 (formed ca. 118000 BC, TMRCA ca 7800 BC), probably corresponding to subclade J2b2a1-L283 (TMRCA ca. 3400 BC), since basal clades are found today in modern populations of southern Italy and Anatolia. These and a later sample of the Late Bronze Age from the Jazinka Cave, near Nečven (ca. 780 BC) show similar ancestry to other available Balkan samples, but with increased Steppe ancestry (ca. 35%), and slightly less WHG (although similar EHG) contribution compared to other Early Bronze Age individuals from the Balkans.

Interestingly, this haplogroup, which probably arrived in the Balkans from a westward expansion through Anatolia during the Chalcolithic or Neolithic, is found later in Armenia MLBA in an individual with Steppe ancestry (see *§viii.14. Caucasians and Armenians*). The finding of haplogroup J-M304 among Mycenaeans (see *§viii.12. Greeks and Philistines*) further suggests a relative infiltration rather than a massive migration of Yamna male lineages in the southern Balkans, probably due in great part to the higher demographic density of south-eastern Europe (Müller and Diachenko 2019).

In the south-east, Messapic-speaking Iapyginians from Botromagno (ca. 7th–4th c. BC) show mainly mtDNA subclades H and U, while the later Romans from nearby Vagnari (ca. AD 1st-4th c.) show more varied mtDNA haplogroups, with closer affinities to eastern Mediterranean populations. This replacement may be associated with the migration of Romans from central and northern Italy, but is likely to represent a direct gene flow from the eastern Mediterranean due to immigration or slave trade (Emery 2018).

VIII.10. Carpathian province

The EBA in the Carpathian area is marked by a great population increase compared to the previous period, suggested by a peaceful lifestyle in tell settlements and the large number of graves in cemeteries. Advanced cultivation skills (grain cultivation supplemented with horticulture) and cattle breeding are probably behind this improvement. Riverine transport and animal transport over land, suggested by spoked wheels and horse cheek-pieces, suggest intense trading networks (Marková and Ilon 2013).

Similar to the findings in the Baltic coast, east Baltic inland and Belarus (see *§VIII.8.2. North-Eastern province – Iwno*), there is a sort of eastern *march* of the Bell Beaker territory that spans from the easternmost Classic Bell Beaker groups (like Moravia or Csepel) to western Ukraine, where the comb–stamp decorated beakers with horizontal band structure are strongly reminiscent of Classical Bell Beakers, even though their shape is clearly original from the Catacomb Grave culture (Heyd 2013).

Bell Beaker findings in this huge eastern area of influence, which covers the Carpathian Basin, include wristguards, *Begleitkeramik*, flint arrowheads, and bone pendants, as well as the preferred comb–stamp decorated vessels and sherds with horizontal zoned decoration. They reflect their late connection with Bell Beaker, as well as cultural adaptations to local or regional cultures. The Csepel group shows often cremation graves instead of inhumation as is common to the west, and features extensive riverbank settlements with boat-shaped buildings and ritual pits. Bell Beaker materials are also encountered in traditional Vučedol territory (Heyd 2013).

Roots of the EBA of the Carpathian region are found in the extensive Makó/Kosihý–Čaka culture, which showed isolated graves featuring cremation in scattered graves and in urns, and sporadic inhumations at the end of the culture. Metallurgy shows a connection with Circum-Pontic cultures, including artefacts and moulds for copper, and shaft–hole axes During the EBA, the Somogyvár–Vinkovci culture dominates over the north and north-western Balkans up to Transdanubia in the west. It shows scattered, short-term open settlements, with post-built or semi-subterranean houses, and varying funeral rites including usually inhumations, and less often urned cremations, with graves in mounds, flat, or with stone packing (Marková and Ilon 2013).

The Nagyrév culture from the Danube–Tisza region to the Carpathians in the north show short-lived, unfortified, sparse settlements, with post-built houses and relief ornamentation in walls and pottery. Burials feature scattered graves and urned cremations, with inhumations proper of its formative phase (Marková and Ilon 2013).

In the north-east Carpathian area, the Nyírség–Zatín culture shows single-phase upland and lowland settlements and tells. Burial rite was cremation in an urn. The Andrid culture represents a transitional group with the Ottomány culture, appearing in settlements before tell sites. It is supposed to have consisted of farmers and stockbreeders. Cremation in pits or urns was the preferred burial rite (Marková and Ilon 2013).

The Kisapostag culture was based on the Makó/Kosihý–Čaka culture, with contributions from the late Somogyvár culture. Cremation is prevalent, with urns and scattered graves. Copper-sheet industry artefacts (like pendants, tubes, diadems) are typical, and imports from this culture are found as far as the Tisza region in the east, and the upper Danube in the west. It was succeeded by the Transdanubian Encrusted Pottery culture (also North Pannonian culture), with a distinction into a northern and a southern group. Settlements are usually short-lived, and cattle breeding is the main subsistence economy. A hierarchy is suggested based on settlement size. Cremation in pits and urns are the norm, they are placed in groups, and elite objects associated with social ranking are deposited in a ritual manner (Marková and Ilon 2013). West of the Danube, the wire-brushed pottery culture (Litzenkeramik) was probably a regional variant of the Kisapostag culture, and the few graves found show bi-ritual funerary practices, i.e. inhumation and cremation.

The Vatya culture forms from the basis of Nagyrév with influences from the Kisapostag culture. Burials show a consistent rite, with cremations laid out in a structured manner, sometimes bounded or covered by stones. Cemeteries comprise several hundred urn burials, and urns were ordered initially in clan groupings. Social differentiation was seen in grave goods in the final phase of the culture. Fortifications appear probably reflecting the formation of social hierarchy, and they show enclosed areas dedicated particular functions, such as metallurgy. Bronze artefacts are abundant. Nagyrév sites are continued in Vatya settlements, which expand to previously unsettled sandy locations (Marková and Ilon 2013).

The Hatvan culture formed from the former Nagyrév culture (with eastern influence evident in its metallurgy), in previous Nagyrév and Nyírség areas. Settlements include tells and tell-like settlements, with small fortified areas surrounded by ditches in settlements which had unfortified annexes or satellite settlements. Small family cemeteries with scattered cremation and urn graves in groups were located around the settlements. Interaction with the Ottomány–Füzesabony complex induced changes in the pottery (Marková and Ilon 2013).

The Early Bronze Age Ottomány I–Füzesabony cultural complex (ca. 2150-1650 BC) spread over a good part of the Pannonian basin, and a quite close interaction with the Hatvan culture. Decorative elements on fine wares mostly geometric, including incised lines and chevrons (Duffy et al. 2019). Regional Füzesabony groups show differences in pottery forms, but they share a common strict burial rite: inhumation burial in crouched position with gender differentiation—males on the right side and females on the left side—and large cemeteries formed by hundreds of graves. Orientation varies depending on phase and region. Grave goods reflect social status, as do the use of a wooden coffin or a grave lining or shroud (Marková and Ilon 2013).

At the end of the culture, urnfields begin (Ottomány–Piliny horizon and Ottomány–Suciu de Sus horizon). Settlement patterns suggest social and economic distinction, and there is evidence of craft production of gold and bronze. In the Middle Bronze Age Gyulavarsánd/Otomani II–III culture (ca. 1750–1450 BC), to the east of the Tisza, Forms become elaborate, flared rims appear on pitchers, cup handles rise high above the rim and smoothed, uniform surfaces become sculpted bas-relief. The culture shows southern influences from the Vatina culture, and ornamental elements similar to the Füzesabony culture, with imports from the eastern Wietenberg culture (in Transilvania). Burial rite shows inhumations in crouched position. Tell settlements appear in new locations, with fortified tells and open settlements with post-built houses (Marková and Ilon 2013).

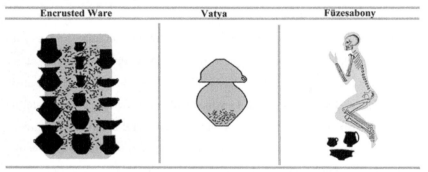

Encrusted Ware	Vatya	Füzesabony

Figure 72. Relationship between pottery and material body in MBA graves. Encrusted Ware: scattered bones, large amount of pottery over the grave, body-sized. Vatya: enclosed bones, pottery as container, urns in pits. Füzesabony: inhumation, sets of pottery annotating parts of the body, body-sized grave pits. Image and text from (Sørensen and Rebay-Salisbury 2008).

It has been argued that important ideological changes in Europe (starting ca. 1600 BC) may have corresponded to the abandonment of tell settlements, but not non-tell sites, in the Great Hungarian Plain, which may also be related to a mass west-to-east migration of the Tumulus group into the area. In the Late Bronze Age, the enormous variety of Ceramic styles across the Carpathian Basin—including forms, techniques, and combinations of elements, such as the vast array of lugs, spirals, chevrons, channels and other motifs and appliqués—fell out of use. The tell system collapses, with densities showing a striking decrease in the early phase (ca. 1450–1200 BC) until a late stage (ca.

1200–900 BC), when the arrival of the Urnfield culture in Central Europe and Transdanubia coincides with large numbers of settlements (Duffy et al. 2019).

viii.10. Carpathian Bell Beakers

After the admixture of Yamna settlers with local populations in Hungary to form the East Bell Beaker group, the genetic picture in the Carpathian Basin in the following centuries (ca. 2500–2200 BC) probably reflects to a great extent the *sink* that the Hungarian Plains represented for Yamna migrants, with high variability in Steppe ancestry and R1b1a1b1-L23 lineages (see *§vii.7. North-West Indo-Europeans*).

During the early phase of the Nagyrév culture in the Csepel island—formed by foreign Bell Beakers gradually merging with local populations and replacing local Bell Beakers—samples from Szigetszentmiklós–Üdülősor (ca. 2500–2200 BC) show a reduction in Steppe ancestry (ca. 19%) compared to the previous Csepel group (which belonged to the Danubian EEBA), and a more mixed haplogroup distribution, among them a child of hg. R1b1a1b1a1a-L151 (xR1b1a1b1a1a1-U106, xR1b1a1b1a1a2-P312), a brother of R1b1a1b1b3-Z2106 lineage, another relative reported as R1b1a1b-M269, and one sample of hg. I2a1a-P37.2, consistent with further admixture with (and resurgence of) locals (Olalde et al. 2018)

Samples of the Vatya culture show a continuation of this trend, with two individuals from Százhalombatta–Földvár (ca. 2200–1600 BC), one of hg. I2a1a-P37.2 and the other of hg. I2a1b1a-CTS616; and four individuals from Erd (ca. 2000–1500 BC), one of hg. I2a1b1a1b1b-S18331 (formed ca. 3400 BC, TMRCA ca. 3200 BC). A similar ancestry is found in samples of the Makó culture from Kompolt–Kigyoser (ca. 2200–2000 BC), of the Hungary MBA from Battonya Vörös (ca. 2000–1800 BC), and in two samples of the Maros group, which belonged to the Danubian Early Bronze Age (Allentoft et al. 2015).

An early sample from Szólád (ca. 1900 BC), of subclade R1a1a1b2a2a1-Z2123 (Amorim et al. 2018) belongs to the westward expansion of Srubna; a sample of the Kyjatice group of the Urnfield culture from Ludas–Varjú dűlő (ca. 1200 BC), of hg. J2a1b-M67, probably reflects a local lineage (Gamba et al. 2014); while a sample of haplogroup N-M231 of the Mezőcsát Culture (ca. 900 BC) belongs to the expanding Cimmerians from the steppes. This and further movements reveal the nature of the Hungarian Plains as the sink of many different migrations since prehistoric times.

VIII.11. Balkan province

VIII.11.1. Balkans EBA

In southern Romania and in Bulgaria, earthen mound-burials of 'ochre' related to the Yamna tradition are still in use during the Early Bronze Age, with stone slab cists—possibly related to the Globular Amphorae tradition—found widespread from east Transylvania to the east and south-east, contrasting with mounds to the west. Up to the Dalmatian hinterland (in Kupreško polje, unrelated to the Cetina culture), tumuli related to steppe cultures can be found. Four-wheeled, rectangular chariots drawn by bovids or horses can be seen from the EBA to the MBA, but disappear in the LBA (Boroffka 2013).

In the eastern Carpathian region, the Baden complex (including the Coţofeni group) give way to the Glina–Schneckenberg culture and early Zimnicea, marked by the disappearance of incised and incrusted (or painted in the Cucuteni–Trypillia) decoration to a dominance of plastic knobs and ribs, as found in Şoimuş, Roşia, the Tumulus grave group of western Transylvania, Glina–Schneckenberg, Folteşti, Delacău–Babino, early Zimnicea, Ezero. Another widespread change is seen in vessel-rims with exterior sleeve-like thickening (Boroffka 2013).

The expansion of the Bell Beaker tradition throughout Europe is seen in its easternmost area with the expansion of small footed bowls, the foot sometimes in the shape of a cross, which can be found in Glina and Ezero contexts to the south and as far east as Romanian Moldova, often together with cord decoration. Metal finds, such as massive golden lock-rings, are found in the Carpathians and the Balkans up to Greece, showing one of the long-distance contacts that appeared during the EBA (Boroffka 2013).

Further to the south-east, marginal remains are also found in the Aegean Early Bronze Age, including Greece and particularly the Peloponnese, with special relations found between Early Helladic III and the Dalmatian Cetina culture: double handled forms sparsely decorated or showing remains of the typical framed decoration in an incised technique. These findings are among the oldest EH III period, but two other notable sherds are found in the previous EH II context, all of them probably under BBC influence after ca. 2500 BC (Heyd 2013).

From EBA in Hungary expanded vessels with brushed or combed lower body, probably with the aim of enlarging the outer surface of cooking vessels for better heat absorption and higher porosity for the cooling of liquid contents by evaporation through the wall. This influence is observed during the EBA in the south in Ezero, Dyadovo, and in the east in Bogdăneşti, Iacobeni, and continues into the MBA with Mureş, Ottomány, and Wietenberg groups (Boroffka 2013).

The other strong influence in the western Balkans during the EBA comes from the Troad in Turkey, which is felt up to south-eastern Bulgaria, although the potter's wheel—well established in Troy itself—was not adopted, the few wheel-thrown fragments being most likely imports. Zooarchaeological material such as the bones of fallow deer, native to Turkey east of the Bosphorus, appears in imports up to the Danube and in the eastern Balkans (Boroffka 2013).

VIII.11.2. Balkans MBA

During the Middle Bronze Age, different groups show the expansion of characteristic EBA pottery shapes, with regional differences in burial rites, settlement structures, economics or ritual elements, with Verbicioara, Tei (later Gîrla Mare/Žuto Brdo), Monteoru, and Costişa groups sharing thus common elements with Ottomány, Wietenberg or Maros groups to the west. In general, the following developments are seen (Boroffka 2013):

1. There is an evolution from spiral to meander motifs.

2. Channelled decoration—usually oblique, but sometimes spiral— appears in the development stages of most MBA cultures.

3. One-handled cups are replaced by other vessels shapes, all presumably for drinking: in eastern Tei and Verbicioara cups are

replaced by kantharoi, in western Wietenberg and Ottomány and Suciu de Sus they are replaced by weakly profiled, shallow open bowls, often with *omphalos* instead of a handle.

Monteoru (which replaced Costişa) in the south-east and Maros in the south-west stand out because of the *kantharoi* that were used along cups (Figure 73), probably because of a southern influence, evidenced by a similar shape and ornament found in southern Romania, Bulgaria, and northern Greece (Boroffka 2013).

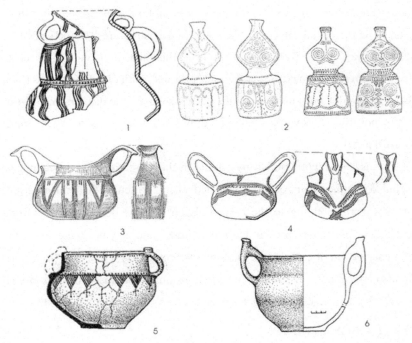

Figure 73. Ceramic from Monteoru culture (1, 3, 4), Komarowo culture (5) and Noua culture (6) with statuette of the Gîrla Mare culture (2). Modified from Dietrich (2011), including images from După Zaharia 1993, Sava 1994, Sava 2002, and Şandor-Chicideanu 2003.

Continued long-distance connections are seen from the west in bar-shaped cheek-pieces, and from the east e.g. in bone psalia (bridle parts), with round plate-shaped variants of the cheek-pieces (as found in Monteoru and Wietenberg), probably originating in the steppes. Especially interesting are bone objects ornamented with spiral-based motifs ('pulley-ornament'), which may be followed as far east as the Ural region, or south to Mycenaean Greece, where they appear much later (Boroffka 2013).

Settlement structures seem to be dependent on the environment rather than on pottery traditions. In Wietenberg, simple cremation appears in burials in urns, rarely with grave goods; in Gîrla Mare/Žuto Brdo, the rule is also cremation and deposition in urns with complex arrangements of vessels and clay figurines; in Monteoru, crouched inhumations with vessels, jewellery and some tools or weapons are the standard, although cremation is also documented, and funerary environment is complex, with simple pits, stone cists, stone rings, and catacomb-like subterranean structures (Boroffka 2013).

Weaponry shows fighting tactics in the Balkan–Carpathian region up to Greece, different from central and western Europe, with disc-butted axes (later also with pointed butt) used as 'battle–axes', in contrast to daggers and swords to the north-west. Swords were probably used mainly as a status object (Boroffka 2013).

The use of wagons pulled by equids in the Carpathian Basin cannot be excluded, with remains of four-wheeled charts (often with a raised front) formally corresponding to the early fighting wagons of the steppes. Light spoked wheels are also present in these cultures, and may be connected to the light chariot, although evidence is scarce. Wagons carry a practical (transport) but also a religious (as transport for the transition to another world) meaning, as well as ideological, marking a special social position (Boroffka 2013).

VIII.11.3. Balkans LBA

During the Late Bronze Age, cultures overlapping with the MBA deepened the east–west divide, with more unified and widely distributed traditions. The western group (Ciumeşti, Lăpuş I, Igriţa, Belegiš–Cruceni, and Bistreţ–Işalniţa groups) shows less variation in vessel shape, and oblique or garland-shaped channelling replaces incised decoration. This process of 'Hallstattisation' caused by influence from Tumulus and Urnfield cultures continues into the Early Iron Age. The dead were cremated and buried in urns (Boroffka 2013).

In the south and south-east, the Čerkovna/Zimnicea– Plovdiv group evolves in central and western Bulgaria from late Tei and Verbicioara, and shows an expansion southward as far as northern Greece. It shows the *kantharoi* as its characteristic shape, a late revival of older pottery shapes, with pottery remains decorated with incised, originally encrusted ornaments, similar to those found in northern Greece. It also features deposition of complete vessels in wells which ceased to function, continuing a Verbicioara tradition. Cremation under mounds seems to be the rule, but crouched inhumation is found in Zimnicea (Boroffka 2013).

Long-distance connections show a clear south-west–north-east axis, illustrated by 'Mycenaean' rapiers found in Bulgaria and Romania during the LBA, and pins with perforated head and knobs on the neck (from the Noua group) found in northern Greece. Stone sceptres of phallic shape and the shape of axe– sceptres with inward curled tip and mushroom-shaped butt have analogies in the south Turkish coast (Boroffka 2013).

The eastern Noua–Sabatinovka–Coslogeni complex shows an eastern intrusion from the steppes, connected to the Srubna culture (see *§VIII.19.2. Srubna and Sabatinovka*), westward into Moldavia and Transylvania, and southward into Dobruja and north-eastern Bulgaria. It features a reduction of the repertoire of vessel forms, with pottery that lacked ornamentation or was sparsely decorated with channelling or incisions. While Balkan axes continue in part previous traditions, the characteristic eastern socketed axes can be traced back to the Eurasian Seima–Turbino phenomenon (Boroffka 2013).

Specific settlement structures—groups of the so-called ash-mound (*zolnik*), round or oval low mounds with whitish-grey soil—and large quantity of animal bones suggesting a pastoralist stockbreeding economy are proof of a highly mobile nomadic society. Nevertheless, the shape and decoration of its pottery partially continues the previous Monteoru culture, and spread into Transylvania. Inhumation in a crouched position with scarce grave goods was the standard burial rite, with cemeteries sometimes including burials in or on older tumuli (Boroffka 2013).

VIII.11.4. Balkans EIA

With the Early Iron Age, the expansion of Hallstatt causes the spread of channelled pottery groups, closely connected to the Urnfield groups further west, and coincident with the demise of steppe influence of Noua–Sabatinovka–Coslogeni in the region. Continuity with the LBA is seen in some ceramic shapes and decorations.

A northern block represented by the Gáva–Holihrady culture spreads from Transylvania to Moldova, while Belegiš II-type pottery spreads through the south into Moldova, including the late eastern variant Chişinău–Corlăteni. In the north, large vessels show exaggerated large hyptertrophic upwards-curving knobs on the body, while Belegiš II urns bear smaller paired knobs pointing upwards and downwards (Boroffka 2013).

In the Dobruja, Bulgaria, and later in Moldova, channelled pottery appears sometimes combined with stamped and incised decoration, representing the origin of the later widespread Basarabi culture, displaying connections with the Gáva–Holihrady culture to the north rather than to the neighbouring Belegiš II type. These elements are found further south in Troy VIIb and in the so-called 'Barbarian Ware' of Greece. While Belegiš II and Gáva–Holihrady display mainly cremation, inhumation graves (and tumuli) coexist in southern Romania and Bulgaria, although it is unclear the actual distribution of the burial rite (Boroffka 2013).

viii.11. Thracians and Albanians

viii.11.2. Thracians

There is scarce data on the Eastern Balkans during the Early Bronze Age. Eastern Balkan cultures likely continued the infiltration of Yamna-related peoples south of the Danube. R1b1a1b1b-Z2103 lineages are found widespread along the Lower Danube, from the east in late Yamna and Catacomb samples (ca. 2500–1950 BC), to the west in Vučedol from Beli Manastir (ca. 2775 BC), in early Nagýrev (ca. 2500–2200 BC), and in some East Bell Beaker groups (ca. 2500–2000 BC).

This overwhelming presence of R1b1a1b1b-Z2103 lineages bears witness to the most likely situation to the south of the Danube, too, where these Yamna-related clans probably replaced in part previous ones of I2a1b1a2a2a-L699 lineages (see *§vii.5. Palaeo-Balkan peoples*), given the scarce presence of this haplogroup in more recent times, including modern populations. The cultural connection of Mycenaeans to Early Bronze Age populations of the Balkans and the Carpathian Basin makes a direct connection of Palaeo-Balkan R1b1a1b1b-Z2103 lineages with the Catacomb culture (e.g. driven by the westward expansion of R1a1a1b2-Z93 and R1a1a1b1a2-Z280 subclades with Srubna) unlikely.

Samples of elevated Steppe ancestry and haplogroup R1a1a1b2-Z93 are found in the Middle Bronze Age along the Danube: one from the Kairyaka necropolis in Merichleri (ca. 1690 BC), ca. 1,000 younger than the other one of hg. I2a1b1a2a2-Y5606 (Mathieson et al. 2018); and one to the west in Szólád, Hungary (ca. 1900 BC), of subclade R1a1a1b2a2a1-Z2123, clustering closely with south-east European samples (Amorim et al. 2018). Both intrusive lineages probably represent male-driven incursions of Srubna-related settlers along the Lower Danube reaching the Hungarian steppes, associated with the appearance of round plate-shaped variants of the cheek-pieces in these territories. These and possibly also later contacts with Cimmerians may explain some recent Indo-Iranian influence in Palaeo-Balkan dialects, like Armenian.

Thracians, traditionally distinguished from nomadic pastoralist Scythians by their agricultural economy, are known to have established urban centres on the right bank of the Danube—beyond their stronghold in Thrace—towards the middle of the 1st millennium BC, with Getae tribes expanding (ca. 650–350 BC) also along the Prut and Dniester, at the same time as Scythians were present south of the Danube. Thraco-Scythian contacts, interaction, and osmosis, their openness to acculturation, and the mixed economy found in different ethnolinguistic group, as well as the potential Sea routes between the north Pontic area and the eastern Balkans, and the incursion of Greeks, complicates the genetic picture.

Two Thracian individuals from Bulgaria show different ancestry, with one showing elevated NWAN ancestry, while another—an aristocratic individual buried with a rich assemblage—clustered closer to the Steppe (Sikora et al. 2014). Both clusters may be tentatively identified with the recently described 'Southern European' and 'Central' clusters among north Pontic Scythians (Krzewińska, Kılınç, et al. 2018), closer to Balkan clusters, and showing increased NWAN contribution: from ca. 5% among Srubna and east Scythians up to 35% (see *§viii.19. Iranians*).

The different haplogroups in these clusters, including two R1b1a1b1b-Z2103 lineages, one of them R1b1a1b1b3-Z2106, one I2a1b1a2a1b-Y7219 (formed ca. 4100 BC, TMRCA ca. 2000 BC) and one E1b1b1a1b1-L618 (formed ca. 10000 BC, TMRCA ca. 6100 BC), also in contrast to eastern Scythians and other previous or later steppe populations, suggest the likely acculturation of the region, and thus the potential spread of Thracian peoples at least partly with R1b1a1b1b-Z2103 lineages.

viii.11.2. Albanians

The lack of close linguistic relationship of Albanian with Illyrian, the lack of Proto-Albanian toponymy in Illyria, and the absence of indigenous sea-faring terminology in the reconstructed language (borrowing corresponding words from Romance or Greek) make it likely that Albanians were unrelated to the ancient Illyrians. It has been proposed that they came from further north, with the settling of Proto-Albanians believed to be in Dacia Ripensis and farther north, in the foothills of the Carpathian Mountains and the Beskidy/Bieszczady (possibly a toponym of Albanian origin), with the migration to Illyria via the eastern slopes of the Balkans taking place before (but not much earlier than) their contact with Romance speakers and the end of the Proto-Albanian period (Orel 1998).

The diversity of haplogroups among modern Albanians reflect their complex ethnogenesis (Peričić et al. 2005; Battaglia et al. 2008): An origin of the Albanoid homeland close to the north-west Pontic region during the Iron Age, before their expansion and subsequent Y-DNA bottlenecks, is supported by the prevalent E1b1b1a1b1-L618 lineages (ca. 24–44%)—mainly V13+ (formed ca. 6100 BC, TMRCA ca. 2800 BC)—a haplogroup found previously in Neolithic Hungary and among Scythians of the north-west Pontic area, with a likely origin in early European farmers; and by hg. R1b1a1b2-M269 (ca. 18–20%), mainly R1b1a1b1b3a1a1c-Y10789 with Z2705+ (formed ca. 700 BC, TMRCA ca. AD 550), a subclade of R1b1a1b1b-Z2103. Their close contact with other Palaeo-Balkan groups, probably through mixture with local peoples of the Balkan and Adriatic regions after their migration from the Carpathians, possibly as early as the 7th century BC (Witczak 2016), is to be inferred from the presence (ca. 15–17%) of J2b2a1-L283 lineages (formed ca. 7700 BC, TMRCA ca. 3400 BC), proper of Balkan populations; but also possibly from hg. R1b1a1b2-PF7562 (ca. 5%)[31], an early offshoot of R1b1a1b2-M269,

---

[31] Data based on reported subclades from the FTDNA group *Albanian Bloodlines*.

associated directly or indirectly to the Yamna expansion to the west (see *§vi.1. Disintegrating Indo-Europeans*).

VIII.12. The Aegean

VIII.12.1. Middle Helladic and Minoan

The Middle Helladic (MH) period starts around 2100 BC or earlier with a severe crisis, which sees the depopulation and destruction in various sites, changes in material culture, burial rite and settlement pattern, hierarchy, and space. Traditionally, these changes have been explained as the consequence of migrations—or at least infiltrations—of ethnic groups probably from the north. Many sites are destroyed or abandoned between 2350 and 2100 BC, and the number of sites in use decreases dramatically. Trade relations are broken, inferred from the lack of circulation of ceramics and chipped stone (Voutsaki 2010).

Especially rural sites are affected, with a decrease in size of the existing settlements and disappearance of site hierarchy. Some sites retain a considerable size, such as Thebes, Argos, or Mycenae. In this new period, few settlements are fortified. Houses are self-standing and positioned in an irregular fashion, with stone foundations and mud-brick superstructure, with ca. 50–60 m². In the following period (ca. 2100–1700 BC) recovery in different regions is seen at different pace, with resettlement of areas and increase in size of the old sites, larger or more complex domestic structures appear, and some accumulation of wealth (Voutsaki 2010).

Slight changes can be seen in burial rite in the early period (ca. 2100–1700 BC), with burials being intramural, and tumuli found with an uneven distribution. There is evidence that tumuli are also places of cult rites. Extramural cemeteries appear later (especially ca. 1900 BC onwards). Grave types include simple pits, cists of various types, and large pithoi, with single, contracted inhumations and rarely offerings. Later, extramural cemeteries become widespread, new tomb types are used (shaft grave, tholos tomb, chamber tomb) and reuse of the grave and secondary treatment of the body become common. This time coincides with the appearance of shrines, at the end of the Middle Helladic period (Voutsaki 2010).

Changes in material culture include the appearance of apsidal buildings, terracotta 'anchors', stone shaft–hole hammer–axes, and tumuli, which point to the influence of northern migrants. Arsenic copper is replaced with bronze metallurgy, and the potter's wheel is adopted. Toward the end of the period (from ca. 1700 BC), the mainland sees an intensification of exchanges within and beyond the Aegean, with diversification of pottery styles and technologies, including Cycladic and Minoan influences, the appearance of a uniform ceramic style, the adoption of figurative elements, and the import of valuable objects (Voutsaki 2010).

New trade contacts appeared soon after ca. 2100 BC between the eastern coast and the Aegean islands, with fluctuating small-scale overlapping networks. Contacts with Epirus and Macedonia included Minyan imports and local imitations, probably related to the newcomers, found also in a few coastal sites. The Adriatic inner and coastal trade was irregular, with some communities or social groups showing more success than others in the different periods. Most of the copper and all of the lead used come from the Aegean, although some may have come from the Aegean Islands, Cyprus, or Rodopi in Thrace (Voutsaki 2010).

The MH society was organised in villages with a subsistence economy based on agriculture and animal husbandry, and limited craft specialisation. This is in contrast to the Aegean Islands, where pottery production was highly organised. The existence of elites is evidenced by the presence of few rich tombs in the early period (ca. 2100–1700 BC), whose rarity may point to different forms of social organisation in the mainland, until the appearance of Shaft Grave elites at the end of the MH period. There is a subtle increase in the complexity of mortuary practices. More radical changes take place after ca. 1700 BC (Voutsaki 2010).

The Middle Minoan period features the appearance of the 'First' or 'Old' palaces (ca. 1900 BC or earlier) in several sites on Crete, probably as an evolution of similar structures with a central court and storage facilities. They represent both the residence of the elite and probably regional redistributive centres linked to an agricultural hinterland, akin to the redistributive temple economy of the Near East, as evidenced by the administrative nature of Linear B tablets. The emergence of similar buildings through Crete point to a hierarchical society. Minoan palaces were probably also minor production centres (e.g. textiles) and concentrated high-status objects, as well as agricultural commodities. Writing and sealing practices are also traditionally associated with the emergence of the palaces (Schoep 2010).

VIII.12.2. Mycenaean Civilisation

The Mycenaean Civilisation (ca. 1700–1100 BC) begins during the late phase of the Middle Helladic period, as a unifying process of the material culture, boosted by the competitive interaction of mainland elites, based on hunting and military prowess, access to external materials, and control of the trade of the mainland with Minoan Crete and the Cyclades, as these cultures intensified contacts (Shelton 2010).

The Early Mycenaean period (ca. 1600–1400 BC) features the first tombs displaying power, wealth, and warfare (such as the Shaft Graves of Mycenae), with pottery, burial customs, and weapons indicating cultural continuity, and thus emerging elites within the previous community. Cemeteries are well defined, organised and divided, and settlements are small, possibly organised into functional or social divisions. Individual regions develop independently, probably under individual chiefs or alliances of chiefs, although common uniform trends are also seen (Shelton 2010).

The palatial system saw a complete stratification of society, with independent settlements gradually consolidated into competing polities organised around larger sites, represented by strong families or chiefs as evidenced by tholoi. Contacts with Minoan palaces was essential for wealth acquisition by Mycenaeans, marking political and social status. Mycenaean styles, arts and beliefs imitate those from Minoans, and it becomes difficult to distinguish them. During the Early Palatial period on the Greek mainland, destructions occur on Crete, and afterward Mycenaean control clearly expands in the southern Aegean, with a takeover of Minoan trade routes and depots. At the end of this period, mainland influence is seen on Crete (Shelton 2010).

The Palatial period (ca. 1400–1200 BC) is marked by the evolution of many previously competing polities into centrally focused and administered states, with stabilisation of the social organisation and institutionalisation of power structures (Figure 74). This period shows an expansion of Mycenaean culture to the north into Mount Olympus, to the west into Epirus, and to the east into the Dodecanese (Shelton 2010).

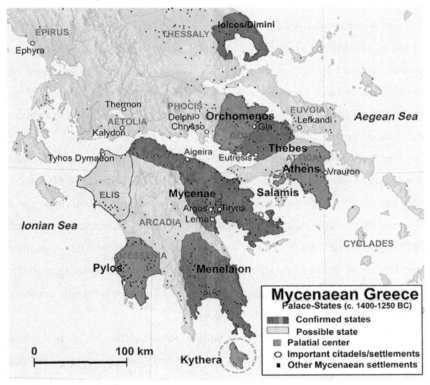

Figure 74. Reconstruction of the political landscape in c. 1400–1250 BC mainland southern Greece, based on Kelder (2010). Image by Alexikoua.

The economic success of Mycenaean palaces reached Asia Minor to the east, Macedonia to the north, Sardinia to the west, and the northern Aegean. Extensive building programs, engineering, and infrastructure support in citadels, palaces, and settlements a large but exclusive elite class and a substantial population at varying distances from the centre, with widespread systematic transportation and communication networks intra- and interregionally (Shelton 2010).

Evidence from the clay tablets written in Linear B script show a power hierarchy with the *wanaks* (king) at the top, as well an administrative system with a power hierarchy, with many administrators being individual landowners, and where material and human resources are mobilised from the centre for the needs of the political economy. Homogeneous Mycenaean pottery ('the Mycenaean koine') appears over much of the Mediterranean, probably necessary for the trade of its content, especially oil and wine (Shelton 2010).

The increasing centralised control was accompanied by localised destructions followed by rebuilding on a large scale. Around 1200 BC, growing isolated instances of destruction and decline and tightening of control gave way to the destruction of all palaces, which are not rebuilt. Many non-palatial sites are abandoned, and the administrative system disappears. Certain sites recover and prosper for a brief time, on a much smaller scale, and regional and local cultural traits develop. The population decreases, and after this small economic recovery, there is a more rapid economic decline in the 11th century BC (Shelton 2010).

viii.12. Greeks and Philistines

The expansion of the first waves of Proto-Greek speakers into the southern tip of the Balkan peninsula must have started at the end of the Early Helladic and beginning of the Middle Helladic period, possibly coinciding with the expanding Minyan pottery style (Beekes 2011), and with the appearance of horse breeding, millet-consuming cultures from the north or north-east, via river valleys leading to the Danube (Valamoti 2016). Mycenaean samples from the Peloponnese show a contribution of Steppe ancestry (ca. 20%), which can only be interpreted as the arrival of peoples from the north, although this ancestry is not found in one Mycenaean individual from Crete (Lazaridis et al. 2017).

These investigated samples from the Peloponnese include: from the eastern site of Galatas Apatheia, one early individual (ca. 2900–1900 BC) in a primary pit–grave buried with two dog carcasses—connected to the social and ideological role of hunting in the Mycenaean society—suggesting that she was a distinguished member of the local community, and a later male (ca. 1700–1200 BC, with estimated range for pottery ca. 1500–1200 BC), of hg. J2a1d-M319, the same found previously among Minoans (see *§vii.4. Aegeans and Anatolians*); to the north of Apatheia, from Agia Kyriaki in Salamina (ca. 1340 BC), a large chamber tomb cemetery belonging to the chief Late Helladic cemetery of the island, corresponding to the Palatial and Post-Palatial periods; and from the western site of Peristeria Tryfilia (ca. 1350 BC), the "Mycenae of the Western Peloponnese", an early Mycenaean settlement which may have served as a seat of a local ruler dynasty, flourished from the 17th to the end of the 13th century BC.

The Late Minoan III Necropolis of Armenoi in Crete (ca. 1390–1190), with two hundred and thirty-two chamber tombs, and one thousand interred individuals, in a site with a stirrup jar with a Linear B inscription, has yielded one sample without detectable Steppe ancestry (Lazaridis et al. 2017). This individual suggests a variable introduction of Steppe ancestry into the different territories that Mycenaeans eventually controlled, and thus potentially the introduction of the language without much genetic change, similar to how southern Balkan J2a1d-M319 lineages may have been incorporated into the Proto-Greek community (at least partially) through exogamy, due to the high demographic density of the Aegean (Müller and Diachenko 2019).

The only reported Y-chromosome haplogroup from Ancient Greeks comes from the Gulf of Amurakia (ca. 470-30 BC), and is R1b1a1-P297[32], which most likely corresponds to the typical Balkan subclade R1b1a1b1b-Z2103. This sampling is from a population before the Roman foundation of Nikopolis, hence from people likely from Anaktorion in Ancient Acarnania, of Corinthian origin. This strengthens the connection of the modern R1b1a1b1b-Z2103 distribution in Greece to the expansion of Dorians, after the Greek Dark Ages.

The twenty-four individuals from the Greek colony of Emporion in northeast Iberia (ca. 500–100 BC) —founded most likely by Phocaean settlers, from western Anatolia—fall into two main ancestry groups: one similar to Iron Age Iberians, and the other similar to Bronze Age Mycenaeans (Olalde et al. 2019). The striking similarity of this eastern Greek population with ancient Mycenaeans from 1,000 years earlier, as well as the presence of two J-M304 lineages in the same cluster, support the likely presence of north-south and west-east clines of Steppe ancestry and typical Yamna lineages in the Ancient Greek-speaking Aegean.

Analysis of modern Greek and Cretan lineages point to a Neolithic expansion of haplogroup R1b1a1b-M269 in the region, which was found nearer to Italian than to Balkan lineages (King et al. 2008). Analysis of Greek-Cypriot modern populations revealed the presence of R1b1a1b1b-Z2103 lineages in easternmost and westernmost sides of the island, with R1b1a1b1b3a1-Z2110 lineages appearing only in the east (Voskarides et al. 2016). The early attestation of Mycenaean Greek in the island points to an early expansion of R1b1a1b1b3a1-Z2110 lineages.

---

[32] Report by Nikolaos Psonis, from the IMBB Joint Colloquia (2018).

Most R1b1a1b-M269 lineages in Greece are probably linked to the Bronze Age expansion associated with the Minyan pottery, in turn linked to an earlier Yamna expansion into south-eastern Europe. Most R1a1a1-M417 lineages, whose proportion in Greece and in historically Greek Anatolia increases with latitude and in peripheral areas, are thus to be linked to the recent migration of southern Balkan populations of R1a1a1b1-Z283 lineages (mainly Slavs, but also Aromanians and Albanians), and to the western spread of Iranian peoples of R1a1a1b2-Z93 lineages (Heraclides et al. 2017).

A potentially older invasion of certain R1a1a1b2-Z93 (and possibly R1a1a1b1-Z283) lineages during the Bronze Age could be supported by the finding of this lineage in Srubna-related settlers along the Danube in the first half of the 2nd millennium BC, although it is unlikely that they reached Greece in sizeable numbers (see *§viii.11. Thracians and Albanians*).

On the controversial ethnicity and language of the Sea Peoples (Figure 75) and the closely related Philistine question, archaeological evidence suggests a large scale immigration to southern Canaan from Anatolia and Cyprus in the 13th–11th c. BC, and material culture of Cypriote, Aegean, and especially Mycenaean influence associated with cultural changes during the transition of the Late Bronze to the Iron Age (Woudhuizen 2006; Maeir, Davis, and Hitchcock 2016; Middleton 2015).

In particular, Monochrome and foreign Bichrome styles contemporaneous in Canaan reflect social interactions during ca. 100 years, supporting the notion that foreigners arrived to Canaan in more than a single event, supporting a "deep change" in the local material culture, including cultural mixing or creolisation and hybridisation. This influence started in Philistia to the south in the late 13th c. BC, during the time of Ramesses III, and diffused to the north after the retreat of the 20th Egyptian Dynasty (Asscher and Boaretto 2018). The turnover in the southern Levantine pig population to European lineages around this time also support increased mobility from west to east (Meiri et al. 2019).

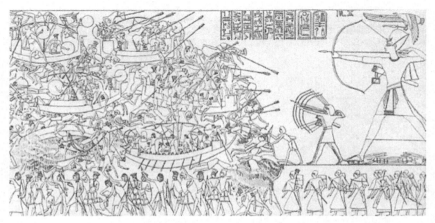

Figure 75. Famous scene from the north wall of Medinet Habu that illustrates the Egyptian campaign against the Sea Peoples in the Battle of the Delta. Egypt's enemies are described simply as being from "northern countries", but early scholars noted the similarities between the hairstyles and accessories worn by the combatants and other reliefs in which such groups are named. Image from Wikipedia.

A Canaanite individual from a clay coffin burial in Tel Shaddud (ca. 1250 BC), reported as of hg. R1b1a1b-M269⁺, has been interpreted as a Canaanite official residing at this site and emulating selected funerary aspects of Egyptian mortuary culture, apparently connected to the administrative centre at Bet She'an during the 19th and 20th Dynasties (van den Brink et al. 2017). This and another contemporary, non-relative individual from a nearby burial pit, of hg. J, show similar estimated ancestry, clustering closely with modern Levantine populations (see *§vi.5. Semites and Berbers*). While the nature of the Egyptian presence in Canaan during the Late Bronze Age is still discussed, the presence of a typically Indo-European lineage in the Levant during the LBA would further support the potential association of Sea Peoples with the Aegean in general, and with Greek speakers in particular.

Genetic research points to a mixture of Steppe ancestry found in the Lebanese population that occurred ca. 1740–160 BC (Haber et al. 2017). Steppe ancestry is found in Roman Period individuals, but not in Bronze Age individuals, which supports its introduction more than 2,000 years ago (Haber et al. 2018). R1b1a1b1b-Z2103 lineages appearing in the region after the Bronze Age are probably of Balkan origin (Greeks or Armenians), while

R1a1a1b2-Z93 lineages are of Indo-Aryan or Iranian origin, although R1b1a1b1b-Z2103 could have also been associated with Indo-Iranians and early Iranians.

VIII.13. Anatolia

VIII.13.1. The Kārum period

During the first centuries of the 2nd millennium BC, Assyrian merchants originating from Assur (Upper Tigris) organised large-scale commercial exchanges with central Anatolia, settling in several fortified towns on the main roads called *kārums*, and smaller trading posts called *wabartums*. Large settlements show an organisation around a huge palace and several temples built on top of the mound, with a lower terrace, where occupation areas are made up of two-storey houses constructed with wood and mudbricks over stone foundations (Michel 2011).

Sociopolitical and economic changes are seen with the new material culture—open wheel-made vessels with coloured geometric decorations— with figurative art (zoomorphological rhyta, lead and ivory figurines), buried bodies under the floors of the houses together with artefacts, all pointing to Assyrian burial customs. The seal industry is the best example of Old Assyrian influence, with Old Anatolian iconography combining elements and filling empty spaces with animal figures. Treaties are documented (ca. 2000–1800 BC) between Assyrian kings and local Anatolian rulers (Michel 2011).

Old Assyrian was used as diplomatic language (with Hittite loanwords since ca. 19th c. BC), and writing continued the Assyrian cuneiform tradition without changes. In family law, husband and wife enjoyed equal status, and they owned house and goods in common. Both could divorce, and contracts were established under the supervision of the local ruler and his second–in– command. Adoption is also attested, with the possibility of adopted individuals to inherit (Michel 2011).

The first generations of Assyrians who came to Anatolia was made up of men who left their families in Assur, temporarily at the beginning, but eventually contracting a second marriage, often with an Anatolian woman, who stayed in Anatolia as 'secondary wife' and brought up their children, taking care of the household, and doing agricultural tasks while their husbands were travelling and trading. When some Assyrians went to retire in Assur, they left their Anatolian wives and drew up a divorce contract, with women keeping usually the house, furniture, and some divorce money, as well as their younger children, with the father paying for their upbringing—although he could also decide to take some of his Anatolian children to Assur (Michel 2011).

VIII.13.2. The Hittite period

Precise archaeological studies do not parallel written accounts, which remain the best source for knowledge of Anatolia during the Bronze and Iron Ages. In the west, the Arzawa territories are assumed to correspond to earlier Luwiya, and refers strictly to the five states or kingdoms constituting the Arzawa Lands: Mira, Šeḫa River Land, Wiluša, and Ḫapalla. It is unclear to what extent these territories formed a social, ethnic, or political unity in the different periods (Bryce 2011).

The eventual presence of Luwian hieroglyphs, the eventual dominance of Mira over western Anatolia, and the succeeding Luwic and Carian groups in the region suggest that at least part of western Anatolia was mainly Luwic-speaking territory in the first half of the 2nd millennium BC. During the mid–2nd millennium, the appearance of Mycenaean settlements—evidenced by fortifications, pottery, domestic architecture, burial practices—suggests that the Hittite form Aḫḫiyawa corresponds to the Greek name *Achaiwia*, Achaean, supporting the close Greek–Anatolian contacts during this period.

The beginning of the Hittite kingdom followed the collapse of the *kārum* period network of Assyrian trade colonies, caused by the struggle of various groups, and eventually the emergence ca. 1650–1600 BC of the Ḫatti kingdom based on Ḫattuša and the area within the Maraššantiya/Kızıl Irmak River. To consolidate their rule, Hittite kings followed an active settlement policy to fund new provincial centres in the semi-arid highlands of Anatolia, bordered by the Pontic Mountains in the north, and the Taurus Mountains to the south, but also including Cilicia in south-eastern Anatolia, and the Upper Euphrates region (Seeher 2011).

Around 1350 BC, during the reign of Tudḫaliya III, enemy attacks from everywhere led to heavy losses of territory and power, and the conflagration of the capital. The recovery of the state was accompanied by the massive development of Hittite rule in the Hittite Empire, evidenced in widespread city growth and monumental architecture, such as the creation of rock reliefs. The collapse of the empire at the end of the Late Bronze Age (ca. 1200/1180 BC) is accompanied by destruction of Empire period sites, with some Early Iron Age sites yielding a pronounced non-Hittite material culture, possibly settlers who took advantage of the deserted landscapes.

viii.13. Assyrians and Hittites

Anatolia EBA individuals from Ovaören (ca. 2300–2000 BC), one of hg. J2a-M410, and later Assyrian and Old Hittite individuals from the MLBA in Kalehöyuk show continuity with Chalcolithic samples, with no statistically significant EHG-related ancestry that could be compatible with a sizeable impact of steppe migrations (de Barros Damgaard, Martiniano, et al. 2018).

Samples from Kalehöyük include individuals from the Assyrian period (ca. 2000–1750 BC), contemporary with the international trade system managed by expatriate Assyrian merchants, one of hg. G2a2b1-M406, mtDNA H6a1b2e, and another of hg. J2a1-L26; and two of the Old Hittite period (ca. 1750–1500 BC), contemporary with the emergence of the Hittite state, one of hg. J2a1-L26. Interestingly, the mtDNA found in one Assyrian sample is of European origin (found also in the steppe), not yet found in any ancient sample of the Near East.

This genetic picture, although as of yet incomplete (lacking a good temporal and regional transect of Anatolia, and Anatolian speakers in particular), is consistent with the description of the Assyrian colony period as one of admixture of Assyrian male settlers with local women, in this case probably Anatolian speakers, who raised their children locally, and the Hittite period representing the emergence of local rulers (of Assyrian patrilineal descent) who spoke the maternal language.

The prevalent presence of non-Indo-European languages of the area, including Hattic, possibly part of the North-West Caucasian group, and Hurrian, part of the Hurro-Urartian family that may have also been related to languages of the Caucasus (see §vi.4. *Northern Caucasians*), is consistent with the appearance of haplogroups G2a-P15 and J2a-M410, both related to migrations through the Fertile Crescent and the Caucasus, and not linked to Indo-Europeans migrating from the steppe.

VIII.14. The Caucasus

The early Trialeti cultural complex (ca. 2000–1700 BC) shows a significant connection of the southern Caucasus with neighbouring lands, in particular Anatolia, and is characterised by their barrow tradition and mobile subsistence economy. The main difference between barrows is the richness displayed. The lavish and grandiose log structures corresponded to the elite social class, who practised cremation with ashes placed in wooden containers, and the only bones appearing in the burial being those of animals, especially cattle. This change in ritual has been associated with a religious change, a transformation of the physical into the metaphysical, which had the effect of entrenching power and authority of the leader and his kin (Sagona 2017).

In the second rank, the dead were interred. Some tombs were also rich, displaying four-wheeled vehicles, and animal remains probably consumed during a ritual feast. The lowest rank is represented by small barrows with poor assemblages. Bronze tools and weapons, which are not found in large numbers in elite burials, are more common in small barrows. Interesting is the deposit of skin of the sacrificed oxen (and later of horses) with its severed forelegs attached, a practice widespread in the Eurasian steppes during the 4th millennium BC, and seen in funerary rites in central and northern Europe up to the medieval period (Sagona 2017).

Wagons and carts, which had been known in the Caucasus since the Kura–Araxes culture, continue to be built and probably represent an important part of the subsistence economy and symbolism in Trialeti, with the practice of burial wagons spreading beyond its borders, and not being gender specific. This tradition was continued in the Late Bronze Age (ca. 1600–1000 BC), with some of the greatest concentrations and highest complexity of carpentry displayed during this time (Sagona 2017). There is no evidence of large-scale regional movements based on isotopic evidence, though, especially to the south into the Ararat Plain, although it is unclear how mobile specific local pastoralist groups may have been (Chazin, Gordon, and Knudson 2019).

Their objects of precious metals and bronze show a fusion of local traits with foreign influences, suggesting its participation in a system of exchange extending to the shores of the eastern Mediterranean during the 2nd millennium BC. The slim sword blade (rapier) found in Trialeti, with its slender, sharply edged and pointed form, 1-meter long and widening at the handle end, is best suited for thrusting attacks. It has been suggested that it represents a local development on the basis of south Caucasian rapiers, that spread to the Aegean via Anatolia (Sagona 2017).

viii.14. Caucasians and Armenians

Individuals of the Late North Caucasus post-Catacomb horizon from Kabardinka (ca. 2200–2000 BC), one of hg. R1b1a1b-Z2103, show typical Steppe ancestry profile, while MBA samples from a site 90 km to the west, Kudachurt (ca. 1950–1775 BC), one of hg. J2b2a1-L283[+], retain the typical 'southern' Caucasus profile. This 'southern' genetic profile is also seen in a recent individual of the western LBA Dolmen culture (ca. 1400–1200 BC), of hg. J2a-M410[+]. Contrasting with these populations, an individual of the Lola culture (ca. 2115–1925 BC), of hg. Q1b2a1a1a-L717[+], resembles the ancestry profile of steppe Maikop individuals, of high ANE ancestry—one of which was of hg. Q1b2b1b-L932[+]—clustering closely to Afontova Gora 3, which suggests the survival of certain isolated pockets in the region since the Epipalaeolithic (Wang et al. 2019).

The language ancestral to Armenian, like Phrygian, is believed to have belonged to the peoples that came from the west and overran the Hittite empire around the 12th century BC (Beekes 2011). The collapse of the Hittite power (ca. 1180 BC) seems to have only impacted regional centres over the next generation (i.e. by mid-12th c. BC), with a radical reorganisation of the economy over a relatively short period (less than 100 years), and a distinctive Early Iron Age material culture suggestinig an increase in population mobility across the region (Kealhofer, Grave, and Voigt 2019). The suggested migration of Balkan peoples through Anatolia, evidenced by the eventual rapid emergence of the Phrygian polity (ca. 9th c. BC) may be related to the intrusion of a population with elevated Steppe ancestry reflected in two sampled individuals of the Hellenistic period from Kalehöyük (ca. 1200–30 BC), although this ancestry is most likely related to later Iron Age Galatians, of Celtic origin (de Barros Damgaard, Martiniano, et al. 2018).

Armenia MLBA samples show an increase in EHG (ca. 10%) and Anatolia Neolithic ancestry (ca. 55%) relative to previous Kura–Araxes and Chalcolithic samples, with an intermediate position between both in the PCA (Allentoft et al. 2015). The diversity of haplogroups and the presence of certain clear outliers of steppe origin suggests close interactions between peoples of the southern and the northern Caucasus.

The sampling of Armenia MLBA includes three individuals of Nerquin Getashen (ca. 1900–1200 BC), one of hg. R1b-M343, two of hg. E1b1-P2; two samples from Kapan (ca. 1200–850 BC), one of hg. R1b-M343; two samples from Norabak (ca. 1200–900 BC), one of hg. J2b2a-M241; and one sample from Noratus (ca. 1050 BC). Interesting is the finding of R1b-M343 subclades in the region—although they may be related to the previously described resurgence of R1b1a-L388—and especially of haplogroup J2b2a-M241, which is also found in the Jazinka Cave in the western Balkans (ca. 780 BC), with elevated Steppe ancestry (ca. 35%), supporting a potential recent Balkan origin of certain typically Neolithic subclades.

An individual of an Iron Age burial at Tepe Hasanlu (ca. 971-832 BC), of haplogroup R1b1a1b1b-Z2103[+], and with contributions of Steppe ancestry, clustering close to previous Armenia MLBA samples (Broushaki et al. 2016), is most likely related to the arrival of Armenian speakers to the region. Another sample of Hajji Firuz Tepe, attributed to the Chalcolithic, but with a date incompatible with its reported haplogroup R1b1a1b1b-Z2103, also shows contribution of Steppe ancestry and a position in the PCA compatible with interactions with populations of the Caucasus (Narasimhan et al. 2018), being thus also likely related to incoming Armenians[33].

The origin of Armenian speakers in the region is complicated with the current data because of the poorly documented archaeological context of samples potentially related to Armenians published from Armenia and Northern Iran; the lack of peer-reviewed studies on the origin of the Steppe ancestry in these samples; and the potential origin of R1b1a1b1b-Z2103 in earlier northern Caucasus populations (potentially integrated in Caucasus populations since the Maikop period), in the Balkans (among Palaeo-Balkan-speaking populations), and probably among certain Indo-Aryan and Iranian groups expanding into the Fertile Crescent. Nevertheless, the clear genetic shift from previous Chalcolithic and EBA (i.e. Kura–Araxes) individuals to Armenia MLBA samples and their outliers is coincident with the expected period of their arrival in the region.

In the case of the Armenian highlands, there is ancestry levelling and genetic continuity in the Middle East during the Neolithic and Chalcolithic (Lazaridis et al. 2016), including ancient mtDNA lineages, also partially during the Bronze Age and Iron Age, which suggests a late and heavily male-biased migration of Armenians (Margaryan et al. 2017). This genetic continuity of Armenians has traditionally been explained by a history of genetic isolation from their surroundings (Haber, Mezzavilla, Xue, et al. 2016). The current data of northern Caucasus populations seems to contradict a late expansion of peoples from the steppe through the Caucasus.

Populations of the western part of the Armenian Highland, Van, Turkey, and Lebanon show genetic affinity with European populations, and their absence in previous studies "should be considered a consequence of the absence in their Armenian datasets of populations from the western region of the Armenian highland" (Hovhannisyan et al. 2014). Ascertaining the origin of Armenians is hindered by the loss of data due to the effects of the Armenian Genocide and massive population displacements of the 19th and 20th centuries.

---

[33] New radiocarbon date reported as corresponding to the Bronze Age – probably close to the Iron Age – by Vagheesh Narasimhan (2019).

VIII.15. Eastern European Forest Zone

VIII.15.1. Balanovo

During the Eneolithic, subsistence economy on the Cis-Urals forest zone was based on the effective hunting of big hoofed animals (reindeer, elk, antelope, wild pig, bear, and beaver), gathering, and productive fishing (sturgeon, grayling, pike, chub, idus, tench, etc.). Large wooden rectangular houses were arranged in rows along the riverbank, and connected to each other and with farmyards by roofed passages. Small settlements were concentrated at the confluence of rivers (Koryakova and Epimakhov 2007).

Groups of the Cis-Urals region—descended from sub-Neolithic Volga–Kama and Kama cultures, and probably related to Volosovo—like Novolin, Garino–Bor, and Yurtik cultures showed late and simple metalwork, limited in forms, made from poor copper of the western Urals region. The eastward diffusion of cattle breeders and farmers of Corded Ware cultures brought a change in pottery design, stone tools, subsistence economy, and funerary ritual—including flat and kurgan burials containing crouched skeletons, accompanied mostly by globular short-necked vessels and stone battle–axes—which can only be explained by the sudden irruption of western settlers (Koryakova and Epimakhov 2007).

The north-east province of the Balanovo culture, a variant of Fatyanovo, was the easternmost group of the Corded Ware culture, occupying the Kama–Vyatka–Vetluga interfluve. Hundreds of sites, including villages, cemeteries, and numerous stone axes found by chance, represent the expansion of the culture in the region, with sites usually located on the high hills of riverbanks, and villages consisting of several above-ground houses (ca. 16–28 m^2) built from wooden logs and saddle roofs, joined by passages (Koryakova and Epimakhov 2007).

Cemeteries contain both individual and collective graves, with men buried on the right side, women on the left side, both in contracted position, and dead wrapped in animal skins or birch bark, and placed into wooden constructions.

Grave assemblages depend on sex, age, and social position, with copper axes accompanying elites, stone axe–hammers with men and teenagers, and flint axes with everyone, except chiefs. Balanovo layers are basically connected or overlap the late Volosovo and Garino layers, which indicates that Balanovo settlers occupied previous Eneolithic sites (Koryakova and Epimakhov 2007).

Balanovo brought a more advanced economic and cultural tradition than that of their neighbours. Their subsistence economy was based on animal husbandry, primarily pigs and sheep, but also later including cattle and horses depending on the local ecological conditions. They used draught cattle and wagons, exploited the local copper sandstone deposits—bringing thus metallurgical tradition to the region—and pioneered the swidden method of farming (Koryakova and Epimakhov 2007).

VIII.15.2. Netted Ware, Chirkovo, Kazan

The Netted Ware or Textile Ware culture (Figure 76) appeared ca. 1900 BC in the Upper Volga–Oka region, derived from Fatyanovo–Balanovo settlers that inhabited previous Volosovo area and interacted with the Seima–Turbino network. It spread ca. 1900–1800 BC to the north into inner Finland, at the same time as the Pozdnyakovo branch of early Srubna exerted its influence on it.

Netted Ware expanded into regions previously occupied by cultures producing asbestos- and organic-tempered wares, reaching the Narva River on the eastern border of Estonia to the west, the Oulu River to the north, and Karelia but did not settle in the coastal zones (Figure 77). The early period of Netted Ware in Finland and Karelia is represented by the Sarsa–Tomitsa ceramics, starting ca. 1700 BC, with a later subgroup of Kalmistonmáki ceramics (Parpola 2018).

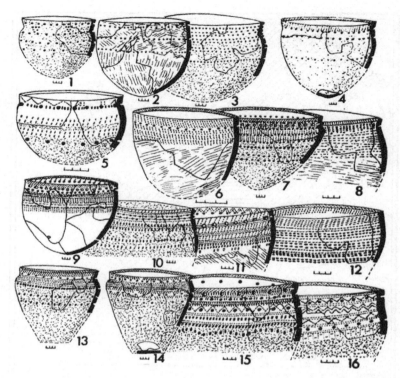

Figure 76. Vessels of the Netted Ware culture from Karelia. Modified from Kosmenko (1996).

It is not clear yet what the relationships between this immigrant tradition and the local populations of inner Finland were, but it is evident that changes took place in all fields of life: settlements, material culture, means of subsistence, and thus *Weltanschauung*. This does not imply a synchronous or abrupt change, or a complete population turnover, because traditional forms of subsistence held their ground alongside slash–and–burn agriculture for centuries and even millennia (Nordqvist 2018).

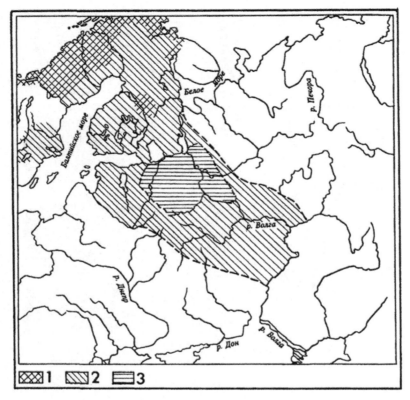

Figure 77. Distribution of eastern Textile Ceramics in northern Europe. 1 'Wafer' ceramics; 2 Area of eastern Textile Ceramics; 3 Area in the early stage. Modified from Kosmenko (1996).

To the east of the textile ceramics area, in the Mid–Volga region, Abashevo settlers fought for the possession of the area between the mouths of the Kama and Vyatka, rich in copper deposits. The Chirkovo culture (ca. 1800–700 BC) formed eventually by the fusion of Abashevo and Balanovo elites over previous Volosovo territory, with Balanovo remains found well into the second half of the 2nd millennium BC. In its early phase, it included the Seima site— one of the type sites for the Seima–Turbino phenomenon, with evidence of materials from as far away as the Krotovo culture—and participated in the Seima–Turbino network, from the forest-steppe of the middle Irtysh to the Baraba steppe on the upper Ob (Parpola 2018).

The Kazan culture (ca. 1900–800 BC) developed in the Vetluga–Volga–Vyatka interfluve based on Balanovo settlers over previous Garino–Bor territory, from which it retained local traditions. Bronzes of the first phase are of the Seima–Turbino type, and it eventually comprised the Kama and Belaya basins, as well as areas of the Middle Volga almost up to Samara to the south, interacting with early Srubna. Its final Maklasheevka phase (ca. 1000–800 BC) immediately preceded its replacement by the Ananyino culture (Parpola 2018).

Similarly, Late Bronze Age groups of the Cis-Urals Prikamsky subarea (Prikazanska, Erzovska, Lugovska, Kurmantau, Buiska), which continued Eneolithic traditions in pottery and house designs, had adopted animal husbandry based on cattle, horse, and to a lesser extent pigs, and sheep, with evidence of cultivation and continuing influence from Andronovo–Cherkaskul, which points to the settlement of Corded Ware-related peoples and partial acculturation of the region (Koryakova and Epimakhov 2007).

VIII.15.3. Ananyino and Akozino

At the turn of the 2nd–1st millennium BC, the Early Iron Age begins in the steppes with the expansion of 'Pre-Scythian' horse-riding nomads. In the Middle Volga area, the Ananyino culture appears in the Kama River and its tributaries Vyatka, Chusovaya, and Belaya, famed for its metallurgy, with revived features of the Seima–Turbino and Eurasian types. It represented the main Cis-Urals metallurgical centre, and features tin, tin–antimony–arsenic, and pure copper alloys, widespread in the Bronze Age. It produced a large number of socketed axes, spearheads, arrowheads, battle hammers, knives-daggers, and plenty of ornaments (Parpola 2013).

It expanded to the north and north-east into the basins of the Pechora, Vychegda, and Mesen' rivers in the first half of the 1st millennium BC. To the south, a buffer zone existed between Ananyino territory and the area of the South Uralian and Volga Sauromatian nomads, although they were in close contact with the north Pontic area, the Caucasus, and Kazakhstan, by this time developing Pre-Sauromatian traditions. Their metallurgical techniques were based in part on technology from the Caucasus, and from the Pontic–Caspian steppes were imported Cimmerian bronzes, such as daggers with cross-linked handles, Koban bronze axes, or two-ring horse bits. Only later (ca. 4th c. BC on) would the local production change its orientation to that of Sauromatian needs (Vasilyev 2002).

Up to eleven territorial variants of the culture can be distinguished, although ceramics are quite homogeneous. Two main interrelated groups can be distinguished: the Post-Maklasheyevo group, at the core of Ananyino expansion to the east; and the Textile group (see below Akozino), both occupying the broad-leafed forests of the Volga–Kama area and being more advanced economically, possessing a quite developed bronze metallurgy. Northern cultural groups occupying the forests of the Kama, Vyatka, and Vetluga rivers under the influence of Ananyino were orientated mainly to hunting and fishing, with an archaic stone industry rooted in the preceding time (Koryakova and Epimakhov 2007).

There are open and fortified settlements, the latter appearing first in the south as a reaction to the nomadic threat and spreading "the Age of Fortresses" in the forest zone, characteristic of the Iron Age throughout eastern Europe and western Siberia. The expansion of a chiefdom-based system is marked thus by the appearance of fortified settlements in the core area of the culture. The Ananyino society shows the greatest degree of militarisation compared to other societies of the Eurasian temperate forest zones, including a great quantity of advanced forms of weaponry. Settlements were divided according to function into a clear hierarchy, with large fortified settlements as administrative centres, smaller sites as watch posts, and open villages of various sizes. Male chiefs probably related by kinship are distinguished by rich and distinguished goods, including imported objects (Koryakova and Epimakhov 2007).

Fortresses are therefore proper of middle and late stages, with earlier settlements being smaller and simpler, in close proximity to water. Fortified settlements were usually located on narrow promontories of high river banks, separated some 20–40 km from each other. They were variable in size, from large administrative and ceremonial centres (up to 30,000 m²) to small fortified subordinated settlements (up to ca. 4,000 m²), and both had usually two sides defended by steep slopes, and a third size limited by a big earthen moat and ditch. There were also seasonal, temporary hunting camps (Koryakova and Epimakhov 2007).

Settlements had numerous rectangular houses with a trend to develop large, above-ground pillar or log wooden constructions, from the early small semisubterranean dwellings. Hearths were located in the central part of a house floor, with one or two entrances to the houses, which were aligned in rows. There could have been a division according to function, with some central structures serving for ritual ceremonies, including sacrifices (e.g. horses, cows), and some exterior zones used for economic activities (Koryakova and Epimakhov 2007).

Ananyino graveyards were located near rivers, on high banks and terraces connected to certain villages. Graves with likely burnt wooden logs above them (in a sort of "mortuary house" above the burial) appear in the dozens or hundreds, organised in rows parallel to the river. The dead were placed in shallow oval or rectangular pits in an extended position, with their legs orientated to the river. Apparently, the Volga and Kama rivers were of great importance for the local population, which could have considered these running waters to be pathways for the dead (Koryakova and Epimakhov 2007).

The Ananyino cosmological model is connected in its upper level with the sun, an image that is repeated on various objects: round discs with the depiction of the face, round plaques with a concentric design, concentrically decorated spindle-whorls, etc. The middle level is associated with animals like elk, bear, wolf, and horse, while the underwater and underground creatures represent the lower level. Communal and tribal ritual centres show remains of fire surrounded by posts with various offerings, great accumulation of ash, charcoal, crushed bones, votive objects, thousands of arrowheads, hundreds of anthropomorphic and zoomorphic figurines, dogs, and bees (Koryakova and Epimakhov 2007).

Individual primary burials were the norm, but there were some collective and double burials, and some secondary burials with cleaned bones or separate skulls only. All graves contained pottery, and there were some practices involving fire cult, based on the charcoal in the grave infilling, possibly from pyres or sacrificial places with cremation. Male graves contained horse bones, weapons (spearheads, arrowheads, battle hammer-axes, socketed axes), tools (knives), decorations (belts with pendants, torques, bracelets). Female burials contained cattle bones, decorations, needles, and spindle whorls. Tombs of chiefs were more complex, with a circle of stone and a wooden roof cover, as well as rich assemblages (Koryakova and Epimakhov 2007).

Pottery is round bottomed, with profiled neck and smooth, sometimes polished surface. Corded and comb decoration combined with holes covers the upper part. Subsistence economy is based on stalled animal husbandry, which make up the majority of animal bones recovered, and—depending on the local environment—included cattle (30–40%), horses (ca. 30%), big pigs (ca. 20–40%) and sheep (ca. 10%), also used a source of wool. Dogs were commonly used, and hunting was common for fur and as an essential dietary complement, together with fishing and gathering. The advanced bronze metallurgy was also complemented by bone- and woodworking and iron production, which eventually replaced bronze production. Its main demographic growth due to the use of natural resources must have happened around the 5th–4th c. BC (Koryakova and Epimakhov 2007).

At the same time as the Ananyino culture begins to expand ca. 1000 BC, the Netted Ware tradition from the middle Oka expanded eastwards into the Oka–Vyatka interfluve of the Middle Volga region, until then occupied by the Chirkovo culture. Eventually, the Akozino and Akhmylovo groups (ca. 800–300 BC) emerged from the area, showing a strong cultural influence from the Ananyino culture (and often considered the *Textile* variant of the culture), by that time already expanding into the north-east forest of the Cis-Urals region (Parpola 2013).

The Akozino culture remained nevertheless linked to the western Forest Zone traditions, showing (Kuzminykh and Chizhevskij 2009):

- Netted Ware ceramics;
- socketed axes of "Akozino–Mälar" type, produced in a special metallurgical furnace distinct from that of the Ananyino culture, related to influences from the Lusatian culture from Poland (Parpola 2013); and
- funeral customs involving the inclusion of the Akozino–Mälar axes and other specific weapons among the grave goods.

An extensive interregional trade system developed during this time in the eastern Baltic area. Celts of Ananyino type and shape are found widespread from ca. 10th to the 5th centuries BC in the eastern Baltic, including Sweden, Finland, and Karelia. Findings with Ananyino origins also include bimetallic, single-edged daggers with iron blade and bronze hilts, characteristic of the second stage of Ananyino development, ca. 8th – 7th centuries BC. On the other hand, Mälar-type celts—so called because of the original belief (as with axes) that they were produced in Mälaren, Sweden—appear with an even wider geographical distribution, including Norway, southern Scandinavia, the Northern European Plains (Paavel et al. 2019), showing in the east a higher concentration on the western area of the Volga–Kama region, which connects it to the Akozino culture (Yushkova 2010).

The Gorodets culture (ca. 800 BC – AD 800) from the forest-steppe zone north and west of the Volga, shows fortified settlements during the Iron Age. Incursions of Gorodets iron makers into the Samara valley are seen by deposits of their typical pottery and a bloom or iron in the region (Kuznetsov and Mochalov 2016). This attests to continued contact between forest and steppe areas in the Cis-Ural region.

In the western region of the Forest Steppe, the Dnieper–Dvina and the Hatched Ware cultures develop with slight differences. Both of them feature jar-shaped and slightly-profiled forms, but while the Dnieper–Dvina culture shows smooth vessels, Early Hatched Ware culture shows mainly hatched vessels. Haching is also seen in Dnieper–Dvina, whose slightly-profiled pots show inverted or vertical rims, in contrast to the elongated and inverted rims of the Hatched Ware. In later stages, during the first centuries AD, carinated pottery features in the Late Hatched Ware, while profiled vessels with elongated rims prevail in the Dnieper–Dvina culture.

The Ananyino culture evolution in the Iron Age can be followed through its zoomorphic styles into Iron Age Pyanobor and Glyadenovo cultures, which partially reject the previous style and 'barbarise' (simplify) the ornamentations, under the influence from Scythian and related styles. The Glyadenov style of flat anthropomorphic and zoomorphic figurines can be followed in morphology and styles to the analogous Ural-Siberian Middle Age cultures—Itkuska, Ust'-Poluiska, Kulaiska cultures—which can in turn be considered as prototypes of Permian styles (Vasilyev 2002).

viii.15. Mordvins and Mari-Permians

The Cis-Uralian forest-steppe zone north of the Pontic–Caspian steppes represents a key prehistorical linguistic and cultural frontier, a north–south ecotone between the pastoral steppes to the south and the forest zone to the north. Pastoral steppe subsistence is associated with dynamic organisations represented by Turkic, before that Iranian, and before that eastern Proto-Indo-European. The Forest Zone is clearly represented pre- and proto-historically by Uralic languages, before they were displaced by Russian (Anthony 2016).

The synchronous appearance of closely related cultures in the forest-steppe and steppe regions, coupled with the emergence of fortified settlements (and thus a chiefdom-based system) in the whole Middle Volga area, should be identified as one of the few cases known where this stable prehistoric linguistic and cultural frontier has been crossed, allowing for the infiltration of Abashevo peoples from the forest into the steppe, probably boosted by the expansion of late Corded Ware groups in the region. This and subsequent interactions between northern and southern Abashevo settlers for centuries left a strong genetic and linguistic impact in both forest and steppe cultures, although each territory eventually retained their own ancestral culture and subsistence economies, which in turn determined their ethnolinguistic identification.

Uralic is widely supported to be spread through the east European forest zone already during the Fatyanovo-Balanovo and Abashevo expansion (Koivulehto 2001, 2003; Kallio 2002, 2017; Parpola 2013). The presence of Proto-Indo-Iranian and Proto-Iranian loanwords in Finno-Ugric (Kallio 2002; Koivulehto 2003; Koivulehto 1991), as well as the Uralic influence in Proto-Indo-Iranian (Kallio 2001), prove that these communities bordered each other in long-lasting contacts. Non-Uralic toponyms in the Volga–Oka and Volga–Kama areas support the admixture of incoming Uralic speakers with non-Uralic-speaking local hunter-gatherers of the Pit–Comb Ware culture (Kallio 2015; Zhivlov 2015), some of which may have survived in northern Russia up to the Common Era, based on topo-hydronyms of the area (Helimski 2001).

The synchronous appearance of Sintashta–Potapovka–Filatovka complex in the steppes, derived in great part from the migration of Abashevo settlers and transformation of southern Abashevo territory (see *§VIII.18.1. Sintashta–Potapovka–Filatovka*), should be identified in part with this interaction area in the forest-steppe and steppe areas. Southern Abashevo and later Pozdnyakovo (from Srubna), as well as the steppes, would then correspond to the Pre- and Proto-Indo-Iranian period, while northern Abashevo and related Fatyanovo and Battle Axe cultures to the north would correspond to the evolving Finno-Ugric community.

While Abashevo has not been sampled yet, the Poltavka outlier from the Sok River in Samara (ca. 2900–2500 BC), of hg. R1a1a1b2a-Z94, clustering closely with Corded Ware, probably represents an Abashevo-related immigrant. Similarly, early Sintashta and Srubna samples, of intrusive

R1a1a1b2-Z93 lineages (and some of hg. R1a1a1b1a2-Z280 in Srubna) suggest the mixture of both haplogroups in Abashevo, probably with a gradient of increasing R1a1a1b1a-Z282 to the north in Fatyanovo–Balanovo.

The expansion of Balanovo- and Abashevo-related groups to the north-east, and the eventual formation of the Ananyino culture, are probably to be associated with the evolution of Proto-Permic. "It is commonly accepted by archaeology, ethnography, and linguistics that the ancestors of the Permian peoples (the Udmurts, Komi-Permians, and Komi-Zyryans) left the sites of Ananyino cultural intercommunity. In the west, in the Middle Volga basin, the Ananyino groups were neighbors of the groups that produced textile ceramics, these were ancestors of the Volga Finns (Goldina 1999; Napolskikh 1997)" (Koryakova and Epimakhov 2007).

The sudden emergence of the Ananyino and Akhmylovo cultures ca. 1000–800 BC is linked to the expansion of Iranian-speaking cultures of the southern steppe, creating a 'push' event that caused the emergence of a chiefdom-based social system in eastern Europe. Ananyino later split into two cultures, the Pyanobor culture (ca. 300 BC – AD 200) on the Vyatka, middle and lower Kama, and lower Balaya river, associated with Proto-Udmurt; and the Glyadenovo culture (ca. 200 BC – AD 500) on the upper Kama, connected with Proto-Komi (Parpola 2013).

The expansion of Ananyino culture into the north-east Cis-Urals region, with the formation of the Northern cultural groups of the Kama, Vyatka, and Vetluga rivers, is probably to be associated with the integration of some N1a1a1a1a-L392 lineages (formed ca. 4400 BC, TMRCA ca. 2900 BC)—by this time probably widely distributed in the Circum-Arctic region and in central and western Siberia (see §§*viii.16. Saami and Baltic Finns, §viii.21.1. Yukaghirs*, and §*viii.21.2. Turkic peoples and Mongols*)—into the Permic genetic stock. The best fit for northern Komi including AP ancestry (Sikora et al. 2018), instead of Baikal-related ancestry (as is common for some eastern

Uralic groups), further supports the integration of distinct Circum-Arctic and Palaeosiberian groups among different expanding Uralic-speaking populations.

The expansion of Netted Ware from Abashevo near the Middle Volga, and its expansion into inner southern Finland, including the Sarsa and Tomitsa groups, possibly represented an expansion of West Uralic peoples, although Textile ceramics in the north are most likely also associated with West Uralic Balto-Finnic and Samic dialects. The emergence of Akozino in Netted Ware territory probably represents the spread of Proto-Mordvinic and closely related Volga-Finnic dialects, while the Gorodets culture can be more specifically correlated with the development of Mordvinians (Parpola 2013).

The expansion of Akozino warrior-traders under influence of Ananyino is probably to be related to a Y-chromosome bottleneck involving N1a1a1a1a1a-VL29 lineages (formed ca. 2100 BC, TMRCA ca. 1600 BC), accompanying migrants to the west into cultures around the Baltic area, likely through alliances and exogamy practices, in an integration facilitated by the emergence of chiefdoms in eastern Europe and the cultural influence and demographic growth of Ananyino and Akozino (see *§viii.16.2. Baltic Finns*). The more intense contacts with forest populations, and later expansion westwards by Akozino may justify a common, recent origin of certain non-Uralic loanwords shared by Balto-Finnic and Mordvinic (Häkkinen 2009).

An origin of haplogroup N1a1a1a1a1a-VL29 in western Siberia, between the Urals and Lake Baikal, can be proposed based on modern (Ilumäe et al. 2016) and ancient DNA (Cui et al. 2013; de Barros Damgaard, Martiniano, et al. 2018). The connection of its upper clade N1a1a1a1-Y6058/CTS10760 (formed ca. 2900 BC) with populations of Northern and Eastern Eurasia, and in particular the expansion of sister clade N1a1a1a1a3a-F4205 with Avars (see *§viii.21.2. Turkic peoples and Mongols*), and N1a1a1a1a-L392 with Northern Asian populations (see *§viii.17.1. Ugrians*), further supports its ancestral connection with Palaeosiberian populations (see *§v.8. Palaeosiberians*) and its

lack of relationship with Uralic peoples, until their gradual incorporation
during the expansion of Uralic dialects to the east and north (Figure 78).

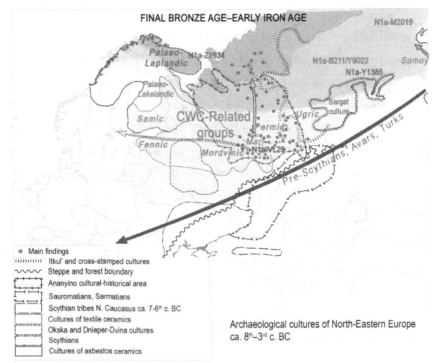

*Figure 78. Map of archaeological cultures in north-eastern Europe ca. 8ᵗʰ–3ʳᵈ centuries
BC. Modified from (Vasilyev 2002). Shaded area represents the Ananyino cultural-
historical society. In pink and purple, Circum-Arctic and Siberian populations. Solid
arrows depict the expansion of Uralic languages to the north, and steppe populations
to the west, while dotted arrows represent the direction of "Siberian" ancestry and
haplogroups from Akozino into the Baltic. Labelled are regions where N1a1-Tat is
probably going to be found, with pink color representing non-N1a1a1a1a-L392
lineages. N1a1a1a1a2-Z1936 shows an ancestral connection between Palaeo-
Laplandic and forest peoples from the Trans-Urals, while N1a1a1a1a1a-CTS10760
connects the Volga region with Altaic peoples. Image modified from Vasilyev (2002).*

In fact, some available ancient DNA samples attributed to steppe nomads
since the LBA–Iron Age transition show likely N1a1-Tat subclades—such as
an LBA individual from Afontova Gora (ca. 1000–850 BC), a Cimmerian from
Hungary (ca. 980–930BC), and Scytho-Siberians (see below §viii.19. Iranians)
—which suggests a potential expansion of lineages ancestral to N1a1a1a1a1a-

VL29 with Pre-Scythian and Scythian populations through a southern route across the Urals, and their integration into the Middle Volga area because of the intense contacts of Ananyino and Akozino–Akhmylovo with steppe peoples.

Mordovians seem to be less affected by the admixture with Palaeosiberian populations from the Circum-Arctic region, showing an ancestry closer to Corded Ware populations of the forest zone, formed by CWC (ca. 79%), WHG (ca. 9%) and Nganasan-like (ca. 12%), compatible with a lesser admixture with Palaeo-Arctic-like populations (Jeong et al. 2019). Mordovians also show more hg. R1a1a-M198 (ca. 27%), with less I-M170 (ca. 20%), N1a1-Tat (ca. 16%), R1b-M343 (ca. 13%), and J-M304 (ca. 12%).

Maris show a north-south cline of N1a2b-P43 (ca. 42% in Bashkirian Maris) against N1a1-Tat (ca. 13% among Bashkirian Maris, with up to 46% in northern Maris), with R1a1a-M198 lineages represented in both populations (ca. 28% in the south, 22% in the north), with approximately half R1a1a1b1a2-Z280 (16%), and half R1a1a1b2-Z93 (16%). None of the N1a1-Tat subclades among Bashkirian Maris investigated belonged to common subclades N1a1a1a1a-VL29 or N1a1a1a1a2-Z1936 (Dudás et al. 2019).

Among Permic peoples, Udmurts and Besermyans show a similar ancestry, formed by CWC (ca. 71–74%) and Nganasan-like (ca. 25–29%), which support closer contacts with Palaeo-Arctic and Trans-Uralian populations (Jeong et al. 2019). Southern Udmurts show more hg. N1a1-Tat (ca. 54%) than R1a1a-M198 (ca. 19%) or N-M231(xN1a1-Tat) (ca. 17%); while northern Komis show less differences between N1a1-Tat (ca. 37%), R1a1a-M198 (ca. 27%) or N-M231(xN1a1-Tat) (ca. 19%).

The cluster formed by modern Mordovians, Estonians, as well as some Finns, Karelians, and Mansis probably represents the original Uralic cluster near Abashevo (Tambets et al. 2018). The presence of N-M231(xN1a1-Tat) lineages suggests contacts with Palaeosiberian peoples to the north, possibly involving migrations from the east (see *§viii.17. Ugrians and* Samoyeds).

VIII.16. Fennoscandia

VIII.16.1. Kiukainen

Late Comb Ware pottery is found especially in coastal areas well into the Corded Ware period (after ca. 2500 BC), probably withstanding cooking and thus used for processing of marine products. Comb Ware settlements, faunal assemblages and the size and fragility of Comb Ware vessels suggest that these populations were sedentary, with a specialised economy based upon coastal resources (Oinonen et al. 2014).

The decrease and even lack of archaeological material from the later 3rd millennium BC onwards has been explained by decreasing population numbers, which would have been caused by the deteriorating climate, characterised by cooler seasons at the end of the 3rd millennium BC. However, the abundant number of burial cairns and pollen analyses showing anthropogenic activities indicate that no complete depopulation took place, so the change was mainly in ways of leaving and material cultures, which left materials difficult to identify archaeologically (Nordqvist 2018).

These changes seem to be connected to external influences. The Corded Ware culture disappears (ca. 2300/2000 BC), and on the coast, the Kiukainen culture appears ca. 2300 BC, coinciding with cultural impulses from the Estonian Western Textile Ceramic tradition – different from the eastern Textile Ceramic or Netted Ware (appearing in eastern Estonia ca. 1700 BC). After ca. 2000 BC, two Corded Ware-related cultures remain in the region: in the coast, the Final Neolithic Kiukais or Kiukainen culture, derived from the original Circum-Baltic Corded Ware settlers, reverts to a subsistence economy which includes hunting and fishing, modest swidden cultivation, and bronze metallurgy, keeping mainly settlements from the best territories along the coast, including the Gulf of Finland (Nordqvist 2018). In inner Finland, another Textile ceramic tradition appears ca. 1900–1800 BC, connected to the northward expansion of Netted Ware from the Mid-Volga area (see *§VIII.15.2. Netted Ware, Chirkovo, Kazan*).

The ceramic inventory of the Kiukainen culture shows similarities with late Corded Ware, but also to local hunter-fisher-forager ware (Pyheensilt and late Comb Ware), and is believed to be a cultural amalgamation and reversion to aquatic foods emerging locally. Pottery residues show a mix of ruminant and non-ruminant/marine products, which suggests that (compared to Corded Ware) this culture used a less-specialised economy, probably reintroducing aquatic resources to complement diminishing terrestrial sources, as is historically common among Scandinavian cultures (Cramp et al. 2014).

Later, the Kiukainen culture probably spread with the custom of burying chiefs in stone cairns to Estonia. The Kiukainen culture evolved into the Paimio ceramics in south-western Finland, and the corresponding Asva Ware of Estonia, whose influence over the area spans ca. 1600–700 BC. This continuity supports the maintenance of close cultural connections through the Gulf of Finland after the demise of the Corded Ware cultural complex (Parpola 2018).

VIII.16.2. Asbestos Ware cultures

Like the isolated Bell Beaker findings of the eastern Baltic, Finland, and Belarus, isolated Bell Beaker findings in the northernmost territories of Norway have to be interpreted in the context of the initial expansive phase of the Bell Beaker peoples, before their integration into distinct regional cultures.

The dichotomy marked by environmental constraints in Scandinavia appears throughout the whole Nordic Bronze Age period, evidenced by the lack of relevance of centres of dominant chiefdoms in northern and mountainous regions, where metal is scarcely known at all. This difference is as relevant between these regions as between the Nordic Bronze Age and Norrland and Finland: for all these groups of foragers and tundra hunters, metal objects and technology must have seemed as fabulous as when bronze was introduced in the south (Thrane 2013). The relationship between southern and northern Scandinavian groups has been described as indirect, based on reciprocal exchange and ideological dominance (Kristiansen 1987).

North Scandinavia shows continuous eastern connections and a Mesolithic way of life, using quartz for flat-based points and scrapers between 1500–500 BC. Small coastal huts were common. Seal oil found in the Nordic EBA was produced in the Åland islands in the Baltic. Asbestos-tempered pots reaching up to central Sweden at the end of the 3ʳᵈ millennium BC show a decoration and technique evidencing connections across the Baltic to Finland via Åland. Containers used in iron smelting are a northern specialty. Burials show southern acculturation, with man-size stone cists and later smaller cists in the cairns along the coast (Thrane 2013).

The border with the southern regions ran through Ångermanland in northern Sweden, coinciding with the modern border between sub-Arctic nomads and the Swedish-speaking population. Here farming and agriculture began during the Late Bronze Age, which is difficult to distinguish from the Early Iron Age (Thrane 2013).

In northern Fennoscandia, pottery is found only sporadically since 4500–4200 BC until the end of the 3ʳᵈ millennium BC, and populations are mainly hunter-gatherer communities characterised by seasonal mobility, apparently with specific resource areas. Asbestos temper ceased in eastern Finland at the same time as it appeared in northern parts of Finland and into Norwegian Finnmark and the Kola peninsula, in the Lovozero Ware, ca. 1900–700 BC (Damm 2012).

VIII.16.3. Textile ceramics

During the 2ⁿᵈ millennium BC, textile impressions appear in pottery as a feature across a wide region, from the Urals through the Volga to the Baltic Sea and beyond, in communities that evolved from late Corded Ware groups without much external influence. It has been traditionally suggested that this stylistic phenomenon was part of a Textile ceramic culture that expanded from the east to the north-west. Nevertheless, the decoration proper of textile ware can be easily copied and spread without much long-term interaction or population movement. In fact, it is possible to see influences proper of horizontal transmission from several directions. In the western area, textile impressions were known since the Corded Ware pottery in Estonia and Finland, and is very common in Kiukainen pottery, immediately preceding Textile wares of Finland. Therefore, groups like Paimio/Asva and western Sarsa show most likely cultural continuity (Lavento 2001).

Figure 79. Stone Cist Graves from the Bronze Age in Northern Estonia. Photo of cultural heritage monument of Estonia number 17543.

Finnish subgroups often related to the Netted Ware, like Sarsa, Tomitsa, or Kainuu developed quite differently, some from local knowledge and traditions (Figure 79) without any necessary new craftsmen, others probably due to some incoming groups or individuals (Lavento 2001). In fact, Late Textile ceramics from the Gulf of Finland show more similarities with Netted Ware, which supports the presence of changing trends. A general preference for textile impression is obviously seen across all these groups, with different stylistic trends—first western, then south-eastern—suggesting a close association between them, but not necessarily much mobility (Damm 2012).

Early Metal Age pottery (ca. 1200–500 BC) shows a strong reliance on dairy products. Increasing population size despite continuing climatic deterioration of the Late Holocene is believed to have arisen from the intensification of agriculture and cattle breeding by the Late Metal Ages, which overcame environmental constraints upon population size (Cramp et al. 2014). While the first cereal grains in mainland Finland occur during the LN or Bronze Age (ca. 1900–1250 BC), the earliest bones of sheep–goat are earlier (ca. 2200–1950 BC). However, finds of Scandinavian bronze artifacts show a likely cultural influx from east-central Sweden, which has been proposed (Vanhanen et al. 2019) as the source of development of agriculture in the East Baltic in the Late Bronze Age (ca. 1400-1150 BC).

On the other hand, the appearance of Textile ware tempered with a variety of materials, but rarely with asbestos, marked a crucial difference with other groups. While Textile ware was widespread into northern Fennoscandia, there are essential regional differences. This phenomenon of abandonment of the traditional asbestos temper probably represents a cultural break, a change in the whole distribution of asbestos through marriage and exchange networks, and thus a reorientation of alliances (Damm 2012).

To the west, in Norway and Sweden, these vessels were predominantly tempered with asbestos, which points to a different transmission of knowledge (learning networks) where the use of asbestos continued, although the copying of textile decorations indicate a positive association with eastern communities. To the north, in northern Finland, the expansion of Textile ware represented an expansion of the technology, contrasting with local traditions of sub-Neolithic Lovozero and Pasvik asbestos-tempered pottery (Damm 2012).

VIII.16.4. Morby/Ilmandu

The influence of Akozino culture reached Finland late, at the end of the Late Bronze Age and beginning of the Early Iron Age, when the influence of the Nordic Bronze Age culture on the Gulf of Finland was already declining. At this time, the Paimio ceramics of the coast evolved into the Morby ceramics in Finland (ca. 700 BC - AD 200 BC), and the corresponding Asva Ware of Estonia evolved into the Ilmandu style ceramics (Figure 80), also including Latvia, and the Mälaren area in Sweden (Parpola 2013).

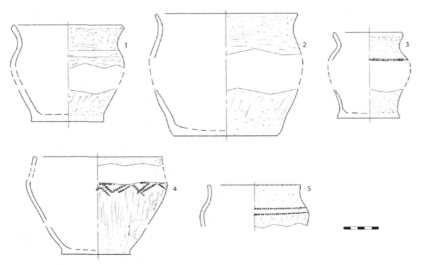

Figure 80. Reconstruction of some clay vessels from a cist grave in Sondlamägi, Muuksi (ca. 1100–800 BC). 1–4 Ilmandu-style pottery; 5 Cord-Impressed Pottery. Modified from Laneman and Lang (2013).

The old Paimio/Asva Ware traditions continued side by side with the new ones, with a clear technical continuity between them, but with ornamentation compared to the EIA cultures of the Upper Volga area. Other pottery types common from Finland and the eastern European forest belt—like the Lüganuse style—also appear in Estonia. Akozino–Mälar axes were introduced into the Baltic area ca. 800–500 BC in such great numbers—especially in south-western Finland, the Åland islands, and the Mälaren area of eastern Sweden—that it is deemed to have involved a movement of people, too (Figure 81). This movement was probably caused by warrior-traders of the Akozino–Akhmylovo culture, following the same waterways that Vikings used more than a thousand years later (Parpola 2013).

At the same time as the new ornamentation appears, early *tarand* graves appear (ca. 800–400 BC) in the coastal areas of northern and western Estonia and on the islands, roughly contemporary with the emergence of similar graves in Ingria, south-western Finland, eastern central Sweden, northern Latvia and Courland. *Tarands* are described as "mortuary houses", corner-joined horizontal log cabins, in which ancestral bones were stored, and it is quite common to find them forming long rows of rectangular 'yards' or 'enclosures'. Such 'houses of the dead' have their origin of similar burial rites in the Akozino–Akhmylovo culture, and grave goods contain ornaments from the Upper and Middle Volga region, while cultural continuity is evidenced by Ilmandu-type pottery (Parpola 2013).

Akozino–Mälar axes are copied in iron in Fennoscandia, with iron being highly valued and rare, and its production technology being a well-guarded secret. Access to this knowledge and to prestige goods was proper of the elites in chiefdom-level societies. Textile ceramic cultures of the Early Iron Age in north-eastern Europe were well armed and possessed hill forts, with those in Finland starting ca. 1000–400 BC, after the Netted Ware expansion. This evolution to a chiefdom-based society—where thousands or tens of thousands formed part of each chiefdom—began slightly earlier than the appearance of Akozino influence and *tarands* (Parpola 2013).

Fortified settlements in the region may have represented visiting warrior-traders settled through matrimonial relationships with local chiefs, eager to get access to coveted goods and become members of a distribution network that could guarantee them even military assistance. Such a system is also seen synchronously in other cultures of the region, e.g. in Vistad in Östergötland, where a fortified settlement within Nordic Bronze Age territory shows Lusatian type pottery and artefacts, suggesting the presence of foreign Lusatian chiefs accommodating long-distance traders in Nordic territory (Parpola 2013).

In the later part of the Early Metal Period and initial Early Iron Age, the use of asbestos temper increased, sign of newly made networks with connections to asbestos sources. Asbestos was used infrequently in Finnish Textile ware during the 2nd millennium BC, but was used in Norwegian Finnmark and the Kola peninsula in the Lovozero ware and in the so-called

Pasvik ware. Asbestos continued to be favoured in Norway and Sweden during the whole period, and was reintroduced in mainland Finnish wares: in the north with the Kjelmøy Ware (ca. 700 BC – AD 300), which replaced the Lovozero Ware; and in the east in inner Finland and Karelia with the Luukonsaari and Sirnihta wares (ca. 700/500 BC – AD 200), where they replaced the previous Sarsa–Tomitsa ceramics (Damm 2012).

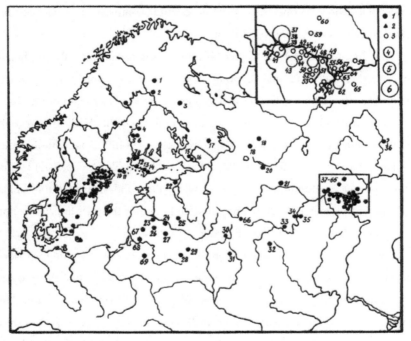

Figure 81. Distribution of the Akozino–Mälar axes in north-eastern Europe according to Sergey V. Kuz'minykh (1996: 8, Fig. 2).

viii.16. Saami and Baltic Finns

R1a1a1b1a-Z282 seems to be the only haplogroup found to the north, in Battle Axe and derived cultures (see *§vii.1. Western and Eastern Uralians*). A late sample also attributed to the Battle Axe culture from Spiginas, Lithuania (ca. 2130–1750 BC) shows subclade R1a1a1b1a2b-CTS1211. Individuals from the Eastern Baltic Bronze Age from Lithuania, Latvia and Estonia (ca. 1230–230 BC) form a common cluster with extra Baltic hunter-gatherer ancestry compared to Late Neolithic samples, a 'northern' shift in the PCA toward WHG, and Baltic haplogroups, none of them stemming necessarily from Comb Ware culture-related samples, which suggests that this population did not play a large role in the ancestry of Bronze Age individuals (Mittnik, Wang, et al. 2018).

In fact, Bronze Age samples need a further source of admixture beyond a Baltic Late Neolihtic population and foragers, including an increase in NWAN-related ancestry, compatible with the arrival of another wave of Battle Axe settlers from east-central European Corded Ware groups, that possibly replaced R1a1a1b1a3-Z284 lineages in the area, or contributed to a Y-chromosome bottleneck different from the one seen in Scandinavia. Another explanation for the presence of R1a1a1b1a3-Z284 in the eastern Baltic area may be continuous contacts with Palaeo-Germanic populations: e.g. through the site of Kivutkalns, a major bronze-working centre located on a trade route that opened to the Baltic Sea on the west and led inland following the Daugava river, and through which surrounding populations might have been in contact (Mittnik, Wang, et al. 2018).

Reported haplogroups include three out of seven samples from the West Baltic site of Turlojiškė, Lithuania (ca. 2000–600 BC), at the border with late Trzciniec (see *§viii.8. Balto-Slavs*), all three of hg. R1a1a1b-Z645, one of them a subclade of R1a1a1b1a2a-Z92, R1a1a1b1a2a1a-YP617 (formed ca. 1400 BC, TMRCA ca. 1400 BC); ten samples from Kivutkalns, Latvia (ca. 810–230 BC) also include only R1a1-M459 lineages, probably all seven of hg. R1a1a1b-

Z645: five of them show hg. R1a1a1b1a2b-CTS1211, including four with mutation Y13467 (formed ca. 2000 BC, TMRCA ca. 2000 BC). One outlier from Turlojiškė (ca. 1075 BC) shows influence from the west (Mittnik, Wang, et al. 2018), probably related to incoming Balto-Slavic populations in the West Baltic through Trzciniec.

In the East Baltic, the sampled population of the Late Bronze Age shows largely continuity with Corded Ware populations, with an ancestry related mainly to Corded Ware samples from the Baltic (ca. 48–65%) and a WHG-like population (ca. 38–52%). They form a common cluster with West Baltic populations, between Corded Ware samples from the Baltic and previous Mesolithic and Neolithic populations from Eastern Europe. Out of nineteen Bronze Age individuals sampled from stone-cist graves in Estonia all sixteen reported haplogroups are R1a-M420, all likely within R1a1a1b-Z645, at least two of hg. R1a1a1b1a2a-Z92 (Saag et al. 2019).

These findings suggest an admixture of incoming Corded Ware migrants of Battle Axe material culture admixing with sub-Neolithic populations of Narva and related eastern Baltic cultures rather than Comb Ceramic groups from the forest zone. Both the origin of males from Corded Ware and their prevalent admixture with western populations in the eastern Baltic area are frontally opposed to the traditional view of Uralic speakers stemming from Volosovo and related hunter-gatherer peoples, and supports the origin of Uralic speakers in Corded Ware migrants instead.

Many R1a1a1b1a2-Z280 lineages (TMRCA ca. 2600 BC) are prevalent in north-eastern European populations around the Baltic: e.g. R1a1a1b1a2a-Z92 (TMRCA ca. 2500 BC), found in ancient samples from Lithuania and in modern north-eastern European populations; R1a1a1b1a2b-CTS1211 (TMRCA ca. 2200), with one ancient sample already found in the Battle Axe culture from Lithuania, and later in Latvia, is found widely distributed in modern populations around the Baltic Sea with basal, early and late subclades. Nevertheless, some late subclades were apparently incorporated into the Slavic expansion, possibly via Trzciniec-mediated interactions, such as R1a1a1b1a2b3-CTS3402 (TMRCA ca. 2200 BC).

Finno-Samic is thought to have developed under strong Nordic Bronze Age influences upon the Baltic coast of Finland and Estonia. The Finno-Samic community, under strong, long-lasting Palaeo-Germanic influence— evidenced by Germanic loanwords representing different dialectal layers— would be thus represented by the transformation of Kiukainen into the Textile ceramic cultures, with Samic probably developing to the north of the Gulf of Finland while Balto-Finnic developed to the south, roughly corresponding to Paimio ceramics and Asva Ware respectively (Kallio 2014).

The conservatism of Finno-Samic phonology relative to Proto-Uralic as late as the Bronze Age further confirms the lack of strong direct external influences, which finds its explanation in the lack of admixture of Corded Ware settlers in the area, and the succeeding contacts mainly with Corded Ware-derived groups, such as Netted Ware and Akozino–Akhmylovo to the east and south-east, Scandinavian peoples (those bilingual communities shifting to a Pre-Germanic language) to the west, and other Finno-Permic populations to the south-west, before their acculturation under expanding Proto-Baltic or Proto-Slavic populations. During the Early Iron Age, the physical separation of Balto-Finnic and Samic communities was probably complete, as reflected by the differing layers of Germanic loanwords in each branch (Kallio 2009, 2012, 2015).

viii.16.1. Saami and Laplandic peoples

To the north of the Gulf of Finland, six individuals of the Lovozero culture from Bolshoy Oleni Ostrov (ca. 1610–1436 BC), two of hg. N1a1a1a1a-L392, show elevated Siberian ancestry—clustering along a Palaeosiberian cline connecting northern Eurasian peoples—and represent most likely a recent expansion of Paleo-Laplandic-speaking hunter-gatherers from west Circum-Arctic Eurasia into the Kola Peninsula, evidenced by the introduction of asbestos-mixed ceramics ca. 2000 BC, and the spread of even-based arrowheads in Lapland from ca. 1900 BC (Lamnidis et al. 2018).

The nearest counterparts of Vardøy ceramics (ca. 1600–1300 BC) can be found on the Taymyr peninsula, much further to the east, compatible with the foreign ancestry found in Lovozero individuals likely related to Neolithic samples from the Cis-Baikal area, as found in modern populations (Jeong et al. 2019). Finally, the Imiyakhtakhskaya culture from Yakutia spread to the Kola Peninsula during the same period, also representing the expansion of Paleosiberian peoples of mainly N1a-L279 lineages across north Eurasia (Lamnidis et al. 2018). The Bolshoy Oleni Ostrov samples cluster in this ancient Palaeosiberian cline near modern Khants, which supports a close original source for both in Circum-Arctic Cis-Urals population.

This movement probably displaced earlier Mesolithic pioneers of the Komsa and Suomusjärvi cultures—probably mainly of Baltic / Scandinavian hunter-gatherer ancestry and of I-M170, R1b1a1-P297(xM269), and R1a1-M459 (xZ645) lineages—from eastern and northern Fennoscandia into central Finland, where they evolved probably with the Kainuu culture. This population probably represents the Palaeo-Lakelandic speakers[34] encountered by Proto-

---

[34] According to Kallio (2015): "No doubt the most convincing substrate theory has recently been put forward by the Saami Uralicist Ante Aikio (2004), who has not only rehabilitated but also improved the old idea of a non-Uralic substrate in Saami. His study shows that there were still non-Uralic languages spoken in Northern Fennoscandia as recently as the first millennium AD. Most of all, they were not only genetically non-Uralic but also typologically non-Uralic-looking, bearing a closer

Samic peoples during their expansion to the north and east, reflected in Samic substrate words (Aikio 2012; Carpelan and Parpola 2017).

The paternal lineages expanded with Palaeo-Laplandic peoples is probably N1a1a1a1a2a-Z1934 (formed ca. 2800 BC, TMRCA ca. 2400 BC), based on its distribution among present-day populations around the Barents Sea, including Finns (ca. 44%), Vepsas (ca. 32%), Karelians, Saamis, North Russians (ca. 20%), and in eastern Russians and Volga-Ural populations such as Komis, Mordvins, and Chuvashes (up to 9%). This haplogroup is in turn connected to parent N1a1a1a1a2-Z1936, also found in Ugric and Altaic populations (see *§viii.17.1. Ugrians*), hence probably related to Paleosiberian and Palaeo-Arctic hunter-gatherers that expanded to the west into the Kola Peninsula, introducing asbestos-mixed ceramics, even-based arrowheads (Lamnidis et al. 2018), and speaking Palaeo-Laplandic, a substrate language of late Samic (Aikio 2012).

An early Samic individual from Levänluhta in western Finland (ca. AD 388-547), with strontium isotope analysis showing mainly marine dietary resources, compatible with coastal resources 25–30 km to the north-west in the Bothnian Sea, shows an admixture similar to previous Battle Axe and Baltic Bronze Age samples, clustering closely to Battle Axe individuals from Scandinavia, and at the one extremity of the ancient Finno-Samic cluster (opposite to the Baltic Iron Age individual, see below), which supports the physical separation of the Saami population from innovations and population contacts that happened to the south, in the eastern Baltic region and the Gulf of Finland. Slightly later samples from the same site (ca. AD 405–555 and ca. AD 662-774) show signs of progressive admixture with Lovozero-like populations, evidenced by their increased Siberian ancestry and their position closer in the PCA (Suppl. Graph. 14) intermediate between Baltic BA and Iron Age samples and Lovozero (Lamnidis et al. 2018).

---

resemblance to the so-called Palaeo-European substrates (for which see e.g. Schrijver 2001; Vennemann 2003)."

This is compatible with the spread of Samic speakers of the Sarsa culture at the same time as it developed into the Luukonsari culture: to the north admixing with Lovozero-derived Kjelmøy Ware peoples, of mainly hg. N1a1a1a1a-L392 (mainly of N1a1a1a1a2-Z1936 lineages); and to the east, admixing with Sirnihta and Anttila culture peoples from inner Finland and Karelia, likely speakers of Samic- or Volga-Finnic-related languages and Palaeo-Lakelandic peoples derived from Tomitsa and Kainuu ceramics, possibly already admixed with Palaeo-Laplandic peoples of Kola during this period.

Two sampled historical Saami from Chalmny Varre (AD 18th – 19th c.), one of hg. I2a1a-P37.2, show similar intermediate ancestry to the mixed Levänluhta samples, between Baltic BA and Lovozero, but on the EHG and Baltic BA side of the previous cluster, with a corresponding increase in Steppe-related ancestry. One modern Saami, of hg. I1a1b3a1-, clusters close to these historical Saami (Lamnidis et al. 2018).

viii.16.2. Baltic Finns

The emergence of a chiefdom-based system, the spread of Celts of Ananyino type and Akozino–Mälar axes, and the expansion of *tarand* graves ca. 1000–400 BC, all can be potentially associated with the intrusion of Akozino warrior-traders of hg. N1a1a1a1a-L392 across chiefdoms all over the Baltic Sea, probably through regional alliances and exogamy practices:

Among seven sampled Iron Age individuals from tarand graves in Estonia, there is largely continuity of Estonian LBA ancestry, with a slight increase of CWC Baltic ancestry (ca. 57–77%) compared to LBA samples, and decreased WHG-like ancestry (ca. 23–43%). This transition also marks the emergence of a variable "Nganasan-like" ancestral component, found in four samples (ca. 1–4%) out of eleven investigated, together with the first samples of hg. N1a1a1a1a1a-VL29 (Saag et al. 2019).

At least two of the three N1a1a1a1a1a-VL29 samples (and three more samples of the Middle Ages) show hg. N1a1a1a1a1a1a-L550 (formed ca. 1100 BC, TMRCA ca. 900 BC), which is today associated with Germanic, Balto-Slavic, and Balto-Finnic populations around the Baltic Sea. This distribution supports the expansion of Akozino warrior-traders through intermarriages and alliances all over the Baltic, without bringing ethnolinguistic change to the region.

Furthermore, Estonian Iron Age samples still show a majority of hg. R1a1a1b-Z645 (five out of eight reported samples), and they form a cluster closer to Corded Ware samples than Baltic Bronze Age individuals, which suggests an origin of migrations close to the steppe, coincident with the influence of Akozino in the region. Samples of haplogroup N1a1a1a1a1a1a-L550 are not particularly linked to that "Nganasan-like ancestry", and the sample with the highest such proportion (ca. 4%) comes from an early R1a1a1b-Z645 sample in Kund. Another early sample from Kunda, of hg. N1a1a1a1a1a-VL29, clusters closer to the Urals in the PCA, both Kunda samples (dated ca. 600 BC) are described as not locally born, with south-western Finland and Sweden excluded.

This arrival and admixture of Akozino warrior-traders could be linked to a number of innovations shared between Proto-Mordvinic and Proto-Balto-Finnic (on the southern Gulf of Finland), but not on Samic (Parpola 2013, 2018), due to the likely elite domination of some among them along the Baltic coast, although cultural contacts between Finland and the Gorodets culture lasted until the AD 7th–8th centuries, evidenced by imports from the Lomovatovo culture (Koryakova and Epimakhov 2007).

A sample of the Baltic Iron Age from northern Lithuania (ca. AD 1–600) shows hg. N1a1a1a1a1a1a1-L1025[+] (formed ca. 900 BC, TMRCA ca. 600 BC) a subclade of hg. N1a1a1a1a1a-VL29, clustering also closely to Corded Ware and Baltic BA samples. This individual corresponds to a period and region of inhumations, among divergent burial traditions that could change abruptly (de Barros Damgaard, Marchi, et al. 2018). The presence of Proto-Baltic loanwords may be dated to the Early Iron Age, which places Balto-Finnic languages in the Gulf of Finland, in close contact with both Germanic and Baltic peoples, once the greater influence of Germanic over Finnic and Samic faded (Kallio 2008).

A late Viking from the town of Sigtuna, in eastern central Sweden (AD 10th–12th century), shows hg. N1a1a1a1a1a1a7-Y4341 (formed ca. 900 BC, TMRCA ca. 600 BC), also subclade of hg. N1a1a1a1a1a-VL29. This individual is of local origin, based on strontium isotope analysis and on his admixture among Nordic peoples (Krzewińska, Kjellström, et al. 2018), hence most likely part of lineages integrated with Proto-Germanic speakers since the expansion of Akozino warrior-traders, rather than a recent intrusion. This lineage supports a Scandinavian origin of Rurik (AD 9th c.), a Varangian prince whose descendants ruled the state of Kievan Rus', and who shows a subclade of N1a1a1a1a1a1a7a-Y4339 (formed ca. 2600 BC, TMRCA ca. AD 250), a haplogroup found primarily in Sweden (ca. 52%), apart from Finland, Russia,

Britain, or Norway, in great part related to the Viking expansions (Volkov and Seslavin 2019).

During AD 5th–10th century, people of present-day north-eastern Belarus, north-western Russia, south-eastern Estonia, and eastern Latvia buried part of their dead in sand barrows, mostly erected in groups on the banks of river valleys, usually in sandy pine forests. These are termed long barrows, and represents a local tradition before the Slavicisation of Russia (Tvauri 2007). A sample from Pskov (AD 8th–10th century), tentatively attributed to the incoming Krivichi Slavic tribe, shows hg. N1a-L279 (Chekunova et al. 2014).

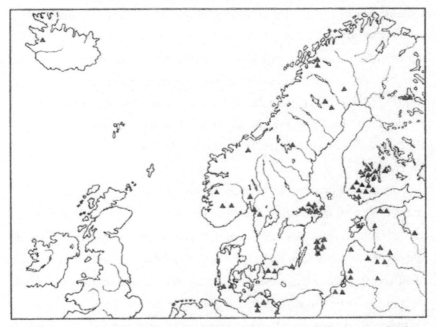

Figure 82. Distribution of finds of similar types of spherical weights, assumed to have been used for trade and transactions during the late Iron Age. Modified from Hedman (2003).

Furthermore, the modern distribution of N1a1a1a1a1a-VL29 reveals a pattern consistent with an Iron Age expansion around the Baltic Sea, with the TMRCA of the most common lineages compatible with Iron Age expansions, found without particular territorial distinction from Kazakhstan and Russia in the east, through Finns, Estonians, Latvians, and Lithuanians, to Swedes,

Norwegians, and Poles in the west. The genetic continuity in Estonia since the Bronze Age supports the late infiltration and expansion of foreign lineages from the east (mainly N1a1a1a1a1a-VL29) without cultural change, similar to the various Bronze Age and Iron Age haplogroup expansions in North-West Indo-European-speaking Europe different from the R1b1a1b1a1a-L151 lineages originally expanded with Bell Beakers.

However, there is no evidence for a non-Uralic substrate in Finnic, and—unlike the substrate words of Saami—no structural non-Uralisms are found in Finnic, which suggests that if Finnic borrowed words it would have been from some genetically related (or at least typologically similar) languages, which agrees with archaeological evidence that the Uralisation of the East Baltic region under Balto-Finnic or a closely related dialect must have occurred no later than the Bronze Age, being a Uralic-speaking region from at least ca. 1900 BC (Kallio 2015). Early Palaeo-Germanic loanwords in Saami and Balto-Finnic, and Balto-Slavic loanwords in Balto-Finnic place all these dialects in close contact with each other, likely around the Baltic Sea, since the Early Bronze Age.

Population genomics show thus largely continuity in the East Baltic, coupled with an incursion of few elite individuals of Corded Ware-derived ancestry from ca. 600 BC on, hence likely Akozino warrior-traders. Supporting late intense cultural contacts in the Baltic during the Iron Age is the distribution of different types of weights used to determine the value of products in a certain amount of silver, suggesting that this was an accepted trading system to exchange goods (Figure 82). The expansion of chiefdom-based systems all over the Baltic in the transition to the Iron Age must have eventually caused the division into ethnolinguistic regions (Figure 83) according to personal and political alliances, mostly disconnected from their genetic make-up (safe for the continuity of previous regional differences).

The assumed separation of Southern Estonian first from the common Balto-Finnic trunk supports the origin of Proto-Balto-Finnic in Estonia, which—

based on the similarities of Finnish and Estonian—is estimated to have spread ca. 2,000 years ago (Kallio 2014). This corresponds to the Early Roman Iron Age, in the first centuries AD, with the appearance of *tarand-* or yard-type cemeteries, as well as new types of iron weapons and ornaments originally from coastal Estonia to the south into inland Estonia and northern Latvia. This expansion must have led to the earliest dialectal splits within Finnic into Inland Finnic (> Chud > South Estonian), including the Long Barrow culture (ca. AD 5th–10th c.); Gulf of Riga Finnic (> Livonian); as well as Gulf of Finland Finnic (> North Estonian, Vote, Veps, Karelian, and Finnish), which clearly represent recent newcomers to the area due to several shared post-Proto-Finnic isoglosses (Kallio 2015).

The expansion of Gulf of Finland Finnic to the east replaced an East Finnic (or Para-Finnic) substrate in the region, which further confirms the presence of Balto-Finnic-related dialects all over the Textile Ware areas around the Gulf of Finland up to Lake Ladoga and Lake Onega. Its expansion to the north was slower, because it was climatically less hopitable. Almost all of eastern Fennoscandia was Saami-speaking before the Finnic northward expansion, and only coastal areas must have had Finnic-speaking colonies before ca. AD 300. They replaced Samic languages of central Finland, and probably displaced part of their population, who in turn must have replaced the remnants of Palaeosiberian and Palaeo-European peoples in northern Fennoscandia up to the Germanic-speaking regions (Kallio 2015).

Estonians can be modelled as CWC Baltic (ca. 60%), WHG (ca. 35%) and Nganasan-like ancestry (ca. 5%); Modern Finns and Karelians show more CWC (ca. 81%), less WHG (ca. 10%) and similar Nganasan-like (ca. 9%), with this higher Steppe-related ancestry also visible in their clusters (Suppl. Graph. 15); while Veps are intermediate, with CWC (ca. 77%), WHG (ca. 10%), and slightly more Nganasan-like ancestry (ca. 13%). Saami are closest to the ancient population from the Kola Peninsula, showing less CWC (ca. 60%), similar WHG (ca. 11%) and more Nganasan-like ancestry (ca. 28%). This is compatible with the ancient expansion of Baltic Finns from a southern homeland to the north and east, respectively, replacing the language and admixing with a more CWC-like Proto-Samic population, less admixed with local WHG-like peoples, in line with the expansion of EBA CWC-like settlers to less populated areas (Jeong et al. 2019).

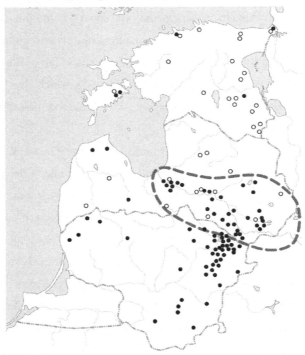

Figure 83. Distribution of fortified settlements (filled circles) and other hilltop sites (empty circles) of the Late Bronze Age and Pre-Roman Iron Ages in the East Baltic region. Tentative area of most intensive contacts between Baltic and Balto-Finnic communities marked with a dashed line. Image modified from (Lang 2016).

While N1a1a1a1a1a-VL29 lineages, already integrated into Balto-Finnic-speaking populations, may have undergone a further Y-chromosome bottleneck during the Finnic expansion, the presence of N1a1a1a1a2-Z1936 lineages (proper of Palaeo-Laplandic peoples) among central Finns suggests either an important role of cultural diffusion into the area, or a less important integration and later bottlenecks due to founder effects. Both options may be supported with the current genetic data, including a bottleneck estimated ca.

AD 500–700 in modern mtDNA among Finns (Översti et al. 2017), and the known several-fold more identity-by-descent segments found in north-east Finns compared to south-west ones, due to the described recent expansion from the Gulf of Finland (Martin et al. 2018).

This bottleneck may be seen in the Iron Age cemetery of Luistari (ca. AD 500–1200), forming a cluster similar to south-western Finns, but where at least four of ten males show haplogroup N-M231, three of them showing mutations linked to Dupuytren's disease.

Sampled medieval Estonians buried in rural cemeteries, representing the local class, cluster with modern Estonians, which in turn continue Iron Age ancestry in the region (between Bronze Age and Corded Ware populations), while certain urban elite individuals associated with the arrival of western Europeans bringing economic, cultural and political networks cluster genetically with modern Germans. Among modern Balto-Finnic populations, Estonians seem to be less affected by Siberian ancestry, showing more hg. R1a1a-M198 (ca. 35%), with less N1a1-Tat (ca. 32%) and I-M170 (ca. 18%).

Karelians also show more R1a1a-M198 (ca. 41%) than N1a1-Tat (ca. 36%) and I-M170 (ca. 10%). Vepsians, clustering closer to eastern groups, show slightly more N1a1-Tat (ca. 38%) than R1a1a-M198 (ca. 36%). Saami show more N1a1-Tat (ca. 40%), with Saami from the Kola Peninsula showing more R1a1a-M198 (ca. 22%), than I-M170 (ca. 17%), and Saami from Sweden more I-M170 (ca. 33%) than R1a1a-M198 (ca. 18%).

The genetic picture among modern Finns, with more N1a1-Tat (ca. 58%) and I-M170 (ca. 29%) than R1a1a-M198 (ca. 7%), is closer thus to modern (and thus probably ancient) Saami, and possibly also influenced by incoming Nordic peoples from Sweden, but there is little difference in the PCA with Vepsians or Karelians (Tambets et al. 2018), evidencing the described recent founder effect.

A medieval warrior from Janakkala in southern Finland (ca. AD 1250), buried with at least two swords, a spear, an axe, and other materials, shows mainly local admixture and hg. R1b1a1b1a1a2c1-L21[35], probably further subclade R1b1a1b1a1a2c1a2a2a1-S5982 (formed ca. 1200 BC, TMRCA ca. 1000 BC), which is almost exclusively found in the British Isles. This may support the initial assessment of the individual as an early crusader, although his admixture suggests the infiltration of this lineage among locals likely during the Crusade Period (Laakso 2017). A contemporary Golden Horde individual of a R1a1a1b1a2a-Z92 subclade, autosomally close to Baltic Bronze and Iron Age samples, is potentially related to the eastern European slave trade or to acculturated Baltic Finns or Volga Finns (see above *§viii.8. Balto-Slavs*). Both mediaeval samples further suggest that the diversity of haplogroups present after the Iron Age in Europe, and especially the bottlenecks under N1a1a1a1a2-Z1936 in Fennoscandia, are a recent phenomenon not associated with the spread of Uralic languages.

---

[35] Preliminary results from the National Board of Antiquities and an archaeological team from the York University shared online, and information appeared on online news.

VIII.17. Eurasian forest-steppes

VIII.17.1. Abashevo

In the forest-steppe zone of the Middle Volga and Upper Don, at the easternmost aspect of the Russian forest zone, the last culture descended from Corded Ware ceramic tradition, the Abashevo group, emerged ca. 2500 BC or later (Anthony 2007), spreading through the forest regions westward to the Upper Don, and eastward substituting the late Volosovo groups that still remained in the region, reaching the Upper Ural basin (Suppl. Fig. 12). Settlements to the south appear up to the Samara valley, in immediate neighbourhood of Poltavka settlements, around 2500–2100 BC, with Abashevo and *Abashevoid* ceramic assemblages appearing in the forest-steppe zone (Kuznetsov and Mochalov 2016).

Abashevo was contemporaneous with Sintashta and Multi-Corded Ware cultures to the south, in Pontic–Caspian forest-steppe and steppe regions, and shares with them similar bronze, flint, stone, and bone objects. Mostly regional ceramics help distinguish the culture, with variants of pots with deep belly and prominent funnel-shaped neck appearing only in Abashevo. Abashevo shows—like Sintashta and Multi-Corded Ware cultures—fortified settlements, enclosed by a ditch (Parzinger 2013), usually located on the promontories of the first river terraces in the high valleys.

The occupied area of the biggest settlements does not exceed several thousand m², with a number of dwellings using supporting and framing posts dug into a slightly deepened foundation pit. Some storage pits and fireplaces are recognised on the floors, and size and interior design seem to be dependent on functional factors, such as small rooms for metalworking activity (Koryakova and Epimakhov 2007).

Animal husbandry is the main subsistence economy, with cattle predominating (ca. 68-78%) over sheep–goats, as was common in Corded Ware groups, and there is no evidence of agriculture. Pigs, usually associated with agriculture (because they can be fed agricultural products) appear only in the Cis-Urals area, where oak forests, and thus acorns, are available. There is a limited presence of horse bones in settlements, with some horse harness details, but only in settlements, not in funeral sites (Koryakova and Epimakhov 2007).

Copper mining and bronze casting appear at a significant scale. Bronze work included large cast bronze shaft–hole axes and small distinctive copper or bronze ornaments worn around the head and face by women. As a cattle-herding pastoralist economy, it probably competed with Poltavka during its expansion to the south into steppe grasslands (Kuznetsov and Mochalov 2016).

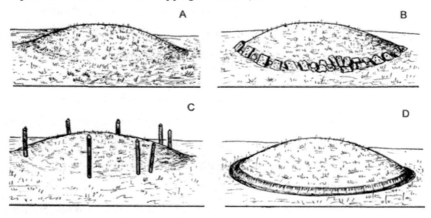

Figure 84. Abashevo kurgan types after Gobunov 1986, image modified from Koryakova and Epimakhov (2007).

Year-round unfortified settlements and seasonal camps are also located near rivers and consist of several houses. Kurgan cemeteries usually occupy river terraces and have several small mounds (80% not higher than 0.5 m, the remaining no more than 1 m) that contain mainly individual inhumations. More than half of the mounds are made of earth, but other elements can be found, such as circular ditches, stone, and wooden fences (Figure 84). Funerary chambers are rectangular and with a dimension connected to the age and number of individuals buried, with average depth less than 1 m. Apart from simple pits without any addition, there are a number of wood and stone inner constructions, such as walling and roofing. The presence of stone is an ethnographic feature of the Cis-Uralian Abashevo sites (Koryakova and Epimakhov 2007).

Grave goods include only limited animal sacrifices in the pit filling, with the majority including pots, some bone and metal objects, including chisels, knives–daggers, sickle-like tools, awls, and hooks, as well as stone and bone arrowheads proper of hunting, and bone "spades". The most characteristic part of the Abashevo assemblage are the numerous ornaments: bracelets, rings, hollow ribbed tubes, rosette-like, and semi-circular plaques (Koryakova and Epimakhov 2007).

Collective burials are rare in both the Cis-Urals and the Middle Volga area. One of this early mass graves is witness to this period of intense conflict and large-scale battles in the region, with 28 violently killed men at Pepkino in the Middle Volga forest-steppe zone, a battle between forces armed with bronze axes and daggers, dated ca. 2130–1950 BC (Figure 85). Analogies of projectile points from the Turbino cemetery allow it to be dated no earlier than ca. 2100–2000 BC (Chechushkov and Epimakhov 2018).

Traces of injuries—broken bones and skulls pierced with metal axes and stone arrowheads of the Balanovo type—detected on the bones of large number of these skeletons suggest that this represents a serious conflict between the Abashevo and forest Balanovo groups. Some of them had been dismembered, and among them there was a bonzesmith, distinguished by his powerful build (Koryakova and Epimakhov 2007).

The Sosnitsa culture succeeded the Middle Dnieper culture in the middle and upper Dnieper regions, although precise radiocarbon dates are lacking. Kurgan and flat graves with inhumation and cremation are found, and vessel forms and their ornamentation (horizontal beaded decoration on the neck and shoulders) show links to Abashevo, Multi-Cordon Ware, and to the succeeding Srubna culture in the region. East European Bronze Age features are seen in bronze findings—spiral bracelets, spiral pendants, socketed axes—in common with East Trzciniec and especially Komarov cultures, with links to eastern

Carpathian cultures (Ottomány, Madarov'ce) whose influence is felt in the north Pontic region ca. 1750–1500 BC (Parzinger 2013).

Figure 85. Pepkino collective burial after Khalikov, Lebedinskaya and Gerasimova 1966, image modified from Koryakova and Epimakhov (2007).

VIII.17.2. The Seima–Turbino phenomenon

The Seima–Turbino inter-cultural network (main finds ca. 1900–1600 BC) is associated with materials present in the Abashevo, Sintashta–Petrovka, Taskovo–Loginovo (on the Middle and Lower Tobol and Middle Irtysh), Samus (on the Upper Ob), Krotovo (forest-steppe of the Middle Irtysh to the Baraba steppe on the Upper Ob), Elunino, and Okunevo cultures. This expansion through Eurasian forest and forest-steppe societies roughly corresponds to the expansions of the Srubna–Andronovo horizon through the Eurasian steppes (Carpelan and Parpola 2001).

While the Okunevo culture belongs to the Early Bronze Age (ca. 2250–1900 BC), most other cultures date to a later period, during the Pre-Andronovo horizon (ca. 2100–1800 BC). The better quality of tin–bronze proper of Seima–Turbino objects makes the source of both copper and tin probably central Asian ores (e.g. Upper Irtysh–Bukhtarta area of tin, copper, and gold ores), which is—apart from the knives with depicted mountain sheep and horses typical of the east—why it has been traditionally considered an east–west movement of objects, and potentially of people (Carpelan and Parpola 2001).

Seima–Turbino metalsmiths were the first to regularly use a tin–bronze alloy, and were masters of lost-wax casting (for decorative figures on dagger handles) and thin-walled hollow-mould casting (for socketed spears and hollow axes). Nevertheless, local Okunevo and Afanasevo metallurgy of the Sayan–Altai area is primitive, and it is unlikely that they developed the advanced technology of casting socketed spearheads as one piece around a blank. On the other hand, spearheads of this type appear first in the Caucasus ca. 2000 BC, diffusing early to the Middle Volga–Kama–southern Urals area, where "it was the experienced Abashevo craftsmen who were able to take up the new techniques and develop and distribute new types of spearheads." The presence of specific animals seems to be a local development, since Seima materials on the Oka river depict European elk types (Carpelan and Parpola 2001).

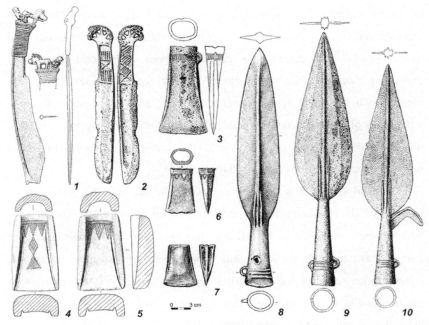

Figure 86. Seima–Turbino objects (4, 5 – stone, the rest are bronze objects) from the burial grounds of southwestern Siberia. Image modified from Marchenko et al. (2017): 3, 9, 10 – Rostovka (Matyushchenko and Sinitsyna 1988); 2 – Elunino 1 (Kiryushin 1987); 4–6 – Sopka 2/4C (Molodin 1983); 7 – Tartas 1 (Molodin et al. 2011), 8 – Preobrazhenka 6 (Molodin et al. 2007).

Sintashta socketed spearheads were made by bending a bronze sheet around a socket form and then forging the seam, while Seima–Turbino types were made by pouring molten metal into a mould that created a seamless cast socket around a suspended core, making a hollow interior, which necessitated tin–bronze rather than arsenical bronze (Anthony 2007). This use of tin–

bronzes, of hollow-mould casting method, and of the lost-wax casting technique were probably learned from BMAC, which is probably explained by the exploratory movements of Abashevo, Sintashta, Srubna, and Andronovo settlers into the tin mining sites of the Zeravshan Valley.

The proportion of tin–bronze, arsenical bronze, and pure copper in Seima–Turbino materials from Europe also speaks in favour of a western origin of the material culture and regional adaptations to ore sources. The presence of pure copper in the Altai supports the presence of Abashevo migrants from the Urals, not yet mining arsenical copper. The main ores for Abashevo metal production were on the Volga–Kama–Belaya area sandstone ores of pure copper, and more easterly Urals deposits of arsenical copper. The Abashevo people, expanding from the Don and Middle Volga to the Urals, developed their metallurgy in the Volga–Kama basin (pure copper) and then moved to the east, where they produced harder weapons and tools of arsenical copper. Further to the south, they contributed to the Sintashta society in a territory richest in copper in the whole Urals region (Parpola 2013).

Arsenical copper was probably connected to the Tash–Kazgan deposits situated on the upper reaches of the Ui River in the southern Trans-Urals, which were transported westward over the low-lying Ural range, for about 250–300 km through the mountains. The rather high variation of arsenic concentration suggests that the Tash–Kazgan ore could be smelted on-site or on the Cis-Urals settlements and then transported to Abashevo and Sintashta areas (Koryakova and Epimakhov 2007).

The finding of Abashevo-like pottery in tin miners' camp at Karnab on the lower Zeravshan, together with contemporary Sintashta-like pottery at Gonur, points to competing exploratory movements including contact and trade from forest-steppe and steppe cultures in Central Asia in look for tin ores near BMAC sites ca. 2100–2000 BC (Anthony 2007).

The Seima–Turbino phenomenon probably shows, therefore, the connection of areas to the west and east of the Urals in a network created by

Abashevo settlers expanding into West Siberia through the forest-steppe and forest regions (Figure 87). Supporting this common expansion is the appearance of similar flint projectile points in Seima–Turbino and Sintashta graves, as well as objects of Petrovka origin, and the contemporary Andronovo expansion through the steppes (Anthony 2007).

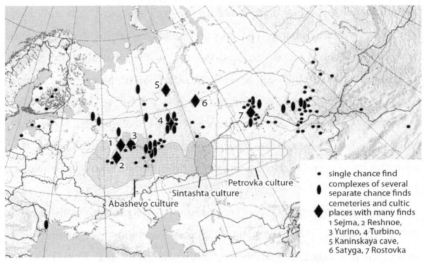

Figure 87. Formative phase of the "Eurasian Metallurgical Province", with the distribution of the Abashevo, Sintashta and Petrovka cultures (the map does not show Petrovka's wider extension to southern Central Asia, Turkmenistan, Tajikistan, Uzbekistan), and the finds of the Seima-Turbino trade network. (After Parpola 2015: 57 Fig. 7.3, based on Chernykh 2007: 77). Image from Parpola (2018).

VIII.17.3. Andronovo-like cultural horizon

Alakul and Fëdorovo material culture appear in the forest-steppe and forest zones of western Siberia, toward the northern taiga, evidenced by numerous settlement sites and decorated ware. They appear as stockbreeders, metallurgists, hunters and fishers, representing a cultural transformation of the vast area east of the Urals. These syncretic cultures are known as "Andronoid" or "Andronovo-like", with apparently stronger connections to Fëdorovo. The horizon is composed of several cultures, including Cherkaskul (middle and southern Trans-Urals), Pakhomovo (Middle Irtysh and Tobol), Suzgun (taiga area of the Middle Irtysh), and Elovka (forest area of the Ob'-Irtysh river basin) (Koryakova and Epimakhov 2007).

All these cultures and smaller groups show similar flat-bottomed pottery with high or middle shoulders, short necks, and compact decoration consisting of alternating geometric motives with recognisable forest "images" and "Andronovo spirit". They share similarities with Cis-, Trans-Urals, and eastern regions of western Siberia. The appearance of Andronovo-type geometric design into the local pottery reduced the area of the local hole and combed ornamental scheme, which still covered the major part of the taiga and Circum-Arctic area. Metallurgy is present, but there is a decrease in the number of metal objects, probably due to the absence of ores. Population density probably remained low, limited by the capacity of the forest ecological niches, with communities concentrated in clusters along rivers (Koryakova and Epimakhov 2007).

The Cherkaskul tradition (ca. 1850–1500 BC) has probably a direct origin in the expansion of Abashevo with the Seima–Turbino phenomenon over the area of the previous Late Garino–Bor and Sayat culture (ca. 2500–1900 BC) of hunter-gatherers, in the middle and south Trans-Urals, with Kazan as its western neighbour. The spread of Cherkaskul materials is thus closely associated with the Seima–Turbino phenomenon, and with the spread of the Fëdorovo tradition of the Andronovo horizon (see above Figure 90), probably as a northern variant directly linked to Abashevo, and not to the Sintashta culture from the steppes (Parpola 2018).

Cherkaskul sites are mainly found concentrated in the southern forest and northern forest-steppe of the Ural Mountains, with some findings as far south as the steppe zone. Cherkaskul materials are also found in thick concentrations on the southern forest and northern forest-steppe of central Asia, including the Upper Irtysh, Upper Ob', and Upper Yenissei rivers, close to the Altai and Sayan mountains. Cherkaskul pottery appears frequently along with Fëdorovo types, and many sites produced pottery mixing both types. About half of the bone finds in Cherkaskul sites come from hunted animals, attesting to a predominantly hunter-gatherer population (Parpola 2018).

Its pottery includes the frequent use of carpet design in ornamentation, in common with Fëdorovo types, but is denser and more sophisticated than the Fëdorovo tradition, with flat-bottomed pots having a smooth and pleasing profile. In the forest, houses show shallow basements with rectangular pits as grounds for small frame-pillar wooden constructions (ca. 22–50 m^2), showing internal hearths. Houses had corridor-like entrances. In the forest-steppe and steppe, houses were larger (ca. 100–200 m^2) with deeper basements (Koryakova and Epimakhov 2007).

Settlements show evidence of a stable and settled life, with tolls for hunting, fishing, and bones of domestic animals, including bone dice, and remains of a developed metallurgy. Funerary tradition includes small kurgans with stone fences and mounds, covering individual burials with traces of cremation in the southern area; and inhumation in shallow pits in contracted left-sided position and modest assemblages in the northern and western regions. From the mid– 2nd millennium on, different cultures without precise radiocarbon dates evolve from the previous expansion of Cherkaskul (Koryakova and Epimakhov 2007).

The Pakhomovo groups constitute the southern part of the Andronovo-like complex, and are located in the northern forest-steppe and forests of the Tobol-Irtysh basin, with pottery similar to Fëdorovo in morphology, decoration, and manner of surface treatment. Pots covered by monotonous ornaments of the forest style with various holes and figured stamps are common. Settlements are not large (ca. 4,500 m^2 in average), with varied large rectangular houses (ca. 100 m^2), wooden built with vertical pillars supporting a pyramidal roof, which include fixed hearths and wooden constructions for economic use. Tools related to hunting, fishing, metallurgy, and metal objects evidence their mainly fishing and hunting activity complemented by cattle and horse breeding (Koryakova and Epimakhov 2007).

The Suzgun groups occupy the area to the north of Pakhonovo, partially overlapping it in the northern Isim and Irtysh forest-steppe. Settlements are located on high promontories of the Irtysh River valley and on low fluvial terraces, with the environment conditioning the economy. A wooden walled enclosure with rectangular houses formed with vertical pillars in perpendicular rows and corridor-like entrances is possibly the model settlement. Mass ritual actions connected to sacrifices and common eating of oblational food are found in common sanctuaries (Koryakova and Epimakhov 2007).

Several individual inhumations and collective burials are found in cemeteries, where dead were buried in the extended supine position, with some apparently Pre-Andronovo and some Andronovo-like customs found in the funerary ritual. Bronze metalworking seems to be a part of ritual actions, and the most common artefact found is pottery, with flat and round bottomed pots with well pronounced profiles decorated with geometric motifs. The subsistence economy was diverse, with hunting and fishing being an essential part, but cattle being also dominant, and horse occupying the second position (Koryakova and Epimakhov 2007).

VIII.17.4. Mezhovska–Irmen cultural horizon

The Mezhovska–Irmen cultural horizon (ca. 1500–800 BC) involves a group of cultures with common stylistic similarities and local differences, in the forest-steppe area on both sides of the Ural Mountains, from the middle Kama and Belaya rivers to the Tobol river in western Siberia, with sites reaching up to the Altai (Suppl. Fig. 13). They emerged from the previous Andronovo-like cultural complex of the forest-steppe and southern forest of western Siberia, with influence coming from cross-stamped cultures of the north, and include Mezhovska and Irmen cultures around the Urals, the Sargary–Alekseevka culture to the south, and the Karasuk culture to the east (Koryakova and Epimakhov 2007).

Mezhovska sites were present in the forest and forest-steppe zones on both sides of the Urals, including the forest-steppe region from the Belaya bend to the Middle Kama up to the Chusovaya river (in the Cis-Urals), the Trans-Urals, the Ishim–Irtysh area. The Irmen cultures were distributed in the Ob-Irtysh forest-steppe, with its influence found in Sargary–Alekseevka culture in northern Kazakhstan (Koryakova and Epimakhov 2007).

All settlements are small or middle-sized open settlements (200–300 individuals), mainly seasonal camps, but also stable long-term habitation settlements. They are situated on river terraces or lake or river promontories, possibly with defensive constructions. The largest pillar-frame structures are found to the south, related to the Sargary culture, while smaller houses (ca. 100 m^2) are proper of the forest zone. There were vertical pillar-frame constructions, and constructions with deep basement and horizontal frame in its low part. Fireplaces and storage pits are found inside houses, and a corridor-like entrance usually faces the water (Koryakova and Epimakhov 2007).

Subsistence economy in both the Cis-Urals and Trans-Urals depends on the specific ecological niche. It usually includes wild species (up to 15%), with a smaller percentage for 'fur' animals; horse and cattle (ca. 30%), and a small percentage of sheep (ca. 13%), as well as fish. Food producing branches were more prevalent in the south, and the high proportion of horses compared to previous periods is probably related to their ability to forge in the winter. Metallurgy was probably not using local ores (as in the succeeding Itkul' culture), and it was most likely based on domestic needs (Koryakova and Epimakhov 2007).

Characteristic is the decoration of the pottery, usually covering the neck and shoulder, with carved (fretted) elements becoming popular, contrasting with the previous comb–stamped techniques of the region. Ornament patterns are simple, and pottery shapes include pots of globular bodies with short straight or turned up necks, and cans and korchags (large earthenware pots). Bronze objects are represented by massive tools, like celts–axes of the Cimmerian type, gouges of Derbeden type, sickles of Derbeden and Kataisk types, daggers of Kardashinsky and Cimmerian types, as well as double-edged knives with smooth passage to tengue, awls, and needles. Bone and stone arrowheads are also numerous (Koryakova and Epimakhov 2007).

There seems to be a kurgan burial tradition, using stone in the erection of mounds, with one to three inhumations for kurgan, and the dead in extended supine or side position. Secondary burials appear on the ancient surface. Graves are shallow with modest wooden arrangement. Animal bones, mainly cattle, represent remains of the funeral feast, and assemblages include pottery, metal daggers, spearheads, knives, and ornaments (Koryakova and Epimakhov 2007).

The eastern part of the Mezhovska–Irmen horizon is formed by the Irmen culture, with material culture intermediate between Mezhovska and Karasuk. Settlements include traditional large house buildings in variable open villages, small camps and, in a later phase, fortified sites. Houses have several hearths and traces of domestic activities, including animal stabling during the winter, and there are separate houses with structures of economic function. Subsistence economy is also based on livestock breeding, with their bones prevalent over wild animals, and only traces of cultivation. Metallurgy developed depending on the sites and raw material resources (Koryakova and Epimakhov 2007).

Pottery includes large flat-bottomed massive pots, and (proper of burials) smaller pots and jars with flat or round bottoms. Ornamentation includes incised techniques, sometimes accompanied by combed stamps and 'pearls', and Andronovo-like motifs appear in funerary pottery. Cemeteries include kurgans with multiple individual burials, with inhumations in crouched right-sided position with southern direction and orientation. Graves are shallow, and wooden frames furnish them. Assemblages consist of metal goods (nail-like pendants, earrings, sewn plaques) and pottery. Collective burials are rare (Koryakova and Epimakhov 2007).

The Sargary culture emerged from Fëdorovo and Cherkaskul traditions in the forest-steppe between Tobol and Irtysh, in northern and central Kazakhstan.

It formed part of the "horizon of cultures of the Valikova pottery tradition" (Chernykh 1992), which comprised cultures from the Don–Volga–Ural steppes (late Srubna), southern Urals and Trans-Urals, and Kazakhstan (Sargary, Trushnikovo, Dandybai–Begazy, Amirabad), characterised by poorly ornamented flat-bottomed pottery with clay rollers stuck around the shoulder or neck. Other similarities involved metal artefacts, economic structure, and funerary ritual.

In the Dandybai–Begazy culture, mausoleums were constructed especially for people of high social status. The characteristic pottery of globular form and very small bottoms and cylindrical necks, often with polished surfaces and black, yellow, or red colour, and both Sargary and this culture probably formed a unity with a core area in central Kazakhstan, where the centres of metallurgy lied. In the Trans-Urals region, Sargary material culture is found with Mezhovska, and some Meshovksa finds contain Sargary material, probably from the 13th century BC on (Koryakova and Epimakhov 2007).

Sargary settlements include large territories (ca. 20,000 m^2) with semisubterranean buildings with deep basements and up to several dozen large houses, and smaller settlements (1,000–2,500 m^2) with up to fifteen houses, yielding a similar number of finds, suggesting that they were inhabited seasonally. Houses are rectangular, frame-pillar constructions with a floor deepened into the ground, and are placed freely along the river bank. Metal tools are numerous (Koryakova and Epimakhov 2007).

Subsistence economy reveals a pattern connected to the steppe area of eastern Europe, with domestic animals predominating, first cattle, then horse and sheep, with likely yearly cycle herding practices. The first trace of agriculture in the region is associated with this culture. Small cemeteries comprising up to three mounds and solitary kurgans of earth and stone are placed on high ground of the initial riverbank and far from river streams, unlike in the preceding period. The dead are placed in contracted position on their side, and assemblages are modest. Funerary rituals are complex and varied, and kurgan ritual and inhumation were reserved for some people, with society tending to atomisation in the forest-steppe, and to concentration in larger settlements in the south (Koryakova and Epimakhov 2007).

The Karasuk culture (ca. 1400–900 BC), genetically at least partly derived from Fëdorovo, flourished around the upper Yenissei, Mongolia and the Ordos region of China. It probably came into being as a result of a migration of different people from the southeast, from the periphery of Shang period China. The beginning of the Karasuk period also marked the return of some Okunevo traditions that did not manifest themselves during the Fëdorovo period (Parpola 2018).

It preceded the transition of the LBA to the EIA Proto-Scythian period, when the use of saddled horse, composite bow, and the 'animal style' art became integral parts of the steppe life. Around 1000 BC, the Eurasiatic steppes became uniform culturally from Mongolia to Hungary (see *§VIII.19.4. Scythians and Sarmatians*), and for a thousand years East Iranian languages were spoken in the region (Parpola 2013). Among the pictorial tradition of petroglyphs in Andronovo-related groups, those of burials of the Karasuk culture in southern Siberia and Kazakhstan represent the latest tradition (Novozhenov 2012).

VIII.17.5. Itkul'–Gamayun and Sargat

The Gamayun and Itkul' cultures evolved (ca. 800–200 BC) from the Mezhovska cultural region in a narrow band (ca. 150 km wide) on the eastern slope of the Urals. Itkul' constituted the main metallurgical centre of the Trans-Urals region during the Iron Age. They were in contact with the Ananyino and Akhmylovo cultures, which were the metallurgical centres of the western Urals, and neighboured the Gorokhovo culture (Parpola 2018).

The Gamayun culture is rather archaic in appearance, featuring open or fortified settlements and early fortified house-refuges (of ca. 600 m^2), having solid wooden walls with a ditch and strengthened by an earthen bank, and a variable living space (ca. 40–400 m^2). Open settlements include small stable villages consisting of several houses, and seasonal short-time hunting-fishing camps. Fortified villages, chiefly concentrated on the periphery of the occupied territory, were variable in size, and occupied the low hills and promontories along riverbanks, with smaller ones representing frontier-guard stations. Houses vary from small hovels and chums to stable pillar-framed wooden houses with one or two sections, and were also used for economic activities (Koryakova and Epimakhov 2007).

Characteristic of the Gamayun culture is the crosslike stamp ornamentation, which was found widespread among the massive of cultures with stamped crosslike ornaments in the southernmost taiga zone and northern forest-steppe, from the Trans-Urals to the Middle Ob'. These cultures emerged from the Late Bronze Age of the Lower Ob' River forest area, represented by the Lozva–Atlym phase of the Late Bronze Age, when some population groups moved southward in search for game due to the humid conditions at the turn of the $2^{nd}/1^{st}$ millennium BC. Most migrating communities of the LBA and Gamayun sites show a rather small size (ca. 20–30 people), perhaps extended families or clans (Koryakova and Epimakhov 2007).

The Itkul' culture represents thus the strict cultural continuation of Mezhovska in the region, and the initial relations with the Gamayun culture seems to be one of conflicts, based on the fortification of houses and on traces of destruction of Gamayun villages. Eventually, both communities formed a symbiotic system based on division of labour and specialisation. Local Itkul' communities, having harnessed local mineral resources for metal production in a previous period, specialised in metallurgy, while Gamayun groups were hunters, fishers, and most likely miners (Koryakova and Epimakhov 2007).

Itkul' sites were fortified villages or fortified metallurgical workshops, with the vast majority occupying high ground of rivers or lake terraces. Fortifications were simple, with a wall, moat, ditch, or grove, and bigger settlements took up very high topographic positions usually with an open-order defensive line. Buildings included houses, workshops, and structures connected with special productive functions. Houses were rectangular semisubterranean and surface-based buildings of a pillar-framed construction, and they were rather small, with a simple interior, including one or two hearths. Small working areas served for copper smelting, iron working, and most often metal processing, while mass production of metal was done on larger dwellings or outdoor (Koryakova and Epimakhov 2007).

Artefacts and structures evidence the intensive dedication of the sites to metallurgical activity, with specialisation mainly in bronze production with local mineral deposits. There is operational division involving metal smelting and casting in mountain clusters (and further divisions into full or limited cycle of production), and metalworking in the periphery. Their distinctive pottery includes round-bottomed pots, of chiefly horizontal proportions, and decorated with rather standard comb–stamped patterns, covering the pot's upper third (Koryakova and Epimakhov 2007).

Itkul' metallurgists had close relations with the Ananyino populations, which used in part Trans-Uralian ores for manufacturing various objects that diffused westwards. Closer connections existed with neighbouring cultures, with Itkul' supplying regularly metal products to Gorokhovo and to the southern Siberian Sargat groups. More or less regular contacts existed also with The Upper Ob' Bolsherechye culture, and with the southern Kazakhstan Saka culture (Koryakova and Epimakhov 2007).

To the east of the Itkul' culture, up to the Ob river, the Nosilovo, Baitovo, Late Irmen, and Krasnoozero cultures (ca. 900–500 BC) developed, some of them in contact with the Akhmylovo culture of the Middle Volga. All these cultures of the forest steppe were later absorbed into the Sargat culture (Parzinger 2006),

The spread of the Suzgun culture with the Baraba trend—marked by the Baraba–Suzgun pottery, featuring slightly and well-profiled pots with a short throat—probably represents a wide-ranging population expansion in pre-taiga and taiga zones in the Irtysh basin. Later, the Berlik tradition expanded with migrants from the south, interacting in certain sites—as in the local Late Irmen cultural tradition—with Late Irmen people inhabiting the citadel of the settlement, and Berlik immigrants inhabiting the surrounding territory (Molodin, Mylnikova, and Kobeleva 2008).

The Sargat culture emerged from the Late Irmen tradition, succeeding the Sargary culture in its territory, comprising all cultural groups between the Tobol–Irtysh forest-steppe interfluve. Apart from the core settlers of the Mezhovska–Irmen horizon of the Final Bronze Age, intercommunity formation was completed by taiga settlers of the Lozva–Atlym LBA from the north, and southern influence from the Valikova pottery horizon and Arzhan phase of the Scythian and Saka confederation. These groups superimposed each other chronologically and territorially, as evidenced in the Chicha settlement. Open and fortified settlements are characteristic (Molodin, Mylnikova, and Kobeleva 2008).

The Gorokhovo cultural group of the Iset–Tobol area also resulted from a population of Sargary–Mezhovska roots, under the influence of climatic, economic, and social factors. With a clear cultural root in the Trans-Uralian forest-steppe, evidenced by its architecture, fortification system, and pottery, they probably adopted pastoral herding under the cultural and possibly political influence of the Saka confederation, evidenced by the funerary ritual. They formed part of a "forest-steppe–steppe system" that involved the Iktul' metallurgical centre, South Urals nomads, and the Sargat culture (Parzinger 2006).

Both Gorokhovo and Sargat eventually developed (ca. 5th c. BC on) the "Golden Age" of the western Siberian forest-steppe, under Sargat dominance coming from the east, and increased influence from steppe nomads from the south. Fortified settlements demonstrate a more complex level of architecture, with large elite barrows including very big kurgans, analogous to those found in the steppes, and mainly individual inhumations. Seminomadic stockbreeding became the main subsistence economy. The expansion of Sargat may have caused an initial expansion of Gorokhovo settlers to the west, until their eventual integration under Sargat (Koryakova and Epimakhov 2007).

viii.17. Ugrians and Samoyeds

Seima–Turbino-related migrations through the Eurasian forest and forest-steppe zones in western Siberia reflect population movements from west to east, coinciding with the arrival of pastoralists in central Asia (Kılınç et al. 2018), which supports the traditional interpretation of Uralic expanding from west to east, originally with Abashevo-related groups, most likely associated with individuals of Steppe MLBA ancestry associated with the Andronovo-like cultural horizon (see *§viii.18.1. Late Indo-Iranians*).

While Mezhovska is the best candidate for the original Proto-Ugric-speaking population, Karasuk has been traditionally proposed as the Pre-Samoyedic-speaking community (Parpola 2013). Both Mezhovska and Tagar samples can be modelled as almost completely of Corded Ware-derived ancestry, in contrast to neighbouring groups like Pazyryk or Zevakino-Chilikta—traditionally considered East Iranian cultures—which show likely contributions from neighbouring Altaic populations.

viii.17.1. Ugrians

Individuals of the Mezhovska culture from the Kapova cave (one dated ca. 1500 BC) are part of the Western Steppe MLBA cluster. It shows mainly Steppe MLBA (ca. 75–84%) and Baikal EBA/Nganasan-like ancestry (ca. 17–20%), with contributions of an ANE-related population (Jeong et al. 2019). One sample is of hg. R1a1a1b1a2-Z280[+], and another of hg. R1b1a1b-M269 (Allentoft et al. 2015). Interesting is the presence of one outlier, with ancestry close to the later South-Eastern Iranian cluster, with increased Near Eastern ancestry, which suggests the potential emergence of this cluster in the Andronovo–Srubna complex, i.e. much earlier than suggested by the available samples. The position of Mezhovska samples is close to later Scythians from

Samara, and also close to modern Finns, northern Russians, Early Sarmatians, Estonians, Mordovians, Lithuanians or Belarusians (Unterländer et al. 2017).

The Sargat culture is probably to be identified (at least partly) with the expansion of Proto-Hungarians, who around the 5th century BC "were caught up in a wave of migrations that swept the steppe... Migrating westwards, they settled between the Urals and the Middle Volga region", staying in Bashkiria until ca. 600 BC, in the so-called *Hungaria Magna* of medieval sources (Suppl. Fig. 18). That Ugric peoples were horsemen is supported by the number of equestrian terms in Ugric languages, including the word for horse (Parpola 2018), and by the presence of horse riding equipment and horse bones in graves of Early Hungarian frequent riders, evidenced by their skeletal hip changes (Berthon et al. 2018).

Seven individuals of the Sargat culture from the Baraba forest (ca. 500 BC – AD 500) show five hg. N-M231, two hg. R1a-M420 (Bennett and Kaestle 2010), which is expected to be found in a late Ugric community integrating with Palaeosiberian peoples from the LBA cultures of the Lower Ob' River forest area, likely expanding with hg. N-M231, and becoming integrated both in the Itkul' culture through its association with Gamayun, and in Sargat through the gradual integration of migrants from the taiga region.

Given the sample of hg. N-M231 from the Mezőcsát Culture (ca. 900 BC) in Hungary (Gamba et al. 2014), belonging to expanding Cimmerians, and the Siberian ancestry expanding with Scythian groups (see *§viii.19. Iranians*) and later with Altaic peoples (see *§viii.21.2. Turkic peoples and Mongols*) it is conceivable that at least part of the N-M231 lineages—and N1a1-Tat in particular, including N1a1a1a1a-L392—integrated among Ugric and part of the Samoyedic peoples accompanied westward steppe migrations (see Suppl. Graph. 15 and Suppl. Graph. 17), which is in line with some known shared traits of Uralic and Altaic (Kortlandt 2010).

Modern Ugric populations include Mansis, in the immediate Trans-Urals region, which have more Steppe MLBA (ca. 38–42%) and less Baikal

EBA/Nganasan-like ancestry (ca. 54–61%) than other Ugric and Samoyedic populations, and show variable contributions of an ANE-like population (ca. 0–8%). They show more N-M231(xN1a1-Tat) (ca. 33–60%) than N1a1-Tat (ca. 16–28%), R1a-Z280 (ca. 19%), other R1a1a-M198 (ca. 6%), I-M170 (ca. 6–8%), R1b-M343 (ca. 4%), or J-M304 (ca. 4%). Eastern Khants, on the other hand, show more N1a1-Tat (ca. 49%) than N-M231(xN1a1-Tat) (ca. 31%) or N1a1-Tat (ca. 16%), but they also show R1b-M343 (ca. 11%), R1a1a-M198 (ca. 6%), I-M170 (ca. 8%), or J-M304 (ca. 4%) (Tambets et al. 2018).

Khants and Nenets share similar ancestry, showing a close affinity with Selkups (in turn intermingled with Yeniseian-speaking Kets), too, which suggests the origin of the admixture among Uralic-speaking peoples in the expansion of Corded Ware-related populations to the east, including language shift of neighbouring Palaeosiberian peoples (Karafet et al. 2018; Dudás et al. 2019; Jeong et al. 2019).

Hungarians, on the other hand, show an ancestry indistinguishable from neighbouring European populations around the Carpathian Basin, and similar contributions of hg. R1a-M420 (ca. 21-60%), R1b-L23 (ca. 15–20%) and I-M170 (ca. 11-26%), with intermediate frequency of J-M304, E1b-P177 and G2a-P15 (ca. 5–15%), and much lesser N-M231(xN1a1-Tat) and N1a1-Tat (ca. 1-6%) (Semino 2000; Csányi et al. 2008; Pamjav et al. 2011; Pamjav et al. 2017).

The closest link between Finno-Ugric populations from around the Urals— including Maris, Mansis, and Hungarians—is found in four different haplotypes of hg. R1a1a1b1a2-Z280 (Csáky et al. 2019), derived from the expansion of Corded Ware groups (see above *§vii.1. Western and Eastern Uralians*), most likely within subclade R1a1a1b1a2b-CTS1211, which appears in modern populations in both West and East Uralic speakers, and is also found in ancient Battle Axe populations.

On the other hand, all Bashkirian Mari R1a1a1b2-Z93 samples (seven haplotypes) formed a very isolated branch, different from a Hungarian sample by seven mutational steps, which support their relative isolation since the initial expansion. Other haplotypes found in Khants or Hungarians are scattered and not particularly related to those of Altaians, Khakassians, or Uzbeks (Csáky et al. 2019).

Another shared Finno-Ugric lineage is hg. N1a1a1a1a2-Z1936 (formed ca. 2900 BC, TMRCA ca. 2300 BC), with the most common Ugric subclade being N1a1a1a1a2a1c-Y13850 (formed ca. 2300 BC, TMRCA ca. 2200 BC): a Y24361 branch (TMRCA ca. 350 BC) is found among Tatars and Bashkirs, and also among Hungarians, while a L1034 branch (TMRCA ca. 2200 BC) is found among Bashkirs and Ugric peoples (Post et al. 2019).

These lineages were likely incorporated into the Ugric stock during their expansion through the forest-steppes and the taiga, and did probably expand further among them during the Turkic migrations through the forest-steppes up to the Middle Volga. In particular, population genetic analyses indicate that Hungarian Conquerors had the closest connection to Volga Tatars (Neparáczki et al. 2019), suggesting that the Y24361 branch belongs to recently assimilated Turkic paternal lines.

An origin of the expansion of N1a1a1a1a2-Z1936 in the central Siberian forests is supported by the likely finding of sister clade N1a1a1a1a2a-Z1934 in Palaeo-Laplandic speakers from Lovozero Ware (ca. 1500 BC), likely stemming from the Taymir Peninsula, and originally from the Imiyakhtakhskaya expansion in Yakutia (see *§viii.16.1. Saami and Laplandic peoples*); the presence of N1a1-Tat subclades in Northern Eurasia likely connected to Neolithic populations to the north of Lake Baikal; their recent TMRCA in the west and the lack of findings in ancient samples, compared to their early split and presence in the east; as well as the presence of both lineages in modern populations of the Siberian Taiga and around the Arctic, up to Lake Baikal in the south.

viii.17.1.1. Hungarians

The distribution of haplogroups among early Hungarian conquerors from Karos (ca. AD 895–950)—without taking into account local paternal lineages—is similar to the expected proportion of N1a1-Tat vs. R1a-M420 lineages, based on the available ancient samples from the Trans-Urals forest-steppes and on modern Ob-Ugric peoples: there are four R1a1a1b1a2-Z280, at least three of them R1a1a1b1a2b-CTS1211, one of them an elite individual from Karos II; two R1a1a1b2a2-Z2124, one of them an elite individual; and one N1a1a1a1a2-Z1936(xL1034)[36], one of them an elite individual.

Likely 'eastern' samples include two N1a1a1a1a4-B2118 (formed ca. 4300 BC, TMRCA ca. 1700 BC), prevalent among Turkic-speaking Yakuts and Dolgans, and linguistically distant Evenks and Evens living in Yakutia, but also appearing around the Urals and particularly scattered among modern Turkic peoples. This patrilineage is a prime example of a male population of broad central Siberian ancestry that is not intrinsic to any linguistically defined group of people, with the deepest branches being represented by a Lebanese and a Chinese sample, and a separate sub-lineage found in Bhutan. This supports a recent strong founder effect primarily in central Siberia (Ilumäe et al. 2016).

A military leader from of Karos II and another elite individual show hg. I2a1a2b-L621(xI2a1a2b1a1a1-S17250). Lineages of likely 'western' origin at Karos1 and Karos2 include two E1b1b-M215, at least one E1b1b1a1b1a-V13, one J1-M267, one G2a2b-L30, and one I1-M253(xI1a1b1-L22).

Samples from a small Karos III cemetery stand out from the rest, with three R1b1a1b1a1a1-U106 lineages, likely stemming from an East Germanic population, and its leader being of hg. I2a1a2b-L621 and brother of the leader

---

[36] Five N1a1a1a1a2-Z1936 samples have been indirectly reported from the study of Fóthi et al. (2019), without reference to its proportion relative to non-N-M231 haplogroups: Three samples in the Upper-Tisza area (Karos II, Bodrogszerdahely/Streda nad Bodrogom) and two in the Middle-Tisza basin cemeteries (Nagykörű and Tiszakécske).

from Karos2, with whom he shares mitogenome and Y-STR haplotypes. The nearby Kenézlő cemetery shows one 'eastern' hg. Q1a-F1096(xQ1a2-M25), one R1b1a1b-L23 (likely R1b1a1b1b-Z2103), and two N1a1a1a1a2-Z1936(xL1034) lineages.

Samples from the small eastern cemetery of Magyarhomorog (ca. AD 10th)—with typical partial horse burials of the early Hungarians containing horse cranium with leg bones and harness objects—show three I2a1a2-M423, at least two of them I2a1a2b-L621(xI2a1a2b1a1a1-S17250). The widespread presence of hg. I2a1a2b-L621 among the elites, as well as the finding of hg. E1b1b1a1b1a-V13 among early conquerors, both lineages found among early Slavs (see *§viii.9.2. Slavs*), suggests that the local population of the Carpathian Basin—home to Slavonic-speaking peoples since the late Avar period, from the 8th century on—became integrated into the new Hungarian-speaking community.

Later samples from Sárrétudvari, representing commoners from the second half of the 10th century, show hg. R1b1a1b1a1a2b-U152 and J2a1a-L26. Unpublished conquerors. Among twelve males from Karos-Eperjesszög (AD 900–1000), at least two are of hg. R1b1a1b-M269, two I2a-L460 (Neparáczki et al. 2017). Another two N1a1-Tat samples have been published (Csányi et al. 2008), one from Szabadkigyos-Palliget (ca. AD 950) and another one from Örménykút[37] (ca. AD 975–1000).

Among early Hungarians interred in Saint Stephen Basilica, Székesfehérvár (AD 12th c.), there are three of hg. R1a-M420, including King Béla III of the Árpád dynasty, of hg. R1a1a1b2a2a1d7-YP451(xYP499)[+], common in modern populations of the northern Caucasus, among Karachays and Balkars; two of hg. R1b-M343, one J1-L255, and one E1b1-P2 (Olasz et al. 2018).

---

[37] This and another conqueror from Tuzsér have been informally reported as of hg. N1a1a1a1a4-M2118, from the unpublished study by Fóthi et al. (2019).

The early mixture found among early Hungarian elites and among modern populations points to the likely domination of a minority of Magyar clans— probably already admixed with Turkic peoples—over a majority of the population of the Carpathian Basin, composed of local lineages, most from Germanic and Slavic populations. The finding of haplogroup R1a1a1b1a2-Z280 (ca. 14-15%) and lesser R1a1a1b2-Z93 (ca. 1%) among modern Hungarians[38] suggests the arrival of some R1a1a1b1a2-Z280 lineages with Magyar tribes, in contrast to the typical Slavic subclades of the area, mainly R1a1a1b1a1a-M458 (ca. 7-20%), I2a1a2b1a1-CTS10228 (ca. 16%), apart from lineages also found among early conquerors.

Further support of the spread of Hungarian conquerors from the Urals region is found in the shared mitogenomes with the ancient populations (AD 6th – 10th c.) of the Volga–Ural region (Szeifert et al. 2018).

viii.17.2. Samoyeds

Seven individuals of the Karasuk culture from Arban, Sabinka and Bystrovka (ca. 1530–1260 BC) form a wide cluster reaching from Western to Eastern Steppe MLBA, and can be modelled as Steppe MLBA (ca. 50–57%) and Baikal EBA/Nganasan-like ancestry (ca. 37–43%), with contributions of an ANE-related population (Jeong et al. 2019), which is compatible with their admixture with populations of the Trans-Uralian and Cis-Baikalic regions, with one particular outlier clustering closely with Khövsgöls in northern Mongolia (see *§viii.21.2. Turkic peoples and Mongols*). Reported haplogroups include two R1a1a1b2a2-Z2124, and one Q1a2a-L712[+] (Allentoft et al. 2015).

The Tagar culture (ca. 1000–200 BC) largely continues the traditions of the Karasuk culture in the Minusinsk basin of the Upper Yenissei. This area is considered the homeland to Proto-Samoyedic, based on the Bulghar Turkic loanwords, and thus the Tagar culture probably represents the expansion of the language (Parpola 2018). Sampled Tagar individuals (probably ca. 9th c. BC)

---

[38] Additional data on subclades taken from the Hungarian-Magyar Y-DNA project of FTDNA.

display increased EHG ancestry compared to other Inner Asian Scythian groups, with unequal ancestry contributions of Steppe MLBA (ca. 83.5%), WSHG (ca. 7.5%), with additional ANE ancestry (ca. 9%), and clear differences of hunter-gatherer ancestry sources with other sampled Sakas, which likely formed a confederation of different peoples (de Barros Damgaard, Marchi, et al. 2018). This is compatible with their origin in the eastern European forest zone, and reported haplogroups include two hg. R1-M173, and one R1a1a1b2a2-Z2124[+].

Modern Samoyedic peoples show a higher admixture of Siberian populations relative to Corded Ware ancestry (Jeong et al. 2019). The southern Selkups show Steppe MLBA (ca. 24%), Baikal EBA (ca. 73%), and ANE ancestry (ca. 3%). with a majority of 'eastern' haplogroups (ca. 58-66%) like P-P295, Q-M242, R-M207 (xR1a1a-M198, xR1b-M343), or R2-M479, but also more R1a1a-M198 (ca. 14-19%), than other Samoyedic peoples, with lesser R1b-M343 (ca. 6-7%), I-M170 (ca. 0–7%), N-M231(xN1a1-Tat) (ca. 7%), N1a1-Tat (ca. 0–2%), or C2-M217 (ca. 2-5%).

Among northern groups, Enets in central regions have similar proportions of Steppe MLBA ancestry (ca. 21–23%), with more Baikal EBA/Nganasan-like (ca. 79–88%) and less ANE-related ancestry (ca. 0–4%), and show hg. N-M231(xN1a1-Tat) (ca. 78%), R1b-M343 (ca. 11%), and N1a1-Tat (ca. 11%). Nenets to the west show N-M231(xN1a1-Tat) (ca. 57%), N1a1-Tat (ca. 41%), while Nganasans to the east, the most recent Palaeosiberian group to adopt Samoyedic languages (Dolgikh 1960, 1962), show N-M231(xN1a1-Tat) (ca. 92%) and N1a1-Tat (ca. 3%), and an elevated "Siberian component" which has the highest frequency in three Karasuk samples (Karafet et al. 2018).

Eastern and western Circum-Arctic nomads show a prevalence of N1a1-Tat lineages, which appear in the western area as N1a1a1a2-B211 lineages (formed ca. 5400 BC, TMRCA 1900 BC) among Khanty and Mansi peoples, and in the east among some Nganasans in contact with Yukaghirs (see *§viii.21.1. Yukaghirs*). Most Nganasans show a deeper N1b-F2905 subclade (formed ca. 16000 BC, TMRCA ca. 13700 BC), though, also found in lesser proportions among Dolgans, Evenks, Evens, as well as in south Siberian Tofalars, Khakassians, Tuvinians, and Shors (Fedorova et al. 2013).

Central Siberian peoples show a majority of N1a2b-P43 lineages (formed ca. 6800 BC, TMRCA ca. 2700 BC), which may suggest an expansion of N1a-F1206 lineages precisely from this central Siberian area. Its western branch N1a2b2-Y3195 (TMRCA ca. 2200 BC) is found in the Cis-Urals region, with Permic peoples and Volga Finns, while its eastern branch N1a2b1-B478/VL64 (formed ca. 2700 BC, TMRCA ca. 1300 BC) is found in central Siberia and East Asia, and N1a2b1b1-B170 in particular coincident with the interaction east of the Urals (Ilumae et al. 2016; Karafet et al. 2018).

VIII.18. Eurasian steppes

VIII.18.1. Sintashta–Potapovka–Filatovka

A markedly cooler, more arid climate began in the Eurasian steppes from western Russia into the Altai ca. 2500 BC, reaching its coolest and driest peak ca. 2250–2000 BC, creating a paleoecological crisis had a significant effect on the economy of Pontic–Caspian tribes, favouring higher mobility and an almost complete transition to nomadic pastoralism (Demkina et al. 2017).

In the Volga–Ural region, forests, lakes, and marshes declined in area and steppes expanded. In northern steppe pastoralism, the most critical resource was winter fodder/grazing and protection from winter ice and snow. This may have led to increased competition for winter access to declining marshes, with mobile herding groups struggling to permanently settle near the most vital resource, in a sort of child's game of musical chairs (Anthony 2016).

In the period around 2400–2300 BC, there is a clear interaction between mobile steppe herders of the Poltavka culture and forest-steppe groups of the Abashevo culture. This interaction is evidenced in the subsequent period by the emergence ca. 2100 BC of Sintashta in the Ural–Tobol steppes, Potapovka in previous Poltavka territory, and Filatovka in the upper Don (Suppl. Fig. 12). Sintashta east of the Urals and the Multi-Corded Ware culture west of the Volga were the first to settle in permanent locations near marshes (Anthony 2016).

These traditions continue in an early phase the previous Abashevo pottery, but also retained and gradually expanded many cultural traits of Poltavka pottery, followed the same burial rites, and settled on top of or incorporated older Poltavka settlements. "It is difficult to imagine that this was accidental. A symbolic connection with old Poltavka clans must have guided these choices" (Anthony 2007).

This transformation was accompanied by an "unprecedented level of population mixing and interregional north–south movement across the steppe/forest-steppe border in the Middle Volga steppes", which is evident in

shared material culture—projectile point styles, pottery, bronze weapons—
closely associated with technical innovations in warfare, sign of increasing
interregional stress (Anthony 2016).

The Sintashta–Potapovka warrior societies were born from a time of
escalating conflict and competition between rival tribal groups in the northern
steppes, where raiding must have been endemic, and intensified fighting led to
the invention of the light chariot (Anthony 2007). The state of intense warfare
was caused by a constant flow of wealth, originating from long-distance metal
trade, with formation and destruction of alliances and gathering of large groups
of warriors, which created a vicious circle of escalation of conflict, and created
new customs, new tactics, and new weapons (Pinheiro 2011).

These harsher conditions and warrying period may also be reflected in
demographic trends, with Sintashta–Potapovka cemeteries dominated by
children (51%), and the population possibly affected by outbreaks of infectious
diseases from domestic animals. However, this trend could simply reflect a
cultural change whereby children were included in the burial rite (Khokhlov
2016). The low proportion of deaths caused by violent injuries, and the high
subadult mortality—population below 18 years representing up to 75% of
buried individuals—further support the scarcity of resources as the most
prevalent cause of death, at least in populations around settlements (Judd et al.
2018).

Most Sintashta–Potapovka kurgan burials present large central burial pits,
accompanied by abundant sacrificial remains in the form of skulls and limbs
of horses, large and small cattle, rich funeral complements including bronze
tools and weapons, artefacts of metal production, and objects related to chariots
(Kitov, Khokhlov, and Medvedeva 2018).

One of the defining innovations of this period was probably the use of
chariots driven into battle, as evidenced by an experimental study on use-wear
of Sintashta–Petrovka shield-like cheekpieces, designed to be used with the
teamed chariot horses for two-wheeled vehicles driven on the steppe

(Chechushkov, Epimakhov, and Bersenev 2018). This improvement in warfare may have helped the expansion of these and succeeding Eurasian steppe cultures, and the rise of elites among them.

Warring groups were strong enough to take and destroy an entire settlement, signalling an age of fully-fledged conflict, with a succession of changes in the defence systems and planning schemes of the settlements, which caused the concentration of the previously dispersed Poltavka mobile herder population around such fortified settlements to the east of the Urals (Anthony 2016).

The Sintashta culture is characterised by carefully laid-out circular shaped settlements (Figure 88) paired with recognisable kurgan cemeteries, and prominent warrior graves furnished with weapons and chariot grave goods. All Sintashta settlements were built near low spots on banks of small steppe streams, usually on the first terrace of a marshy, meandering stream close to winter grazing, in spite of the obvious concerns for security. In the Middle Volga steppes, similar settlements—with a preference for low terraces beside the wet floodplain, preferably behind a large marsh—begin later, ca. 1900 BC (Anthony 2016).

Figure 88. Description of archaeological site of Arkaim, Russia (Wikipedia).

The chronology of Sintashta–Petrovka is short, about 300 years, and can be divided into an earlier Sintashta phase (ca. 2050–1850 BC), and a later Petrovka phase (ca. 1850–1750 BC). Sintashta–Petrovka local communities of nucleated settlements include fortifications with ditches and earth walls, strengthened by wooden and stone constructions. Within settlements, houses are closely packed together in rows or circles in such a way that they share walls. Domestic artefact assemblages do not allow the separation of elites and commoners, even though stratification is visible in burial contexts (Chechushkov and Epimakhov 2018).

Potapovka (ca. 1950–1750 BC) appears in the Volga–Ural steppes as a variant of the Sintashta–Potapovka–Filatovka culture, also under strong Abashevo influence. Its main difference with the groups east of the Urals is the lack of fortified settlements, and thus the mobile nature of its economy, probably based on wagon camps. Nevertheless, domesticated animals are the basic diet of all groups, and there is no evidence for the production of domesticated cereals (Hanks et al. 2018).

Poltavka and Sintashta–Potapovka share nevertheless almost identical metals, ceramics (both similar to Abashevo), and mortuary rituals featuring horse cheek-pieces, paired horse sacrifices including whole horses, and some new ornaments, as well as very similar metal weapons (such as socketed spearpoints and waisted-blade daggers), which support their close relatedness. Distinct from the previous Poltavka period are the lavish graves, with far richer assemblages, featuring more weapons (Anthony 2016; Khokhlov 2016).

Social complexity arose in Sintashta–Petrovka based on herding economy. People who were skilful at managing walled villages, as well as those skilful warriors able to protect from military threats, probably formed the core of the chiefdoms that were created. The majority of the permanent population was involved in craft activities, though, including extraction of copper ores, metallurgy, bone, leather, and woodwork. The most labour-intensive part of the economy was haymaking. Control of craft by clans of miners, metallurgists, blacksmiths and casters also provided a source of power for elites in the fortified settlements. Their highly developed craft allowed for the improvement of the complex technology and substantial resources necessary to build two-wheeled vehicles (Chechushkov et al. 2018).

The fortifications of Sintashta represent only a portion of the population (also evidenced by the lack of them in Potapovka), whereas ordinary semi-mobile people, dedicated to herding—the main subsistence economy— inhabited the outside part of fortifications during the winter. This way, herds were grazed during the summer, and protected in portable shelters during the winter, in the best (fortified) spots dominated by the elites. Their activities and lack of rich assemblages suggest a less prestigious status of herders. Kuzmina (1994) cited a connection of the common Indo-Aryan word for a permanent village, *grāmas*, earlier meaning a circle of mobile wagon homes, situated together for defensive purposes for an overnight camp (Chechushkov 2018), which is compatible with an evolution of the word from highly mobile herders to its adoption as the designation of a permanent settlement.

Elites were imbued of a high social prestige that could be transferred to their children. This is reflected in the elaborate tombs (Figure 89) and sculptures, suggesting supernatural powers and ritual roles as much more important bases of their social prominence than control or accumulation of wealth, which seems nevertheless to have been prevalent within fortifications. Semi-mobile herders possibly represented ca. 30–60% of the population, while the local community represented ca. 40–70%. About 5% of them seem to have had the right to be buried under kurgans, and elites represented no more than 2–3% of the population, based on their extremely rich assemblages (Chechushkov 2018).

The social system of Sintashta (and probably also Potapovka) demonstrate a three-part social order, which seems to follow the same order of the Varna system of ancient India (similar also the ancient Iranian system) which consisted of priests (Brahmanis), rulers and warriors (Kshatriyas), free producers (Vaishyas) and laborers and service providers (Shudras) (Kuzmina 1994). In Sintashta–Petrovka chiefdoms, the elite consisted of priests and warriors (2-5%), dominating over local dependent producers (48-55%) and mobile herders (ca. 50–60%) of lower social rank (Chechushkov 2018).

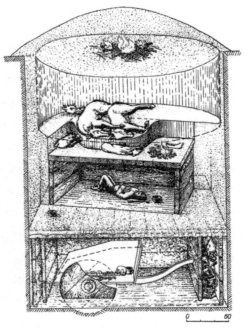

Figure 89. Aristrocratic burial at Sintashta in the southern Urals (ca. 2200–1800 BC). The warrior lies in the chariot with solid wheels, beneath two horses accompanied by the groom or charioteer. Image modified from Gering et al. 1992: 154, fig. 72, as it appears in Parpola and Carpelan (2005).

This social organisation, apart from being inherited from the similar Late Proto-Indo-European system, was reorganised into a system that favoured incoming Abashevo settlers, who were already skilled craftsmen, and probably emerged as the elite of warriors and priests among leading clans in each fortification. This happened probably during the aridification period and the associated massive migration of Poltavka herders north into the previous forest-zone, and east into the southern Urals, zones which became dominated by Abashevo settlers.

Sintashta–Potapovka emerged thus as a transcultural phenomenon associated with predominant clans of craftsmen—under the jurisdiction of warrior and priest elites—in what was most likely a social organisation based on local chiefdoms. Their variety of reinterpreted cultural traditions incorporated to local funeral rites and ceramic complexes point to interregional family and marriage relations, in particular with Abashevo and (in Sintashta) with quasi-Eneolithic cultures of the southern Urals and northern Kazakhstan (Vinogradov 2018)

To the west, Abashevo influence is felt especially in the eastern part of the Multi-Corded Ware tradition, near the Don–Volga interfluve, which points to the limit of the massive southward migration of Corded Ware-related groups (mostly from Abashevo) into the Pontic–Caspian steppe cultures since the mid–3rd millennium BC. Rituals performed for people of distinctive position have been excavated in kurgans along the Don River within the traditional Abashevo area, in particular the Filatovka and Vlasovo cemeteries, characterised by the composition of elements connected with the Late Catacomb and Multi-Cordoned Ware cultures, as well as to Sintashta and Alakul (Koryakova and Epimakhov 2007).

From the social point of view, these Filatovka-like burials display distinctive elements of a system of prestige good and warrior attributes, and have been interpreted as a western 'back-migration' of eastern Abashevo groups, as a Potapovka-related version of the Sintashta tradition, or as a component of the Novokumaksky horizon, representing in any of these cases a westward movement of Abashevo-related peoples from the Volga–Ural area. The newcomers possessed a powerful social and political organisation, as well as chariots, and probably encountered Late Catacomb and Abashevo settlers in the Don area. They most likely represent the original population from which early Srubna formed in its Pokrovka (east) and Berezhnovka (west) variants (Koryakova and Epimakhov 2007).

The phenotypic change in the steppe during this time is mentioned as the clearest example (since the Neolithic and until the Iron Age) of race—and thus probably ethnic—mixing of heterogeneous groups in Sintashta and Potapovka, compared to Yamna. Some other noticeable phenotypic changes occur related to 'eastern' features of the Trans-Uralian steppes arriving in Sintashta, possibly through the Seima–Turbino phenomenon, but also through its expansionist waves to the east (Khokhlov 2016).

VIII.18.2. Andronovo

Pottery, weapons, bone cheek-pieces for chariot driving, and graves of Sintashta style evolved into Petrovka ceramics, weapons, and ornaments, which in turn represent the origin of Alakul (ca. 2000 – 1700 BC), the earliest phase of Andronovo, which was mainly distributed in the whole steppe and forest-steppe of the Trans-Urals and northern, western and central Kazakhstan and Chorasmia (Anthony 2016).

Alakul represents thus the expansion of a cattle- and sheep-herding economy everywhere in the grasslands east of the Urals. It continued thus many customs and styles inherited from Sintashta, such as small family kurgan cemeteries, settlements with 10–40 houses built closely together, similar spear and dagger types, ornaments, and the same decorative motifs on pottery, such as meanders, hanging triangles, "pine-tree" figures, stepped pyramids and zig-zags (Anthony 2007). The petroglyph tradition of Andronovo people consists of depictions of everyday life, showing the importance of the wheeled transport (Novozhenov 2012).

Bearers of the Alakul tradition assimilated all the Trans-Uralian forest-steppe cultures included in its northern area, evidenced by burial rituals, and in the south it was limited by the steppe zone. Alakul settlements are located on the first river terraces or in the low lake banks, usually close to a large valley, and only rarely on high ground. The biggest settlements are located in the eastern territory, with general settlement surface not exceeding 10,000 m^2. Their planning structure is linear, houses organised into one or (rarely) two rows running along the river bank. Houses are rectangular postframe constructions, with internal space divided into partitions, containing wells, storage pits, and fireplaces, including metallurgical furnaces (Koryakova and Epimakhov 2007).

Alakul cemeteries involve some dozens of kurgans or multigrave funeral sites with one or two big graves in the centre, and many others in the periphery. They appear in the same area as settlements, without a visible demarcation of the "world of dead" and "world of living", as in Sintashta. Pottery in assemblages have flat bottoms with a ledge between the neck and shoulder, and their surface carefully treated, with more than half decorated, usually in the neck and shoulder with flat or comb stamps. The dominant burial rite is inhumation. Sacrifices are connected to large burials, and are represented by separate animal bones, usually head and extremities, with a composition similar to Petrovka: first cattle, then sheep, then horse. Dog sacrifices are characteristic of the Trans-Urals region, and fire played a significant role in Alakul rituals (Koryakova and Epimakhov 2007).

The Andronovo horizon then included the (at least partially unrelated) Fëdorovo style (ca. 1850–1450 BC), which covered essentially the whole of Turkmenistan and Kazakhstan, connected in the north to the forest-steppe, and in the west to eastern Kazakhstan and the Upper Yenissei. Fëdorovo ceramic and grave types represented an eastern or northern style with which the Alakul style interacted in many regions. Stratigraphic sequences show either Alakul turning into Fëdorovo, or mixed Alakul and Fëdorovo traits, which support the earlier appearance of the Alakul tradition. Alakul showed inhumation beneath earth kurgans, while Fëdorovo showed cremation graves with stone constructions (Anthony 2016).

The Fëdorovo shape and ornamentation are nevertheless distinct from the preceding Okunevo culture (ca. 2400–1950 BC), and continue therefore at least in part the Petrovka tradition from the southern Urals into northern, central, and eastern Kazakhstan, to the east into Tian Shan and Xingjian, mostly through the southern Siberia, connected to forest-steppe landscapes. It is found among Alakul sites in eastern Kazakhstan, Altai, and the Minusinsk lowland, and with mixed Alakul appearance in central Kazakhstan. It is also found to the south into southern Turkmenistan, which points to a long-range migration, possibly with the aim of obtaining control of local copper and tin resources, important for the production of high quality weapons (Parzinger 2006).

Known settlements are found on the first river terraces, near large river valleys, and can comprise several dozen houses following a linear pattern. Inhabited constructions vary from 30–300 m^2, having usually storage pits, niches, wells, and hearths. There are two building types: daylight framework dwellings, proper of central Asia (evidenced by pottery of Namazga tradition), and big, semi-subterranean multiroomed buildings of local origin. Metal objects include socketed arrowheads, chisels, awls, hooked sickles, knife–daggers, etc. and bone inventory include instruments for wool and leather processing, and bone arrowheads (Koryakova and Epimakhov 2007).

Kurgan cemeteries, containing dozens to hundreds of mounds, occupy the flat banks of water reservoirs, in contrast to the previously preferred flat terraces. They are usually surrounded by circular or rectangular fences, made of stone by cyst or masonry lying, or covered by an earthen mound along the outer contour. Fëdorovo kurgans are oval-shaped barrows smaller than Alakul mounds but with better expressed relief, containing one rectangular grave pit. Burials include cremation, when the deceased was burned somewhere outside the area and remains and ashes were placed into a grave (Koryakova and Epimakhov 2007).

The characteristic Fëdorovo material culture are well-made pots, thin-sided and with a smooth profile, with a technique that involved starting with the body (whereas Alakul vessels were manufactured on a model), with surfaces carefully treated, sometimes polished. The Fëdorovo decorative system, consisting of three zones, was designed according to a canon. Fëdorovo also shows imported central Asian pots made with white or red clay fabrics, largely undecorated, in forms such as pedestaled dishes, which point to the creation of stable, long-range exchange routes (Koryakova and Epimakhov 2007).

The expansion of the early Srubna–Andronovo pan-continental, macro-cultural horizon over central Asia (see Figure 90) brought innovations like bronze casting, chariotry, and aspects of pastoral economy and sedentary settlement types (based on year-round residence in timber houses) that connected territories isolated until then. The Andronovo cultural-historical community, or horizon, is the eastern branch of this entity, although mixed Srubna–Alakul settlements are found in the Cis-Ural region (Anthony 2016).

Interregional networks include trade of copper, tin, and horses, while material culture shows a patchier diffusion, with differences in rituals and distinctive elite behaviours suggesting also distinct ethnolinguistic groups. In the east, it interacted with north-western China across Tian Shan during the rise of the earliest Chinese state (Quijia, Erlitou, and early Shang periods), and with central Asia during the declining period (ca. 1800–1600 BC) of the BMAC and Namazga VI cultures (Anthony 2016).

The idea of simplistic 'waves' of eastward movement creating 'cultural clusters' is not clear, though, based on the quite early radiocarbon dates from eastern sites of the Fëdorovo type, which may range from ca. 2000 BC. Nevertheless, typological definitions of Fëdorovo can be ambiguous. The long-term localised regional development; the disparate distribution and technological patterns for metal artefacts, ceramics, burial practices and architectural styles; and local variations dependent on specific microregions, all question the validity of a simple demic diffusion model for all Andronovo-type material cultures in central Asia (Jia et al. 2017). Similarly, early Alakul-type funeral rituals included Abashevo elements in the Trans-Urals region, which suggests a multi-ethnic expansion of the culture, supported by the emergence of the Andronovo-like cultural horizon in the Trans-Uralian forest zone (Koryakova and Epimakhov 2007).

Continuation of the social organisation based on elites and kinship is reflected in indirect data: while labour invested in funeral rituals is reduced, symbols of prestige (maces, spearheads, axes, and chariotry complexes) maintain a similar trend, and cemeteries suggest a lineage-based organisation: in Alakul, based on the contraposition of central and peripheral burials. Bones of horses are found more often accompanying adults in central graves, while cattle are found accompanying adults and juveniles, while sheep and goats appear with infants (Koryakova and Epimakhov 2007).

Andronovo settlements in Kazakhstan were generally larger and more organised than those of Srubna in the Volga–Ural region. Pottery from settlements usually show multiple ceramic phases, interpreted as indicating a cyclical pattern of abandonment and reoccupation. In Andronovo settlements studied to date, the diet was based mainly on sheep–goats and cattle (with conflicting reports as to which predominated in which area), then horses; this suggests a more mobile pastoralism east of the Urals, based at least in part on sheepherding, in contrast to the mainly cattle-breeding economy in Srubna (Kuzmina 2008).

While livestock breeding was the main subsistence economy for both Alakul and Fëdorovo, and agriculture was not essential, fishing and hunting (basically elk) played quite a notable role in the northern zone. Around ca. 1400–1200 BC, steppe herders from central Asia were cultivating grain, including pastoralists of semi-alpine pastures of the Karasuk culture in the western Altai. The oldest evidence of agriculture in Andronovo comes from Tasbas in the Dzhungarian Mountains of eastern Kazakhstan This trend continued into the Iron Age (Koryakova and Epimakhov 2007).

Metallurgy was quite advanced and concentrated in several centres, whose products were distributed throughout temperate Eurasia. Tin–bronzes are prevalent in Andronovo (more than 90%), contrasting with Srubna (Chernykh 1992) probably due to central Asian tin deposits like those of the Zeravshan Valley near BMAC settlements, and on the middle Irtysh River in the western

Altai piedmont near Cherkaskul settlements. Large copper mines exploited during this period include Atasu and Dzezkazgan (Koryakova and Epimakhov 2007).

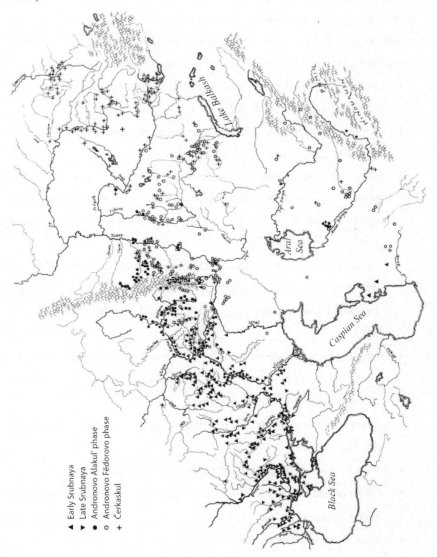

Figure 90. Distribution of the Srubnaya, Alakul Andronovo, Fëdorovo Andronovo and Cherkaskul monuments. Image modified from Parpola (2015): 62 Fig. 7.6, based on Chlenova 1984: map facing page 100.

VIII.18.3. Chemurchek

The Chemurchek culture (late 3rd – early 2nd millennium BC) emerged in the northern Xinjiang region of China, between eastern Kazakhstan and western Mongolia. It shows connections with Afanasevo, Okunevo, Andronovo and Karasuk, but represents a different Bronze Age culture. Relevant features described to date include (Jia and Betts 2010):

- Rectangular enclosures built using large stone slabs, with a size varying from 28 x 30 m to 10.5 x 4.4 m.

- Almost life-sized anthropomorphic stelae erected along one side of the stone enclosures.

- Single enclosures tend to contain one or more than one burial, all or some with stone cist coffins usually built with five large stone slabs (four for the sides and one on the top), sometimes with painted designs on the inside.

- Primary and secondary burials, with two potential orientations (of ca. 20° or 345°), sometimes decapitated bodies (up to 20) associated with the main burial, and bodies placed on the back or side with legs drawn up.

- Grave goods include stone and bronze arrowheads, hand-made gray or brown round-bottomed ovoid jars (together with clay lamps) and small numbers of flat-bottomed jars.

- Complex incised decoration in ceramics is common, but some vessels are undecorated.

- Stone vessels distinctive for the high quality of manufacture.

- Stone moulds show a relatively sophisticated metallurgical expertise.

- Some artefacts are made of pure copper.

- Sheep knucklebones (astragali) imply a tradition of keeping them for ritual or other purposes, indicating an economy based on domestic sheep.

viii.18.1. Late Indo-Iranians

Sintashta eventually transformed into the Petrovka–Alakul economy as part of eastward-expanding Andronovo horizon, while Potapovka and western groups evolved into Pokrovka and the expanding early Srubna culture. The identification of Srubna and some Andronovo complex-related groups with expanding Proto-Iranians, and the expansion of Proto-Indo-Aryans coincident with other groups of the Andronovo complex leads to a direct identification of the emergence of Sintashta–Potapovka–Filatovka cultures as the classic Proto-Indo-Iranian community (Anthony 2007; Mallory and Adams 2007; Beekes 2011).

This origin of the Sintashta–Potapovka–Filatovka population in Abashevo migrants mixing with indigenous East Yamna and Catacomb/Poltavka herders is evidenced by the intrusive Corded Ware-like ancestry and R1a1a1b-Z645 lineages (mainly of R1a1a1b2-Z93 subclades) in an area previously dominated by Yamna ancestry and R1b1a1b1b-Z2103 lineages. Nevertheless, there seems to be a clear genetic difference between eastern (southern Urals) and western (Volga–Ural) groups coincident with cultural ones (Allentoft et al. 2015; Narasimhan et al. 2018).

Four Potapovka samples from the Samara region, from Utyevka and Grachevka (ca. 2200–1800 BC), one reported as of hg. R1-M173, another R1a1a1b-Z645, form a wide cluster between Yamna and Corded Ware samples (Allentoft et al. 2015; Narasimhan et al. 2018). The admixture and PCA shift of Potapovka–Srubna samples relative to Sintashta–Andronovo individuals is compatible with more WHG and less EEF (ca. 28%) contribution (Wang et al. 2019), as found in north Pontic forest-steppe and probably forest samples near the Middle and Upper Dnieper regions.

Eight Sintashta–Petrovka individuals from varied settlements of the southern Urals (ca. 2200–1750 BC), one of hg. R1a1a1b2a2-Z2124 from Bulanovo, another R1a1a1b2a2a1-Z2123 from Stepnoe, form a tight cluster close to central European Corded Ware samples (Mathieson et al. 2015;

Narasimhan et al. 2018), with elevated EEF ancestry (ca. 42%), which may suggest less admixture of certain eastern Abashevo groups with forest-steppe peoples. Forty individuals from the Kamennyi Ambar V cemetery (ca. 2130–1750 BC) form also part of this cluster, with fifteen samples of hg. R1a1-M459, probably most R1a1a1b2-Z93; two R1b-M343, probably R1b1a1b1b-Z2103; and one I2-M438, probably I2a1b1a2a2-Y5606 (Narasimhan et al. 2018).

Ten outliers out of fifty individuals, usually interred on the margins of investigated kurgans, evidence the heterogeneity of the Kamennyi Ambar population, consistent with its interaction with neighbouring populations (Narasimhan et al. 2018). Increased Steppe ancestry is found in four individuals (ca. 2000–1700 BC), three brothers of 1–5 years, moderate outliers, probably of hg. R1a1a1b2-Z93, and one young male, a full outlier clustering with Yamna and Afanasevo, probably of hg. R1b1a1b1b3-Z2106. Ancestry related to Khvalynsk Eneolithic individuals is found in two males (ca. 2050–1650 BC), one of hg. R1b1a1-P297, the other R1b1a1a-M73, without archaeological context (see *§ii.3. Indo-Uralians* and *§viii.21.1. Yukaghirs*). West Siberian Neolithic ancestry is found in four individuals (ca. 2130–1750 BC), one probably of hg. R1b1a1b-M269, two Q1a2-M25, probably related to eastern populations with elevated 'Siberian' component, found later in steppe LBA samples. All these outliers with elevated proportions of different ancestries (and direct dates that are contemporaneous with the other individuals) show that this fortified site harboured peoples of diverse ancestries living side–by–side (Narasimhan et al. 2018).

Based on later samples from Iranian peoples in the steppes and Indo-Aryans from central Asia, and considering that sampled Sintashta–Potapovka individuals come from fortified settlements and higher status burials (most showing animal sacrifices), commoners of the Sintashta–Potapovka–Filatovka community were probably mainly descendants of Poltavka herders, and thus mainly of R1b1a1b1-L23 and I2a1b1a2a2-Y5606 subclades, whereas elites were mainly descendants of Abashevo migrants, and showed thus an increasing Y-chromosome bottleneck under R1a1a1b-Z645 lineages, in particular R1a1a1b2-Z93 subclades.

This integration of Abashevo elites, originally Uralic speakers, among Poltavka herders, of Pre-Proto-Indo-Iranian language, is conceivable in a region of highly fortified settlements, evolving through alliances of different groups against each other, akin to the situation found in Bronze Age Europe: a minority of Abashevo chiefs and their families would dominate over certain successful fortified settlements and wage war against other, neighbouring tribes for control over the best economic areas. After a certain number of generations, where the majority of the population—including commoners, females among the elites, and possibly slaves— retained the original Poltavka culture, the integrated elites would have replaced the paternal lineages of the region.

This explains the language shift of Corded Ware lineages from Abashevo in the steppe, and is supported by the archaeological continuity of Sintashta-Potapovka with Poltavka in terms of material and symbolic culture (Anthony 2007). The strong influence of Uralic speakers on Indo-Iranian pronunciation, visible in the characteristic phonetic Uralisms of Proto-Indo-Iranian, have to be put in relation with the strong influence of Indo-Iranian loanwords on northern Abashevo peoples—who probably maintained close contacts with their southern relatives as they became bilingual—visible in Finno-Ugric loanwords (see *§viii.15. Mordvins and Mari-Permians*).

The Andronovo cultural complex represents a complex historical phenomenon encompassing a large number of cultures from the Eurasian steppes, between the Ural Mountains in the west and the Minusinks Basin in the east, without clear ethnolinguistic borders. The most important Andronovo cultures, probably to be identified roughly with expanding Indo-Iranians, are Alakul and Fëdorovo, from central Kazakhstan to the Yenisei river in present-day Russia. Different genetic clusters have been found among Andronovo-related groups (Narasimhan et al. 2018), some of them likely representing distinct ethnolinguistic communities.

A common cluster with Sintashta–Petrovka is found in most Andronovo samples of the Trans-Urals steppes (ca. 2000–1400 BC). This "Western Steppe MLBA" cluster shows similar EEF contribution (ca. 26%) and haplogroup distribution. A subcluster of "Eastern Steppe MLBA" peoples is formed by certain samples which show statistically significant differences with the Western Steppe MLBA cluster, consisting mainly of additional West Siberian HG ancestry contribution (ca. 8%), suggesting that peoples of Western Steppe MLBA admixed with West Siberian HG-related peoples as they spread further east (Narasimhan et al. 2018).

Western Steppe MLBA samples include, apart from those of Sintashta–Petrovka, mainly samples from Alakul and derived groups: from central-east Kazakhstan, there is one from Ak Moustafa (ca. 1770 BC), of hg. R1a1a1b-Z93; six from Kairan, near the Ak-Koitas and Kara-Koitas mountain in Karaganda (ca. 1930–1630 BC), two of hg. R-M207; seven from Maitan (ca. 1880–1640 BC), including three likely R1a1a1b-Z645; one from Satan (ca. 1780 BC), of hg. R1a1a1b-Z93; one female from Alpamsa (ca. 1550 BC); three males from Karagash (ca. 1880–1600 BC), of hg. R1a1a1b-Z93. Other samples include two from Lisakovskiy, northern Kazakhstan (ca. 1870–1690 BC); six from Oy-Dzhaylau, southern Kazakhstan (ca. 1900–1400 BC), three of them likely R1a1a1b-Z93; one from Solyanka, western Kazakhstan (ca. 1640 BC); and four from Aktogai, south-east Kazakhstan (ca. 1600–1500 BC), three of them hg. R1a-M420, probably R1a1a1b-Z93 (Narasimhan et al. 2018). Other Western Steppe MLBA samples include individuals of the Mezhovska culture (see *§viii.17. Ugrians and Samoyeds*).

Eastern Steppe MLBA samples include four from Kytmanovo in the Altai Krai (ca. 1700–1300 BC), one of hg. R1a1a1b2a2-Z2124 (Allentoft et al. 2015); three from Dali (ca. 1900–1300 BC), one of hg. R1a1a1b2-Z93; four from Kazakh Mys (ca. 1730–1530), two likely of hg. R1a1a1b-Z645; one from

Zevakino (ca. 2000 BC) of hg. R1a1a1b2-Z93, before the Fëdorovo stage; fifteen from the easternmost area in Orak Ulus and near the Minusinsk Basin in Krasnoyarsk (ca. 1900–1400 BC), with eleven samples of hg. R-M207, ten of them probably R1a1a1b-Z645, including at least three R1a1a1b2-Z93, and a clear outlier from the Orak Ulus site (ca. 2000–900 BC), of hg. Q-M242, clustering with West Siberian Neolithic samples (Narasimhan et al. 2018).

Other likely Eastern Steppe MLBA samples include a group north of the Altai (ca. 1800–1400 BC), one of hg. R1a1a-M198 from Oust-Abakansty, Khakassia, one of hg. R1a1a-M198 from Solenoozernaya IV, Krasnoyarsk, and one of hg. C-M130(xC2-M217) from Tatarka cemetery, Charypovsky (Keyser et al. 2009); one from Mityurino in the central steppe (ca. 1590 BC) showing contribution from East Asian populations (de Barros Damgaard, Marchi, et al. 2018).

viii.18.2. Tocharians

It has been suggested that Afanasevo and Chemurchek find their "missing link" with the migration of Tocharians to the Tarim Basin in the sites of Gumuguo and Xiaohe in the Taklamakan desert of southern Xinjiang, based on the *Caucasoid* features of the investigated individuals. The finding of haplogroup R1a1a1b-Z645 (xR1a1a1b2-Z93) in 11 out of 12 investigated Tarim Basin mummies of the Xiaohe necropolis (Li et al. 2010), dated probably ca. 1700–1400 BC (Qiu et al. 2014), increases the doubts of the connection of these mummies to Afanasevo on one hand, and to speakers of Tocharian on the other (Mallory 2015). In fact, the penetration of Andronovo cultural influence is found in the western Tian Shan and the Ili River valley, but also further east and south (Kuzmina 2007).

If the Tarim Basin mummies actually belonged to ancestors of later Tocharian speakers, this would support a cultural assimilation of Pre-Tocharian peoples into expanding Asian clans of R1a1a1b-Z645 lineages (see above), and also that the migration of the Proto-Tocharian language to the Tarim Basin was coincident with the Andronovo expansion, which "had transformed the steppes from a series of isolated cultural ponds to a corridor of communication" (Anthony 2007). The likely presence of early contacts between Tocharian and Samoyedic (to the north), as well as the especially intense contacts with Indo-Iranian, support the close interactions of these groups around the Tian Shan and Altai mountains during the Bronze Age.

In particular, there are early contacts of Common Tocharian with one or several unknown Old Iranian dialects (which are not Avestan or Old Persian), which must date to the 2nd millennium BC, before the contacts of Tocharians with Middle Iranian languages (like Khotanese, Sogdian, and Bactrian). The prevalent terms related to specific concepts of merchandise or administration indicate that Iranians influenced Tocharians by imposing an administrative infrastructure (Carling 2005).

Investigated samples of the Sagsai tombs ("Mongun Taiga" culture for Russian archaeologists) from the Altai show an early sample from Takhilgat-Uzuur 5 (ca. 2700 BC), contemporary with late Afanasevo, of hg. Q-M242, with western and eastern genetic components, which supports an early infiltration of steppe ancestry in the region. Later individuals of the Middle and Late Bronze (ca. 1400–900 BC) show four samples of hg. R1b1a1b1-Z93, and three samples of hg. Q1b1a-L54, apart from a late one of hg. C-M130, which supports the arrival of R1b1a1b1-Z93 lineages in the region during the MBA (Hollard et al. 2014).

Nevertheless, from the paternal lineages found in modern Uyghurs (Zhong et al. 2013), those of haplogroup R1b1a1b-M269 could be explained only by either Afanasevo or Indo-Iranian R1b1a1b1b-Z2103 lineages. The presence of R1b1a1b-M269 (23%) among modern Yaghnobis of the Upper Zeravshan Valley (Cilli et al. 2019) also support the ancient distribution of this haplogroup in central Asia, potentially related to the Tocharian expansion.

VIII.19. Pontic–Caspian steppes

VIII.19.1. Multi-Cordoned Ware

The Babino or Multi-Cordoned Ware (MCW) culture succeeds the Catacomb culture in the north Pontic area, and is characterised by ceramics with cord-marked decorations (horizontal lines, diagonally hatched triangles) on their upper surfaces. It continues in the same region as Catacomb, expanding northward into the southern forest area of the Middle Dnieper culture. Metal objects show continuity with Catacomb tradition, but become more developed. Bronze adzes are longer, slimmer, and more curved, as are bronze shaft–hole axes, flange-hilted daggers, and polished stone axes. Round disc-toggles and extensively retouched flint arrowheads feature also prominently (Parzinger 2013).

Some of these objects—e.g. flange-hilted daggers, shaft–hole axes, round disc-toggles and flint arrowheads—have correlates in Sintashta burials. The leading MCW form is the outwardly round, in cross-section curved, bone disc with a large centre hole and an additional hole bored in the side, which occurs in the Abashevo culture. Both Abashevo and Sintashta are synchronous developments of the Pontic–Caspian steppe and forest-steppe regions, pointing to their interwoven cultural dynamics, probably through the expansionist Abashevo population (Parzinger 2013).

Kurgan earth-banks are not very high, and as a rule contain one to three burials in a pit with vertical walls. Stone cists and timber fittings in building-block fashion anticipate the construction of the succeeding Srubna culture. The dead are not uniformly orientated or placed, with supine and crouched on the side being frequent positions. Grave goods are scarce, as is ceramic (Parzinger 2013).

The number of settlements increases compared to previous periods, primarily on river terraces, with occasional fortified settlements on elevations pointing to more sedentary centres and higher interregional conflict than in previous periods. Houses include sunken earth-houses and ground-level wooden-post buildings with a rectangular plan. Animal husbandry is the main subsistence economy—mainly cattle, also sheep, goats, horses, and pigs—with no evidence of agriculture. Bridle cheek-pieces prove the use of horses for transport, probably to reach further pastures (Parzinger 2013).

VIII.19.2. Srubna and Sabatinovka

The LBA starts in the Eurasian steppes ca. 1900–1800 BC, contemporary with the central European Únětice EBA and Middle Helladic cultures of the Aegean MBA, and is represented by the rapid spread of a settled form of agropastoralism from a previous Sintashta–Potapovka–Filatovka core over a vast area to the east of the Urals, into the western Tian Shan and Altai Mountains, and to the west into the Danube River. This developing Srubna–Andronovo horizon has the Ural River and southern Ural steppes as its rough boundary, with some Andronovo (Alakul-type) materials on eastern Srubna settlements, and mixed Andronovo–Srubna settlements on the easternmost headwaters of the Samara River (Anthony 2016).

In the forest-steppe and steppe zones of the Don–Volga interfluve, reaching as far as the Samara Valley, the latest variant of Abashevo is often referred to as the Pokrovka type, dating to ca. 2000–1700 BC. Both the Abashevo culture and Pokrovka type are often seen as, respectively, the formative and terminal periods of the same cultural complex, successor of the Corded Ware culture and predecessor of the Timber Grave phenomenon. However, its relationship with the Catacomb, Fatyanovo, Balanovo and Sintashta is widely debated (Chechushkov and Epimakhov 2018).

The Pokrovka or early Srubna burials appeared first in the Middle Volga region as a transition of Potapovka pottery shapes, fabrics, and decorative motifs, representing thus an evolution of Potapovka potters. Pokrovka pottery and bronze weapon styles and grave types spread from the Volga–Ural steppes westward into the north Pontic steppes ca. 1800–1700 BC, probably thanks to the new warrior technology and also through intermarriages, as suggested by the adoption of local pottery-making customs. Compared to the previous period, it represents a transition to sedentary life, with the first permanent settlements, at the same time as pottery evolves to simpler ceramic types (Mochalov 2008).

The group shows usually several kurgans in each cemetery, with each kurgan displaying one to three burials, being the first period in the region with cemeteries containing entire social groups, individuals of both sexes and all ages. Burial pits are rectangular, and they tend to be fairly large in size. Bodies are usually interred placed on their left side in a contracted position, with their arms bent and hands in front of their faces, and orientated to the north. Burials are often lined with organic mats, and remains of large domesticated animals and ochre (and sometimes chalk) are frequent (Popova, Murphy, and Khokhlov 2011).

Some elite burials are marked by vessels with elaborated decoration and animal remains, and each separate cemetery seems to have vessels that copy ornamentation from bone rings found in burials with weapons. Burials of those with social power and prestige (such as Staroyurievo Cemetery, the Filatovka kurgan, etc.) are also accompanied by weapons, the insignia of power, and gold jewellery, and are conspicuously different from the rest of the graves of ordinary people. The same graves provide indirect evidence of the wide use of wheeled transport, such as bones of domesticated horse as draft animal, and studded elk-antler cheekpieces, the earliest artefacts of this kind in Eastern Europe, ca. 2000–1700 BC. Pokrovka is thus seen as an important part of the 'chariot horizon', representing a rapid extension of the chariot complex to vast areas of North Eurasia (Chechushkov and Epimakhov 2018).

The Srubna or Timber-Grave culture (ca. 1600–1200 BC) represents thus a unified culture of the Pontic–Caspian steppes after the expansion of Pokrovka groups from the Volga replaced the previous cultures up to Crimea (Suppl. Fig. 13). In the east, most Pokrovka settlements continue to be occupied during the mature Srubna period. In the west, Srubna settlements appear in steppe and forest-steppe regions, in areas previously occupied by Multi-Corded Ware groups; to the north, southern Abashevo groups are replaced by Srubna. Further north, northern Abashevo groups—from the forest region between the Oka and Vetluga rivers—transition to the Pozdnyakovo culture (Parzinger 2013).

Srubna (and Pozdnyakovo) pottery show vessel shape and ornamentation in common with Andronovo–Fёdorovo ware, although there is also some regional continuity of Srubna with Abashevo and MCW traditions. Ceramic comprises round to hour-glass shaped cups, bowls, and pots, as well as shoulder decorated (carved, pricked, impressed) with triangles, diamonds, and zigzag bands. Pottery shows homogeneous features with little regional or temporal variation, which is also common in Andronovo–Fёdorovo. The synchronous appearance and similarities of Pozdnyakovo (ca. 1850 BC) to the north of the forest-steppe in the Upper Don, Srubna to the west of the Urals, and Andronovo–Fёdorovo to the east, point to an expansion of related populations in eastern Europe (Parzinger 2013).

Copper objects like spearheads, hooked sickles, flange-hilted daggers, narrow shaft–hole axes, and bracelets with spiral ends may have been made with copper from Kargaly in the Urals, where there was intensive copper mining (as previously in Yamna). Kargaly may have been the largest mining complex in the 2nd millennium BC Europe, which implies a substantial export trade. Arsenical and antimony bronzes predominate in Srubna, in contrast to the tin–bronzes prevalent in Andronovo, which are probably responsible in part for the tin–bronzes (ca. 25% of the total bronze objects) found in Srubna, especially in elite burials (Chernykh 1992).

The scale of mining and metalworking displayed by Srubna–Andronovo materials suggest a complex organisation of the subsistence economy and trade networks beyond a simple herding economy. Kargaly copper was probably traded with help from wagons and traction animals (as suggested by specific pathologies) and through waterways up to Troy and the Aegean. Bone bridle attachments and bone discs with wavy ornamentation shows connections with the Mycenaean world through LBA cultures from the Carpathian Basin (Parzinger 2013).

Common burial rite includes simple earth pits covered with an earth mound. Some burials show timber-lined grave chambers, while others show simple branches covering the grave. Bodies were in the contracted position on the side, orientated to the north, and few grave goods if any are deposited. Elites are not marked in the burial ritual, and only rarely are richer graves with weapons found (Parzinger 2013). The Srubna society was probably hierarchical in nature, dominated by tribal chiefs, although the specialised organisation probably determined different, equally important heterarchical relationships.

This period represents a stabilisation of the population, with increased average life span (ca. 20 years, with men ca. 37 years, women ca. 39 years) compared to the previous period. A lesser proportion of children (ca. 30%) compared to the previous period and high survivorship to adolescence bring this period closer to those previous to the Sintashta–Potapovka crisis (Khokhlov 2016).

In the north Pontic area, agriculture remained important, with Noua–Sabatinovka showing full agropastoral economy with a wide variety of cultivated grains. To the east of the Dnieper and on the Donets, some settlements were also agropastoral, but agriculture featured less importantly in the subsistence economy, and domestic grains were mostly millet. Settlements in the west show fortifications—either embankments or trenches—with farmstead-like clusters of houses (Figure 91) which could be earth-houses, dugouts (*zemlyanki*), built in partially sunken areas (*poluzemlyanki*), or ground-level wooden-post buildings (Parzinger 2013).

In the east, settlements are small and unplanned, suggesting an extended family at each site. Herders from three or four distinct permanent settlements could occupy the same herding seasonal camps. Riverine bottomlands near marshes are preferred, either on the floodplain or on the first terrace. Subsistence economy in the Volga–Ural area does not show indications of agricultural diet, with agriculture having probably faded completely in this period. The main diet was cattle (50–60%), sheep, and goats for meat and dairy products (and occasionally pigs), apart from rare gathering and hunting traits, which frequently involve wolfs (Anthony 2016).

Figure 91. Reconstruction of house from Berezhnovka Srubna culture, between the Dnieper and the Volga, in the Ternopil history museum. Photo by Vodnik.

Srubna shows a multiscalar regional organisation represented by three circles of relationship, namely *obligation* (for copper mining), *cooperation* (for herding), and *affiliation* (for shared rituals). For example, a mining settlement would be supported by surrounding pastoral communities, and would contribute in turn ore to surrounding communities which had firewood for smelting (Anthony 2016). Long-ranging contacts are supported by the presence of Srubna settlers in the Low Amu-Dary'a (Chorasmia), where Srubna elements appear mixed with the Alakul material culture, representing the Tazabagyab culture, the southernmost extension of the culture (Koryakova and Epimakhov 2007).

The earliest date for horseback riding in warfare seems to have originated in this period, because of the rod-shaped artefacts (evolved from the tubular-bone-made cheekpieces used for chariots in Sintashta), suitable for rigid control of a ridden horse. The earliest specimens of that class, along with metal bits and weapons of a mounted warrior, date back to ca. 1200–1000 BC, which points to the Bronze Age as the emergence of this use (Chechushkov, Epimakhov, and Bersenev 2018). The first signs of bronze snaffle bit, improving control for horseback riding in more stressful and difficult activities (such as warfare), and developing horse dentistry among nomadic pastoralists ca 750 BC (Taylor, Bayarsaikhan, et al. 2018), point to continued innovations in the north-east Asian steppes after the expansion of Andronovo.

Their repeated violation of the canid-eating taboo across generations, at least in the Volga–Ural region, point to the connection of dog/wolf–as–warrior myth associated with violent death and war, identified with the symbol of the savage fury that the warrior desired in battle (Anthony and Brown 2017). This tradition was thus more likely associated with war–bands, but maybe also with the Indo-European myth of dogs guarding the entrance to the afterlife, and thus with the ancient dog–as–death symbolism.

The Sabatinovka culture (ca. 1500–1200 BC) appears as a western continuation of Srubna—overlapping with it—bounded by the steppe zone, from the Sea of Azov across the lower Dnieper until the lower Danube Valley. Ceramics show dishes, pots, and storage vessels with conical or slightly curved sides, simple bowls, and single and double-lugged vessels. The Noua culture (appearing ca. 1400–1300 BC) in the forest-steppes from the Dniester to Transylvania, appears at the same time as Sabatinovka, and with extensive similarities to it (see *§VIII.11. Balkan province*) supporting their common origin as part of the Srubna-like population expanding to the west (Parzinger 2013).

Beaded decoration on the neck and shoulders links the Sabatinovka culture to the Sargary–Alekseevka culture (part of Andronovo) east of the Urals, and other western Siberian groups ca. 1500–900 BC. The European custom of depositing bronze objects in hoards gained acceptance in the Pontic–Caspian steppe and forest-steppe regions reaching as far as the Urals, probably through the intermediary Noua culture in the west (Parzinger 2013).

Settlements in the north Pontic steppe and forest-steppe continued the previous MCW trend to grow, with houses becoming larger, multi-roomed complexes, and settlements divided in living and working quarters. Agriculture becomes part of the subsistence economy. Kurgans and flat cemeteries with the dead lying on the side (usually the left one) and head orientated to the east are the standard. Only exceptional rich warrior graves are seen (Parzinger 2013).

VIII.19.3. Simple-Relief-Band Ware

Around 1200 BC, new cultures emerge in the Pontic–Caspian region and beyond, showing largely continuity with the previous period, and an expansion of a common type pottery called Simple-Relief-Band Ware (SRBW), also *roller pottery* (*valikovaya keramika*), the steppes and into Central Asia (Suppl. Fig. 13). This period is coincident with Hallstatt A in central Europe and sub-Mycenaean materials in Greece. It is characterised by an increased aridity that may have caused a crisis of the subsistence economy, with a gradual extension of seasonal herding movements eventually leading to a decline in settled pastoralism, increased residential mobility (Parpola 2013).

SRBW cultures expanded the Srubna area westwards, northwards (to the Kamar River basin) and eastwards. In the east, the Alekseevka or Sargary culture (ca. 1500–900 BC) appeared in the steppe and forest steppe, with roller pottery remains occupying the whole Kazakhstan and Turkmenistan – previously occupied by the Andronovo culture (Parpola 2013).

In southern and central Asia, the Yaz I-related cultures (ca. 1450–1000 BC) replace the BMAC, but continue many of its traditions, among them fortifications, evidenced in Tillya Tepe. No burials are found in south-central Asia between ca. 1500–500 BC, which suggests that these cultures adopted the custom of exposing their dead to vultures and other carrion animals, a practice common in Zoroastrianism, whose first text—the Avesta, oldest Iranian composition known—is supposed to have been composed in this region at the end of the 2nd millennium BC (Parpola 2013).

The large-scale adoption of horse-riding warfare in central Asia and in the Iranian plateau, replacing chariotry, is probably associated with the rapid spread of the SRBW culture, and thus early Iranian languages. Terracotta figurines of horse rider in Pirak (ca. 1500 BC), in Pakistani Baluchistan, show anthropomorphic riders with bird's beaks, which has been related to pointed felt caps of mounted Saka warriors from frozen tombs of the Altai mountains (ca. 500–200 BC) featuring at the top the shape of a bird's head (Parpola 2013).

In the Pontic–Caspian steppes, this period is associated with a movement northward away from the steppe border, and the first evidence of agriculture (already ca. 1400–1200 BC) in the Don–Volga–Ural region as part of the subsistence economy. The volume of mining and metal production also declined (Kuzmina 2008).

The Belozerka culture (1200–900 BC) is a north Pontic culture with settlements scattered from the Don to the Danube. It shows partial continuity with Srubna-related traditions, but new ceramics are distinguishable, such as pot decoration with engraved, incised, and pricked diagonally hatched bands, or multi-line zigzag patterns. Also new are one- and two-looped curved brooches made of fine wire, while socketed axes, spearheads with semicircular blades, and grip-tongue daggers with lancet-shaped blades continue the Sabatinovka tradition (Parzinger 2013).

Settlements lay on high terraces above rivers and estuaries, with traditional *poluzemlyanki* houses coexisting with a new type, ground-level wattle-and-daub houses with stone cladding. Animal husbandry continues as the main subsistence economy, while agriculture is uncertain. Burial rite consist of flat inhumation cemeteries and kurgans, with side-crouched position predominant and scarce grave goods, also continuing the Sabatinovka culture (Parzinger 2013).

The Belogrudovka culture (ca. 1200–1000 BC) of the forest-steppe between the Dnieper and the Dniester shows inhumation and cremation in kurgans or flat cemeteries, with pottery continuing Noua and Sabatinovka traditions, while small and later finds show similarities with Belozerka in the steppe (Parzinger 2013).

Between the Dnieper and the Don, the forest-steppe and adjacent forest areas are occupied by the Bondarikha culture, with the eastern Prikazanskaya culture corresponding to the same tradition in the Volga–Kama region. It shows a distinct pottery with pricked- and comb–stamped traditions, but also clear connections with Belozerka and Belogrudovka wares in its round-bellied cylindrical-necked vessels and biconical pots with hatched triangles and angular multi-lined patterns (Parzinger 2013).

VIII.19.4. Scythians and Sarmatians

In the Early Iron Age, Simple-Relief-Band Ware cultures of the Eurasian steppes were succeeded by the early phases of likely Iranian-speaking mounted nomads (Suppl. Fig. 15).

The Proto-Scythian period in the north Pontic steppe features the appearance of horse-riding nomads associated with Cimmerian assemblages. These early groups are represented by the Chernogorovka tradition (ca. 1000–800 BC) and by Novochrekassk (ca. 800–700 BC), with differences based on grave construction, deposition of the body, and artefact form, with the later period showing Assyrian-influenced finds in warrior elite graves (Parzinger 2013).

To the north, in the Dnieper forest-steppes, Belogrudovka is replaced by the Chernoles culture, contemporaneous with Chernogorovka. It is in turn replaced by Zhabotin I (ca. 900–800 BC), contemporaneous with Novochrekassk, and contains pottery connecting it with the late Chernoles culture but also to the Cozia-Sakharna and Bessarabi I cultures of the lower

Danube. Zhabotin II forms a bridge to Bessarabi II, while Zhabotin III (beginning ca. 700 BC) represents a bridge into the early Scythian period, with the first Greek imported ceramics (Parzinger 2013).

On the Volga, the appearance of horse-borne nomads is identified as the Pre-Sauromatian tradition, characterised by weapons, horse harness, clothing, and pottery associated with the early Ananyino culture of the Middle Volga and traditions from the north Pontic area.

At the beginning of the Iron Age (ca. 850 BC) a rapid cooling and humidification of the steppes provided a fertile region that allowed for an increasingly mobile pastoral economy to expand into steppe regions that were too arid to exploit. The Early Scythian period in southern Siberia (ca. 800–700 BC) represents a new form of nomadic pastoralism based on cavalry-based warfare, armed with new recurve bows and mass-produced socketed arrowheads. Scythians expand rapidly from Tian Shan and the Altai Mountains to the Pontic–Caspian steppes and the Kuban region during the early 7th century BC (Koryakova and Epimakhov 2007).

This period is marked by broadly shared artistic styles (the "Animal Style"), and styles of horse trappings and weapons; by a return of the Pontic–Caspian steppes to mobile settlements in wagon camps; and is especially marked by lavish graves (Figure 92) of princes and kings (Parzinger 2013; Anthony 2016). Different groups (including Sarmatians and Saka) show cultural similarities but also differences in settlement, subsistence economy, political organisation, and mobility. For example, certain Scythian groups in the north Pontic forest-steppe apparently form some non-mobile, agriculturally-orientated urban societies concentrated in fortified settlements.

Scythians and Sarmatians are traditionally identified as eastern Iranian peoples, judging from personal and god names and words attested from Greek and Persian sources, as well as by toponyms in the steppes and archaeological remains that correlate with rituals specified in later Persian texts (Parpola 2018).

Figure 92.Scythian warriors drawn after figures on an electrum cup from the Kul'Oba kurgan burial (ca. 400–350 BC) near Kerch. The man on the leftwearing a diadem is likely to be the Scythian king. Hermitage Museum, St. Petersburg.

To the north, the Gorodets culture from the forest-steppe zone (north and west of the Volga) shows fortified settlements during the Iron Age. Incursions of Gorodets iron makers into the Samara valley are seen by deposits of their typical pottery and a bloom or iron in the region (Kuznetsov and Mochalov 2016). This attests to continued contact between forest and steppe in the Cis-Ural region.

viii.19. Iranians

The language spoken by peoples of the Pokrovka–Srubna culture of the Pontic–Caspian steppes, developed from Potapovka–Filatovka and late Abashevo groups, was most likely Iranian. The presence of some early Proto-Iranian loanwords in Finno-Ugric supports the continued presence of early Iranian tribes in contact with the north-eastern European forest zone, and the absence of clear Proto-Indo-Aryan borrowings suggests that this community was already separated, probably expanding with Andronovo into central Asia.

Sampled individuals of Srubna include one of the Pokrovka phase from Mikhailovsky, in Samara (ca. 1900–1750 BC), of hg. R1a1a1b2-Z93, clustering close to Srubna and Sintashta samples, showing the first lineage of *Yersinia pestis* that possessed all vital genetic characteristics required for flea-borne transmission of plague in rodents, humans and other mammals. It belongs to a different strain from that found in European samples associated with earlier steppe migrations (see *§vii.1. Western and Eastern Uralians*), suggesting a further development and origin of expansion of the disease in the Bronze Age Pontic–Caspian steppes (Spyrou et al. 2018).

Classical Srubna individuals from Samara (ca. 1900–1200 BC) show a continuation of the wide Potapovka cluster, with slightly more EEF ancestry than Potapovka (ca. 32%), consistent with increased Abashevo-related contribution. The ancestry of Srubna samples show an intermediate position between Sintashta and Yamna (Mathieson et al. 2015; Narasimhan et al. 2018; Krzewińska, Kılınç, et al. 2018; Järve et al. 2019), with a slight 'northern' shift relative to Sintashta-Andronovo, compatible with their increased WHG due to admixture with forest-steppe peoples, supported by the finding of an earlier north Pontic outlier close to Neolithic samples (see *§VI.2.2. Catacomb*).

Reported haplogroups are dominated by R1-M173, in particular R1a1a1b2-Z93 (seven samples), with one R1a1a1b2a2-Z2124, one R1a1a1b2a2a1-Z2123. Two outliers from the Samara region, one from Barinovka, of hg. R1a1a1b2-Z93, and one from Spiridonovka (ca. 1850 BC), show more ANE ancestry, clustering closer to Afontova Gora (Mathieson et al. 2015), in line with West Siberian-like outliers of Sintashta (see *§viii.18.1. Late Indo-Iranians*).

Most Srubna–Alakul samples from Kazburun and Muradym in the Trans-Volga forest-steppe (ca. 1900–1600 BC) show high genetic diversity, and an admixture similar to Srubna samples from Samara, clustering with them. All five Srubna–Alakul samples are reported of hg. R1a1-M459, two are probably of hg. R1a1a1b1a2-Z280$^+$, and four of hg. R1a1a1b2-Z93$^+$, including one R1a1a1b2a-Z94$^+$, one R1a1a1b2a2a1-Z2123$^+$, and one R1a1a1b2h-YP5585$^+$. This heterogeneity of lineages, including 'northern' R1a1a1b1a2-Z280, probably reflects closer contacts of this region with neighbouring Abashevo and Balanovo settlers, also consistent with the longer contacts of Iranian with Finno-Ugric.

There is a Srubna–Alakul outlier (ca. 1745–1620 BC) showing more Near Eastern ancestry, clustering between modern Mordovians and northern Caucasus, in a new Iranian Steppe cluster 'south' of Yamna, later shared also by some Cimmerians, most Sarmatians, and some Scythians (Krzewińska, Kılınç, et al. 2018). The admixture found in this late outlier may be thus related to the expansion of Srubna peoples into the Lower Danube, evidenced by the contribution of EEF ancestry and 'south-eastern' PCA position of samples from Merichleri (ca. 1690 BC), and from Szólád, Hungary (ca. 1900 BC), of subclade R1a1a1b2-Z93 (Mathieson et al. 2018) and R1a1a1b2a2a1-Z2123 (Amorim et al. 2018) respectively, both most likely related to vanguard Srubna settlers that developed the Noua–Sabatinovka culture (see *§viii.11. Thracians and Albanians*).

Whereas Srubna probably represented part of the earliest Proto-Iranian community, at the same time as other (probably early Western Iranian) groups migrated to the south into the Zeravshan valley (see *§viii.20. Dravidians and Indo-Aryans*), it is likely that early Eastern Iranian tribes like Scythians or Sarmatians emerged from regions near the southern Urals (Krzewińska, Kılınç, et al. 2018), given the contribution of WSHG ancestry (up to 25%) found. Similar ancestry is found to the east in different Andronovo sites, mainly east Alakul or Fëdorovo individuals from east Kazakhstan and the Altai: two outliers from Alakul Maitan (ca. 1880–1640 BC), two from Kairan (ca. 1750–1550 BC), and two from Oy-Dzhaylau, one early male (ca. 1675 BC) of hg. R1a1a1b2-Z93, and one female (ca. 1500 BC); and Zevakino in eastern Kazakhstan, continuing previous Fëdorovo stage with one MLBA male (ca. 1500 BC) of hg. R1a1a1b2-Z93, and six later LBA–Iron Age individuals (ca. 1200–900 BC), four of hg. R1a1a1b-Z645, including two R1a1a1b2-Z93, one of hg. R1b-M173, and one Q-M242.

Sampled Cimmerians from the north Pontic steppe show a correspondingly increased amount of Siberian component, sharing more drift with the far eastern Karasuk population compared to the geographically closer Srubna. Pre-Scythian nomads from the Pontic–Caspian steppes include one from Mokra (ca. 923 BC), one from Glinoe Sad (ca. 873 BC), of hg. Q1a1a1a-Y558, and one individual from the Mezőcsát culture (ca. 980–830 BC), of hg. N-M231

(Gamba et al. 2014). Three more recently reported samples include a Thraco-Cimmerian one clustering with south-east Europeans in the PCA, but with 55% of 'Asian' alleles; and two samples from Ukraine clustering between Srubna and Saka samples, of hg. R1a1a1b-Z645 and R1a1a1b2a2-Z2124 (Järve et al. 2019). The distinct ancestry and divergence of lineages may support the existence of a 'Karasuk-Cimmerian cultural-historical community' clearly distinct from East Iranian peoples (Krzewińska, Kılınç, et al. 2018).

There is thus more genetic diversity in Cimmerians compared to earlier and later groups of the steppe, with increasing Near Eastern admixture through time reflecting admixture with Srubna-like populations, and the most recent sample from Glinoe Sad (ca. 860 BC) showing the typical Iranian Steppe cluster and hg. R1a1a1b2-Z93. The heterogeneity of Cimmerians and their original genetic links to Karasuk and East Asians obscure their ethnolinguistic identification, although the relationship of this culture with the emergence of Ananyino in the Middle Volga may be related to certain Altai traits in Uralic languages, including the spread of some N-M231(xN1a1-Tat) lineages among Cis-Urals (Finno-Permic) and Trans-Urals (Ugric) populations, up to Hungary.

Early Scythians show a corresponding loose cluster between Okunevo and Karasuk samples (see *§viii.17. Ugrians and* Samoyeds), evidencing the admixture of Steppe MLBA with WSHG. Early Scythians include those from the Zevakino-Chilikta group (ca. 9th–7th c. BC), early Central Sakas (ca. 800–750 BC), one of hg. E-M96; later Central Sakas, of the Tasmola culture (ca. 760–680 BC), two of hg. R1a1a1b2a2-Z2124; and individuals from Andy Bel (ca. 7th–6th c. BC). There is a clear separation in admixture between eastern and western Scythians, and among Inner Asian groups, with Central Sakas showing the highest WSHG admixture (ca. 50%), supporting the confederal nature of the Scythian organisation (de Barros Damgaard, Marchi, et al. 2018).

Forty-four later samples from Pazyryk in eastern Kazakhstan (ca. 4th–3rd c. BC), one of hg. R1a1a1b2a2-Z2124+, and ten Sakas from the Tian Shan region (ca. 450–80 BC), including two R-M207, three R1-M173, and one R1a1-M459, show contributions from CHG/IN-related ancestry (ca. 5%), apart from Steppe MLBA (ca. 70%) and WSHG (ca. 25%), with a corresponding 'southern' shift in the PCA (Unterländer et al. 2017). This is compatible with the migration of peoples from Turan into the Kazakh steppes and forest-steppe region in the mid–2nd millennium BC (see *§viii.20. Dravidians and Indo-Aryans*), since this ancestry is also found in the Mezhovska culture from the Trans-Urals forest region (ca. 1500 BC, see *§viii.17. Ugrians and Samoyeds*), and later among Scythians from the southern Trans-Urals and north Pontic area, in a "Southern Steppe MLBA cluster" (de Barros Damgaard, Marchi, et al. 2018).

Other two Pazyryk samples from a "frozen grave" in Ak-Alakha-1, both presumably of a high social status, show hg. N (Pilipenko, Trapezov, and Polosmak 2015), with haplotypes shared with modern Yakutian populations (Tikhonov et al. 2019), which may indicate the infiltration of this haplogroup (possibly N1a1a1a1a-L392) among Scythian populations close to Lake Baikal. Similarly, sampled Scytho-Siberians of Aldy-Bel and Sagly show typically East Asian mtDNA compared to western Scythians, and more diverse mitochondrial haplotypes close to southern Siberia. In terms of Y-DNA, they show nine R1a-M420, at least two of them R1a1a1b2a-Z93, probably five Q1b1a3-L330, and one N-M231. This diversity has been interpreted as proof of the multicultural nature of eastern Scythian groups, with those close to the Altai potentially representing Altaic speakers (Tikhonov et al. 2019).

Sampled *Scythians* from Kazakhstan are more spread out and drawn towards East Asian populations, although still positioned 'west' of the Central Saka—despite originating from neighbouring burial mounds of the same Tasmola culture—and most of the Eastern Scythians, itself a very heterogeneous group both culturally and genetically (Järve et al. 2019). The shift to east Asian ancestry compared to Srubna is accompanied by mtDNA lineages, which show equal proportion of east and west Eurasian origin in eastern Scythians, but increasing eastern origin in western Scythians, from zero in early samples to 18-26% in later periods (Unterländer et al. 2017).

Sampled Scythians from Nadezhdinka, in the Samara region (ca. 375–203 BC), of hg. R1a1a1b2a2a1-Z2123 (Mathieson et al. 2015), as well as three sampled Scythians from the north Pontic region near the Dnieper (ca. 790–115 BC), one of hg. R1a1a1b2a2a1-Z2123+, form part of the Iranian Steppe cluster, although one shows a high genetic drift with previous Srubna samples. This Western Iranian Steppe cluster is also shared by the previous Mezőcsát sample from Hungary, and have East Asian ancestry shared with Cimmerians and Sarmatians.

North Pontic Scythians close to the described Southern Steppe MLBA cluster, showing more Near Eastern ancestry, includes one South-Eastern Steppe cluster, in common with south-eastern Europeans, one of hg. R1b1a1b1b3-Z2106+, one E1b1b1a1b1-L618+; and an intermediate cluster between Iranian Steppe and south-eastern Europeans, with one hg. R1b1a1b1a2c-Z2103+ and one I2a1b1a2a1b-Y7219+. A northern European cluster among Scythians, including one sample of hg. R1b1a1b1a1a2-P312+, suggests close contacts of the north-west Pontic area with Celtic populations from Hallstatt. Similar clusters can be seen in Scythian samples from Ukraine, which show four hg. R1a1a1-M417 (one of them R1a1a1b-Z645, another R1a1a1b2a-Z93), one hg. J2a1a1a2b1b-M319, and one Q1b1a3-L330 (Järve et al. 2019).

This high intragroup diversity compared to Bronze Age groups is also found in sampled Hungarian Scythians (ca. 756-370 BC), one of hg. R1-M173, who falls between Iranian Steppe, South-Eastern Steppe, and northern European clusters (de Barros Damgaard, Marchi, et al. 2018), while recently sampled Scythians from south-central Ukraine form part of three similarly described clusters (Järve et al. 2018). This temporal and geographical transect of Scythians offers a picture of variable admixture in the north Pontic area, proper of migrating nomadic settlers interacting with local populations, and of cultural dominance rather than population replacement (see *§viii.21.2. Turkic peoples and Mongols* for more on central Asian nomads).

Sampled Sarmatians from the southern Urals show a cluster similar to the described Iranian Steppe one, showing genetic continuity over centuries despite the supposed cultural shift and suspected earlier population replacement between early and middle/late Sarmatians (Krzewińska, Kılınç, et al. 2018). Assessed individuals include Early Sarmatians from Pokrovka in the southern Urals (ca. 500–100 BC), one of hg. R1b1a1b1b-Z2103 (Veeramah et al. 2018); Sarmatians from the central Asian steppe (ca. 50–15 BC), one of hg. I2b-L415, from the Caspian steppe (ca. 85 BC – AD 15), three of hg. R1-M173, one of hg. R1a1a1b2a2a-Z2125 (de Barros Damgaard, Marchi, et al. 2018); and late Sarmatians from the south-east and south-west Urals (ca. AD 55–320), three of hg. R1a1a1b2a2-Z2124[+], one R1a1a1b2a2a1-Z2123[+] and the other R1a1a1b2a2b-Z2122[+] (Krzewińska, Kılınç, et al. 2018). Other reported Scythian-Sarmatian samples from the southern Urals show a very compact cluster (except for one outlier drawn to East Asia), poisitioned between Scythians from Ukraine and Tagar samples; three of them are of hg. R1a1a1b-Z645, and one hg. E2b1-M90, and they cluster close to a Sarmatian sample from the North Caucasus, of hg. Q1b1a3-L330 (Järve et al. 2019).

The Wusun and Kangju are probably also East Iranian groups that became isolated after the expansion of Xiongnu-related nomads, and re-emerged into the central steppe from south-east of the Tian Shan mountains, evidenced by their Iran Neolithic-related ancestry and the lack of East Asian admixture compared to Iron Age Sakas. This interpretation of resurging East Iranian population is also supported by their position in the PCA, between Sarmatians and Sakas (de Barros Damgaard, Marchi, et al. 2018).

Ancient Alans (AD 4th–14th c.) and individuals of Saltovo-Mayatsk culture (AD 8–10th c.) from the northern Caucasus and Middle Don basin cluster with Near Eastern / Caucasus individuals. Saltovo-Mayatsk shows six samples of hg. G2-P287, one J2a-M410, and two R1-M173, one among them R1a1a1b2a2-Z2124. Among six samples from the northern Caucasus one shows hg. R1a1a1b2a2a3-S23592[+] (de Barros Damgaard, Marchi, et al. 2018); and among two other samples also from North Ossetia (AD 300-400), there is one of hg. R1a1a1b2a2-Z2124, and one G2a-P15 (Afanas'ev et al. 2014).

VIII.20. Turan and South Asia

The Namazga culture of farming towns (Namazga, Anau, Altyn-Depe, Geoksur) was situated on alluvial fans where rivers that flowed off the Iranian plateau emerged in central Asia. Turquoise deposits were found in middle Zeravshan, near the farming colony of Sarazm (founded before ca. 3500 BC).

Late Kelteminar (ca. 3000–2000 BC) pottery was found there, and it had turquoise workshops in the desert near Lower Zeravshan, as well as metal deposits of copper, lead, silver, and tin. Turquoise was traded—along with sources in north-eastern Iran—into Mesopotamia, the Indus Valley, and even Maikop. Arsenical bronze is found, but objects show mostly pure copper, while tin-copper appear only rarely if at all.

The Bactria and Margiana Archaeological Complex (BMAC), also called Oxus Civilisation (ca. 2200–1450 BC), was a hierarchical society based on intensive agriculture and specialised craft production of metal and precious stone objects for prestige display and long-distance exchange. Their economy based on water management was likely favoured by the aridification event ca. 4.2 ka BP that also affected Europe (Luneau 2019). Immigrants probably came from the northern Iranian plateau to colonise the Murghab River delta, with their early pottery showing similarities with Namazga V-types. They built large towns surrounded by thick yellow-brick walls, with narrow gates and high corner towers. In the centre of walled palaces or citadels, temples were also built (Anthony 2007).

The early BMAC colonisation phase was followed by a much richer period ca. 2000–1800 BC, with new walled towns spreading to the upper Amu Darya valley. Trade and crafts flourished in the crowded streets of fortified towns, with metalsmiths making beautiful objects of bronze, lead, silver, and gold, such as metal figures, crested bronze shaft–hole axes with down-curved blades, tanged daggers, mirrors, pins, and distinctive metal compartmented seals (Anthony 2007).

A mixed agropastoral economy including cattle and goat emerges in Turan at least ca. 2200 BC, transitioning from the previously prevalent sheep–goat herding economy (Taylor, Shnaider, et al. 2018). Evidence of the appearance of horses in funeral rites and imagery—but never for meat consumption—is seen from ca. 2100–2000 BC, with scattered samples of Sintashta- and Abashevo-type pottery in the Zeravshan Valley. Until that moment, the typical BMAC equids were onagers, as in most of the Near East, and wagons—found in funeral remains—were pulled by cattle (Anthony 2007). The colonisation of the Ili delta in southern Kazakhstan had begun before 2000 BC by groups of hunter-fishermen and early shepherds, possibly semi-settled in niches of the upper course, while the bulk of the Bronze Age findings belongs to a second phase after 2000 BC, with groups already acquainted with seasonal transhumances between summer camps in mountain meadows, autumn and spring transitions across piedmonts, and winter camps in the green alluvial plains of the lower part of the delta system (Deom, Sala, and Laudisoit 2019).

The BMAC culture expanded to the Gorgan area of northern Iran, where a horse-drawn chariot is depicted on a cylinder seal from Tepe Hissar III B. Tin–bronze appear especially in Bactria, closer to Zeravshan, after ca. 2000 BC, suggesting an establishment or expansion of tin mines of Zeravshan during this time. With the emergence of tin trade between BMAC and Assyrians from Cappadocia, in the 20th century BC, the horse-drawn chariot appeared in the Near East. This expansion from south-central Asia through northern Iran into the Near East has been associated with the arrival of Mitanni Aryans into Syria (Parpola 2013).

Contacts with steppe pastoralists becomes evident ca. 1900–1800 BC, with materials of early Andronovo (Alakul) types among tin miners. Also, an elite grave on the Zeravshan Valley in Tajikistan (Figure 93) shows a horse-drawn chariot with Sintashta–Arkaim-type bits and bone cheek-pieces, as well as a bronze sceptre topped with the image of a horse, but typically BMAC ceramics (Bochkarev 2010). It is likely that Petrovka had a metalworking colony at

Tugai already ca. 1900 BC, with steppe tribes eventually taking control of the ore sources of Zeravshan (Anthony 2007).

Between 2000–1800 BC, BMAC styles and objects (small jars made of carved steatite) appear in sites and cemeteries across the Iranian plateau, with many elements on the border between the Harappan and Elamite Civilisations suggesting a movement of BMAC peoples into Baluchistan. Chariots were simultaneously introduced in BMAC, Iran and the Near East ca. 2000–1900 BC (Anthony 2007).

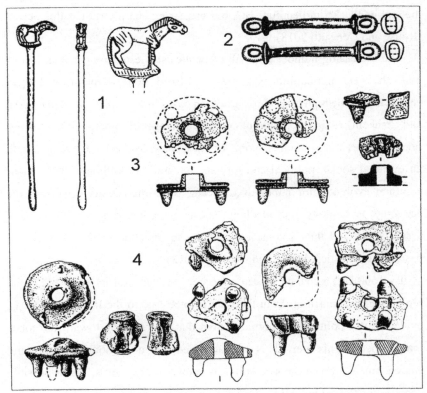

Figure 93. Materials from an aristocratic burial at Zardcha Khalifa in the Zeravshan Valley. (1) Horse-head sceptre pin of bronze of the same type as those found in Sintashta (4) [not to scale]. (2) two horse bits of bronze. (3) fragments of cheek-pieces of bone. Modified from Parpola and Carpelan (2005), where images from Bobomulloev 1997 and Gening et al. 1992 are used.

By 1800 BC, political centralisation fades, suggesting loosening of state-level structures. The late BMAC period (ca. 1800–1600 BC) shows a shift from a tiered system of urban centres, villages and hamlets to a more dispersed pattern of smaller-scale agricultural settlements. Walled towns decrease sharply in size, with each settlement developing its own pottery, and Andronovo–Tazabagyab coarse-incised pottery appearing widely in the BMAC countryside (Anthony 2007).

The first evidence of campsites with a distinct ceramic tradition supports an influx of mobile pastoralists from the central Eurasian steppes and foothills—and thus farmer-pastoralist interactions—appearing rather early, at the end of the 2nd millennium BC, but increasing sharply during this period (Rouse and Cerasetti 2018).

The increasing number of small campsites suggests stronger interactions with the new agricultural settlements. Mixed pottery found in kurgan cemeteries of the highlands above Bactrian oases in modern Tajikistan (Vaksh and Bishkent). This is a period of combined control of mineral trade (copper, tin, turquoise) and pastoral economy (horses, dairy, leather) in the region, with an eventual social, political and military integration (Anthony 2007). Their common evolution for hundreds of years, with interactions in subsistence economy, technology, and ideology, attests nevertheless also to the lack of assimilation, and thus a conscious attempt to maintain distinct farmer and pastoralist identities (Rouse and Cerasetti 2018).

By 1600 BC, a change is seen in access to water—essential for life in the region—in the transition from the Late Bronze Age to the Iron Age (Yaz I), evidence of a political–economic system that was shifting toward territorial management. This period is characterised by a combination of sand encroachment from the north, shifts in known watercourses, and a possible decrease in flows, as well as the invasion of people represented by 'steppe' pottery, with declines and abandonment of major population centres (Rouse and Cerasetti 2016).

Many settlements of the old BMAC region, as well as trading settlements and outposts in eastern Iran, are abandoned. Sites remaining in the agricultural heartland of the southern Mughab region are campsites with non-Oxus pastoral economy, although some evidence exists as to the persistence of some agricultural activities (Rouse and Cerasetti 2018).

Pastoral economies spread across Iran and into Baluchistan, and are followed by the Gurgan Buff Ware (ca. 1100–1000 BC), which appears in south-central Asia, probably an expansion of the Yaz-I related cultures. This is followed by the Late West Iranian Buff Ware, which appeared ca. 950 BC in the regions where Median and Old Persian were first attested (Parpola 2013).

BMAC-related settlements expand to the borderlands of south Asia, including the Gandhara Grave culture (ca. 1600–900 BC) around the Swat Valley, the first local culture to have domesticated horses. The horse and chariot are essential in Rigvedic hymns, which were potentially composed ca. 1200–1000 BC in the northern Indus Valley (Parpola 2013).

viii.20. Dravidians and Indo-Aryans

Thirteen individuals of the Chalcolithic–to–Bronze Age urban settlement from Tepe Hissar in eastern Iran (ca. 3700–2000 BC) show homogeneous Iran Neolithic-like ancestry without significant genetic drift over the whole period, suggesting little impact of migrations and a substantial population size. In spite of this, varied haplogroups have been reported, including J2a-M410, T1a-M70, L2-L595, all with connections to the Fertile Crescent area (Narasimhan et al. 2018).

Two samples from Sarazm (ca. 3600–3500 BC), and twelve samples of the East Anau group of tribes from the Geoksiur Oasis (ca. 3500–3000 BC), three of hg. J-M304, one of hg. I2-M438, and one of hg. Q-M242, also belong to this Iranian Neolithic-like cluster, and evidence the likely dispersal of tribes from south-eastern Iran. Samples from the Sumbar Valley also show a similar ancestry, from the Eneolithic to the LBA Sumbar culture, in samples from Tepe Anau (ca. 4000–3000 BC), two of hg. R2-M479; from Parkhai (ca. 3500–1000 BC), one of hg. G-M201; and one from Sumbar (ca. 1300 BC), of hg. R2a-M124. A Bronze Age Turan sample from Darra-i-kur (ca. 2700 BC), probably of hg. R1b1a1a-M73, and two from Shahr-i-Sokhta, Iran (ca. 2800–2500 BC), of hg. J2a1-L26, also show similar ancestry (Narasimhan et al. 2018).

A cline of Anatolian agriculturalist-related admixture ranging from ca. 70% in Chalcolithic Anatolia, to ca. 33% in eastern Iran, to ca. 3% in far eastern Turan was probably established early, consistent with the spread of wheat and barley agriculture from west to east (ca. 7th–6th millennia BC), which suggests that Anatolian agriculturalists may have contributed to spreading farming economies into central Asia as they contributed to Early European farmers (Narasimhan et al. 2018).

Two outliers from Shahr-i-Sokhta, one early (ca. 3100 BC) the other late (ca. 2500 BC), both of hg. J-M304, show a distinctive ancestry found also in a BMAC outlier from Gonur (ca. 2300 BC), with AASI-related ancestry (ca. 14-

42%) and the rest related to Iran Neolithic and West Siberian Neolithic, without Anatolian Neolithic ancestry. Based on later samples from the Swat region, these early outliers, so-called Indus Periphery samples, are the best proxies for the population of the Indus Valley Civilisation, with an ancestry formed from Iranian Neolithic migrants—likely originating from an eastern region, given the lack of Anatolia Neolithic-related ancestry—and a population migrating from South Asia (Narasimhan et al. 2018).

The admixture of both groups is estimated ca. 4700–3000 BC (Narasimhan et al. 2018), which is consistent with the migration of populations from eastern Iran into territories occupied by AASI-like people causing the emergence of the Harappan Civilisation. The language spoken in the Indus Valley was probably Proto-Dravidian, based on the later finding of this ancestry to the south, and on the dispersal of the culture (ca. 2000 BC) coinciding with linguistic guesstimates of the proto-language. It is unclear if this language was brought by migrants from Iran, or if it was adopted by them from the local AASI-like populations, especially without a proper sampling and reported haplogroups directly from the culture, although the former seems a priori more likely, based on the different languages associated with AASI in south Asia.

Sixty-eight individuals belonging to the BMAC culture show a genetic cluster similar to preceding groups in Turan, showing Iran Neolithic ancestry (ca. 60%) with lesser contributions of Anatolian Neolithic (ca. 21%) and WSHG ancestry (ca. 13%), suggesting that the culture emerged from preceding pre-urban populations in Turan, in turn likely from earlier eastward migrations from Iran. A close cluster with little Steppe ancestry is found in thirty-four samples from Gonur Depe (ca. 2300–1600 BC), including three of hg. J-M304, two E1b1-P2, one I2-M438, and one R-M207; seven samples from Dzharkutan (one ca. 2100–1800 BC, six ca. 1750–1450 BC), one of hg. R1b-M343; thirteen samples from the MBA Sapalli Tepe (ca. 2000–1600 BC), two of hg. J-M304, two of hg. R2-M479, one of hg. G-M201, and one of hg. L-M20; and six samples from the Bustan catacomb-type burials of a culture similar to

Dzharkutan, but with a complex funerary ritual related to the usage of fire, including one early individual (ca. 1900–1700 BC), of hg. L-M20, and five post-BMAC MBA samples (ca. 1600–1300 BC), three of hg. J-M304, one G-M201 (Narasimhan et al. 2018).

Two early BMAC outliers (ca. 2500–2000 BC), one of hg. J-M304, show significant amounts of WSHG ancestry, including one female from a pit, and one female from a large rectangular pit in the 'Royal Cemetery'. This ancestry comes probably from indigenous populations of the Kelteminar culture, native hunter-gatherers of the region before the emergence of BMAC, and represent thus the most likely donors of the WSHG ancestry present in BMAC (Narasimhan et al. 2018).

Substantial Steppe ancestry is found in two outliers from Gonur, a male from a shaft tomb (ca. 2150 BC), of hg. P-M45 (hence potentially R-M207), and a female from a pit (ca. 2050 BC); in two early outliers from Dzharkutan (ca. 2100–1800 BC), both females; and in one individual from Sapalli (ca. 2000–1600 BC), of hg. Q-M242. This clearly documents a southward movement of steppe migrants through the region (Suppl. Graph. 13), with an admixture starting probably at the turn of the $2^{nd}/1^{st}$ millennium BC (Narasimhan et al. 2018).

At the same time as steppe migrants were moving further south, three sites to the north of BMAC showed evidence of significant admixture with Iranian Neolithic-related populations (ca. 1600–1500 BC), suggesting mobility of disintegrating BMAC peoples north and south through the Inner Asian Corridor. Samples include three steppe individuals from Dashti-Kozy, near Sarazm (ca. 1700–1400 BC); one late sample from Kyzlbulak, southern Kazakhstan (ca. 1570 BC), of hg. Q-M242, contrasting with an earlier female (ca. 1680 BC), of Steppe ancestry; and one ancient metallurgist of Taldysay, in central Kazakhstan (ca. 1500 BC), of hg. J-M304, contrasting with another later male from the same site (ca. 1300 BC), of hg. R1a-M420 and Steppe ancestry (Narasimhan et al. 2018). Especially interesting is the temporal transect depicted by Taldysay and Kyzlbulak, suggesting the start and the end to the incursion of Turan-related peoples into the southern steppes.

Early samples from the Swat Valley in northern Pakistan (ca. 1200–800 BC) are genetically very similar to Indus Periphery individuals, but harbouring Steppe MLBA ancestry (ca. 22%), which supports the integration of steppe peoples in south Asian groups likely coincident with the appearance of this ancestry in early BMAC samples. Later samples from the Swat Valley of the 1st millennium BC had higher proportions of Steppe MLBA and AASI ancestry, more similar to that found in the modern Indian cline, supporting the intrusion of more Steppe ancestry in the region and additional admixture with Ancestral South Indians (see below).

Swat proto-historic graves (SPGT) from the Gandhara Grave culture include twenty-one individuals from Udegram (ca. 1200–800 BC), nine likely of hg. E1b1-P2, two from Gogdara (ca. 1300–900 BC), one of hg. H1a-M69, apart from individuals from sites with similar grave architecture, burial features, and grave furnishing (ca. 1000–800 BC): four from Katelai, one of hg. J-M304, another R2-M479; one from Arkoktila; and four from the southern site of Barikot, one of hg. H-L901. Other samples include nine individuals from Loebanr, one early (ca. 1300–1000 BC), of hg. L-M20, eight late (ca. 1000–800 BC), two of hg. L-M20, one R1b-M343, one R2-M479, one Q-M242, one C-M130; one from Aligrama (ca. 1000–500 BC). Samples from Aligrama also include non-SPGT samples (ca. 970–550 BC), one of hg. G2a-P15, one R2a-M124.

Early historic graves of the Swat Valley include twelve individuals from the Buddhist site of Saidu Sharif I (ca. 500–300 BC), one R1a1a1b-Z645, one Q-M242, one L-M20, with one outlier showing mainly Iran Neolithic and AASI ancestry; and five later samples from Butkara (ca. 200 BC – AD 100), including two of hg. J1-L255. While the arrival of R1a1a1b2-Z93 lineages and subsequent Y-chromosome bottleneck in India remains unexplored, the Turan region hosted communities with a majority of hg. R1a1a1b2-Z93 already since the Late Bronze Age, as evidenced by two samples of the late Kayrakkum culture (Ferghana variant of Andronovo) from Kashkarchi (ca. 1200–1000 BC), both of hg. R1a1a1b-Z645 with fully Western Steppe MLBA ancestry.

The modern Indian Cline can be modelled as a mixture of two populations, Ancestral North Indian (ANI) and Ancestral South Indian (ASI), none of them existing today in unmixed form, and both contributing a variable amount of the ancestry of South Asians (Reich et al. 2009). ANI can be modelled as a mix of ancestry related to both Iranian farmers and people from the Bronze Age Eurasian steppe, close to Middle Easterners, Central Asians, and Europeans (Lazaridis et al. 2016). The maximum Indus Periphery ancestry found in ANI is ca. 72%, with a population from northern Pakistan, the Kalash, close to the minimum, and Steppe MLBA ancestry (ca. 50%) close to modern eastern Europeans.

ASI can be modelled as a mixture of Iranian farmers and AASI, harbouring a minimum of 39% Indus Periphery ancestry, with the closest groups to maximum Indus Periphery contribution found in four Dravidian tribal groups from southern India: Palliyar, Ulladan, Malayan and Adiyan (Narasimhan et al. 2018). Among ethnolinguistic and social groups, there seems to be an influence of north Eurasian admixture (potentially from ancient Indo-European-speaking populations) in forward castes, diminishing in backward castes and Dravidian-speaking peoples (Bose et al. 2017).

Using admixture linkage disequilibrium, the Palliyar and the Kalash show that their admixture was largely unformed at the beginning of the 2nd millennium BC, and imply that ASI—and thus the expansion of Dravidian languages—may have formed either with the spread of West Asian domesticates into peninsular India (starting ca. 3000 BC), or alternatively in association with the spread of material culture from the Indus Valley after the Harappan Civilisation declined.

This spread to the south-east is also supported by the finding of a higher ratio of AASI–to–Iranian farmer-related ancestry in Austroasiatic-speaking groups in India (like the Juang) than the ASI (Narasimhan et al. 2018), with an early admixture of AASI with a south-east Asian substrate—and prevalent O2a-M95 lineages—suggesting an arrival in the 3rd millennium BC (Tätte et al. 2018), coinciding with hill cultivation systems (Silva et al. 2018).

The modern distribution of R1a1a1b2-Z93 lineages shows a clear division between western and eastern subclades, with basal R1a1a1b2-Z93 located east of the Andronovo horizon (Underhill et al. 2015). Whereas the western R1a1a1b2a1a-L657 subclade has an expected peak in the northern part of the Indian subcontinent, broadly coincident with the spread of Proto-Indo-Aryan and Indo-Aryan languages, the eastern R1a1a1b2a2-Z2124 subclade peaks at the core of the Proto-Iranian Yaz culture and East Iranian expansion (of languages related to old Bactrians, Sogdians, and Scytho-Sarmatian peoples). The spread of Iranian to the west into the Iranian Plateau, however, was probably complicated by this region's higher demographic density, as is the case with the genetic make-up of the Balkans.

A quite late expansion of Indo-Aryans from a southern Turan region, suggested by the available ancient DNA samples, is also consistent with the greater linguistic diversity in the Hindu Kush–Himalayan area, including: Burushaski, a language isolate, with a majority of R1a1a1b2-Z93 and R2a-M124 subclades among the modern Burusho people (Thangaraj et al. 2010); the controversial *centum* nature of the Bangani language or its substrate; the presence of a third Indo-Iranian branch, Nuristani, in the southern Hindukush mountains; and the likely expansion of West Iranian languages from the Yaz core area, to the west of the Hindu Kush. This region seems also potentially at the origin of the distinction between expansions of R1a1a1b2a2-Z2124 to the north and R1a1a1b2a1a-L657 to the south-west (Underhill et al. 2015).

The simplified linguistic situation to the south-west, dominated by Indo-Aryan languages, is consistent with the Y-chromosome bottleneck of R1a1a1b2a1a-L657 lineages representing recently expanding Indo-Aryan speakers. Nevertheless, modern populations from the Indus Valley show a high proportion (ca. 41–76%) of South Asian lineages like C1b1a1-M356, H1a-M69, R2a-M124, J-M172, L-M11, or Q-M242 (Pathak et al. 2018; Ullah et al. 2017), which supports the mixture of haplogroups in the expanding early Indo-Aryan community, or their expansion from a south-eastern source. Supporting this interpretation is the distribution of Y-chromosome haplogroups among modern Yaghnobis of the Upper Zeravshan Valley, who show J2-M172 (30%), R1a1a-M198 (30%), R1b1a1b-M269 (23%), and K-M9 (12%), apart from other minor lineages (Cilli et al. 2019). The multiple ANI-related admixture events are probably coincident with population movements associated with the complex caste organisation based on the Indo-European-like varna and indigenous jati systems of social stratification.

Whereas the prevalent presence of R1a1a1b2-Z93, especially R1a1a1b2a2-Z2124, among modern populations of Xinjiang—who also show typical central Asian lineages—may support the early expansion of Indo-Iranian or Iranian peoples from the east, the finding of R1a1a1b2a1a L657.1 (ca. 8%) in the western site of Dolan (Liu et al. 2018) may be related to a recent expansion of the Indo-Aryan Gāndhārī to the region.

VIII.21. Siberia

VIII.21.1. West Siberia

The Middle Bronze Age Pre-Andronovo cultural horizon of the beginning of the 2nd millennium BC in south-western Siberia was constituted by all of the forest-steppe and southern forests from the Trans-Urals to the Yenisei River, which were occupied by several cultures and groups: Tashkovo (Middle Tobol), Loginovo (Middle Ishim), Odino, Krotovo, and Elunino (the Middle Irtysh, Upper Ob', and Altai areas), as well as the Samus' culture (Tom–Chulym rivers) (Koryakova and Epimakhov 2007).

They display clear evidence of the diversified economy contributed by the productive and non-productive branches. Their similar pottery morphology and decoration shows alternating holed and combed motifs that cover the entire pot's surface and reach back to an earlier epoch when they were dominant. These cultures remained rather distinctive and were only slightly touched by steppe influence (Koryakova and Epimakhov 2007).

The Tashkovo and Krotovo are more significant, contributing to later cultural formations in western Siberia, with the latter continuing into the Late Bronze Age. The Tashkovo culture is represented by villages with a circular or semi-circular layout, of ten to twelve houses on the banks of small rivers or lakes, whereas Krotovo shows open dispersed settlements with one- or two-chamber houses of the semisubterranean type and flat burial grounds (Koryakova and Epimakhov 2007).

The eastern Krotovo–Elunino territory (Middle Irtysh and Upper Ob') shows flat burial grounds situated on elevated riverbanks or terraces, with sprinkled ochre, burials of separated skulls or skeletons without skulls, collective multi-layered burials, and secondary fractured burials. Some graves show rich metal objects, among which are some of Seima–Turbino type (Koryakova and Epimakhov 2007).

The arrival of Andronovo-like cultural horizon in the forest-steppe and southern forest regions replaced these cultures or displaced them to the north and east into the taiga.

viii.21.1. Yukaghirs

Based on proposed Indo-Uralic community (Kortlandt 2002; Kloekhorst 2008; Hyllested 2009), a macro-family formed by Indo-European, Uralic, and Yukaghir is quite likely to have migrated back from the Trans-Urals region with hunter-gatherer pottery (see *§ii.3. Indo-Uralians*). Remnant populations from this migration probably include two Sintashta outliers of Khvalynsk Eneolithic-like ancestry (ca. 2000–1650 BC), one R1b1a1-P297, the other R1b1a1a-M73 (Narasimhan et al. 2018), both lineages probably related to westward migrations through the Urals. Similarly, there is a possible sample of hg. R1b1a1-P297 in Darra-e Kūr, Afghanistan (ca. 2700 BC), with fully Iran Neolithic-like ancestry. The presence of hg. R1b1a1a-M73 lineages among diverse central Asian populations, in particular among Turkic-speaking groups (see below), also suggest potential remnant groups of hg. R1b1a1-P297 in West Siberia during the Neolithic.

Nevertheless, the continuous population expansions and replacements in Siberia have obscured the potential migration routes for Yukaghirs, whose language has been recorded only recently. Ancient DNA sampled from historical central Siberian peoples show certain discordances with a simplistic model of a macro-Yeniseian community in the taiga zone and southern Siberia up to the Altai–Sayan zone (Kim et al. 2018), and this complexity is in turn compatible with ancient Eurasian and Indo-Uralic population movements through Siberia . Modern Yukaghirs show among ten sampled individuals—in a similar distribution to Tungusic Evenks and Evens—four hg. C2-M217, three N1a-L279, two R1a-M420, as well as (not present in Tungusic peoples) one I2a-L460 and one O-M175 (Fedorova et al. 2013).

Four samples of the Bronze Age Glazkovo culture, from the Lake Baikal (ca. 18th–13th c. BC), one of hg R1-M173, show ancestry compatible with modern north-east Siberian populations, compatible with their later described spread to the north (de Barros Damgaard, Marchi, et al. 2018).

A medieval individual near the Yana river (ca. AD 1350) shows hg. N1a1a1a1a4a1-M1993 (formed ca. 1700 BC, TMRCA ca. AD 450), and falls within the widespread Neosiberian cline evidenced by a recent sample from Ust'Belaya (ca. AD 1300) near Lake Baikal (Sikora et al. 2018). The prevalent presence of N1a1a1a1a4-M2019 (formed ca. 4400 BC, TMRCA 1700 BC) in central Siberia and Yakutia, and at lower frequencies in Khants and Mansis (Ilumae et al. 2016), is most likely the result of the expansion of Yukaghir-and Altaic-related languages with acculturated Palaeosiberian clans.

The complex evolution of north-east Asia can be seen in the replacement of lineages from Ekven Iron Age samples (ca. 400 BC – AD 400), predominantly of hg. Q-M242, at least one within the Q1b1a1a-M3 tree (formed ca. 13200 BC, TMRCA ca. 11400 BC), prevalent in the Americas, and two samples of hg. C2a-L1373, at least one within the C2a1a1a2-F3918 tree (formed ca. 12400 BC, TMRCA ca. 10800 BC), prevalent today in Eurasian populations likely related to Altaic expansions (Sikora et al. 2018).

The expansion of Yukaghir was probably then coincident with Bronze Age migrations, likely continued to the east with N1a1a1a1a4a-M1993 during the Iron Age–Early Middle Ages, as Ugrians and Samoyeds expanded to the north (see *§viii.17. Ugrians and Samoyeds*). This later expansion probably displaced populations of mainly N1a1a1a1a3b-B202 lineages (formed ca. 2800, TMRCA ca. 600 BC) to the extreme north-eastern Siberia, where they retained their Chukotko-Kamchatkan languages, supported by their prevalent N1a1a1a-L708 lineages (ca. 92%).

Turkic-speaking Evenks cluster together and overlap with Yukaghirs, and both in turn cluster closely to Nganasans from the Taymyr Peninsula and to Chukchi-speaking Koryaks, revealing a complex acculturation of different East Asian peoples in recent times (Karafet et al. 2018). The wide cluster formed by modern Yukaghirs, including southern Samoyedic speakers in the west and Chukotko-Kamchatkan speakers in the east (see Suppl. Graph. 15) further supports the relatively recent expansion of Yukaghir into the Circum-Arctic region.

viii.21.2. Turkic peoples and Mongols

Cultures succeeding Afanasevo in the Altai region show different lineages and the partial resurgence of WSHG ancestry coupled with different Afanasevo-, Steppe MLBA-, AP-, and AEA-related contributions, suggesting the emergence of different local West Siberian populations (Hollard et al. 2018): the Chemurchek culture (ca. 2300–1800 BC), with one hg. C-M130; the Okunevo culture (ca. 2300–1800 BC), with one hg. R1b1a1b1-L23, three likely N-Z4813, and three likely Q1b1a-L54; the Elunino culture (ca. 2300–1700 BC), with one hg. Q-M242, and one Q1b-M346; the Munkh-Khairkhan culture (ca. 1700–1400 BC), with two N-M231 lineages; and the Sagsai culture (ca. 1400–800 BC), with four hg. Q1b1a-L54, four R1a1a1b2-Z93, and one C-M130.

MBA sites Takhilgat Uzuur and Tsagaan Asga in the Mongolian Altai Mountains also show apparent succeeding replacements from hg. Q1b1a-L54 in the 3rd millennium BC to R1a1a1b2-Z93 in the late 2nd millennium BC, to C-M130 in the early 1st millennium BC (Hollard et al. 2014).

To the east, near Lake Baikal, a resurgence of AP ancestry (up to ca. 50%) coupled with Afanasevo-related ancestry (ca. 10%) found in EBA individuals is continued during the LBA. Samples of the Deer Stone-Khirigsuur Complex from Khövsgöl in northern Mongolia (ca. 1200–800 BC) show a slightly higher contribution of AP ancestry evidenced by a 'northern' shift in the PCA, similar to Karasuk or Okunevo samples (Jeong, Wilkin, et al. 2018). In terms of haplogroups, there are ten probably Q1b-L56, possibly all of Q1b1a-L54 subclade Q1b1a3-L330 (formed ca. 16000 BC, TMRCA ca. 5900 BC), with an estimated successful dispersal of these subclades starting in the Mesolithic ca. 6300 BC from central Asia (Grugni et al. 2019), possibly initially accompanying Dene-Yeniseian-related languages (see *§v.8. Palaeosiberians*).

A small contribution of Steppe MLBA ancestry (ca. 4-7%) suggests close contacts with Andronovo-related peoples. In particular, the presence of one outlier (ca. 1130–900 BC), of hg. R1a1a1b2a2a1-Z2123, is consistent with the appearance of admixed forest-steppe populations of Eastern Steppe MLBA ancestry like Karasuk in the Altai (ca. 1200–800 BC). Supporting these contacts of Karasuk with eastern Asian steppes is also the Karasuk outlier and the sample of hg. Q1a2a-L712. This points to the spread of pastoralism in the region mediated by acculturation and exogamy more than population replacement (Jeong, Wilkin, et al. 2018). Another sample (ca. 1420-1130 BC) of hg. N1a1a-M178, mtDNA U5a2d1, suggests—like the different groups succeeding Afanasevo in the Altai region—the acculturation of northern Eurasian communities with post-Neolithic expansions.

To the south-east of Lake Baikal, in the Houtaomuga site from Manchuria, there is genetic continuity from ca. 10000 BC until the Iron Age, but haplogroup N1b1-CTS582, found in the Early Neolithic (ca. 5430–5320 BC), is replaced in the Bronze Age by C2b-L1373, which continues in the Early Iron Age (Ning 2018). Twelve Donghu individuals from the Jinggouzi site (ca. 770–476 BC) show C2a1a-F4032 lineages (formed ca. 12700 BC, TMRCA ca. 12300 BC), as do four samples from Xianbei (ca. AD 4th–10th c.) (Zhang, Wu, et al. 2018; Li et al. 2018). The expansion of the Donghu seems to have caused the expansion of C2-M217 lineages in the Trans-Baikal area.

The first Turkic-speaking community is usually identified with the Xiongnu confederation, with ancient Y-chromosomal data indicating a heterogeneous multi-ethnic cultural organisation, likely emerging initially from local East Asian groups to the east of the Tian Shan Mountains, who showed admixture with central steppe nomads. A more recent West Eurasian ancestry is found among western Xiongnu groups, with Central Sakas being the closest source for their admixture (de Barros Damgaard, Marchi, et al. 2018).

Sampled Xiongnu individuals (ca. 300 BC – AD 200) include hg. R1a1a-M198 and C2-M217 in Duurlig Nars, and hg. N1a1-Tat and Q-M52 and in Egyin Gol Valley (Kim et al. 2010; Petkovski 2006); two likely hg. O2a2b-P164 from Omnogobi, one early sample from the West Xiongnu in Khövsgöl (ca. 330 BC), of hg. R1b2-PH155, and one from an aristocratic burial in Arkhangai (ca. AD 1), likely of hg. R1b2b-PH200^{+} (de Barros Damgaard, Marchi, et al. 2018).

The homeland of Turkic peoples is difficult to pinpoint based on scarce samples through wide temporal transects, due to the multiple population replacements in the central and eastern Asian steppes, forest-steppes, and forests, and to the linguistic data and complex ethnogenesis legends pointing to a composite grouping of diverse elements since the reconstructible stage of the language (Golden 1992).

Based on Indo-European (Iranian and Tocharian) and Uralic influences, Proto-Turkic is supposed to have been spoken ca. 1000 BC in some area from the Trans-Urals area to the Altai, with the forest zones of West Siberia being the most likely candidate based on the Indo-Iranian expansions through the steppes, as well as the Uralic expansions through the forest-steppe and forest regions. From there, the ancestors of the Turks migrated east into the Baikal area, where the Xiongnu confederation eventually emerged, and Huns later migrated to West Eurasia (Golden 1992).

The two Sintashta outliers of Khvalynsk Eneolithic-like ancestry, of reported haplogroups R1b1a1-P297 and R1b1a1a-M73, probably correspond to ancient populations of R1b1a1a-M73 lineages widespread from the west in the southern Urals up to the Lake Baikal in the east since the Neolithic, following a WSHG ancestry cline. This is compatible with the Mesolithic expansion of Eurasian through Inner Asia (see *§ii.1. Eurasians*), and the isolated development of Altaic in the Neolithic (see *§v.8. Palaeosiberians*).

Haplogroup R1b1a1a-M73 is reported with low frequencies among modern Siberian populations, such as Ugric and Samoyedic peoples, especially southern Selkups (Tambets et al. 2018), and with increasing frequencies among south Siberian populations, in particular among Turkic-speaking Bashkirs (Jeong, Balanovsky, et al. 2018) and Teleuts near the Altai (Karafet et al. 2018), which suggests its presence among Turkic-speaking peoples before their expansion into the Trans-Baikal area and the creation of a community integrating diverse local populations.

The earlier emergence of Turkic-speaking peoples from the forming multi-ethnic groups in the Trans-Baikal area further supports that Turko–Mongolic, and not only Turkic, expanded from the west. Similarly, the link of different Altaic-related expansions since the early first millennium BC associated with bottlenecks of West Siberian N1a1a1a1a-L1026/L392 lineages (see *§v.8. Palaeosiberians*) further supports the connection of Altaic with the West Siberian forest-steppes. The adaptation of horseback riding for more stressful and difficult activities such as warfare—characteristic of these nomadic groups—in the eastern steppes, started probably at the end of the Deer Stone–Khirigsuur Complex or slightly later, evidenced by findings from the Altai to the Baikal region, including the appearance of the bronze snaffle bit and innovations in equine dentistry (Taylor, Bayarsaikhan, et al. 2018).

The Huns, likely representatives of the earliest Turkic-speaking groups in Eurasia, emerged following minor male-driven East Asian gene flow into the preceding Sakas that they invaded, ca. 2,000 years ago. They displaced Iranian-speaking groups (ancestors of the Wusun and Kangju) to the south-east of the Tian Shan mountains, where they became isolated (see *§viii.19. Iranians*). Sampled nomads from the Kargaly in the Tian Shan region include two early ones (ca. 800–700 BC), one of hg. Q-M242, clustering with Siberian peoples (close to Yeniseians), one intermediate (ca. 425 BC), of hg. R1a1a1b2a2-Z2124, and a later one (ca. 35 BC), of hg. R1b1a1a1b-Y20750 (formed ca. 5300 BC, TMRCA ca. 3300 BC), a subclade of R1b1a1a-M73 (de Barros Damgaard, Marchi, et al. 2018).

This variability is also found later among Huns from Tian Shan (ca. AD 60–600), with three hg. R1a1a1b2a2-Z2124, two R1-M173, one hg. R1b2b-PH200, one N1a1a-M178, and one Q1a2a1-L715$^+$, in contrast to Tian Shan Sakas, who were all of R1-M173 subclades. Nomads from the central steppe (ca. AD 360), either Huns or Sarmatians, show one sample of hg. R1a1a1b2-Z93. Huns sampled from the Carpathian Basin (AD 5th c.) show hg. Q1a2-M25, one R1b1a1b1a1a1-U106, and one R1a1a1b2a2-Z2124 (Neparáczki et al. 2019). All Huns show an increased shared drift with West Eurasians compared to Xiongnu (de Barros Damgaard, Marchi, et al. 2018).

A sample of the Mongolian Rouran Khaganate from Khermen Tal shows the continuation of haplogroup C2a1a-F4032 in the region (Li et al. 2018), probably expanding with Mongolian-speaking peoples in the eastern steppes. Samples from Baiyin Huangwan Han dynasty tombs from a north-western Chinese farming area near the Xiongnu states, spanning from the Western Han Dynasty (202 BC – AD 8) to the Eastern Han Dynasty (AD 25–220), show significant genetic contribution from the northern Eurasian populations, as well as an accommodation to the nomadic lifestyle, which supports the acculturation of the Xiongnu population to the Han culture (Li, Ma, and Wen 2018).

After the defeat of the Xiongnu (ca. AD 552), a part of their population migrated to Pannonia, where they became known as the Avars and allied with the Longobards to defeat the Gepids, creating the Avar Khaganate (AD 567-805). Two early female Avars from Szólád (ca. AD 540–640) show an ancestry similar to Eastern Europeans, with contributions of East Asian ancestry, clustering close to modern West Slavs, which justifies the Central Asian admixture found in a Gepid and a medieval Bavarian individual of the region (Amorim et al. 2018). Twenty-three individuals from a group of elite burials in Hungary (AD 7th–8th c.) show a majority of Inner Asian origin (up to 64%) of their mtDNA (Csáky et al. 2018), although there is high intergroup variation (Šebest et al. 2018).

In terms of Y-chromosome haplogroups, early Avars (ca. AD 570–660) show the intrusion of N1a1a-M178, found among six out of eleven males, with at least four of them subclades of N1a1a1a1a3-Y16323 (formed ca. 2900 BC, TMRCA ca. 2900 BC), in turn a subclade of N1a1a1a1a-L392 (formed ca. 4300 BC, TMRCA ca. 2900 BC). At least one of them estimated to be N1a1a1a1a3a-F4205[+] (TMRCA ca. 500 BC), a haplogroup confirmed in all seventeen sampled males from the Avar Khaganate in the Danube–Tisza Interfluve (ca. 600–775 BC). Haplotypes confirm that these samples share their closes relatives today among Siberian populations, including Buryats, Mongolians, Yakuts, Mansis and Khants, in line with the presence of hg. N1a1a-M178 in Bronze Age Inner Mongolia and late medieval Yakuts (Csáky et al. 2019).

Two individuals from a secondary power centre east of the Tisza (ca. 650-700 BC) show hg. Q1a-F1096 and Q1b-M346, the latter of likely Altaian or South Siberian paternal origin (Csáky et al. 2019). Other early haplogroups include one C2-M217 and one R1a1a1b2a2-Z2124. All these samples support an original Siberian expansion of this haplogroup from a region close to Lake Baikal. Samples probably related originally to European paternal lines include one early Avar of hg. G2a-P15, and another one of hg. I1-M253 (Neparáczki et al. 2019).

Middle or Late Avar samples (ca. 650-710 BC) show one hg. C2-M217 and one N1a1a1a3-Y16323, showing continuity with the previous period, but also one E1b1b1a1b1a-V13. Given the nature of the Avar polity as a Slavic-speaking territory during the last century of its existence (ca. 700–800 BC), and the finding of E1b1b1a1b1a-V13 lineages later during the Hungarian Conqueror period (see *§viii.17.1. Ugrians*) and among early Slavs, it is highly likely that the expansion of hg. E1b1b1a1b1a-V13 from the Carpathian Basin is related to the Slavonic expansion to neighbouring regions (Neparáczki et al. 2019).

The Turkic Khaganate assumed military and political organisation of the steppes as the Hunnic Empire broke up and dispersed (AD 6th c.), following the emergence of the Turks, the blacksmiths of the Rourans (Suppl. Fig. 17). Their elite soldiers are genetically closer to East Asians than the preceding Huns of the Tian Shan mountains, with one sample from Berygavoya (ca. 690 BC), of hg. R1-M173. A genetic outlier of the central steppe (ca. AD 270), of hg. R1-M173, shows pronounced European ancestry, and thus ongoing contacts with Europe (de Barros Damgaard, Marchi, et al. 2018).

The Turkic Khaganate was eventually replaced by short-lived steppe cultures, such as the Kipchak and the Tungusik Kimak poulations, which spread southwards towards the Tian Shan mountains and westward towards the Ural Mountains to form the Kimak Khaganate in the central steppe (ca. 8th– 11th c.). One sample from Kimak nomads of the Central Steppes (ca. AD 665), of hg. R1b1a1a1a-Y14051, does not show elevated East Asian ancestry (de Barros Damgaard, Marchi, et al. 2018).

The Kima Khaganate was replaced by local Kipchak groups allied with the Cuman of West Eurasia, hence probably originating near the area of Tuva. Two individuals dating to the Cuman–Kipchak alliance (ca. AD 1050) show one hg. C-M130 and increased East Asian ancestry, and the other one pronounced European ancestry, which is compatible with the incorporation of western and eastern steppe populations. The Karakhanid Khaganate from Turan incorporated some of these groups, with three samples (ca. AD 950–1250) showing further East Asian influx compared to earlier Turks (de Barros Damgaard, Marchi, et al. 2018).

Other unassigned early medieval Turkic samples show different proportions of East Asian ancestry, including nine from Tian Shan, among them one early (ca. AD 800–1000), of hg. J2a-M410, and one later (ca. AD 1170) of hg. C2a1a1b1b1-Y12825[+] (formed ca. 1000 BC, TMRCA ca. 100 BC); one from the Central Steppe (ca. AD 735) of hg. R1b1a1a1a-Y14051[+]; and one from the Caspian Steppe (ca. AD 700) of hg. R1a1a1b2a2-Z2124[+].

Among two samples (ca. AD 1250) of the medieval Jochi Khan's Golden Horde in the central steppes, there is one of clearly East Asian ancestry and corresponding PCA cluster, of hg. C2-M217, and one of West Eurasian descent, of hg. R1a1a1b1a2a-Z280, which is further proof of the assimilation of different groups into succeeding Turkic organisations (de Barros Damgaard, Marchi, et al. 2018).

Among modern Tatars, descendants from elite clans of the Golden Horde belong to haplogroup R1b1a1a-M73 (Akchurin et al. 2018). There seems to be a general trend during the Iron Age and medieval times to a distribution of R1a1a1b2a2-Z2124 lineages in the Pontic–Caspian steppes, of R1b1a1a-M73 lineages in the central steppes, and of R1-M173 (likely R1b2-PH155) and C2a1a1b1b1-Y12825 in the eastern steppes, which may reflect to some extent the different alliances formed by multi-ethnic groups since the time of the formation of the Xiongnu confederacy and the Hunnic expansion, although it may also reflect the initial contacts between peoples of the eastern steppe before the formation of the Xiongnu community. Modern peoples from investigated Xinjiang sites show hg. R1b-M343 including R1b1a1-P297, R1b1a1a-M73 (up to 9%), and R1b2-PH155 subclades, among a majority of typically central Asian lineages, including hg. R1a1a1b2-Z93, especially R1a1a1b2a2-Z2124 (Liu et al. 2018), whose origin cannot be properly interpreted without specific subclades.

Eventually, these khaganates were conquered by the Mongol Empire, which emerged through the unification of East Mongolian and Trans-Baikal tribes, expanding under the rule of Genghis Khan (ca. AD 13th c.). Modern Mongolian tribes show a mixture of East Asian lineages, mainly C2 subclades (ca. 42%), including C2b-F1067 (ca. 29%) and C2a-L1373 (ca. 13%), but also O-M175 (ca. 24%) and N-M231 (ca. 18%). In the PCA, Mongolians cluster in close genetic proximity to a group of North Asian Siberians, including Altaians, Tuvinians, Evenki, and Yakut, with eastern tribes Abaga, Khalkha, Oirat, and Sonid showing the least differentiation, with close interaction between northern Eurasian populations (Bai et al. 2018). Common Mongols likely expanded mainly with a Y-chromosome bottleneck of haplogroup C2a1a1c1-F3796 (TMRCA ca. 500 BC), whose expansion pattern is consistent with the diffusion of most Mongolic-speaking populations (Wei et al. 2018).

Manchu-Tungusic is proposed to have spread either from the Trans-Baikal area or from the Amur River region. Ancient samples from the West Liao River region shows high dynamism, similar to Trans-Baikal areas[39], which may support the emergence of Tungusic-speaking peoples from previous population movements through the eastern steppes. The presence of shared isoglosses with Turkic and Mongolic to the west, forming a likely Altaic family, and with Koreanic (and Japonic) to the east, with less clear links to Altaic, makes the identification of Tungusic still more complicated. The Proto-Tungusic society has been associated either with the Donghu or with an ancestral group from the Amur River region sharing links with eastern peoples. The potential attribution of vowel harmony in Proto-Tungusic to contacts with Mongolic languages (Ko, Joseph, and Whitman 2014) makes the identification of the language with one or the other group still harder.

Present-day Tungusic-speaking peoples, of varied lineages and ancestry, share a similar history to that found among Palaeosiberian peoples integrated among Finnic, Samic, Samoyedic, or Yukaghir-speaking populations, of acculturated Palaeosiberians adopting languages in recent times (Fedorova et al. 2013). This tradition of exogamy notwithstanding, it seems that the recent expansion of C2a1a1b1-M86 lineages among some southern Tungusic groups (as well as other C2-M217 lineages) may have been associated with their expansion from the south-east (Balanovska et al. 2018).

---

[39] Upcoming communication by Ning et al. at Eurasia3Angle conference (2019).

References

Ache, Mireia, Selina Delgado-Raack, Elena Molina, Roberto Risch, and Antoni Rosell-Melé. 2017. Evidence of bee products processing: A functional definition of a specialized type of macro-lithic tool. *Journal of Archaeological Science: Reports* 14:638-650.

Adamov, Dmitry, Vladimir M. Guryanov, Sergey Karzhavin, Vladimir Tagankin, and Vadim Urasin. 2015. Defining a New Rate Constant for Y-Chromosome SNPs based on Full Sequencing Data. *The Russian Journal of Genetic Genealogy (Русская версия)* 7 (1):68-89.

Adrados, F.R. 1998. La reconstrucción del indoeuropeo y de su diferenciación dialectal. In *Manual de lingüística indoeuropea*, edited by F. R. Adrados, A. Bernabé and J. Mendoza. Madrid: Ediciones clásicas.

Afanas'ev, G. E., M. V. Dobrovol'skaya, D. S. Korobov, and I. K. Reshetova. 2014. O kul'turnoi, antropologicheskoi i geneticheskoi spetsifike donskikh Alan. *Institut arkheologii RAN, Moskva.*

Aikio, Ante. 2012. An essay on Saami ethnolinguistic prehistory. In *A Linguistic Map of Prehistoric Northern Europe*. Helsinki.

Akchurin, M.M., M.R. Isheev, A.V. Belyakov, T.A. Abdurakhmanov, and R.R. Salikhov. 2018. Kasimov Tatars of the Kypchak tribe. *UDK* 94 (47):312-241.

Allentoft, Morten E., Martin Sikora, Karl-Goran Sjogren, Simon Rasmussen, Morten Rasmussen, Jesper Stenderup, Peter B. Damgaard, Hannes Schroeder, Torbjorn Ahlstrom, Lasse Vinner, Anna-Sapfo Malaspinas, Ashot Margaryan, Tom Higham, David Chivall, Niels Lynnerup, Lise Harvig, Justyna Baron, Philippe Della Casa, Pawel Dabrowski, Paul R. Duffy, Alexander V. Ebel, Andrey Epimakhov, Karin Frei, Miroslaw Furmanek, Tomasz Gralak, Andrey Gromov, Stanislaw Gronkiewicz, Gisela Grupe, Tamas Hajdu, Radoslaw Jarysz, Valeri Khartanovich, Alexandr Khokhlov, Viktoria Kiss, Jan Kolar, Aivar Kriiska, Irena Lasak, Cristina Longhi, George McGlynn, Algimantas Merkevicius, Inga Merkyte, Mait Metspalu, Ruzan Mkrtchyan, Vyacheslav Moiseyev, Laszlo Paja, Gyorgy Palfi, Dalia Pokutta, Lukasz Pospieszny, T.

Douglas Price, Lehti Saag, Mikhail Sablin, Natalia Shishlina, Vaclav Smrcka, Vasilii I. Soenov, Vajk Szeverenyi, Gusztav Toth, Synaru V. Trifanova, Liivi Varul, Magdolna Vicze, Levon Yepiskoposyan, Vladislav Zhitenev, Ludovic Orlando, Thomas Sicheritz-Ponten, Soren Brunak, Rasmus Nielsen, Kristian Kristiansen, and Eske Willerslev. 2015. Population genomics of Bronze Age Eurasia. *Nature* 522 (7555):167-172.

Amorim, Carlos Eduardo G., Stefania Vai, Cosimo Posth, Alessandra Modi, István Koncz, Susanne Hakenbeck, Maria Cristina La Rocca, Balazs Mende, Dean Bobo, Walter Pohl, Luisella Pejrani Baricco, Elena Bedini, Paolo Francalacci, Caterina Giostra, Tivadar Vida, Daniel Winger, Uta von Freeden, Silvia Ghirotto, Martina Lari, Guido Barbujani, Johannes Krause, David Caramelli, Patrick J. Geary, and Krishna R. Veeramah. 2018. Understanding 6th-century barbarian social organization and migration through paleogenomics. *Nature Communications* 9 (1):3547.

Anthony, David W. 1990. Migration in archeology: the baby and the bathwater. *American Anthropologist* 92 (4):895-914.

Repeated Author. 2007. *The Horse, the Wheel, and Language: How Bronze-Age Riders from the Eurasian Steppes Shaped the Modern World.* Princeton and Oxford: Princeton University Press.

Repeated Author. 2016. The Samara Valley Project and the Evolution of Pastoral Economies in the Western Eurasian Steppes. In *A Bronze Age Landscape in the Russian Steppes. The Samara Valley Project*, edited by D. W. Anthony, D. R. Brown, O. D. Mochalov, A. A. Khokhlov and P. F. Kuznetsov. Los Angeles: The Cotsen Institute of Archaeology Press at UCLA.

Anthony, David W., and Dorcas R. Brown. 2017. The dogs of war: A Bronze Age initiation ritual in the Russian steppes. *Journal of Anthropological Archaeology* 48:134-148.

Arboledas-Martínez, Luis, and Eva Alarcón-García. 2018. Redefining the role of metal production during the Bronze Age of south-eastern Iberia. The mines of eastern Sierra Morena. *Documenta Praehistorica* 45:138-153.

Asscher, Yotam, and Elisabetta Boaretto. 2018. Absolute Time Ranges in the Plateau of the Late Bronze to Iron Age Transition and the Appearance of Bichrome Pottery in Canaan, Southern Levant. *Radiocarbon*:1-25.

Ávila-Arcos, María. 2015. Assessment of Whole-Genome capture methodologies on single-and double-stranded ancient DNA libraries from Caribbean and European archaeological human remains. In *Biology of Genomes*. Cold Spring Harbor, New York.

Bai, Haihua, Xiaosen Guo, Narisu Narisu, Tianming Lan, Qizhu Wu, Yanping Xing, Yong Zhang, Stephen R. Bond, Zhili Pei, Yanru Zhang, Dandan Zhang, Jirimutu Jirimutu, Dong Zhang, Xukui Yang, Morigenbatu Morigenbatu, Li Zhang, Bingyi Ding, Baozhu Guan, Junwei Cao, Haorong Lu, Yiyi Liu, Wangsheng Li, Ningxin Dang, Mingyang Jiang, Shenyuan Wang, Huixin Xu, Dingzhu Wang, Chunxia Liu, Xin Luo, Ying Gao, Xueqiong Li, Zongze Wu, Liqing Yang, Fanhua Meng, Xiaolian Ning, Hashenqimuge Hashenqimuge, Kaifeng Wu, Bo Wang, Suyalatu Suyalatu, Yingchun Liu, Chen Ye, Huiguang Wu, Kalle Leppälä, Lu Li, Lin Fang, Yujie Chen, Wenhao Xu, Tao Li, Xin Liu, Xun Xu, Christopher R. Gignoux, Huanming Yang, Lawrence C. Brody, Jun

Wang, Karsten Kristiansen, Burenbatu Burenbatu, Huanmin Zhou, and Ye Yin. 2018. Whole-genome sequencing of 175 Mongolians uncovers population-specific genetic architecture and gene flow throughout North and East Asia. *Nature Genetics*.

Balanovska, E. V., Y. V. Bogunov, E. N. Kamenshikova, O. A. Balaganskaya, A. T. Agdzhoyan, A. A. Bogunova, R. A. Skhalyakho, I. E. Alborova, M. K. Zhabagin, S. M. Koshel, D. M. Daragan, E. B. Borisova, A. A. Galakhova, O. V. Maltceva, Kh Kh Mustafin, N. K. Yankovsky, and O. P. Balanovsky. 2018. Demographic and Genetic Portraits of the Ulchi Population. *Russian Journal of Genetics* 54 (10):1245-1253.

Battaglia, Vincenza, Simona Fornarino, Nadia Al-Zahery, Anna Olivieri, Maria Pala, Natalie M. Myres, Roy J. King, Siiri Rootsi, Damir Marjanovic, Dragan Primorac, Rifat Hadziselimovic, Stojko Vidovic, Katia Drobnic, Naser Durmishi, Antonio Torroni, A. Silvana Santachiara-Benerecetti, Peter A. Underhill, and Ornella Semino. 2008. Y-chromosomal evidence of the cultural diffusion of agriculture in southeast Europe. *European Journal Of Human Genetics* 17:820.

Beekes, R.S.P. 2003. *The Origin of the Etruscans*. Amsterdam: Koninklijke Nederlandse Akademie vanWetenschappen.

Beekes, Robert S.P. 2011. *Comparative Indo-European Linguistics. An introduction*. 2nd ed. Amsterdam / Philadelphia: John Benjamins.

Bennett, Casey C., and Frederika A. Kaestle. 2010. Investigation of Ancient DNA from Western Siberia and the Sargat Culture. *Human Biology* 82 (2):143-156.

Bernabò Brea, M. 2009. Le terramare nell'Età del Bronzo. In *Acqua e civiltà nelle terramare. La vasca votiva di Noceto*, edited by M. Bernabò Brea and M. Cremaschi. Milan: Skira.

Bertemes, François, and Volker Heyd. 2002. Der Übergang Kupferzeit / Frühbronzezeit am Nordwestrand des Karpatenbeckens - kulturgeschichtliche und paläometallurgische Betrachtungen. In *Die Anfänge der Metallurgie in der Alten Welt*, edited by M. Bartelheim. Rahden/Westfalen: Leidorf.

Repeated Author. 2015. Innovation or Evolution: Genesis of the Danubian EBA. In *2200 BC – A climatic breakdown as a cause for the collapse of the old world? 7th Arch. Conference Central Germany, Oct. 23–26, 2014*. Halle: Tagungen Landesmus. Vorgesch.

Berthon, William, Balázs Tihanyi, Luca Kis, László Révész, Hélène Coqueugniot, Olivier Dutour, and György Pálfi. 2018. Horse Riding and the Shape of the Acetabulum: Insights from the Bioarchaeological Analysis of Early Hungarian Mounted Archers (10th Century). *International Journal of Osteoarchaeology* 0 (ja).

Biagini, Simone Andrea, Neus Solé-Morata, Elizabeth Matisoo-Smith, Pierre Zalloua, David Comas, and Francesc Calafell. 2019. People from Ibiza: an unexpected isolate in the Western Mediterranean. *European Journal of Human Genetics*.

Bietti Sestieri, Anna Maria. 2013. The Bronze Age in Sicily. In *The Oxford Handbook of the European Bronze Age*, edited by H. Fokkens and A. Harding. Oxford: Oxford University Press.

Bietti Sestieri, Anna Maria 2013. Peninsular Italy. In *The Oxford Handbook of the European Bronze Age*, edited by H. Fokkens and A. Harding. Oxford: Oxford University Press.

Bilger, Michael. 2019. Der Glockenbecher in Europa – eine Kartierung. *Journal of Neolithic Archaeology* (Special Issue 4): Think Globla, Act Local! Bell Beakers in Europe:203-270.

Blanco-González, A., K. T. Lillios, J. A. López-Sáez, and B. L. Drake. 2018. Cultural, Demographic and Environmental Dynamics of the Copper and Early Bronze Age in Iberia (3300–1500 BC): Towards an Interregional Multiproxy Comparison at the Time of the 4.2 ky BP Event. *Journal of World Prehistory* 31 (1):1-79.

Blasco Ferrer, Eduardo. 2010. *Paleosardo: Le radici linguistiche della Sardegna neolitica*. Edited by G. Holtus, *Beihefte zur Zeitschrift für romanische Philologie*. Berlin/New York: Walter de Gruyter.

Blevins, Juliette. 2018. *Advances in Proto-Basque Reconstruction with Evidence for the Proto-Indo-European-Euskarian Hypothesis*. Edited by C. Bowern, *Routledge Studies in Historical Linguistics*: Routledge.

Bochkarev, Vadim Sergeevich. 2010. *Koni, kolesnitsy i kolesnichie stepej Evrazii / Horses, chariots and chariot's drivers of Eurasian steppes*. . Yekaterinburg, Samara, Donetsk: Rossijskaja Akademija Nauk, Ural'skoe Otdelenie, Institut Ėkologii Rastenij i Životnych.

Bogdanowicz, W., M. Allen, W. Branicki, M. Lembring, M. Gajewska, and T. Kupiec. 2009. Bogdanowicz, W. et al. (2009), Genetic identification of putative remains of the famous astronomer Nicolaus Copernicus, Proceedings of the National Acadamy of Sciences of the USA (Published online before print July 7, 2009). *Proceedings of the National Academy of Sciences* 106 (30):12279-12282.

Boroffka, Nikolaus. 2013. Romania, Moldova, and Bulgaria. In *The Oxford Handbook of the European Bronze Age*, edited by H. Fokkens and A. Harding. Oxford: Oxford University Press.

Bose, Aritra, Daniel E. Platt, Laxmi Parida, Peristera Paschou, and Petros Drineas. 2017. Dissecting Population Substructure in India via Correlation Optimization of Genetics and Geodemographics. *bioRxiv*.

Briquel, D. 1999. *La civilisation etrusque*.

Brisighelli, F., C. Capelli, V. Alvarez-Iglesias, V. Onofri, G. Paoli, S. Tofanelli, A. Carracedo, V. L. Pascali, and A. Salas. 2009. The Etruscan timeline: a recent Anatolian connection. *Eur J Hum Genet* 17 (5):693-6.

Brodie, N. 2001. Technological frontiers and the emergence of the Beaker Culture. In *Bell Beakers today: pottery, people, culture, symbols in prehistoric Europe*, edited by F. Nicolis. Trento: Servicio Beni Culturali, Provincia Autonoma di Trento.

Broushaki, Farnaz, Mark G Thomas, Vivian Link, Saioa López, Lucy van Dorp, Karola Kirsanow, Zuzana Hofmanová, Yoan Diekmann, Lara M. Cassidy, David Díez-del-Molino, Athanasios Kousathanas, Christian Sell, Harry K. Robson, Rui Martiniano, Jens Blöcher, Amelie Scheu, Susanne Kreutzer, Ruth Bollongino, Dean Bobo, Hossein Davudi, Olivia Munoz, Mathias Currat, Kamyar Abdi, Fereidoun Biglari, Oliver E. Craig, Daniel G Bradley, Stephen

Shennan, Krishna R Veeramah, Marjan Mashkour, Daniel Wegmann, Garrett Hellenthal, and Joachim Burger. 2016. Early Neolithic genomes from the eastern Fertile Crescent. *Science*.

Brück, Joanna, and Alex Davies. 2018. The Social Role of Non-metal 'Valuables' in Late Bronze Age Britain. *Cambridge Archaeological Journal* 28 (4):665-688.

Brunel, Samantha. 2018. Paléogénomique des dynamiques des populations humaines sur le territoire Français entre 7000 et 2000, Bio Sorbonne Paris Cité (BIOSPC) & Institut Jaques Monod, Sorbonne Paris Cité, Paris.

Bryce, Trevor. 2011. The Late Bronze Age in the West and the Aegean. In *The Oxford Handbook of Ancient Antolia 10,000-323 B.C.E.*, edited by S. R. Steadman and G. McMahon. Oxford: Oxford University Press.

Bueno Ramirez, Primitiva, Rodrigo de Balbín Behrmann, Rosa Barroso Bermejo, Enrique Cerrillo Cuenca, Antonio Gonzalez Cordero, and Alicia Prada Gallardo. 2011. Megaliths and stelae in the inner basin of Tagus River: Santiago de Alcántara, Alconétar and Cañamero (Cáceres, Spain). In *From the Origins: The Prehistory of the Inner Tagus Region*, edited by P. B. Ramirez, E. C. Cuenca and A. G. Cordero.

Burmeister, Stefan. 2016. Archaeological Research on Migration as a Multidisciplinary Challenge. In *The Genetic Challenge to Medieval History and Archaeology*, edited by W. Pohl and A. Gingrich: Austrian Academy of Sciences Press.

Butler, J.J., S. Arnoldussen, and H. Steegstra. 2011/2012. Single-edged socketed Urnfield knives in the Netherlands and western Europe. *Palaeohistoria* 53/54:65-107.

Bycroft, Clare, Ceres Fernández-Rozadilla, Clara Ruiz-Ponte, Iéns Quintela-García, Ángel Carracedo, Peter Donnelly, and Simon Myers. 2018. Patterns of genetic differentiation and the footprints of historical migrations in the Iberian Peninsula. *bioRxiv*.

Cardarelli, Andrea. 2009. The Collapse of the Terramare Culture and growth of new economic and social System during the late Bronze Age in Italy. In *Scienze dell'Antichità. Storia archeologia antropologia*. Roma: Quasar.

Carling, Gerd. 2005. Proto-Tocharian, Common Tocharian, and Tocharian - on the value of linguistic connections in a reconstructed language. Paper read at Proceedeings of the Sixteenth Annual UCLA Indo-European Conference, at Los Angeles.

Carpelan, Chr., and A. Parpola. 2001. Emergence, Contacts and Dispersal of Proto-Inda-European, Proto-Uralic and Proto-Aryan in Archaeological Perspective. In *Early Contacts between Uralic and Indo-European: Linguistic and Archaeological Considerations*, edited by A. Parpola and P. Koskikallio. Helsinki: Memoires de la Societé Finno-Ougrienne.

Carpelan, Christian, and Asko Parpola. 2017. On the emergence, contacts and dispersal of Proto-Indo-European, Proto-Uralic and Proto-Aryan in an archaeological perspective. In *Language and Prehistory of the Indo-European Peoples*, edited by A. Hyllested, B. N. Whitehead, T. Olander and B. A. Olsen. Copenhagen: Museum Tusculanum Press.

Cassidy, L. M., R. Martiniano, E. M. Murphy, M. D. Teasdale, J. Mallory, B. Hartwell, and D. G. Bradley. 2016. Neolithic and Bronze Age migration to Ireland and establishment of the insular Atlantic genome. *Proc Natl Acad Sci U S A* 113 (2):368-73.

Cassidy, Lara. 2018. A Genomic Compendium of an Island: Documenting Continuity and Change across Irish Human Prehistory, School of Genetics & Microbiology, Trinity College Dublin., Dublin.

Chadwick, Nora. 1970. *The Celts*. London: Folio Society.

Chazin, Hannah, Gwyneth W. Gordon, and Kelly J. Knudson. 2019. Isotopic perspectives on pastoralist mobility in the Late Bronze Age South Caucasus. *Journal of Anthropological Archaeology* 54:48-67.

Chechushkov, I. V., A. S. Yakimov, O. P. Bachura, Yan Chuen Ng, and E. N. Goncharova. 2018. Social Organization of the Sintashta-Petrovka Groups of the Late Bronze Age and a Cause for Origin of Social Elites (Based on Materials of the Settlement of Kamenny Ambar). *Stratum plus* 2:149-166.

Chechushkov, Igor V. 2018. Bronze Age Human Communities in the Southern Urals Steppe: Sintashta-Petrovka Social and Subsistence Organization, Graduate Faculty of The Dietrich School of Arts and Sciences, University of Pittsburgh, PIttsburgh.

Chechushkov, Igor V., and Andrei V. Epimakhov. 2018. Eurasian Steppe Chariots and Social Complexity During the Bronze Age. *Journal of World Prehistory*.

Chechushkov, Igor V., Andrei V. Epimakhov, and Andrei G. Bersenev. 2018. Early horse bridle with cheekpieces as a marker of social change: An experimental and statistical study. *Journal of Archaeological Science* 97:125-136.

Chekunova, E.M., N.V. Yartseva, M.K. Chekunov, and A.N. Mazurkevich. 2014. The First Results of the Genotyping of the Aboriginals and Human Bone Remains of the Archeological Memorials of the Upper Podvin'e. // Archeology of the lake settlements of IV—II Thousands BC: The chronology of cultures and natural environment and climatic rhythms. Paper read at Proceedings of the International Conference, Devoted to the 50-year Research of the Pile Settlements on the North-West of Russia., 13-15 November, at St. Petersburg.

Chernykh, E. N. 1992. *Ancient Metallurgy in the USSR*. Cambridge: Cambridge University Press.

Chiang, Charleston W. K., Joseph H. Marcus, Carlo Sidore, Arjun Biddanda, Hussein Al-Asadi, Magdalena Zoledziewska, Maristella Pitzalis, Fabio Busonero, Andrea Maschio, Giorgio Pistis, Maristella Steri, Andrea Angius, Kirk E. Lohmueller, Goncalo R. Abecasis, David Schlessinger, Francesco Cucca, and John Novembre. 2018. Genomic history of the Sardinian population. *Nature Genetics* 50 (10):1426-1434.

Cilli, Elisabetta, Stefania Sarno, Guido Alberto Gnecchi Ruscone, Patrizia Serventi, Sara De Fanti, Paolo Delaini, Paolo Ognibene, Gian Pietro Basello, Gloria Ravegnini, Sabrina Angelini, Gianmarco Ferri, Davide Gentilini, Anna Maria Di Blasio, Susi Pelotti, Davide Pettener, Marco Sazzini, Antonio Panaino, Donata Luiselli, and Giorgio Gruppioni. 2019. The genetic legacy of the Yaghnobis: A witness of an ancient Eurasian ancestry in the historically reshuffled central Asian gene pool. *American Journal of Physical Anthropology*:1-12.

Coromines, Joan. 1976. Els ploms sorotàptics d'Arles. In *Entre dos llenguatges*, edited by J. Coromines. Barcelona: Curial Edicions Catalanes.

Cramp, Lucy J. E., Richard P. Evershed, Mika Lavento, Petri Halinen, Kristiina Mannermaa, Markku Oinonen, Johannes Kettunen, Markus Perola, Päivi Onkamo, and Volker Heyd. 2014. Neolithic dairy farming at the extreme of agriculture in northern Europe. *Proceedings of the Royal Society B: Biological Sciences* 281 (1791).

Csáky, Veronika, Dániel Gerber, István Koncz, Gergely Csiky, Balázs G. Mende, Antónia Marcsik, Erika Molnár, György Pálfi, András Gulyás, Bernadett Kovacsóczy, Gabriella M. Lezsák, Gábor Lőrinczy, Anna Szécsényi-Nagy, and Tivadar Vida. 2018. Inner Asian maternal genetic origin of the Avar period nomadic elite in the 7th century AD Carpathian Basin. *bioRxiv*.

Csáky, Veronika, Dániel Gerber, István Koncz, Gergely Csiky, Balázs G. Mende, Bea Szeifert, Balázs Egyed, Horolma Pamjav, Antónia Marcsik, Erika Molnár, György Pálfi, András Gulyás, Bernadett Kovacsóczy, Gabriella M. Lezsák, Gábor Lőrinczy, Anna Szécsényi-Nagy, and Tivadar Vida. 2019. Genetic insights into the social organisation of the Avar period elite in the 7th century AD Carpathian Basin. *bioRxiv*:415760.

Csányi, B., E. Bogácsi-Szabó, Gy Tömöry, Á Czibula, K. Priskin, A. Csõsz, B. Mende, P. Langó, K. Csete, A. Zsolnai, E. K. Conant, C. S. Downes, and I. Raskó. 2008. Y-Chromosome Analysis of Ancient Hungarian and Two Modern Hungarian-Speaking Populations from the Carpathian Basin. *Annals of Human Genetics* 72 (4):519-534.

Cui, Yinqiu, Hongjie Li, Chao Ning, Ye Zhang, Lu Chen, Xin Zhao, Erika Hagelberg, and Hui Zhou. 2013. Y Chromosome analysis of prehistoric human populations in the West Liao River Valley, Northeast China. *BMC Evolutionary Biology* 13 (1):216.

Curry, Andrew. 2016. Slaughter at the bridge: Uncovering a colossal Bronze Age battle. *Science News*.

Curta, Florin. 2001. *The Making of the Slavs: History and Archaeology of the Lower Danube Region, c. 500-700, Cambridge Studies in Medieval Life and Thought: Fourth Series*. Cambridge: Cambridge University Press.

Repeated Author. 2019. *Eastern Europe in the Middle Ages (500-1300), Brill's Companions to European History*. Leiden/Boston: Brill.

Czebreszuk, J. 2001. *Schyłek neolitu i początki epoki brązu w strefie południowozachodniobałtyckiej (III i początki II tys. przed Chr.). Alternatywny model kultur*. Poznań: Adam Mickiewicz University.

Czebreszuk, Janusz. 1998. "Trzciniec". An alternative view. In *The Trzciniec area of the Early Bronze Age civilization: 1950-1200 BC*. Poznan.

Repeated Author. 2013. The Bronze Age in the Polish Lands. In *The Oxford Handbook of the European Bronze Age*, edited by H. Fokkens and A. Harding. Oxford: Oxford University Press.

Czebreszuk, Janusz, and Marzena Szmyt. 2011. Identities, Differentiation and Interactions on the Central European Plain in the 3rd millennium BC. In *Sozialarchäologische Perspektive: Gesellschaftlicher Wandel 5000-1500 v.*

Chr. zwichen Atlantik und Kaukasus, edited by S. Hansen and J. Müller. Darmstadt: philipp von Zabern.

Repeated Author. 2012. Bell Beakers and the cultural milieu of north European plain. In *Background to Beakers. Inquiries into regional cultural backgrounds of the Bell Beaker complex*, edited by H. Fokkens and F. Nicolis. Leiden: Sidestone Press.

Damm, Charlotte. 2012. From entities to interaction. Replacing pots and people with networks of transmission. In *A Linguistic Map of Northern Europe*, edited by R.Grünthal and P.Kallio. Helsinki: The Finno-Ugrian Society.

de Barros Damgaard, Peter, Nina Marchi, Simon Rasmussen, Michaël Peyrot, Gabriel Renaud, Thorfinn Korneliussen, J. Víctor Moreno-Mayar, Mikkel Winther Pedersen, Amy Goldberg, Emma Usmanova, Nurbol Baimukhanov, Valeriy Loman, Lotte Hedeager, Anders Gorm Pedersen, Kasper Nielsen, Gennady Afanasiev, Kunbolot Akmatov, Almaz Aldashev, Ashyk Alpaslan, Gabit Baimbetov, Vladimir I. Bazaliiskii, Arman Beisenov, Bazartseren Boldbaatar, Bazartseren Boldgiv, Choduraa Dorzhu, Sturla Ellingvag, Diimaajav Erdenebaatar, Rana Dajani, Evgeniy Dmitriev, Valeriy Evdokimov, Karin M. Frei, Andrey Gromov, Alexander Goryachev, Hakon Hakonarson, Tatyana Hegay, Zaruhi Khachatryan, Ruslan Khaskhanov, Egor Kitov, Alina Kolbina, Tabaldiev Kubatbek, Alexey Kukushkin, Igor Kukushkin, Nina Lau, Ashot Margaryan, Inga Merkyte, Ilya V. Mertz, Viktor K. Mertz, Enkhbayar Mijiddorj, Vyacheslav Moiyesev, Gulmira Mukhtarova, Bekmukhanbet Nurmukhanbetov, Z. Orozbekova, Irina Panyushkina, Karol Pieta, Václav Smrčka, Irina Shevnina, Andrey Logvin, Karl-Göran Sjögren, Tereza Štolcová, Angela M. Taravella, Kadicha Tashbaeva, Alexander Tkachev, Turaly Tulegenov, Dmitriy Voyakin, Levon Yepiskoposyan, Sainbileg Undrakhbold, Victor Varfolomeev, Andrzej Weber, Melissa A. Wilson Sayres, Nikolay Kradin, Morten E. Allentoft, Ludovic Orlando, Rasmus Nielsen, Martin Sikora, Evelyne Heyer, Kristian Kristiansen, and Eske Willerslev. 2018. 137 ancient human genomes from across the Eurasian steppes. *Nature* 557 (7705):369-374.

de Barros Damgaard, Peter, Rui Martiniano, Jack Kamm, J. Víctor Moreno-Mayar, Guus Kroonen, Michaël Peyrot, Gojko Barjamovic, Simon Rasmussen, Claus Zacho, Nurbol Baimukhanov, Victor Zaibert, Victor Merz, Arjun Biddanda, Ilja Merz, Valeriy Loman, Valeriy Evdokimov, Emma Usmanova, Brian Hemphill, Andaine Seguin-Orlando, Fulya Eylem Yediay, Inam Ullah, Karl-Göran Sjögren, Katrine Højholt Iversen, Jeremy Choin, Constanza de la Fuente, Melissa Ilardo, Hannes Schroeder, Vyacheslav Moiseyev, Andrey Gromov, Andrei Polyakov, Sachihiro Omura, Süleyman Yücel Senyurt, Habib Ahmad, Catriona McKenzie, Ashot Margaryan, Abdul Hameed, Abdul Samad, Nazish Gul, Muhammad Hassan Khokhar, O. I. Goriunova, Vladimir I. Bazaliiskii, John Novembre, Andrzej W. Weber, Ludovic Orlando, Morten E. Allentoft, Rasmus Nielsen, Kristian Kristiansen, Martin Sikora, Alan K. Outram, Richard Durbin, and Eske Willerslev. 2018. The first horse herders and the impact of early Bronze Age steppe expansions into Asia. *Science*.

della Casa, Philippe. 2013. Switzerland and the Central Alps. In *The Oxford Handbook of the European Bronze Age*, edited by H. Fokkens and A. Harding. Oxford: Oxford University Press.

Demkina, T. S., A. V. Borisov, V. A. Demkin, T. E. Khomutova, T. V. Kuznetsova, M. V. El'tsov, and S. N. Udal'tsov. 2017. Paleoecological crisis in the steppes of the Lower Volga region in the Middle of the Bronze Age (III–II centuries BC). *Eurasian Soil Science* 50 (7):791-804.

Deom, Jean-Marc, Renato Sala, and Anne Laudisoit. 2019. The Ili River Delta: Holocene Hydrogeological Evolution and Human Colonization. In *Socio-Environmental Dynamics along the Historical Silk Road*, edited by L. E. Yang, H.-R. Bork, X. Fang and S. Mischke. Cham: Springer International Publishing.

Di Cristofaro, Julie, Stéphane Mazières, Audrey Tous, Cornelia Di Gaetano, Alice A. Lin, Paul Nebbia, Alberto Piazza, Roy J. King, Peter Underhill, and Jacques Chiaroni. 2018. Prehistoric migrations through the Mediterranean basin shaped Corsican Y-chromosome diversity. *PLOS ONE* 13 (8):e0200641.

Dietrich, Laura. 2011. Gânduri asupra dimensiunilor sociale ale vaselor de tip kantharos din cultura Noua (Gedanken über die sozialen Dimensionen der Kantharos-Gefäße der Noua-Kultur). In *Archaeology. Making of and practice. Studies in honor of Mircea Babeş at his 70th anniversary*, edited by D. Măgureanu, D. Măndescu and S. Matei. Piteşti: Ordessos.

Dolgikh, B.O. . 1960. *Rodovoi i plemennoi sostav narodov Sibiri v XVII veke [The clans and Tribes of the Peoples of Siberia in the 17th century]*. Moscow.

Repeated Author. 1962. *Rodovaya ekzogamiya y nganasan i entsev [The Clan Exogamy among the Nganasans and the Enets]*, *Siberian Ethnographic Collection*. Moscow: Publishing house of the Academy of Sciences of the USSR.

Dolukhanov, P. M. 1989. Prehistoric ethnicity in the north-east of Europe. *Fennoscandia Archaeologica* 6:81-84.

Dudás, Eszter, Andrea Vágó-Zalán, Anna Vándor, Anastasia Saypasheva, Péter Pomozi, and Horolma Pamjav. 2019. Genetic history of Bashkirian Mari and Southern Mansi ethnic groups in the Ural region. *Molecular Genetics and Genomics*.

Duffy, Paul R., Györgyi M. Parditka, Julia I. Giblin, and László Paja. 2019. The problem with tells: lessons learned from absolute dating of Bronze Age mortuary ceramics in Hungary. *Antiquity* 93 (367):63-79.

Dzięgielewski, Karol. 2017. Late Bronze and Early Iron Age communities in the northern part of the Polish Lowland (1000-500 BC). In *The Past Societies. Polish lands from the first evidence of human presence to the early Middle Ages. Volume 3: 2000–500 BC*, edited by U. Bugaj. Warszawa.

Earle, T., J. Ling, C. Uhnér, Z. Stos-Gale, and L. Melheim. 2015. The Political Economy and Metal Trade in Bronze Age Europe: Understanding Regional Variability in Terms of Comparative Advantages and Articulations. *European Journal of Archaeology* 18 (4):633-657.

Ebenesersdóttir, S. Sunna, Marcela Sandoval-Velasco, Ellen D. Gunnarsdóttir, Anuradha Jagadeesan, Valdís B. Guðmundsdóttir, Elísabet L. Thordardóttir, Margrét S. Einarsdóttir, Kristjan H. S. Moore, Ásgeir Sigurðsson, Droplaug N. Magnúsdóttir, Hákon Jónsson, Steinunn Snorradóttir, Eivind Hovig, Pål Møller, Ingrid Kockum, Tomas Olsson, Lars Alfredsson, Thomas F. Hansen, Thomas Werge, Gianpiero L. Cavalleri, Edmund Gilbert, Carles Lalueza-Fox, Joe W. Walser, Steinunn Kristjánsdóttir, Shyam Gopalakrishnan, Lilja Árnadóttir,

Ólafur Þ. Magnússon, M. Thomas P. Gilbert, Kári Stefánsson, and Agnar Helgason. 2018. Ancient genomes from Iceland reveal the making of a human population. *Science* 360 (6392):1028-1032.

Eisenmann, Stefanie, Eszter Bánffy, Peter van Dommelen, Kerstin P. Hofmann, Joseph Maran, Iosif Lazaridis, Alissa Mittnik, Michael McCormick, Johannes Krause, David Reich, and Philipp W. Stockhammer. 2018. Reconciling material cultures in archaeology with genetic data: The nomenclature of clusters emerging from archaeogenomic analysis. *Scientific Reports* 8 (1):13003.

Emery, Matthew. 2018. Assessing Migration and Demographic Change in pre-Roman and Roman Period Southern Italy Using Whole-Mitochondrial DNA and Stable Isotope Analysis, Anthropology, McMaster University, Hamilton, Ontario.

Fedorova, Sardana A., Maere Reidla, Ene Metspalu, Mait Metspalu, Siiri Rootsi, Kristiina Tambets, Natalya Trofimova, Sergey I. Zhadanov, Baharak Hooshiar Kashani, Anna Olivieri, Mikhail I. Voevoda, Ludmila P. Osipova, Fedor A. Platonov, Mikhail I. Tomsky, Elza K. Khusnutdinova, Antonio Torroni, and Richard Villems. 2013. Autosomal and uniparental portraits of the native populations of Sakha (Yakutia): implications for the peopling of Northeast Eurasia. *BMC Evolutionary Biology* 13 (1):127.

Fernandes, D. M., D. Strapagiel, P. Borówka, B. Marciniak, E. Żądzińska, K. Sirak, V. Siska, R. Grygiel, J. Carlsson, A. Manica, W. Lorkiewicz, and R. Pinhasi. 2018. A genomic Neolithic time transect of hunter-farmer admixture in central Poland. *Scientific Reports* 8 (1):14879.

Fernandes, Daniel M., Alissa Mittnik, Iñigo Olalde, Iosif Lazaridis, Olivia Cheronet, Nadin Rohland, Swapan Mallick, Rebecca Bernardos, Nasreen Broomandkhoshbacht, Jens Carlsson, Brendan J. Culleton, Matthew Ferry, Beatriz Gamarra, Martina Lari, Matthew Mah, Megan Michel, Alessandra Modi, Mario Novak, Jonas Oppenheimer, Kendra A. Sirak, Kirstin Stewardson, Stefania Vai, Edgard Camarós, Carla Calò, Giulio Catalano, Marian Cueto, Vincenza Forgia, Marina Lozano, Elisabetta Marini, Margherita Micheletti, Roberto M. Miccichè, Maria R. Palombo, Damià Ramis, Vittoria Schimmenti, Pau Sureda, Luís Teira, Maria Teschler-Nicola, Douglas J. Kennett, Carles Lalueza-Fox, Nick Patterson, Luca Sineo, David Caramelli, Ron Pinhasi, and David Reich. 2019. The Arrival of Steppe and Iranian Related Ancestry in the Islands of the Western Mediterranean. *bioRxiv*:584714.

Fitzpatrick, A. P. 2011. *The Amesbury Archer and the Boscombe Bowmen. Bell Beaker Burials on Boscombe Down, Amesbury, Wiltshire*. Salisbury: Wessex Archaeology.

Fokkens, Harry, and David Fontijn. 2013. The Bronze Age in the Low Countries. In *The Oxford Handbook of the European Bronze Age*, edited by H. Fokkens and A. Harding. Oxford: Oxford University Press.

Forni, Gianfranco. 2013. Evidence for Basque as an Indo-European Language. *JIES* 41 (1 & 2):1-142.

Fóthi, E., T. Fehér, Á. Fóthi, and C. Keyser. 2019. Európai És Ázsiai Apai Genetikai Vonalak A Honfoglaló Magyar Törzsekben. *Avicenna Institute of Middle Eastern Studies*.

Fraser, Magdalena, Federico Sanchez-Quinto, Jane Evans, Jan Storå, Anders Götherström, Paul Wallin, Kjel Knutsson, and Mattias Jakobsson. 2018. New insights on cultural dualism and population structure in the Middle Neolithic Funnel Beaker culture on the island of Gotland. *Journal of Archaeological Science: Reports* 17:325-334.

Fraser, Magdalena, Per Sjödin, Federico Sanchez-Quinto, Jane Evans, Gustaf Svedjemo, Kjel Knutsson, Anders Götherström, Mattias Jakobsson, Paul Wallin, and Jan Storå. 2018. The stone cist conundrum: A multidisciplinary approach to investigate Late Neolithic/Early Bronze Age population demography on the island of Gotland. *Journal of Archaeological Science: Reports* 20:324-337.

Freder, Janine. 2010. Die mittelalterlichen Skelette von Usedom. Anthropologische Bearbeitung unter besonderer Berücksichtigung des ethnischen Hintergrundes, Fachbereich Biologie, Chemie, Pharmazie, Freie Universität Berlin, Berlin.

Furmanek, Mirosław, Agata Hałuszko, Maksym Mackiewicz, and Bartosz Myslecki. 2015. New data for research on the Bell Beaker Culture in Upper Silesia, Poland. In *2200 BC – Ein Klimasturz als Ursache für den Zerfall der Alten Welt? 2200 BC – A climatic breakdown as a cause for the collapse of the old world? 7. Mitteldeutscher Archäologentag vom 23. bis 26. Oktober 2014 in Halle (Saale)*, edited by H. Meller, H. W. Arz, R. Jung and R. Risch. Halle (Saale).

Gamba, C., E. R. Jones, M. D. Teasdale, R. L. McLaughlin, G. Gonzalez-Fortes, V. Mattiangeli, L. Domboroczki, I. Kovari, I. Pap, A. Anders, A. Whittle, J. Dani, P. Raczky, T. F. Higham, M. Hofreiter, D. G. Bradley, and R. Pinhasi. 2014. Genome flux and stasis in a five millennium transect of European prehistory. *Nat Commun* 5:5257.

Gilbert, Edmund, Seamus O'Reilly, Michael Merrigan, Darren McGettigan, Anne M. Molloy, Lawrence C. Brody, Walter Bodmer, Katarzyna Hutnik, Sean Ennis, Daniel J. Lawson, James F. Wilson, and Gianpiero L. Cavalleri. 2017. The Irish DNA Atlas: Revealing Fine-Scale Population Structure and History within Ireland. *Scientific Reports* 7 (1):17199.

Golden, Peter B. 1992. The Türk Empires of Eurasia. In *An Introduction to the History of the Turkic Peoples. Ethnogenesis and State-Formation in Medieval and Early Modern Eurasia and the Middle East*. Wiesbaden: Otto Harrasowitz.

González-Fortes, G., F. Tassi, E. Trucchi, K. Henneberger, J. L. A. Paijmans, D. Díez-del-Molino, H. Schroeder, R. R. Susca, C. Barroso-Ruíz, F. J. Bermudez, C. Barroso-Medina, A. M. S. Bettencourt, H. A. Sampaio, A. Grandald'Anglade, A. Salas, A. de Lombera-Hermida, R. Fabregas Valcarce, M. Vaquero, S. Alonso, M. Lozano, X. P. Rodríguez-Alvarez, C. Fernández-Rodríguez, A. Manica, M. Hofreiter, and G. Barbujani. 2019. A western route of prehistoric human migration from Africa into the Iberian Peninsula. *Proceedings of the Royal Society B: Biological Sciences* 286 (1895):20182288.

Górski, Jacek. 2012. Transcarpathian elements in the Trzciniec culture Wanderings of people or ideas? In *Václav Furmánek a doba bronzová : zborník k sedemdesiatym narodeninám*, edited by R. Kujovský and V. Mitáš: Nitra.

Grugni, Viola, Alessandro Raveane, Francesca Mattioli, Vincenza Battaglia, Cinzia Sala, Daniela Toniolo, Luca Ferretti, Rita Gardella, Alessandro Achilli, Anna Olivieri, Antonio Torroni, Giuseppe Passarino, and Ornella Semino. 2018. Reconstructing the genetic history of Italians: new insights from a male (Y-chromosome) perspective. *Annals of Human Biology* 45 (1):44-56.

Grugni, Viola, Alessandro Raveane, Linda Ongaro, Vincenza Battaglia, Beniamino Trombetta, Giulia Colombo, Marco Rosario Capodiferro, Anna Olivieri, Alessandro Achilli, Ugo A. Perego, Jorge Motta, Maribel Tribaldos, Scott R. Woodward, Luca Ferretti, Fulvio Cruciani, Antonio Torroni, and Ornella Semino. 2019. Analysis of the human Y-chromosome haplogroup Q characterizes ancient population movements in Eurasia and the Americas. *BMC Biology* 17 (1):3.

Gunther, T., C. Valdiosera, H. Malmstrom, I. Urena, R. Rodriguez-Varela, O. O. Sverrisdottir, E. A. Daskalaki, P. Skoglund, T. Naidoo, E. M. Svensson, J. M. Bermudez de Castro, E. Carbonell, M. Dunn, J. Stora, E. Iriarte, J. L. Arsuaga, J. M. Carretero, A. Gotherstrom, and M. Jakobsson. 2015. Ancient genomes link early farmers from Atapuerca in Spain to modern-day Basques. *Proc Natl Acad Sci U S A* 112 (38):11917-22.

Günther, Torsten, Helena Malmström, Emma Svensson, Ayça Omrak, Federico Sánchez-Quinto, Gülşah M. Kılınç, Maja Krzewińska, Gunilla Eriksson, Magdalena Fraser, Hanna Edlund, Arielle R. Munters, Alexandra Coutinho, Luciana G. Simões, Mário Vicente, Anders Sjölander, Berit Jansen Sellevold, Roger Jørgensen, Peter Claes, Mark D. Shriver, Cristina Valdiosera, Mihai G. Netea, Jan Apel, Kerstin Lidén, Birgitte Skar, Jan Storå, Anders Götherström, and Mattias Jakobsson. 2017. Genomics of Mesolithic Scandinavia reveal colonization routes and high-latitude adaptation. *bioRxiv*.

Haak, W., I. Lazaridis, N. Patterson, N. Rohland, S. Mallick, B. Llamas, G. Brandt, S. Nordenfelt, E. Harney, K. Stewardson, Q. Fu, A. Mittnik, E. Banffy, C. Economou, M. Francken, S. Friederich, R. G. Pena, F. Hallgren, V. Khartanovich, A. Khokhlov, M. Kunst, P. Kuznetsov, H. Meller, O. Mochalov, V. Moiseyev, N. Nicklisch, S. L. Pichler, R. Risch, M. A. Rojo Guerra, C. Roth, A. Szecsenyi-Nagy, J. Wahl, M. Meyer, J. Krause, D. Brown, D. Anthony, A. Cooper, K. W. Alt, and D. Reich. 2015. Massive migration from the steppe was a source for Indo-European languages in Europe. *Nature* 522 (7555):207-11.

Haber, M., M. Mezzavilla, Y. Xue, D. Comas, P. Gasparini, P. Zalloua, and C. Tyler-Smith. 2016. Genetic evidence for an origin of the Armenians from Bronze Age mixing of multiple populations. *Eur J Hum Genet* 24 (6):931-6.

Haber, Marc, Claude Doumet-Serhal, Christiana Scheib, Yali Xue, Petr Danecek, Massimo Mezzavilla, Sonia Youhanna, Rui Martiniano, Javier Prado-Martinez, Michał Szpak, Elizabeth Matisoo-Smith, Holger Schutkowski, Richard Mikulski, Pierre Zalloua, Toomas Kivisild, and Chris Tyler-Smith. 2017. Continuity and admixture in the last five millennia of Levantine history from ancient Canaanite and present-day Lebanese genome sequences. *bioRxiv*.

Haber, Marc, Y. Xue, C. Scheib, C. Doumet-Serhal, T. Kivisild, and C. Tyler-Smith. 2018. Mount Lebanon provides an opportunity to study DNA from the ancient Near East. Paper read at American Society of Human Genetics Annual Meeting 2018. October 16-20, at San Diego.

Häkkinen, Jaakko. 2009. Kantauralin ajoitus ja paikannus: perustelut puntarissa. *SUSA/JSFOu* 92:9-56.

Hanks, Bryan, Alicia Ventresca Miller, Margaret Judd, Andrey Epimakhov, Dmitry Razhev, and Karen Privat. 2018. Bronze Age diet and economy: New stable isotope data from the Central Eurasian steppes (2100-1700 BC). *Journal of Archaeological Science* 97:14-25.

Harrison, Richard, and Volker Heyd. 2007. The Transformation of Europe in the Third Millennium BC: the example of 'Le Petit-Chasseur I + III' (Sion, Valais, Switzerland). *Praehistorische Zeitschrift* 82 (2).

Hedman, Sven-Donald. 2003. *Boplatser och offerplatser. Ekonomisk strategi och boplatsmönster bland skoggsamer 700–1600 AD, Studia archaeologica Universitatis Umensis.* Umeå.

Helimski, Eugene. 2001. Уральцы и их предшественники: белые пятна на этноисторической карте Северной Евразии и уральские языки. Paper read at Congressus Nonus Internationalis Fenno-Ugristarum IV. Dissertationes sectionum: Linguistica I,, at Tartu.

Heraclides, Alexandros, Evy Bashiardes, Eva Fernández-Domínguez, Stefania Bertoncini, Marios Chimonas, Vasilis Christofi, Jonathan King, Bruce Budowle, Panayiotis Manoli, and Marios A. Cariolou. 2017. Y-chromosomal analysis of Greek Cypriots reveals a primarily common pre-Ottoman paternal ancestry with Turkish Cypriots. *PLOS ONE* 12 (6):e0179474.

Heyd, Volker. 2007. Families, Prestige Goods, Warriors & Complex Societies: Beaker Groups of the 3rd Millennium cal BC Along the Upper & Middle Danube. *Proceedings of the Prehistoric Society* 73:327-379.

Repeated Author. 2013. Europe at the Dawn of the Bronze Age. In *Transition to the Bronze Age*, edited by V. Heyd, G. Kulcsár and V. Szeverényi. Budapest: Archaeolingua.

Heyd, Vollker. 2007. When the West meets the East: The Eastern Periphery of the Bell Beaker Phenomenon and its Relation with the Aegean Early Bronze Age. In *Between the Aegean and Baltic Seas*, edited by I. Galanaki. Liège: Aegaeum.

Hollard, C., C. Keyser, P. H. Giscard, T. Tsagaan, N. Bayarkhuu, J. Bemmann, E. Crubezy, and B. Ludes. 2014. Strong genetic admixture in the Altai at the Middle Bronze Age revealed by uniparental and ancestry informative markers. *Forensic Sci Int Genet* 12:199-207.

Hollard, Clémence, Vincent Zvénigorosky, Alexey Kovalev, Yurii Kiryushin, Alexey Tishkin, Igor Lazaretov, Eric Crubézy, Bertrand Ludes, and Christine Keyser. 2018. New genetic evidence of affinities and discontinuities between bronze age Siberian populations. *American Journal of Physical Anthropology* 167 (1):97-107.

Hoole, M., A. Sheridan, A. Boyle, T. Booth, S. Brace, Y. Diekmann, I. Olalde, M. Thomas, I. Barnes, J. Evans, C. Chenery, H. Sloane, H. Morrison, S. Fraser, S. Timpany, and D. Hamilton. 2018. 'Ava': a Beaker-associated woman from a cist at Achavanich, Highland, and the story of her (re-)discovery and subsequent study. *Proceedings of the Society of Antiquaries of Scotland* 147:73-118.

Horváth, Csaba Barnabás. 2014. The story of two northward migrations - origins of Finno-Permic and Balto-Slavic languages in northeast Europe, based on Y-chromosome haplogroups. *European Scientific Journal* 2:531-538.

Hovhannisyan, A, Z Khachatryan, M Haber, P Hrechdakian, T Karafet, P Zalloua, and L Yepiskoposyan. 2014. Different waves and directions of Neolithic migrations in the Armenian Highland. *Investig Genet* 5 (1):15.

Hyllested, Adam. 2009. Internal reconstruction vs. external comparison: the case of the Indo-Uralic larnygeals. In *Internal reconstruction in Indo-European: Methods, results and problems. Section papers from the XVIth International Conference on Historical Linguistics held at the University of Copenhagen*, edited by J. E. Rasmussen and T. Olander. Copenhagen: Museum Tusculanum.

Ilumae, A. M., M. Reidla, M. Chukhryaeva, M. Jarve, H. Post, M. Karmin, L. Saag, A. Agdzhoyan, A. Kushniarevich, S. Litvinov, N. Ekomasova, K. Tambets, E. Metspalu, R. Khusainova, B. Yunusbayev, E. K. Khusnutdinova, L. P. Osipova, S. Fedorova, O. Utevska, S. Koshel, E. Balanovska, D. M. Behar, O. Balanovsky, T. Kivisild, P. A. Underhill, R. Villems, and S. Rootsi. 2016. Human Y Chromosome Haplogroup N: A Non-trivial Time-Resolved Phylogeography that Cuts across Language Families. *Am J Hum Genet* 99 (1):163-73.

Ilumäe, Anne-Mai, Maere Reidla, Marina Chukhryaeva, Mari Järve, Helen Post, Monika Karmin, Lauri Saag, Anastasiya Agdzhoyan, Alena Kushniarevich, Sergey Litvinov, Natalya Ekomasova, Kristiina Tambets, Ene Metspalu, Rita Khusainova, Bayazit Yunusbayev, Elza K Khusnutdinova, Ludmila P Osipova, Sardana Fedorova, Olga Utevska, Sergey Koshel, Elena Balanovska, Doron M Behar, Oleg Balanovsky, Toomas Kivisild, Peter A Underhill, Richard Villems, and Siiri Rootsi. 2016. Human Y Chromosome Haplogroup N: A Non-trivial Time-Resolved Phylogeography that Cuts across Language Families. *The American Journal of Human Genetics* 99 (1):163-173.

ISOGG. 2018. Y-DNA Haplogroup Tree. Version: 13.270 . Date: 13 November 2018. International Society of Genetic Genealogy.

Jantzen, Detlef; Gundula Lidke, Jana Dräger, Joachim Krüger, Knut Rassmann, Sebastian Lorenz, and Thomas Terberger. 2017. An early Bronze Age causeway in the Tollense Valley, Mecklenburg-Western Pomerania – The starting point of a violent conflict 3300 years ago? In *Bericht der römisch-germanischen Komission*. Frankfurt a.M.: Römisch-Germanische Kommission des Deutschen Archäologischen Instituts.

Jarosz, P., M. Mazurek, J. Okoński, and A. Szczepanek. 2011. Bell Beaker influence in the Early Bronze Age on the basis of latest discoveries in Rozbórz, in south. Paper read at Current researches on Bell Beakers. Proceedings of the 15th International Bell Beaker Conference: From Atlantic to Ural. 5th-9th May 2011, at Poio (Pontevedra, Galicia, Spain).

Järve, M., C. L. Scheib, L. Saag, A. Kriiska, I. Shramko, S. Zadnikov, N. Savelev, O. Utevska, L. Varul, A. K. Pathak, L. Pagani, J. R. Flores, F. Montinaro, L. Saag, K. Tambets, T. Kivisild, and R. Villems. 2018. Genetic continuity in the western Eurasian Steppe broken not due to Scythian dominance, but rather at the transition to the Chernyakhov culture (Ostrogoths). Paper read at 8th

International Symposium on Biomolecular Archaeology ISBA 2018. 18th – 21st September, at Jena, Germany.

Järve, Mari, Lehti Saag, Christiana Lyn Scheib, Ajai K. Pathak, Francesco Montinaro, Luca Pagani, J. Rodrigo Flores, Meriam Guellil, Lauri Saag, Kristiina Tambets, Alena Kushniarevich, Anu Solnik, Liivi Varul, Stanislav Zadnikov, Oleg Petrauskas, Maryana Avramenko, Boris Magomedov, Serghii Didenko, Gennadi Toshev, Igor Bruyako, Denys Grechko, Vitalii Okatenko, Kyrylo Gorbenko, Oleksandr Smyrnov, Anatolii Heiko, Roman Reida, Serheii Sapiehin, Sergey Sirotin, Aleksandr Tairov, Arman Beisenov, Maksim Starodubtsev, Vitali Vasilev, Alexei Nechvaloda, Biyaslan Atabiev, Sergey Litvinov, Natalia Ekomasova, Murat Dzhaubermezov, Sergey Voroniatov, Olga Utevska, Irina Shramko, Elza Khusnutdinova, Mait Metspalu, Nikita Savelev, Aivar Kriiska, Toomas Kivisild, and Richard Villems. 2019. Shifts in the Genetic Landscape of the Western Eurasian Steppe Associated with the Beginning and End of the Scythian Dominance. *Current Biology* In Review, Available at SSRN.

Jensen, J. 2003. *The prehistory of Denmark*. London and New York: Routledge.

Jeong, Choongwon, Oleg Balanovsky, Elena Lukianova, Nurzhibek Kahbatkyzy, Pavel Flegontov, Valery Zaporozhchenko, Alexander Immel, Chuan-Chao Wang, Olzhas Ixan, Elmira Khussainova, Bakhytzhan Bekmanov, Victor Zaibert, Maria Lavryashina, Elvira Pocheshkhova, Yuldash Yusupov, Anastasiya Agdzhoyan, Sergey Koshel, Andrei Bukin, Pagbajabyn Nymadawa, Shahlo Turdikulova, Dilbar Dalimova, Mikhail Churnosov, Roza Skhalyakho, Denis Daragan, Yuri Bogunov, Anna Bogunova, Alexandr Shtrunov, Nadezhda Dubova, Maxat Zhabagin, Levon Yepiskoposyan, Vladimir Churakov, Nikolay Pislegin, Larissa Damba, Ludmila Saroyants, Khadizhat Dibirova, Lubov Atramentova, Olga Utevska, Eldar Idrisov, Evgeniya Kamenshchikova, Irina Evseeva, Mait Metspalu, Alan K. Outram, Martine Robbeets, Leyla Djansugurova, Elena Balanovska, Stephan Schiffels, Wolfgang Haak, David Reich, and Johannes Krause. 2019. The genetic history of admixture across inner Eurasia. *Nature Ecology & Evolution*.

Jeong, Choongwon, Oleg Balanovsky, Elena Lukianova, Nurzhibek Kahbatkyzy, Pavel Flegontov, Valery Zaporozhchenko, Alexander Immel, Chuan-Chao Wang, Olzhas Ixan, Elmira Khussainova, Bakhytzhan Bekmanov, Victor Zaibert, Maria Lavryashina, Elvira Pocheshkhova, Yuldash Yusupov, Anastasiya Agdzhoyan, Koshel Sergey, Andrei Bukin, Pagbajabyn Nymadawa, Michail Churnosov, Roza Skhalyakho, Denis Daragan, Yuri Bogunov, Anna Bogunova, Alexandr Shtrunov, Nadezda Dubova, Maxat Zhabagin, Levon Yepiskoposyan, Vladimir Churakov, Nikolay Pislegin, Larissa Damba, Ludmila Saroyants, Khadizhat Dibirova, Lubov Artamentova, Olga Utevska, Eldar Idrisov, Evgeniya Kamenshchikova, Irina Evseeva, Mait Metspalu, Martine Robbeets, Leyla Djansugurova, Elena Balanovska, Stephan Schiffels, Wolfgang Haak, David Reich, and Johannes Krause. 2018. Characterizing the genetic history of admixture across inner Eurasia. *bioRxiv*.

Jeong, Choongwon, Shevan Wilkin, Tsend Amgalantugs, Abigail S. Bouwman, William Timothy Treal Taylor, Richard W. Hagan, Sabri Bromage, Soninkhishig Tsolmon, Christian Trachsel, Jonas Grossmann, Judith Littleton,

Cheryl A. Makarewicz, John Krigbaum, Marta Burri, Ashley Scott, Ganmaa Davaasambuu, Joshua Wright, Franziska Irmer, Erdene Myagmar, Nicole Boivin, Martine Robbeets, Frank J. Rühli, Johannes Krause, Bruno Frohlich, Jessica Hendy, and Christina Warinner. 2018. Bronze Age population dynamics and the rise of dairy pastoralism on the eastern Eurasian steppe. *Proceedings of the National Academy of Sciences.*

Jia, Peter W., Alison Betts, Dexin Cong, Xiaobing Jia, and Paula Doumani Dupuy. 2017. Adunqiaolu: new evidence for the Andronovo in Xinjiang, China. *Antiquity* 91 (357):621-639.

Jia, Peter Wei Ming, and Alison V. G. Betts. 2010. A re-analysis of the Qiemu'erqieke (Shamirshak) cemeteries, Xinjiang, China. *JIES* 38 (3 & 4):275-317.

Jiráň, Luboš, Milan Salaš, and Alexandra Krenn-Leeb. 2013. The Czech Lands and Austria in the Bronze Age In *The Oxford Handbook of the European Bronze Age*, edited by H. Fokkens and A. Harding. Oxford: Oxford University Press.

Jockenhövel, Albrecht. 2013. Germany in the Bronze Age In *The Oxford Handbook of the European Bronze Age*, edited by H. Fokkens and A. Harding. Oxford: Oxford University Press.

Johansen, K. L., S. T. Laursen, and M. K. Holst. 2004. Spatial patterns of social organization in the Early Bronze Age of South Scandinavia. *Journal of Anthropological Archaeology* 23:33-55.

Jones, Jennifer R., Cristina Vega Maeso, Eduardo Carmona Ballestero, Luis Villanueva Martín, Maria Eugenía Delgado Arceo, and Ana B. Marín-Arroyo. 2019. Investigating prehistoric diet and lifeways of early farmers in central northern Spain (3000–1500 CAL BC) using stable isotope techniques. *Archaeological and Anthropological Sciences.*

Judd, Margaret A., Jessica L. Walker, Alicia Ventresca Miller, Dmitry Razhev, Andrey V. Epimakhov, and Bryan K. Hanks. 2018. Life in the fast lane: Settled pastoralism in the Central Eurasian Steppe during the Middle Bronze Age. *American Journal of Human Biology* 30 (4):e23129.

Juras, Anna, Maciej Chyleński, Edvard Ehler, Helena Malmström, Danuta Żurkiewicz, Piotr Włodarczak, Stanisław Wilk, Jaroslav Peška, Pavel Fojtík, Miroslav Králík, Jerzy Libera, Jolanta Bagińska, Krzysztof Tunia, Viktor I. Klochko, Miroslawa Dabert, Mattias Jakobsson, and Aleksander Kośko. 2018. Mitochondrial genomes reveal an east to west cline of steppe ancestry in Corded Ware populations. *Scientific Reports* 8 (1):11603.

Kadrow, Sławomir. 1998. The Central European Dimension of the Decline of the Early Bronze Age Civilization. The Trzciniec Socio-cultural System at the Outset of ist Career. In *The Trzciniec area of the Early Bronze Age Civilization: 1950-1200 BC.* Poznan.

Repeated Author. 2007. Soziale Strukturen und ethnische Identitäten der Bronzezeit Ostpolens, Auf der Suche nach Identitäten: Volk – Stamm – Kultur – Ethnos. Internationale Tagung der Universität Leipzig vom 8.- 9. Dezember 2000. In *Auf der Suche nach Identitäten: Volk – Stamm – Kultur – Ethnos. Internationale Tagung der Universität Leipzig vom 8.- 9. Dezember 2000*, edited by S. Rieckhoff and U. Sommer. Oxford.

Repeated Author. 2017. What Happened in Iwanowice at the End of the 3rd Millennium BC? Did a Rebellion Break Out? In *Rebellion and Inequality in Archaeology. Proceedings of the Kiel Workshops "Archaeology of Rebellion" (2014) and "Social Inequality as aTopic in Archaeology" (2015)*, edited by S. Hansen and J. Müller. Bonn: Dr. Rudolf Habelt.

Kajtoch, Łukasz, Elżbieta Cieślak, Zoltán Varga, Wojciech Paul, Miłosz A. Mazur, Gábor Sramkó, and Daniel Kubisz. 2016. Phylogeographic patterns of steppe species in Eastern Central Europe: a review and the implications for conservation. *Biodiversity and Conservation* 25 (12):2309-2339.

Kallio, Petri. 2001. Phonetic Uralisms in Indo-European? In *Early Contacts between Uralic and Indo-European: Linguistic and Archaeological Considerations*, edited by C. Carpelan, A. Parpola and P. Koskikallio. Helsinki: Société Finno-Ougrienne.

Repeated Author. 2002. Prehistoric Contacts between Indo-European and Uralic. In *Proceedings of the Thirteenth Annual UCLA Indo-European Conference*, edited by K. Jones-Bley, M. E. Huld, A. D. Volpe and M. R. Dexter. Washington, DC: Institute for the Study of Man.

Repeated Author. 2008. On the 'Early Baltic' loanwords in Common Finnic. In *Evidence and Counter-Evidence, Festschrift Frederik Kortlandt*. Amsterdam - New York: Rodopi.

Repeated Author. 2009. Stratigraphy of Indo-European loanwords in Saami. In *Máttut - máddagat: The Roots of Saami Ethnicities, Societies and Spaces / Places*, edited by T. Äikäs. Oulu: Publications of the Giellagas Institute 12.

Repeated Author. 2012. The Prehistoric Germanic Loanword Strata in Finnic. In *A Linguistic Map of Prehistoric Northern Europe*. Helsinki: Suomalais-Ugrilainen Seura.

Repeated Author. 2014. The Diversification of Proto-Finnic. In *Fibula, Fabula, Fact: The Viking Age in Finland*, edited by J. A. Frog and C. Tolley Helsinki.

Repeated Author. 2015. The Language Contact Situation in Prehistoric Northeastern Europe. In *The Linguistic Roots of Europe: Origin and Development of European Languages*, edited by R. Mailhammer, T. Vennemann and B. A. Olsen. Copenhagen: Museum Tusculanum Press.

Repeated Author. 2015. The Stratigraphy of the Germanic Loanwords in Finnic. In *Early Germanic Languages in Contact*, edited by J. O. Askedal and H. F. Nielsen. Amsterdam - Philadelphia: John Benjamins.

Repeated Author. 2017. The Indo-Europeans and the Non-Indo-Europeans in Prehistoric Northern Europe. In *Language and Prehistory of the Indo-European Peoples: A Cross-Disciplinary Perspective*, edited by A. Hyllested, B. N. Whitehead, T. Olander and B. A. Olsen. Copenhagen: University of Chicago Press.

Kaňáková, Ludmila, Jozef Bátora, and Vojtěch Nosek. 2019. Use-wear and ballistic analyses of arrowheads from the burial ground of the Nitra culture in Ludanice - Mýtna Nová Ves. *Journal of Archaeological Science: Reports* 23:25-35.

Karafet, Tatiana M., Ludmila P. Osipova, Olga V. Savina, Brian Hallmark, and Michael F. Hammer. 2018. Siberian genetic diversity reveals complex origins of the Samoyedic-speaking populations. *American Journal of Human Biology* 0 (0):e23194.

Kealhofer, Lisa, Peter Grave, and Mary M. Voigt. 2019. Dating Gordion: the timing and tempo of Late Bronze and Early Iron Age political transformation. *Radiocarbon*:1-20.

Kelder, Jorrit M. 2010. *The Kingdom of Mycenae: A Great Kingdomin the Late Bronze Age Aegean*. Bethesda, Maryland: CDL Press.

Keyser, C., C. Bouakaze, E. Crubézy, V. G. Nikolaev, D. Montagnon, and T. Reis. 2009. Ancient DNA provides new insights into the history of south Siberian Kurgan people. *Hum Genet* 126.

Khokhlov, Aleksandr A. 2016. Demographic and Cranial Characteristics of the Volga-Ural Population in the Eneolithic and Bronze Age. In *A Bronze Age Landscape in the Russian Steppes. The Samara Valley Project*, edited by D. W. Anthony, D. R. Brown, O. D. Mochalov, A. A. Khokhlov and P. F. Kuznetsov. Los Angeles: Cotsen Institute of Archaeology Press.

Kiesslich, Jan, Franz Neuhuber, Harald J. Meyer, Max P. Baur, and Jutta Leskovar. 2004. KiDNA Analysis on Biological Remains from Archaeological Findings–Sex Identification and Kinship Analysis on Skeletons from Mitterkirchen, Upper Austria. *na*.

Kilinc, G. M., A. Omrak, F. Ozer, T. Gunther, A. M. Buyukkarakaya, E. Bicakci, D. Baird, H. M. Donertas, A. Ghalichi, R. Yaka, D. Koptekin, S. C. Acan, P. Parvizi, M. Krzewinska, E. A. Daskalaki, E. Yuncu, N. D. Dagtas, A. Fairbairn, J. Pearson, G. Mustafaoglu, Y. S. Erdal, Y. G. Cakan, I. Togan, M. Somel, J. Stora, M. Jakobsson, and A. Gotherstrom. 2016. The Demographic Development of the First Farmers in Anatolia. *Curr Biol* 26 (19):2659-2666.

Kılınç, Gülşah Merve, Natalija Kashuba, Reyhan Yaka, Arev Pelin Sümer, Eren Yüncü, Dmitrij Shergin, Grigorij Leonidovich Ivanov, Dmitrii Kichigin, Kjunnej Pestereva, Denis Volkov, Pavel Mandryka, Artur Kharinskii, Alexey Tishkin, Evgenij Ineshin, Evgeniy Kovychev, Aleksandr Stepanov, Aanatolij Alekseev, Svetlana Aleksandrovna Fedoseeva, Mehmet Somel, Mattias Jakobsson, Maja Krzewińska, Jan Storå, and Anders Götherström. 2018. Investigating Holocene human population history in North Asia using ancient mitogenomes. *Scientific Reports* 8 (1):8969.

Kim, A., T. Savenkova, Y. Reis, S. Smushko, S. Mallick, N. Rohland, R. Bernardos, and D. Reich. 2018. Yeniseian hypotheses in light of genome-wide ancient DNA from historical Siberia. Paper read at 8th International Symposium on Biomolecular Archaeology ISBA 2018. 18th – 21st September, at Jena, Germany.

Kim, Kijeong, Charles H. Brenner, Victor H. Mair, Kwang-Ho Lee, Jae-Hyun Kim, Eregzen Gelegdorj, Natsag Batbold, Yi-Chung Song, Hyeung-Won Yun, Eun-Jeong Chang, Gavaachimed Lkhagvasuren, Munkhtsetseg Bazarragchaa, Ae-Ja Park, Inja Lim, Yun-Pyo Hong, Wonyong Kim, Sang-In Chung, Dae-Jin Kim, Yoon-Hee Chung, Sung-Su Kim, Won-Bok Lee, and Kyung-Yong Kim. 2010. A western Eurasian male is found in 2000-year-old elite Xiongnu cemetery in Northeast Mongolia. *American Journal of Physical Anthropology* 142 (3):429-440.

King, R. J., S. S. Ozcan, T. Carter, E. Kalfoglu, S. Atasoy, C. Triantaphyllidis, A. Kouvatsi, A. A. Lin, C. E. Chow, L. A. Zhivotovsky, M. Michalodimitrakis, and P. A. Underhill. 2008. Differential Y-chromosome Anatolian influences on the Greek and Cretan Neolithic. *Ann Hum Genet* 72 (Pt 2):205-14.

Kitov, E. P., A. A. Khokhlov, and P. S. Medvedeva. 2018. Paleoanthropological Data as a Source of Reconstruction of the Process of Social Formation and Social Stratifi cation (based on the Sintashta and Potapovo sites of the Bronze Age). *Stratum plus* 2:225-243.

Klochko, Viktor, and Aleksander Kośko. 1998. "Trzciniec" – Borderland of Early Bronze Civilization of Eastern and Western Europe? In *The Trzciniec Area of the Early Bronze Age Civilization: 1950-1200 BC*. Poznan.

Kloekhorst, Alwin. 2008. Some Indo-Uralic Aspects of Hittite. *JIES* 36 (1 & 2).

Knipper, Corina, Alissa Mittnik, Ken Massy, Catharina Kociumaka, Isil Kucukkalipci, Michael Maus, Fabian Wittenborn, Stephanie E. Metz, Anja Staskiewicz, Johannes Krause, and Philipp W. Stockhammer. 2017. Female exogamy and gene pool diversification at the transition from the Final Neolithic to the Early Bronze Age in central Europe. *Proceedings of the National Academy of Sciences*.

Ko, Seongyeon, Andrew Joseph, and John Whitman. 2014. Comparative consequences of the tongue root harmony analysis for proto-Tungusic, proto-Mongolic, and proto-Korean. In *Paradigm Change: In the Transeurasian languages and beyond*, edited by M. Robbeets and W. Bisang: John Benjamins.

Kobyliński, Zbigniew. 2005. The Slavs. In *The New Cambridge Medieval History, Vol. 1: c. 500-c. 700*, edited by P. Fouracre. Cambridge: Cambridge University Press.

Koch, John T. 2009. A case for tartessian as a celtic language. *Palaeohispanica* 9:339-351.

Repeated Author. 2013. Is Basque an Indo-European Language? *JIES* 41 (1 & 2).

Koivulehto, J. . 1991. *Uralische Evidenz für die Laryngaltheorie*. Vol. 566. Viena: Österreichische Akademie der Wissenschaften.

Koivulehto, Jorma. 2001. The Earliest Contacts between Indo-European and Uralic Speakers in the Light of Lexical Loans. Christian Carpelan,. In *Early Contacts between Uralic and Indo-European: Linguistic and Archaeological Considerations*, edited by A. Parpola and P. Koskikallio. 2001: Societé Finno-Ougrienne.

Repeated Author. 2003. Frühe Kontakte zwischen Uralisch und Indogermanisch im nordwestindogermanischen Raum. In *Languages in Prehistoric Europe*, edited by A. Bammesberger and T. Vennemann. Heidelberg: Universitätsverlag Winter.

Repeated Author. 2006. Wie alt sind die Kontakte zwischen Finnisch-Ugrisch und Balto-Slavisch? In *The Slavicization of the Russian North. Mechanisms and Chronology*, edited by J. Nuorluoto. Helsinki.

Korpela, Jukka. 2019. Eastern European Slave Trade. In *Slaves from the North. Finns and Karelians in the East European Slave Trade, 900-1600*. Leiden/Boston: Brill.

Kortlandt, Frederik. 2002. The Indo-Uralic verb. In *Finno-Ugrians and Indo-Europeans: Linguistic and literary contacts*. Maastricht: Shaker.

Repeated Author. 2010. Indo-Uralic and Altaic revisited. In *Transeurasian verbal morphology in a comparative perspective: genealogy, contact, chance*. Wiesbaden: Harrassowitz.

Repeated Author. 2016. Baltic, Slavic, Germanic. *Baltistica* 51 (1):81-86.

Koryakova, Ludmila, and Andrej Epimakhov. 2007. *The Urals and Western Siberia in the Bronze and Iron Ages, Cambridge World Archaeology*. Cambridge: Cambridge University Press.

Kośko, Aleksander. 1979. *Rozwój kulturowy społeczeństw Kujaw w okresie schyłkowego neolitu i wczesnego brązu*. Poznań.

Kosmenko, M. G. 1996. The culture of Bronze Age Net Ware in Karelia. *Fennoscandia Archaeologica* XIII:51-67.

Krahe, H. 1949. Alteuropäische Flußnamen. *Beiträge zur Namenforschung* 1:24–51, 247–266 (and cont. in following volumes).

Repeated Author. 1964. *Unsere ältesten Flußnamen*. Wiesbaden: Harrassowitz.

Kristiansen, Kristian. 1987. From stone to bronze - the evolution of social complexity in Northern Europe, 2300-1200 BC. In *Specialization, exchange and complex societies*, edited by E. M. Brumfiel and T. K. Earle. Cambridge: Cambridge University Press.

Repeated Author. 2000. *Europe Before History*. Cambridge: Cambridge University Press.

Repeated Author. 2009. Proto-Indo-European Languages and Institutions: An Archaeological Approach. In *Journal of Indo-European Studies Monograph Series, No. 56*, edited by M. V. Linden and K. Jones-Bley. Washinton: Institute for the Study of Man.

Repeated Author. 2016. Bronze Age Vikings? A Comparative Analysis of Deep Historical Structures and their Dynamics. In *Comparative Perspectives on Past Colonisation, Maritime Interaction and Cultural Integration. New Directions in Anthropological Archaeology*, edited by L. Melheim, Z. T. Glørstad and H. Glørstad. Sheffield: Equinox.

Kristiansen, Kristian, and Thomas B. Larsson. 2005. *The Rise of Bronze Age Society: Travels, Transmissions and Transformations*. Cambridge: Cambridge University Press.

Kristiansen, Kristian, and Paulina Suchowska-Ducke. 2015. Connected Histories: the Dynamics of Bronze Age Interaction and Trade 1500–1100 bc. *Proceedings of the Prehistoric Society* 81:361-392.

Krzewińska, Maja, Gülşah Merve Kılınç, Anna Juras, Dilek Koptekin, Maciej Chyleński, Alexey G. Nikitin, Nikolai Shcherbakov, Iia Shuteleva, Tatiana Leonova, Liudmila Kraeva, Flarit A. Sungatov, Alfija N. Sultanova, Inna Potekhina, Sylwia Łukasik, Marta Krenz-Niedbała, Love Dalén, Vitaly Sinika, Mattias Jakobsson, Jan Storå, and Anders Götherström. 2018. Ancient genomes suggest the eastern Pontic-Caspian steppe as the source of western Iron Age nomads. *Science Advances* 4 (10).

Krzewińska, Maja, Anna Kjellström, Torsten Günther, Charlotte Hedenstierna-Jonson, Torun Zachrisson, Ayça Omrak, Reyhan Yaka, Gülşah Merve Kılınç, Mehmet Somel, Veronica Sobrado, Jane Evans, Corina Knipper, Mattias Jakobsson, Jan Storå, and Anders Götherström. 2018. Genomic and Strontium

Isotope Variation Reveal Immigration Patterns in a Viking Age Town. *Current Biology* 28 (17):2730-2738.e10.

Kuhn, Hans, Rolf Hachmann, and Georg Kossack. 1986. *Völker zwischen Germanen und Kelten. Schriftquellen, Bodenfunde und Namengute zur Geschichte des nördlichen Westdeutschlands um Christi Gebur.* Neumünster: Karl Wachholz.

Künnap, Ago. 1997. *Breakthrough in Present-Day Uralistics.* Tartu, Estonia: Tartu University Press.

Kushniarevich, A., O. Utevska, M. Chuhryaeva, A. Agdzhoyan, K. Dibirova, I. Uktveryte, M. Mols, L. Mulahasanovic, A. Pshenichnov, S. Frolova, A. Shanko, E. Metspalu, M. Reidla, K. Tambets, E. Tamm, S. Koshel, V. Zaporozhchenko, L. Atramentova, V. Kucinskas, O. Davydenko, O. Goncharova, I. Evseeva, M. Churnosov, E. Pocheshchova, B. Yunusbayev, E. Khusnutdinova, D. Marjanovic, P. Rudan, S. Rootsi, N. Yankovsky, P. Endicott, A. Kassian, A. Dybo, Consortium Genographic, C. Tyler-Smith, E. Balanovska, M. Metspalu, T. Kivisild, R. Villems, and O. Balanovsky. 2015. Genetic Heritage of the Balto-Slavic Speaking Populations: A Synthesis of Autosomal, Mitochondrial and Y-Chromosomal Data. *PLoS One* 10 (9):e0135820.

Kuzmina, E.E. 1994. *Otkuda prishli indoarii? [Whence the Indo-Aryans Came From?].* Moscow: Vostochnaya Literatura.

Kuzmina, Elena E. 2007. *The Origin of the Indo-Iranians.* Leiden: Brill.

Repeated Author. 2008. *The Prehistory of the Silk Road.* Edited by V. H. Mair. Philadelphia: University of Pennsylvania Press.

Kuzminykh, S. V. , and A. A. Chizhevskij. 2009. Anan'inskij mir: Vzglyad na sovremennoe sostoyanie problemi. In *U istokov arkheologii Volgo-Kam'ya: K 150-letiyu otkrytiya Anan'inskogo mogil'nika. Arkheologiya Evrazijskikh stepej, vypusk 8,* edited by S. V. Kuz'minykh, A. A. Chizhevskij and G. R. Rudenko. Elabuga: Institut Arkheologii AN RT.

Kuznetsov, Pavel F., and Oleg D. Mochalov. 2016. The Samara Valley in the Bronze Age: A Review of Archaeological Discoveries. In *A Bronze Age Landscape in the Russian Steppes. The Samara Valley Project,* edited by D. W. Anthony, D. R. Brown, O. D. Mochalov, A. A. Khokhlov and P. F. Kuznetsov. Los Angeles: The Cotsen Institute of Archaeology Press at UCLA.

Laakso, Ville. 2017. Continuity or Change? Selecting the Sites for Early Medieval Churches in Finland. In *Sacred Monuments and Practices in the Baltic Sea Region. New Visits to Old Churches,* edited by J. Harjula, S. Hukantaival, V. Immonen, A. Randla and T. Ratilainen. Cambridge: Cambridge Scholars.

Lamnidis, Thiseas C., Kerttu Majander, Choongwon Jeong, Elina Salmela, Anna Wessman, Vyacheslav Moiseyev, Valery Khartanovich, Oleg Balanovsky, Matthias Ongyerth, Antje Weihmann, Antti Sajantila, Janet Kelso, Svante Pääbo, Päivi Onkamo, Wolfgang Haak, Johannes Krause, and Stephan Schiffels. 2018. Ancient Fennoscandian genomes reveal origin and spread of Siberian ancestry in Europe. *Nature Communications* 9 (1):5018.

Laneman, Margot, and Valter Lang. 2013. New radiocarbon dates for two stone-cist graves at Muuksi, Northern Estonia. *Estonian Journal of Archaeology* 17 (2):89-122.

Lang, Valter. 2016. Early Finni-Baltic contacts as evidenced by archaeological and linguistic data. *ESUKA - JEFUL* 7 (1):11-38.

Lavento, Mika. 2001. *Textile Ceramics in Finland and on the Karelian Isthmus. Nine variations and Fugue on a Theme of C. F.Meinander, Suomen Muinaismuisto yhdistuksen Aikakauskirja / Finska Fornminnseföreningens Tidsskrift.* Helsinki.

Lazaridis, I., D. Nadel, G. Rollefson, D. C. Merrett, N. Rohland, S. Mallick, D. Fernandes, M. Novak, B. Gamarra, K. Sirak, S. Connell, K. Stewardson, E. Harney, Q. Fu, G. Gonzalez-Fortes, E. R. Jones, S. A. Roodenberg, G. Lengyel, F. Bocquentin, B. Gasparian, J. M. Monge, M. Gregg, V. Eshed, A. S. Mizrahi, C. Meiklejohn, F. Gerritsen, L. Bejenaru, M. Bluher, A. Campbell, G. Cavalleri, D. Comas, P. Froguel, E. Gilbert, S. M. Kerr, P. Kovacs, J. Krause, D. McGettigan, M. Merrigan, D. A. Merriwether, S. O'Reilly, M. B. Richards, O. Semino, M. Shamoon-Pour, G. Stefanescu, M. Stumvoll, A. Tonjes, A. Torroni, J. F. Wilson, L. Yengo, N. A. Hovhannisyan, N. Patterson, R. Pinhasi, and D. Reich. 2016. Genomic insights into the origin of farming in the ancient Near East. *Nature* 536 (7617):419-24.

Lazaridis, Iosif, Alissa Mittnik, Nick Patterson, Swapan Mallick, Nadin Rohland, Saskia Pfrengle, Anja Furtwängler, Alexander Peltzer, Cosimo Posth, Andonis Vasilakis, P. J. P. McGeorge, Eleni Konsolaki-Yannopoulou, George Korres, Holley Martlew, Manolis Michalodimitrakis, Mehmet Özsait, Nesrin Özsait, Anastasia Papathanasiou, Michael Richards, Songül Alpaslan Roodenberg, Yannis Tzedakis, Robert Arnott, Daniel M. Fernandes, Jeffery R. Hughey, Dimitra M. Lotakis, Patrick A. Navas, Yannis Maniatis, John A. Stamatoyannopoulos, Kristin Stewardson, Philipp Stockhammer, Ron Pinhasi, David Reich, Johannes Krause, and George Stamatoyannopoulos. 2017. Genetic origins of the Minoans and Mycenaeans. *Nature* 548 (7666):214-218.

Leonardi, Michela, Anna Sandionigi, Annalisa Conzato, Stefania Vai, Martina Lari, Francesca Tassi, Silvia Ghirotto, David Caramelli, and Guido Barbujani. 2018. The female ancestor's tale: Long-term matrilineal continuity in a nonisolated region of Tuscany. *American Journal of Physical Anthropology* 167 (3):497-506.

Li, C., H. Li, Y. Cui, C. Xie, D. Cai, W. Li, V. H. Mair, Z. Xu, Q. Zhang, I. Abuduresule, L. Jin, H. Zhu, and H. Zhou. 2010. Evidence that a West-East admixed population lived in the Tarim Basin as early as the early Bronze Age. *BMC Biol* 8:15.

Li, Jiawei, Ye Zhang, Yongbin Zhao, Yongzhi Chen, A. Ochir, Sarenbilige, Hong Zhu, and Hui Zhou. 2018. The genome of an ancient Rouran individual reveals an important paternal lineage in the Donghu population. *American Journal of Physical Anthropology* 166 (4):895-905.

Li, X., M. Ma, and S. Wen. 2018. Archaeological and ancient DNA evidence reveals the early population admixture between Han farmers and steppes nomads in northwest China. Paper read at American Geophysical Union, Fall Meeting 2018, at Washington, D.C.

Lindstedt, Jouko Sakari, and Elina Salmela. 2019. Migrations and language shifts as components of the Slavic spread. In *Language contact and the early Slavs*, edited by T. Klír and V. Boček. Heidelberg: Universitätsverlag Winter.

Ling, J., Per Cornell, and K. Kristiansen. 2017. Bronze Economy and Mode of Production: The Role of Comparative Advantages in Temperate Europe during the Bronze Age.

Lipson, Mark, Anna Szécsényi-Nagy, Swapan Mallick, Annamária Pósa, Balázs Stégmár, Victoria Keerl, Nadin Rohland, Kristin Stewardson, Matthew Ferry, Megan Michel, Jonas Oppenheimer, Nasreen Broomandkhoshbacht, Eadaoin Harney, Susanne Nordenfelt, Bastien Llamas, Balázs Gusztáv Mende, Kitti Köhler, Krisztián Oross, Mária Bondár, Tibor Marton, Anett Osztás, János Jakucs, Tibor Paluch, Ferenc Horváth, Piroska Csengeri, Judit Koós, Katalin Sebők, Alexandra Anders, Pál Raczky, Judit Regenye, Judit P. Barna, Szilvia Fábián, Gábor Serlegi, Zoltán Toldi, Emese Gyöngyvér Nagy, János Dani, Erika Molnár, György Pálfi, László Márk, Béla Melegh, Zsolt Bánfai, László Domboróczki, Javier Fernández-Eraso, José Antonio Mujika-Alustiza, Carmen Alonso Fernández, Javier Jiménez Echevarría, Ruth Bollongino, Jörg Orschiedt, Kerstin Schierhold, Harald Meller, Alan Cooper, Joachim Burger, Eszter Bánffy, Kurt W. Alt, Carles Lalueza-Fox, Wolfgang Haak, and David Reich. 2017. Parallel palaeogenomic transects reveal complex genetic history of early European farmers. *Nature* 551:368.

Liu, Shuhu, Yilihamu Nizam, Bake Rabiyamu, Bupatima Abdukeram, and Matyusup Dolkun. 2018. A study of genetic diversity of three isolated populations in Xinjiang using Y-SNP. *Acta Anthropologica Sinica* 37 (1):146-156.

Lo Schiavo, Fulvia. 2013. The Bronze Age in Sardinia In *The Oxford Handbook of the European Bronze Age*, edited by H. Fokkens and A. Harding. Oxford: Oxford University Press.

Luca, F., F. Di Giacomo, T. Benincasa, L. O. Popa, J. Banyko, A. Kracmarova, P. Malaspina, A. Novelletto, and R. Brdicka. 2007. Y-chromosomal variation in the Czech Republic. *American Journal of Physical Anthropology* 132 (1):132-139.

Lull, V., R. Micó, C. Rihuete Herrada, and R. Risch. 2013. The Bronze Age in the Balearic Islands Oxford Handbooks. In *The Oxford Handbook of the European Bronze Age*, edited by H. Fokkens and A. Harding. Oxford.

Lull, Vicente, Rafael Micó, Cristina Rihuete Herrada, and Roberto Risch. 2013. Bronze Age Iberia. In *The Oxford Handbook of the European Bronze Age*, edited by H. Fokkens and A. Harding. Oxford: Oxford University Press.

Luneau, Élise. 2019. Climate Change and the Rise and Fall of the Oxus Civilization in Southern Central Asia. In *Socio-Environmental Dynamics along the Historical Silk Road*, edited by L. E. Yang, H.-R. Bork, X. Fang and S. Mischke. Cham: Springer International Publishing.

Maeir, Aren M., Brent Davis, and Louise A. Hitchcock. 2016. Philistine Names and Terms Once Again: A Recent Perspective. *Journal of Eastern Mediterranean Archaeology & Heritage Studies* 4 (4):321-340.

Magness, Jodi. 2001. A Near Eastern Ethnic Element Among the Etruscan Elite? *Etruscan Studies* 8 (4):79-117.

Maisano Delser, Pierpaolo, Metka Ravnik-Glavač, Paolo Gasparini, Damjan Glavač, and Massimo Mezzavilla. 2018. Genetic Landscape of Slovenians: Past Admixture and Natural Selection Pattern. *Frontiers in Genetics* 9 (551).

Makarowicz, Przemysław. 2010. The Creation of New Social Space. Barrows of the Corded Ware Culture and Trzciniec Circle as markers of a mental map in the upland parts of Poland and western Ukraine. In *Landscapes and Human Development: The Contribution of European Archaeology. Proceedings of the International Workship "Socio-Environmental Dynamics over the Last 12,000 Years: The Creation of Landscapes (1st-4th April 2009)"*, edited by K. G. School. Bonn: Dr. Rudolf Habelt.

Malin-Boyce, Susan. 2004. Hallstatt and La Tène. In *Ancient Europe, 8000 B.C. to A.D. 1000: An Encyclopedia of the Barbarian World*, edited by P. Bogucki and P. J. Crabtree. New York: Charles Scribner.

Mallory, J., and D.Q. Adams. 2007. Reconstructing the Proto-Indo-Europeans. In *The Oxford Introduction to Proto-Indo-European and the Proto-Indo-European World*. Oxford: Oxford University Press.

Mallory, J.P. 2013. The Indo-Europeanization of Atlantic Europe. In *Celtic From the West 2: Rethinking the Bronze Age and the Arrival of Indo-European in Atlantic Europe*, edited by J. T. Koch and B. Cunliffe. Oxford: Oxbow Books.

Repeated Author. 2014. Indo-European dispersals and the Eurasian Steppe. In *Reconfiguring the Silk Road: New Research on East-West Exchange in Antiquity*, edited by V. H. Mair and J. Hickman. Philadelphia: University of Pennsylvania Museum of Archaeology and Anthropology.

Mallory, J.P., and Douglas Q. Adams. 1997. *Encyclopedia of Indo-European Culture*. London: Fitzroy Dearborn Publishers.

Mallory, James P. 2015. The problem of Tocharian origins: An archaeological perspective. In *Sino-Platonic Papers*. Philadelphia: University of Pennsylvania.

Marchenko, Z. V., S. V. Svyatko, V. I. Molodin, A. E. Grishin, and M. P. Rykun. 2017. Radiocarbon Chronology of Complexes With Seima-Turbino Type Objects (Bronze Age) in Southwestern Siberia. *Radiocarbon* 59 (5):1381-1397.

Marchesini, Simona. 2012. The Elymian language. In *Language and Linguistic Contact in Ancient Sicily*, edited by O. Tribulato. Cambridge: Cambridge University Press.

Marcus, Joseph H., Cosimo Posth, Harald Ringbauer, Luca Lai, Robin Skeates, Carlo Sidore, Jessica Beckett, Anja Furtwängler, Anna Olivieri, Charleston Chiang, Hussein Al-Asadi, Kushal Dey, Tyler A. Joseph, Clio Der Sarkissian, Rita Radzevičiūtė, Maria Giuseppina Gradoli, Wolfgang Haak, David Reich, David Schlessinger, Francesco Cucca, Johannes Krause, and John Novembre. 2019. Population history from the Neolithic to present on the Mediterranean island of Sardinia: An ancient DNA perspective. *bioRxiv*:583104.

Margaryan, Ashot, Miroslava Derenko, Hrant Hovhannisyan, Boris Malyarchuk, Rasmus Heller, Zaruhi Khachatryan, Pavel Avetisyan, Ruben Badalyan, Arsen Bobokhyan, Varduhi Melikyan, Gagik Sargsyan, Ashot Piliposyan, Hakob Simonyan, Ruzan Mkrtchyan, Galina Denisova, Levon Yepiskoposyan, Eske Willerslev, and Morten E. Allentoft. 2017. Eight Millennia of Matrilineal Genetic Continuity in the South Caucasus. *Current Biology*.

Marin Aguilera, Beatriz, Esther Rodriguez-Gonzalez, Sebastian Celestino, and Margarita Gleba. 2019. Dressing the sacrifice: textiles, textile production and the sacrificial economy at Casas del Turuñuelo, in the fifth century BC Iberia. *Antiquity* (Accepted manuscript).

Marková, Klára, and Gábor Ilon. 2013. Slovakia and Hungary. In *The Oxford Handbook of the European Bronze Age*, edited by H. Fokkens and A. Harding. Oxford: Oxford University Press.

Martin, Alicia R., Konrad J. Karczewski, Sini Kerminen, Mitja I. Kurki, Antti-Pekka Sarin, Mykyta Artomov, Johan G. Eriksson, Tõnu Esko, Giulio Genovese, Aki S. Havulinna, Jaakko Kaprio, Alexandra Konradi, László Korányi, Anna Kostareva, Minna Männikkö, Andres Metspalu, Markus Perola, Rashmi B. Prasad, Olli Raitakari, Oxana Rotar, Veikko Salomaa, Leif Groop, Aarno Palotie, Benjamin M. Neale, Samuli Ripatti, Matti Pirinen, and Mark J. Daly. 2018. Haplotype Sharing Provides Insights into Fine-Scale Population History and Disease in Finland. *The American Journal of Human Genetics* 102 (5):760-775.

Martiniano, Rui, Anwen Caffell, Malin Holst, Kurt Hunter-Mann, Janet Montgomery, Gundula Müldner, Russell L. McLaughlin, Matthew D. Teasdale, Wouter van Rheenen, Jan H. Veldink, Leonard H. van den Berg, Orla Hardiman, Maureen Carroll, Steve Roskams, John Oxley, Colleen Morgan, Mark G. Thomas, Ian Barnes, Christine McDonnell, Matthew J. Collins, and Daniel G. Bradley. 2016. Genomic signals of migration and continuity in Britain before the Anglo-Saxons. *Nature Communications* 7:10326.

Martiniano, Rui, Lara M. Cassidy, Ros Ó'Maoldúin, Russell McLaughlin, Nuno M. Silva, Licinio Manco, Daniel Fidalgo, Tania Pereira, Maria J. Coelho, Miguel Serra, Joachim Burger, Rui Parreira, Elena Moran, Antonio C. Valera, Eduardo Porfirio, Rui Boaventura, Ana M. Silva, and Daniel G. Bradley. 2017. The population genomics of archaeological transition in west Iberia: Investigation of ancient substructure using imputation and haplotype-based methods. *PLOS Genetics* 13 (7):e1006852.

Matasović, Ranko 2009. *Etymological Dictionary of Proto-Celtic*. Vol. 9, *Leiden Indo-European Etymological Dictionary Series*. Leiden/Boston: Brill.

Mathieson, I., I. Lazaridis, N. Rohland, S. Mallick, N. Patterson, S. A. Roodenberg, E. Harney, K. Stewardson, D. Fernandes, M. Novak, K. Sirak, C. Gamba, E. R. Jones, B. Llamas, S. Dryomov, J. Pickrell, J. L. Arsuaga, J. M. de Castro, E. Carbonell, F. Gerritsen, A. Khokhlov, P. Kuznetsov, M. Lozano, H. Meller, O. Mochalov, V. Moiseyev, M. A. Guerra, J. Roodenberg, J. M. Verges, J. Krause, A. Cooper, K. W. Alt, D. Brown, D. Anthony, C. Lalueza-Fox, W. Haak, R. Pinhasi, and D. Reich. 2015. Genome-wide patterns of selection in 230 ancient Eurasians. *Nature* 528 (7583):499-503.

Mathieson, Iain, Songül Alpaslan-Roodenberg, Cosimo Posth, Anna Szécsényi-Nagy, Nadin Rohland, Swapan Mallick, Iñigo Olalde, Nasreen Broomandkhoshbacht, Francesca Candilio, Olivia Cheronet, Daniel Fernandes, Matthew Ferry, Beatriz Gamarra, Gloria González Fortes, Wolfgang Haak, Eadaoin Harney, Eppie Jones, Denise Keating, Ben Krause-Kyora, Isil Kucukkalipci, Megan Michel, Alissa Mittnik, Kathrin Nägele, Mario Novak, Jonas Oppenheimer, Nick Patterson, Saskia Pfrengle, Kendra Sirak, Kristin Stewardson, Stefania Vai, Stefan Alexandrov, Kurt W. Alt, Radian Andreescu, Dragana Antonović, Abigail Ash, Nadezhda Atanassova, Krum Bacvarov, Mende Balázs Gusztáv, Hervé Bocherens, Michael Bolus, Adina Boroneanţ, Yavor Boyadzhiev, Alicja Budnik, Josip Burmaz, Stefan Chohadzhiev,

Nicholas J. Conard, Richard Cottiaux, Maja Čuka, Christophe Cupillard, Dorothée G. Drucker, Nedko Elenski, Michael Francken, Borislava Galabova, Georgi Ganetsovski, Bernard Gély, Tamás Hajdu, Veneta Handzhyiska, Katerina Harvati, Thomas Higham, Stanislav Iliev, Ivor Janković, Ivor Karavanić, Douglas J. Kennett, Darko Komšo, Alexandra Kozak, Damian Labuda, Martina Lari, Catalin Lazar, Maleen Leppek, Krassimir Leshtakov, Domenico Lo Vetro, Dženi Los, Ivaylo Lozanov, Maria Malina, Fabio Martini, Kath McSweeney, Harald Meller, Marko Menđušić, Pavel Mirea, Vyacheslav Moiseyev, Vanya Petrova, T. Douglas Price, Angela Simalcsik, Luca Sineo, Mario Šlaus, Vladimir Slavchev, Petar Stanev, Andrej Starović, Tamás Szeniczey, Sahra Talamo, Maria Teschler-Nicola, Corinne Thevenet, Ivan Valchev, Frédérique Valentin, Sergey Vasilyev, Fanica Veljanovska, Svetlana Venelinova, Elizaveta Veselovskaya, Bence Viola, Cristian Virag, Joško Zaninović, Steve Zäuner, Philipp W. Stockhammer, Giulio Catalano, Raiko Krauß, David Caramelli, Gunita Zariņa, Bisserka Gaydarska, Malcolm Lillie, Alexey G. Nikitin, Inna Potekhina, Anastasia Papathanasiou, Dušan Borić, Clive Bonsall, Johannes Krause, Ron Pinhasi, and David Reich. 2018. The genomic history of southeastern Europe. *Nature* 555:197.

Matisoo-Smith, E., A. L. Gosling, D. Platt, O. Kardailsky, S. Prost, S. Cameron-Christie, C. J. Collins, J. Boocock, Y. Kurumilian, M. Guirguis, R. Pla Orquín, W. Khalil, H. Genz, G. Abou Diwan, J. Nassar, and P. Zalloua. 2018. Ancient mitogenomes of Phoenicians from Sardinia and Lebanon: A story of settlement, integration, and female mobility. *PLOS ONE* 13 (1):e0190169.

McEvoy, Brian P., and Daniel G. Bradley. 2010. Irish Genetics and Celts. In *Celtic from the West: Alternative Perspectives from Archaeology, Genetics, Language and Literature*, edited by B. Cunliffe and J. T. Koch. Oxford: Oxbow Books.

Meiri, Meirav, Philipp W. Stockhammer, Peggy Morgenstern, and Joseph Maran. 2019. Mobility and trade in Mediterranean antiquity: Evidence for an 'Italian connection' in Mycenaean Greece revealed by ancient DNA of livestock. *Journal of Archaeological Science: Reports* 23:98-103.

Melheim, Lene, Johan Ling, Zofia A. Stos-Gale, Eva Hjärthner-Holdar, and Lena Grandin. 2018. The role of pre-Norsemen in trade and exchange of commodities in Bronze Age Europe. In *Metal, Minds and Mobility. Integrating scientific data with archaeological theory*, edited by X.-L. Armada, M. Murillo-Barroso and M. Charlton. Oxford & Philadelphia: Oxbow books.

Meller, Harald. 2017. Armies in the Early Bronze Age? An alternative interpretation of Únětice Culture axe hoards. *Antiquity* 91 (360):1529-1545.

Michel, Cécile. 2011. The Kārum Period on the Plateau. In *The Oxford Handbook of Ancient Antolia 10,000-323 B.C.E.*, edited by S. R. Steadman and G. McMahon. Oxford: Oxford University Press.

Middleton, Guy D. 2015. Telling Stories: The Mycenaean Origins of the Philistines. *Oxford Journal of Archaeology* 34 (1):45-65.

Mihovilić, Kristina. 2013. Castellieri-Gradine of the Northern Adriatic. In *The Oxford Handbook of the European Bronze Age*, edited by H. Fokkens and A. Harding. Oxford: Oxford University Press.

Mikhailova, Tatyana A. 2015. Celtic origin: location in time and space? Reconsidering the "East-West Celtic" debate. *Journal of Language Relationship* 13 (3):257-279.

Mittnik, A., K. Massy, C. Knipper, R. Friedrich, W. Haak, S. Schiffels, P. W. Stockhammer, and J. Krause. 2018. Ancient genomes from the Lech Valley, Bavaria, suggest socially stratified households in the European Bronze Age. Paper read at 8th International Symposium on Biomolecular Archaeology ISBA 2018. 18th – 21st September, at Jena, Germany.

Mittnik, Alissa, Chuan-Chao Wang, Saskia Pfrengle, Mantas Daubaras, Gunita Zariņa, Fredrik Hallgren, Raili Allmäe, Valery Khartanovich, Vyacheslav Moiseyev, Mari Tõrv, Anja Furtwängler, Aida Andrades Valtueña, Michal Feldman, Christos Economou, Markku Oinonen, Andrejs Vasks, Elena Balanovska, David Reich, Rimantas Jankauskas, Wolfgang Haak, Stephan Schiffels, and Johannes Krause. 2018. The genetic prehistory of the Baltic Sea region. *Nature Communications* 9 (1):442.

Mochalov, Oleg D. 2008. *Keramika Pogrebal'nykh Pamiatnikov Epokhi Bronzy Lesostepi Volgo-Ural'skogo Mezhdurech'ya.* Samara: Samarskii Gosudarstvennyi Pedagogicheskii Universitet.

Molodin, V. I., L. N. Mylnikova, and L. S. Kobeleva. 2008. Stages in the settlement history of Chicha-1: The results of ceramic analysis. *Archaeology, Ethnology and Anthropology of Eurasia* 35 (3):54-67.

Mordant, Claude. 2013. The Bronze Age in France In *The Oxford Handbook of the European Bronze Age*, edited by H. Fokkens and A. Harding. Oxford: Oxford University Press.

Moroni, Adriana, Vincenzo Spagnolo, Jacopo Crezzini, Francesco Boschin, Marco Benvenuti, Samuele Gardin, Silvia Cipriani, and Simona Arrighi. 2019. Settlement, space organization and land-use of a small Middle Bronze Age community of central Italy. The case study of Gorgo del Ciliegio (Arezzo-Tuscany). *Quaternary International*.

Müller, Johannes, and Aleksandr Diachenko. 2019. Tracing long-term demographic changes: The issue of spatial scales. *PLOS ONE* 14 (1):e0208739.

Murillo-Barroso, Mercedes, and Ignacio Montero-Ruiz. 2017. The Social Value of Things. In *Key Resources and Socio-Cultural Developments in the Iberian Chalcolithic*, edited by M. Bartelheim, P. B. Ramírez and M. Kunst. Tübingen: Tübingen Library Publishing.

Narasimhan, Vagheesh M, Nick J Patterson, Priya Moorjani, Iosif Lazaridis, Lipson Mark, Swapan Mallick, Nadin Rohland, Rebecca Bernardos, Alexander M. Kim, Nathan Nakatsuka, Inigo Olalde, Alfredo Coppa, James Mallory, Vyacheslav Moiseyev, Janet Monge, Luca M. Olivieri, Nicole Adamski, Nasreen Broomandkhoshbacht, Francesca Candilio, Olivia Cheronet, Brendan J. Culleton, Matthew Ferry, Daniel Fernandes, Beatriz Gamarra, Daniel Gaudio, Mateja Hajdinjak, Eadaoin Harney, Thomas K. Harper, Denise Keating, Ann-Marie Lawson, Megan Michel, Mario Novak, Jonas Oppenheimer, Niraj Rai, Kendra Sirak, Viviane Slon, Kristin Stewardson, Zhao Zhang, Gaziz Akhatov, Anatoly N. Bagashev, Baurzhan Baitanayev, Gian Luca Bonora, Tatiana Chikisheva, Anatoly Derevianko, Enshin Dmitry, Katerina Douka, Nadezhda Dubova, Andrey Epimakhov, Suzanne Freilich, Dorian Fuller, Alexander

Goryachev, Andrey Gromov, Bryan Hanks, Margaret Judd, Erlan Kazizov, Aleksander Khokhlov, Egor Kitov, Elena Kupriyanova, Pavel Kuznetsov, Donata Luiselli, Farhad Maksudov, Chris Meiklejohn, Deborah C. Merrett, Roberto Micheli, Oleg Mochalov, Zahir Muhammed, Samridin Mustafakulov, Ayushi Nayak, Rykun M. Petrovna, Davide Pettner, Richard Potts, Dmitry Razhev, Stefania Sarno, Kulyan Sikhymbaevae, Sergey M. Slepchenko, Nadezhda Stepanova, Svetlana Svyatko, Sergey Vasilyev, Massimo Vidale, Dima Voyakin, Antonina Yermolayeva, Alisa Zubova, Vasant S. Shinde, Carles Lalueza-Fox, Matthias Meyer, David Anthony, Nicole Boivin, Kumarasmy Thangaraj, Douglas Kennett, Michael Frachetti, Ron Pinhasi, and David Reich. 2018. The Genomic Formation of South and Central Asia. *bioRxiv.*

Neparáczki, Endre, Zoltán Juhász, Horolma Pamjav, Tibor Fehér, Bernadett Csányi, Albert Zink, Frank Maixner, György Pálfi, Erika Molnár, Ildikó Pap, Ágnes Kustár, László Révész, István Raskó, and Tibor Török. 2017. Genetic structure of the early Hungarian conquerors inferred from mtDNA haplotypes and Y-chromosome haplogroups in a small cemetery. *Molecular Genetics and Genomics* 292 (1):201-214.

Neparáczki, Endre, Zoltán Maróti, Tibor Kalmár, Kitti Maár, István Nagy, Dóra Latinovics, Ágnes Kustár, György Pálfi, Erika Molnár, Antónia Marcsik, Csilla Balogh, Gábor Lőrinczy, Szilárd Sándor Gál, Péter Tomka, Bernadett Kovacsóczy, László Kovács, István Raskó, and Tibor Török. 2019. Y-chromosome haplogroups from Hun, Avar and conquering Hungarian period nomadic people of the Carpathian Basin. *bioRxiv*:597997.

Nicolaisen, W. 1957. Die alteuropäischen Gewässernamen der britischen Hauptinsel. *Beiträge zur Namenforschung*:211-268.

Nicolis, Franco. 2013. Northern Italy In *The Oxford Handbook of the European Bronze Age*, edited by H. Fokkens and A. Harding. Oxford: Oxford University Press.

Ning, C. 2018. Genomic insight into the Neolithic transition peopling of Northeast Asia. Paper read at 8th International Symposium on Biomolecular Archaeology ISBA 2018. 18th – 21st September, at Jena, Germany.

Noble, Gordon, Martin Goldberg, and Derek Hamilton. 2018. The development of the Pictish symbol system: inscribing identity beyond the edges of Empire. *Antiquity* 92 (365):1329-1348.

Nordqvist, Kerkko. 2018. The Stone Age of north-eastern Europe 5500–1800 calBC : bridging the gap between the East and the West, Human Sciences, University of Oulu, Oulu.

Novozhenov, Victor A. 2012. *Communications and the Earliest Wheeled Transport of Eurasia.* Edited by E. E. Kuzmina. Moscow: Taus Publishing.

Oinonen, Markku, Petro Pesonen, Teija Alenius, Volker Heyd, Elisabeth Holmqvist-Saukkonen, Sanna Kivimäki, Tuire Nygrén, Tarja Sundell, and Päivi Onkamo. 2014. Event reconstruction through Bayesian chronology: Massive mid-Holocene lake-burst triggered large-scale ecological and cultural change. *The Holocene* 24 (11):1419-1427.

Ojārs, Bušs. 2014. The Finno-Ugric influence on the Latvian place names: the history of the research and current challenges. In *Международной научной* конференции *«Uralo-indogermanica», посвященной лингвисту Р.-П. Риттеру (1938–2011). (16–17 октября 2014 г., Нарвский колледж, филиал Тартуского ун-та.).*

Olalde, Iñigo, Selina Brace, Morten E. Allentoft, Ian Armit, Kristian Kristiansen, Thomas Booth, Nadin Rohland, Swapan Mallick, Anna Szécsényi-Nagy, Alissa Mittnik, Eveline Altena, Mark Lipson, Iosif Lazaridis, Thomas K. Harper, Nick Patterson, Nasreen Broomandkhoshbacht, Yoan Diekmann, Zuzana Faltyskova, Daniel Fernandes, Matthew Ferry, Eadaoin Harney, Peter de Knijff, Megan Michel, Jonas Oppenheimer, Kristin Stewardson, Alistair Barclay, Kurt Werner Alt, Corina Liesau, Patricia Ríos, Concepción Blasco, Jorge Vega Miguel, Roberto Menduiña García, Azucena Avilés Fernández, Eszter Bánffy, Maria Bernabò-Brea, David Billoin, Clive Bonsall, Laura Bonsall, Tim Allen, Lindsey Büster, Sophie Carver, Laura Castells Navarro, Oliver E. Craig, Gordon T. Cook, Barry Cunliffe, Anthony Denaire, Kirsten Egging Dinwiddy, Natasha Dodwell, Michal Ernée, Christopher Evans, Milan Kuchařík, Joan Francès Farré, Chris Fowler, Michiel Gazenbeek, Rafael Garrido Pena, María Haber-Uriarte, Elżbieta Haduch, Gill Hey, Nick Jowett, Timothy Knowles, Ken Massy, Saskia Pfrengle, Philippe Lefranc, Olivier Lemercier, Arnaud Lefebvre, César Heras Martínez, Virginia Galera Olmo, Ana Bastida Ramírez, Joaquín Lomba Maurandi, Tona Majó, Jacqueline I. McKinley, Kathleen McSweeney, Balázs Gusztáv Mende, Alessandra Modi, Gabriella Kulcsár, Viktória Kiss, András Czene, Róbert Patay, Anna Endrődi, Kitti Köhler, Tamás Hajdu, Tamás Szeniczey, János Dani, Zsolt Bernert, Maya Hoole, Olivia Cheronet, Denise Keating, Petr Velemínský, Miroslav Dobeš, Francesca Candilio, Fraser Brown, Raúl Flores Fernández, Ana-Mercedes Herrero-Corral, Sebastiano Tusa, Emiliano Carnieri, Luigi Lentini, Antonella Valenti, Alessandro Zanini, Clive Waddington, Germán Delibes, Elisa Guerra-Doce, Benjamin Neil, Marcus Brittain, Mike Luke, Richard Mortimer, Jocelyne Desideri, Marie Besse, Günter Brücken, Mirosław Furmanek, Agata Hałuszko, Maksym Mackiewicz, Artur Rapiński, Stephany Leach, Ignacio Soriano, Katina T. Lillios, João Luís Cardoso, Michael Parker Pearson, Piotr Włodarczak, T. Douglas Price, Pilar Prieto, Pierre-Jérôme Rey, Roberto Risch, Manuel A. Rojo Guerra, Aurore Schmitt, Joël Serralongue, Ana Maria Silva, Václav Smrčka, Luc Vergnaud, João Zilhão, David Caramelli, Thomas Higham, Mark G. Thomas, Douglas J. Kennett, Harry Fokkens, Volker Heyd, Alison Sheridan, Karl-Göran Sjögren, Philipp W. Stockhammer, Johannes Krause, Ron Pinhasi, Wolfgang Haak, Ian Barnes, Carles Lalueza-Fox, and David Reich. 2018. The Beaker phenomenon and the genomic transformation of northwest Europe. *Nature* 555:190.

Olalde, Iñigo, Swapan Mallick, Nick Patterson, Nadin Rohland, Vanessa Villalba-Mouco, Marina Silva, Katharina Dulias, Ceiridwen J. Edwards, Francesca Gandini, Maria Pala, Pedro Soares, Manuel Ferrando-Bernal, Nicole Adamski, Nasreen Broomandkhoshbacht, Olivia Cheronet, Brendan J. Culleton, Daniel Fernandes, Ann Marie Lawson, Matthew Mah, Jonas Oppenheimer, Kristin Stewardson, Zhao Zhang, Juan Manuel Jiménez Arenas, Isidro Jorge Toro Moyano, Domingo C. Salazar-García, Pere Castanyer, Marta Santos, Joaquim Tremoleda, Marina Lozano, Pablo García Borja, Javier Fernández-Eraso, José Antonio Mujika-Alustiza, Cecilio Barroso, Francisco J. Bermúdez, Enrique

Viguera Mínguez, Josep Burch, Neus Coromina, David Vivó, Artur Cebrià, Josep Maria Fullola, Oreto García-Puchol, Juan Ignacio Morales, F. Xavier Oms, Tona Majó, Josep Maria Vergès, Antònia Díaz-Carvajal, Imma Ollich-Castanyer, F. Javier López-Cachero, Ana Maria Silva, Carmen Alonso-Fernández, Germán Delibes de Castro, Javier Jiménez Echevarría, Adolfo Moreno-Márquez, Guillermo Pascual Berlanga, Pablo Ramos-García, José Ramos-Muñoz, Eduardo Vijande Vila, Gustau Aguilella Arzo, Ángel Esparza Arroyo, Katina T. Lillios, Jennifer Mack, Javier Velasco-Vázquez, Anna Waterman, Luis Benítez de Lugo Enrich, María Benito Sánchez, Bibiana Agustí, Ferran Codina, Gabriel de Prado, Almudena Estalrrich, Álvaro Fernández Flores, Clive Finlayson, Geraldine Finlayson, Stewart Finlayson, Francisco Giles-Guzmán, Antonio Rosas, Virginia Barciela González, Gabriel García Atiénzar, Mauro S. Hernández Pérez, Armando Llanos, Yolanda Carrión Marco, Isabel Collado Beneyto, David López-Serrano, Mario Sanz Tormo, António C. Valera, Concepción Blasco, Corina Liesau, Patricia Ríos, Joan Daura, María Jesús de Pedro Michó, Agustín A. Diez-Castillo, Raúl Flores Fernández, Joan Francès Farré, Rafael Garrido-Pena, Victor S. Gonçalves, Elisa Guerra-Doce, Ana Mercedes Herrero-Corral, Joaquim Juan-Cabanilles, Daniel López-Reyes, Sarah B. McClure, Marta Merino Pérez, Arturo Oliver Foix, Montserrat Sanz Borràs, Ana Catarina Sousa, Julio Manuel Vidal Encinas, Douglas J. Kennett, Martin B. Richards, Kurt Werner Alt, Wolfgang Haak, Ron Pinhasi, Carles Lalueza-Fox, and David Reich. 2019. The genomic history of the Iberian Peninsula over the past 8000 years. *Science* 363 (6432):1230-1234.

Olasz, Judit, Verena Seidenberg, Susanne Hummel, Zoltán Szentirmay, György Szabados, Béla Melegh, and Miklós Kásler. 2018. DNA profiling of Hungarian King Béla III and other skeletal remains originating from the Royal Basilica of Székesfehérvár. *Archaeological and Anthropological Sciences*.

Olivieri, Anna, Carlo Sidore, Alessandro Achilli, Andrea Angius, Cosimo Posth, Anja Furtwängler, Stefania Brandini, Marco Rosario Capodiferro, Francesca Gandini, Magdalena Zoledziewska, Maristella Pitzalis, Andrea Maschio, Fabio Busonero, Luca Lai, Robin Skeates, Maria Giuseppina Gradoli, Jessica Beckett, Michele Marongiu, Vittorio Mazzarello, Patrizia Marongiu, Salvatore Rubino, Teresa Rito, Vincent Macaulay, Ornella Semino, Maria Pala, Gonçalo R. Abecasis, David Schlessinger, Eduardo Conde-Sousa, Pedro Soares, Martin B. Richards, Francesco Cucca, and Antonio Torroni. 2017. Mitogenome Diversity in Sardinians: A Genetic Window onto an Island's Past. *Molecular Biology and Evolution* 34 (5):1230-1239.

Orel, Vladimir. 1998. *Albanian Etymological Dictionary*. Leiden / Boston / Köln: Brill.

Översti, Sanni, Päivi Onkamo, Monika Stoljarova, Bruce Budowle, Antti Sajantila, and Jukka U. Palo. 2017. Identification and analysis of mtDNA genomes attributed to Finns reveal long-stagnant demographic trends obscured in the total diversity. *Scientific Reports* 7 (1):6193.

Paavel, Kristiina, Aivar Kriiska, Valter Lang, and Alexander Kulkov. 2019. Three bronze axes with wooden haft remains from Estonia. *Estonian Journal of Archaeology* 23 (1):3-19.

Pacciarelli, Marco, Teodoro Scarano, and Anita Crispino. 2015. The transition between the Copper and Bronze Ages in southern Italy and Sicily. Paper read at 2200 BC – A climatic breakdown as a cause for the collapse of the old world? 7. Mitteldeutscher Archäologentag vom 23. bis 26. Oktober 2014, at Halle (Saale).

Pamjav, Horolma, Á Fóthi, T. Fehér, and Erzsébet Fóthi. 2017. A study of the Bodrogköz population in north-eastern Hungary by Y chromosomal haplotypes and haplogroups. *Molecular Genetics and Genomics* 292 (4):883-894.

Pamjav, Horolma, Andrea Zalán, Judit Béres, Melinda Nagy, and Yuet Meng Chang. 2011. Genetic structure of the paternal lineage of the Roma People. *American Journal of Physical Anthropology* 145 (1):21-29.

Parker Pearson, Mike, Andrew Chamberlain, Mandy Jay, Mike Richards, Alison Sheridan, Neil Curtis, Jane Evans, Alex Gibson, Margaret Hutchison, Patrick Mahoney, Peter Marshall, Janet Montgomery, Stuart Needham, Sandra O'Mahoney, Maura Pellegrini, and Neil Wilkin. 2016. Beaker people in Britain: migration, mobility and diet. *Antiquity* 90 (351):620-637.

Parpola, A. 2015. *The Roots of Hinduism: The Early Aryans and the Indus Civilization.* New York: Oxford University Press.

Parpola, Asko. 2013. Formation of the Indo-European and Uralic (Finno-Ugric) language families in the light of archaeology: Revised and integrated 'total' correlations. In *A Linguistic Map of Prehistoric Northern Europe.* Helsinki: Société Finno-Ougrienne.

Repeated Author. 2018. Finnish vatsa ~ Sanskrit vatsá and the formation of Indo-Iranian and Uralic languages. *Suomalais-Ugrilaisen Seuran Aikakauskirja* 96:245-286.

Parpola, Asko, and Christian Carpelan. 2005. The cultural counterparts to Proto-Indo-European, Proto-Uralic and Proto-Aryan: matching the dispersal and contact patterns in the linguistic and archaeological record. In *The Indo-Aryan controversy. Evidence and inference in Indian history.*, edited by E. F. Bryant and L. L. Patton. London and New York: Routledge.

Parzinger, Hermann. 2006. *Die frühen Völker Eurasiens: Vom Neolithikum bis zum Mittelalter.* München: Verlag C. H. Beck.

Repeated Author. 2013. Ukraine and South Russia in the Bronze Age. In *The Oxford Handbook of the European Bronze Age*, edited by H. Fokkens and A. Harding. Oxford: Oxford University Press.

Pathak, Ajai K., Anurag Kadian, Alena Kushniarevich, Francesco Montinaro, Mayukh Mondal, Linda Ongaro, Manvendra Singh, Pramod Kumar, Niraj Rai, Jüri Parik, Ene Metspalu, Siiri Rootsi, Luca Pagani, Toomas Kivisild, Mait Metspalu, Gyaneshwer Chaubey, and Richard Villems. 2018. The Genetic Ancestry of Modern Indus Valley Populations from Northwest India. *The American Journal of Human Genetics* 103 (6):918-929.

Perdikaris, Sophia. 2004. Pre-Roman Iron Age Scandinavia. In *Ancient Europe, 8000 B.C. to A.D. 1000: An Encyclopedia of the Barbarian World*, edited by P. Bogucki and P. J. Crabtree. New York: Charles Scribner.

Peričić, Marijana, Lovorka Barać Lauc, Irena Martinović Klarić, Siiri Rootsi, Branka Janićijević, Igor Rudan, Rifet Terzić, Ivanka Čolak, Ante Kvesić, Dan Popović, Ana Šijački, Ibrahim Behluli, Dobrivoje Đorđević, Ljudmila

Efremovska, Đorđe D. Bajec, Branislav D. Stefanović, Richard Villems, and Pavao Rudan. 2005. High-Resolution Phylogenetic Analysis of Southeastern Europe Traces Major Episodes of Paternal Gene Flow Among Slavic Populations. *Molecular Biology and Evolution* 22 (10):1964-1975.

Perra, M. 2009. Osservazioni sull'evoluzione sociale e politica in età nuragica. *Rivista di Scienze Preistoriche* LIX:355-368.

Petkovski, Elizabet. 2006. Polymorphismes ponctuels de séquence et identification génétique: étude par spectrométrie de masse MALDI-TOF, Université Louis Pasteur, Strasbourg.

Pilipenko, A.S., R.O Trapezov, and N.V. Polosmak. 2015. Paleogenetic study of Pazyryk people buried at Ak-Alakha-1, the Altai mountains. *Archaeol Ethnol Anthrop Eurasia* 43:144-150.

Pimenta, João, Alexandra M. Lopes, Angel Carracedo, Miguel Arenas, António Amorim, and David Comas. 2019. Spatially explicit analysis reveals complex human genetic gradients in the Iberian Peninsula. *Scientific Reports* 9 (1):7825.

Pinheiro, Elias. 2011. The Sintashta cultural particulars and the origin of the war chariot. *Res Antiquitatis : journal of ancient history Vol. 2 (2011) p. 149-168* 2:149-168.

Pleinerová, I. . 1992. Les Habitats et les maisons du Bronze Ancien en Bohême du Nordouest. In *L' Habitat et l' occupation du sol a l âge du Bronze en Europe*, edited by C. Mordant and A. Richard. Paris: éditions du Comité des Travaux Historiques et Scientifiques.

Poccetti, Paolo. 2012. Language relations in Sicily - Evidence for the speech of the Σικανοί, the Σικελοί, and others. In *Language and Linguistic Contact in Ancient Sicily*, edited by O. Tribulato. Cambridge: Cambridge University Press.

Pokutta, Anna. 2013. Population Dynamics, Diet and Migrations of the Únětice culture in Poland, Gothernburg, Department of Archaeology, University of Gothenburg, Gothenburg.

Popova, Laura M., Eileen M. Murphy, and Aleksandr A. Khokhlov. 2011. Standardization and Resistance: Changing Funerary Rites at Spiridonovka (Russia) during the Beginning of the Late Bronze Age. In *The Archaeology of Politics: The Materiality of Political Practice and Action in the Past*, edited by P. G. Johansen and A. M. Bauer: Cambridge Scholars Publishing.

Post, Helen, Endre Németh, László Klima, Rodrigo Flores, Tibor Fehér, Attila Türk, Gábor Székely, Hovhannes Sahakyan, Mayukh Mondal, Francesco Montinaro, Monika Karmin, Lauri Saag, Bayazit Yunusbayev, Elza K. Khusnutdinova, Ene Metspalu, Richard Villems, Kristiina Tambets, and Siiri Rootsi. 2019. Y-chromosomal connection between Hungarians and geographically distant populations of the Ural Mountain region and West Siberia. *Scientific Reports* 9 (1):7786.

Prescott, C., and E. Walderhaug. 1995. The Last Frontier? Processes of Indo-Europeanization in Northern Europe. The Norwegian Case. *JIES* 23 (2):257-278.

Prescott, Christopher. 2009. History in prehistory - the later Neolithic / Early Metal Age, Norway. In *Neolithisation as if History mattered. Process of Neolithisation in North-Western Europe*, edited by H. Glørstad and C. Prescott. Lindome: Bricoleur.

Repeated Author. 2012. No longer north of the Beakers. Modeling an interpretative platform for third millennium transformations in Norway. In *Background to Beakers: Inquiries in Regional Cultural Backgrounds of the Bell Beaker Complex* edited by H. Fokkens and F. Nicolis. Leiden: Sidestone Press.

Prescott, Christopher, Anette Sand-Eriksen, and Knut Ivar Austvoll. 2018. The Sea and Bronze Age Transformations Water and Power in Past Societies. In *Water and Power in Past Societies*, edited by E. Holt. Albany: State University of New York Press.

Prøsch-Danielsen, Lisbeth, Christopher Prescott , and Mads Kähler Holst. 2018. Economic and social zones during the Late Neolithic/Early Bronze Age in Jaeren, Southwest Norway. Reconstructing large-scale land-use patterns. *Praehistorische Zeitschrift* 93 (1).

Prósper, Blanca María. 2013. Is Basque an Indo-European language? Possibilities and limits of the comparative method when applied to isolates. *JIES* 41 (1 & 2):239-245.

Repeated Author. 2017. Proto-Italic laryngeals in the context CLHC- and new Italic and Celtic etymological connections. *Rivista Italiana di Linguistica e Dialettologia, Roma*.

Qiu, Zhenwei, Yimin Yang, Xue Shang, Wenying Li, Yidilisi Abuduresule, Xingjun Hu, Yan Pan, David K. Ferguson, Yaowu Hu, Changsui Wang, and Hongen Jiang. 2014. Paleo-environment and paleo-diet inferred from Early Bronze Age cow dung at Xiaohe Cemetery, Xinjiang, NW China. *Quaternary International* 349:167-177.

Radivojević, Miljana, Benjamin W. Roberts, Ernst Pernicka, Zofia Stos-Gale, Marcos Martinón-Torres, Thilo Rehren, Peter Bray, Dirk Brandherm, Johan Ling, Jianjun Mei, Helle Vandkilde, Kristian Kristiansen, Stephen J. Shennan, and Cyprian Broodbank. 2018. The Provenance, Use, and Circulation of Metals in the European Bronze Age: The State of Debate. *Journal of Archaeological Research*.

Rahkonen, Pauli. 2011. Finno-Ugrian hydronyms of the River Volkhov and Luga catchment areas. *SUSA/JSFOu* 93:205-266.

Raveane, Alessandro, Serena Aneli, Francesco Montinaro, Georgios Athanasiadis, Simona Barlera, Giovanni Birolo, Giorgio Boncoraglio, Anna Maria Di Blasio, Cornelia Di Gaetano, Luca Pagani, Silvia Parolo, Peristera Paschou, Alberto Piazza, George Stamatoyannopoulos, Andrea Angius, Nicolas Brucato, Francesco Cucca, Garrett Hellenthal, Antonella Mulas, Marine Peyret-Guzzon, Madzia Zoledziewska, Abdellatif Baali, Clare Bycroft, Mohammed Cherkaoui, Christian Dina, Jean-Michel Dugoujon, Pilar Galan, Joanna Giemza, Toomas Kivisild, Mohammed Melhaoui, Mait Metspalu, Simon Myers, Luisa Mesquita Pereira, Francois-Xavier Ricaut, Francesca Brisighelli, Irene Cardinali, Viola Grugni, Hovirag Lancioni, Vincenzo Lorenzo Pascali, Antonio Torroni, Ornella Semino, Giuseppe Matullo, Alessandro Achilli, Anna Olivieri, and Cristian Capelli. 2018. Population structure of modern-day Italians reveals patterns of ancient and archaic ancestries in Southern Europe. *bioRxiv*:494898.

Rębała, Krzysztof, Begoña Martínez-Cruz, Anke Tönjes, Peter Kovacs, Michael Stumvoll, Iris Lindner, Andreas Büttner, H. Erich Wichmann, Daniela Siváková, Miroslav Soták, Lluís Quintana-Murci, Zofia Szczerkowska, David

Comas, and Consortium the Genographic. 2012. Contemporary paternal genetic landscape of Polish and German populations: from early medieval Slavic expansion to post-World War II resettlements. *European Journal Of Human Genetics* 21:415.

Rebay-Salisbury, Katharina. 2019. Personal relationships between co-buried individuals in the central European early Bronze Age. In *Giving New meaning to Cultural Heritage - The Old and the Young in Past Societies.*, edited by E. Murphy and G. Lillehammer. Stavanger: Museum of Archaeology, University of Stavanger/Society for the Study of Childhood in the Past.

Reguera-Galan, A., T. Barreiro-Grille, M. Moldovan, L. Lobo, M. Á de Blas Cortina, and J. I. García Alonso. 2018. A Provenance Study of Early Bronze Age Artefacts Found in Asturias (Spain) by Means of Metal Impurities and Lead, Copper and Antimony Isotopic Compositions. *Archaeometry* 0 (0).

Reich, David, Kumarasamy Thangaraj, Nick Patterson, Alkes L. Price, and Lalji Singh. 2009. Reconstructing Indian Population History. *Nature* 461 (7263):489-494.

Rhys, Guto. 2015. Approaching the Pictish language: historiography, early evidence and the question of Pritenic, School of Humanities. College of Arts., University of Glasgow, Glasgow.

Risch, Roberto, Vicente Lull, Rafael Micó, and Cristina Rihuete. 2015. Transitions and conflict at the end of the 3rd millennium BC in south Iberia. In *2200 BC – A climatic breakdown as a cause for the collapse of the old world?*, edited by H. Meller, H. Arz, R. Jung and R. Risch. Halle: Landesmuseum für Vorgeschichte Halle.

Roberts, Benjamin W. 2013. Britain and Ireland in the Bronze Age: Farmers in the Landscape or Heroes on the High Seas? In *The Oxford Handbook of the European Bronze Age*, edited by H. Fokkens and A. Harding. Oxford: Oxford University Press.

Rodríguez-Corral, Javier. 2018. Arming landscapes: Connectivity and resistance in northwestern Iberia in Late Prehistory. *Journal of Anthropological Archaeology*.

Rouse, Lynne M., and Barbara Cerasetti. 2016. Micro-dynamics and macro-patterns: Exploring new archaeological data for the late Holocene human-water relationship in the Murghab alluvial fan, Turkmenistan. *Quaternary International*.

Repeated Author. 2018. Mixing metaphors: sedentary-mobile interactions and local-global connections in prehistoric Turkmenistan. *Antiquity* 92 (363):674-689.

Saag, Lehti, Margot Laneman, Liivi Varul, Martin Malve, Heiki Valk, Maria A. Razzak, Ivan G. Shirobokov, Valeri I. Khartanovich, Elena R. Mikhaylova, Alena Kushniarevich, Christiana Lyn Scheib, Anu Solnik, Tuuli Reisberg, Jüri Parik, Lauri Saag, Ene Metspalu, Siiri Rootsi, Francesco Montinaro, Maido Remm, Reedik Mägi, Eugenia D'Atanasio, Enrico Ryunosuke Crema, David Díez-del-Molino, Mark G. Thomas, Aivar Kriiska, Toomas Kivisild, Richard Villems, Valter Lang, Mait Metspalu, and Kristiina Tambets. 2019. The Arrival of Siberian Ancestry Connecting the Eastern Baltic to Uralic Speakers further East. *Current Biology* 29 (10):1701-1711.e16.

Sagona, Antonio. 2017. The Emergence of Elites and a New Social Order (2500–1500 BC). In *The Archaeology of the Caucasus: From Earliest Settlements to the Iron Age*. Cambridge: Cambridge University Press.

Sand-Eriksen, Anette. 2017. Mjeltehaugen: Europe's northernmost Bell Beaker expression? In *New Perspectives on the Bronze Age: Proceedings of the 13th Nordic Bronze Age Symposium Held in Gothenburg 9th to 13th June 2015*, edited by S. Bergerbrant and A. Wessman. Oxford: Archaeopress.

Scheeres, Mirjam. 2014. High mobility rates during the period of the "Celtic migrations"? $^{87}Sr/^{86}Sr$ and $\delta^{18}O$ evidence from Early La Tène Europe, Fachbereich Biologie, Johannes Gutenberg–Universität Mainz, Mainz.

Schilz, Felix. 2006. Molekulargenetische Verwandtschaftsanalysen am prähistorischen Skelettkollektiv der Lichtensteinhöhle, Johann Friedrich Blumenbach Institut für Zoologie und Anthropologie, Abteilung Historische Anthropologie und Humanökologie, Georg-August-Universität Göttingen, Göttingen.

Schoep, Ilse. 2010. Middle Bronze Age: Crete. In *The Oxford Handbook of the Bronze Age Aegean*, edited by E. H. Cline. Oxford: Oxford University Press.

Schrijver, Peter. 2000. Varia V. Non-Indo-European Surviving in Ireland in the First Millennium AD. *Ériu* 51:195-199.

Repeated Author. 2005. Varia I. More on Non-Indo-European Surviving in Ireland in the First Millennium AD. *Ériu* 55:137-144.

Repeated Author. 2014. *Language Contact and the Origins of the Germanic Languages, Routledge Studies in Linguistics*. New York and London: Routledge.

Šebest, Lukáš, Marian Baldovič, Adam Frtús, Csaba Bognár, Klaudia Kyselicová, Ľudevít Kádasi, and Radoslav Beňuš. 2018. Detection of mitochondrial haplogroups in a small avar-slavic population from the eigth–ninth century AD. *American Journal of Physical Anthropology* 165 (3):536-553.

Seeher, Jürgen. 2011. The Plateau: The Hittites. In *The Oxford Handbook of Ancient Antolia 10,000-323 B.C.E.*, edited by S. R. Steadman and G. McMahon. Oxford: Oxford University Press.

Sell, Christian. 2017. Addressing Challenges of Ancient DNA Sequence Data Obtained with Next Generation Methods, Faculty of Biology, Johannes Gutenberg University Mainz, Mainz.

Semino, O. 2000. The Genetic Legacy of Paleolithic Homo sapiens sapiens in Extant Europeans: A Y Chromosome Perspective. *Science* 290 (5494):1155-1159.

Shelton, Kim. 2010. Late Bronze Age: Mainland Greece. In *The Oxford Handbook of the Bronze Age Aegean*, edited by E. H. Cline. Oxford: Oxford University Press.

Sikora, Martin, Meredith L. Carpenter, Andres Moreno-Estrada, Brenna M. Henn, Peter A. Underhill, Federico Sánchez-Quinto, Ilenia Zara, Maristella Pitzalis, Carlo Sidore, Fabio Busonero, Andrea Maschio, Andrea Angius, Chris Jones, Javier Mendoza-Revilla, Georgi Nekhrizov, Diana Dimitrova, Nikola Theodossiev, Timothy T. Harkins, Andreas Keller, Frank Maixner, Albert Zink, Goncalo Abecasis, Serena Sanna, Francesco Cucca, and Carlos D. Bustamante. 2014. Population Genomic Analysis of Ancient and Modern Genomes Yields

New Insights into the Genetic Ancestry of the Tyrolean Iceman and the Genetic Structure of Europe. *PLOS Genetics* 10 (5):e1004353.

Sikora, Martin, Vladimir Pitulko, Vitor Sousa, Morten E Allentoft, Lasse Vinner, Simon Rasmussen, Ashot Margaryan, Peter de Barros Damgaard, Constanza de la Fuente Castro, Gabriel Renaud, Melinda Yang, Qiaomei Fu, Isabelle Dupanloup, Konstantinos Giampoudakis, David Bravo Nogues, Carsten Rahbek, Guus Kroonen, Michael Peyrot, Hugh McColl, Sergey Vasilyev, Elizaveta Veselovskaya, Margarita Gerasimova, Elena Pavlova, Vyacheslav Chasnyk, Pavel Nikolskiy, Pavel Grebenyuk, Alexander Fedorchenko, Alexander Lebedintsev, Boris Malyarchuk, Morten Meldgaard, Rui Martiniano, Laura Arppe, Jukka Palo, Tarja Sundell, Kristiina Mannermaa, Mikko Putkonen, Verner Alexandersen, Charlotte Primeau, Ripan Mahli, Karl-Göran Sjögren, Kristian Kristiansen, Anna Wessman, Antti Sajantila, Marta Mirazohn Lahr, Richard Durbin, Rasmus Nielsen, David Meltzer, Laurent Excoffier, and Eske Willerslev. 2018. The population history of northeastern Siberia since the Pleistocene. *bioRxiv*.

Silva, Fabio, Alison Weisskopf, Cristina Castillo, Charlene Murphy, Eleanor Kingwell-Banham, Ling Qin, and Dorian Q. Fuller. 2018. A tale of two rice varieties: Modelling the prehistoric dispersals of japonica and proto-indica rices. *The Holocene* 28 (11):1745-1758.

Simkin, Oliver. 2012. Coins and Language in Ancient Sicily. In *Language and Linguistic Contact in Ancient Sicily*, edited by O. Tribulato. Cambridge: Cambridge University Press.

Solé-Morata, Neus, Patricia Villaescusa, Carla García-Fernández, Neus Font-Porterias, María José Illescas, Laura Valverde, Francesca Tassi, Silvia Ghirotto, Claude Férec, Karen Rouault, Susana Jiménez-Moreno, Begoña Martínez-Jarreta, Maria Fátima Pinheiro, María T. Zarrabeitia, Ángel Carracedo, Marian M. de Pancorbo, and Francesc Calafell. 2017. Analysis of the R1b-DF27 haplogroup shows that a large fraction of Iberian Y-chromosome lineages originated recently in situ. *Scientific Reports* 7 (1):7341.

Sørensen, Marie Louise Stig, and Katharina Rebay-Salisbury. 2008. Landscapes of the body: burials of the Middle Bronze Age in Hungary. *European Journal of Archaeology* 11 (1):49-74.

Spatzier, André, and François Bertemes. 2018. The ring sanctuary of Pömmelte, Germany: a monumental, multi-layered metaphor of the late third millennium BC. *Antiquity* 92 (363):655-673.

Spyrou, Maria A., Rezeda I. Tukhbatova, Chuan-Chao Wang, Aida Andrades Valtueña, Aditya K. Lankapalli, Vitaly V. Kondrashin, Victor A. Tsybin, Aleksandr Khokhlov, Denise Kühnert, Alexander Herbig, Kirsten I. Bos, and Johannes Krause. 2018. Analysis of 3800-year-old Yersinia pestis genomes suggests Bronze Age origin for bubonic plague. *Nature Communications* 9 (1):2234.

Stolarek, I., L. Handschuh, A. Juras, W. Nowaczewska, H. Kóčka-Krenz, A. Michalowski, J. Piontek, P. Kozlowski, and M. Figlerowicz. 2019. Goth migration induced changes in the matrilineal genetic structure of the central-east European population. *Scientific Reports* 9 (1):6737.

Stolarek, Ireneusz, Anna Juras, Luiza Handschuh, Malgorzata Marcinkowska-Swojak, Anna Philips, Michal Zenczak, Artur Dębski, Hanna Kóčka-Krenz, Janusz Piontek, Piotr Kozlowski, and Marek Figlerowicz. 2018. A mosaic genetic structure of the human population living in the South Baltic region during the Iron Age. *Scientific Reports* 8 (1):2455.

Sureda, Pau. 2018. The first metallurgy in the Pityusic Islands (Balearic archipelago, Mediterranean Sea). *Archaeological and Anthropological Sciences*.

Szecsenyi-Nagy, Anna, Christina Roth, Brandt Guido, Cristina Rihuete-Herrada, Cristina Tejedor-Rodriguez, Petra Held, Inigo Garcia-Martinez-de-Lagran, Hector Arcusa Magallon, Stephanie Zesch, Corina Knipper, Eszter Banffy, Susanne Friedrich, Harald Meller, Primitiva Bueno-Ramirez, Rosa Barroso Bermejo, Rodrigo de Balbin Behrmann, Ana M. Herrero-Coral, Raul Flores Fernandez, Carmen Alonso Fernandez, Javier Jimenez Echevarria, Laura Rindlisbacher, Camila Oliart, Maria-Ines Fregeiro, Ignacio Soriano, Oriol Vincente, Rafael Mico, Vincente Lull, Jorge Soler Diaz, Juan Antonio Lopez Padilla, Consuelo Roca de Togores Munoz, Mauro S. Hernandez Perez, Francisco Javier Jover Maestre, Joaquin Lomba Maurandi, Azucena Aviles Fernandez, Katina T. Lillios, Ana Maria Silva, Miguel Magalhaes Ramalho, Luiz Miguel Oosterbeek, Claudia Cunha, Anna J Waterman, Jordi Roig Buxo, Andres Martinez, Juana Ponce Martinez, Mark Hunt Ortiz, Juan Carlos Mejias-Gracia, Juan Carlos Pecero Espin, Rosario Cruz-Aunon Briones, Tiago Tome, Eduardo Carmona Ballestero, Joao Luis Cardoso, Ana Cristina Araujo, Corina Liesau von Lettow-Vorbeck, Conception Blasco Bosqued, Patricia Rios Mendoza, Ana Pujante, Jose I. Royo-Guillen, Marco Aurelio Esquembre Bevia, Victor Manuel Dos Santos Goncalves, Rui Parreira, Elena Moran Hernandez, Elena Mendez Izquierdo, Jorge Vega de Miguel, Roberto Menduina Garcia, Victoria Martinez Calvo, Oscar Lopez Jimenez, Johannes Krause, Sandra L. Pichler, Rafael Garrido-Pena, Michael Kunst, Roberto Risch, Manuel A. Rojo-Guerra, Wolfgang Haak, and Kurt W. Alt. 2017. The maternal genetic make-up of the Iberian Peninsula between the Neolithic and the Early Bronze Age. *bioRxiv*.

Szeifert, Bea, Veronika Csakyova, Balazs Stegmar, Daniel Gerber, Balazs Egyed, S. G. Botalov, R. D Goldina., A. V. Danich, Attila Tiirk, Balazs G. Mende, and Anna Szecsenyi-Nagy. 2018. Maternal genetic. *Archeologiya evraziiskikh stepei* 6:202-222.

Tambets, Kristiina, Bayazit Yunusbayev, Georgi Hudjashov, Anne-Mai Ilumäe, Siiri Rootsi, Terhi Honkola, Outi Vesakoski, Quentin Atkinson, Pontus Skoglund, Alena Kushniarevich, Sergey Litvinov, Maere Reidla, Ene Metspalu, Lehti Saag, Timo Rantanen, Monika Karmin, Jüri Parik, Sergey I. Zhadanov, Marina Gubina, Larisa D. Damba, Marina Bermisheva, Tuuli Reisberg, Khadizhat Dibirova, Irina Evseeva, Mari Nelis, Janis Klovins, Andres Metspalu, Tõnu Esko, Oleg Balanovsky, Elena Balanovska, Elza K. Khusnutdinova, Ludmila P. Osipova, Mikhail Voevoda, Richard Villems, Toomas Kivisild, and Mait Metspalu. 2018. Genes reveal traces of common recent demographic history for most of the Uralic-speaking populations. *Genome Biology* 19 (1):139.

Tätte, Kai, Luca Pagani, Ajai Kumar Pathak, Sulev Kõks, Binh Ho Duy, Xuan Dung Ho, Gazi Nurun Nahar Sultana, Mohd Istiaq Sharif, Md Asaduzzaman, Doron M. Behar, Yarin Hadid, Richard Villems, Gyaneshwer Chaubey, Toomas Kivisild, and Mait Metspalu. 2018. The genetic legacy of continental scale admixture in Indian Austroasiatic speakers. *bioRxiv*.

Taylor, William, Svetlana Shnaider, Aida Abdykanova, Antoine Fages, Frido Welker, Franziska Irmer, Andaine Seguin-Orlando, Naveed Khan, Katerina Douka, Ksenia Kolobova, Ludovic Orlando, Andrei Krivoshapkin, and Nicole Boivin. 2018. Early pastoral economies along the Ancient Silk Road: Biomolecular evidence from the Alay Valley, Kyrgyzstan. *PLOS ONE* 13 (10):e0205646.

Taylor, William Timothy Treal, Jamsranjav Bayarsaikhan, Tumurbaatar Tuvshinjargal, Scott Bender, Monica Tromp, Julia Clark, K. Bryce Lowry, Jean-Luc Houle, Dimitri Staszewski, Jocelyn Whitworth, William Fitzhugh, and Nicole Boivin. 2018. Origins of equine dentistry. *Proceedings of the National Academy of Sciences* 115 (29):E6707-E6715.

Terradas, Xavier, Bernard Gratuze, Josep Bosch, Roser Enrich, Xavier Esteve, F. Xavier Oms, and Genís Ribé. 2014. Neolithic diffusion of obsidian in the western Mediterranean: new data from Iberia. *Journal of Archaeological Science* 41:69-78.

Teržan, Biba, and Snježana Karavanić. 2013. The Western Balkans in the Bronze Age. In *The Oxford Handbook of the European Bronze Age*, edited by H. Fokkens and A. Harding. Oxford: Oxford University Press.

Thangaraj, Kumarasamy, B. Prathap Naidu, Federica Crivellaro, Rakesh Tamang, Shashank Upadhyay, Varun Kumar Sharma, Alla G. Reddy, S. R. Walimbe, Gyaneshwer Chaubey, Toomas Kivisild, and Lalji Singh. 2010. The Influence of Natural Barriers in Shaping the Genetic Structure of Maharashtra Populations. *PLOS ONE* 5 (12):e15283.

Thrane, Henrik. 2013. Scandinavia In *The Oxford Handbook of the European Bronze Age*, edited by H. Fokkens and A. Harding. Oxford: Oxford University Press.

Tikhonov, Dmitrii G., Cemal Gurkan, Gokce Y. A. Peler, and Victor M. Dyakonov. 2019. Matrilineal Patrilineal Genetic Continuity of Two Iron Age Individuals from a Pazyryk Culture Burial. *International Journal of Human Genetics* 19 (1):29-47.

Torelli, M. 2000. *Gli Etruschi*. Venezia.

Trump, D. H. 2014. The Apennine Culture of Italy. *Proceedings of the Prehistoric Society* 24:165-200.

Tvauri, Andres. 2007. Migrants or Natives? The Research History of Long Barrows in Russia and Estonia in the 5th– 10th Centuries. *Slavica Helsingiensia* 32:247-285.

Udolph, Jürgen. 1994. *Namenkundliche Studien zum Germanenproblem*. Edited by H. Beck, H. Steuer and D. Timpe, *Ergänzungsbände zum Reallexikon der Germanischen Altertumskunde*. Berlin/New York: Walter de Gruyter.

Repeated Author. 1997. Alteuropäische Hydronymie und urslavische Gewässernamen. *Onomastica* XLII:21-70.

Repeated Author. 2016. Expansion slavischer Stämme aus namenkundlicher und bodenkundlicher Sicht. *Onomastica* 60:215-231.

Ugas, Giovanni. 2005. *L'Alba dei Nuraghi*. Cagliari: Fabula.

Ullah, Inam, Jill K. Olofsson, Ashot Margaryan, Melissa Ilardo, Habib Ahmad, Martin Sikora, Anders J. Hansen, Muhammad Shahid Nadeem, Numan Fazal, Murad Ali, Anders Buchard, Brian E. Hemphill, Eske Willerslev, and Morten E. Allentoft. 2017. High Y-chromosomal Differentiation Among Ethnic Groups of Dir and Swat Districts, Pakistan. *Annals of Human Genetics* 81 (6):234-248.

Underhill, P. A., G. D. Poznik, S. Rootsi, M. Jarve, A. A. Lin, J. Wang, B. Passarelli, J. Kanbar, N. M. Myres, R. J. King, J. Di Cristofaro, H. Sahakyan, D. M. Behar, A. Kushniarevich, J. Sarac, T. Saric, P. Rudan, A. K. Pathak, G. Chaubey, V. Grugni, O. Semino, L. Yepiskoposyan, A. Bahmanimehr, S. Farjadian, O. Balanovsky, E. K. Khusnutdinova, R. J. Herrera, J. Chiaroni, C. D. Bustamante, S. R. Quake, T. Kivisild, and R. Villems. 2015. The phylogenetic and geographic structure of Y-chromosome haplogroup R1a. *Eur J Hum Genet* 23 (1):124-31.

Unterländer, Martina, Friso Palstra, Iosif Lazaridis, Aleksandr Pilipenko, Zuzana Hofmanová, Melanie Groß, Christian Sell, Jens Blöcher, Karola Kirsanow, Nadin Rohland, Benjamin Rieger, Elke Kaiser, Wolfram Schier, Dimitri Pozdniakov, Aleksandr Khokhlov, Myriam Georges, Sandra Wilde, Adam Powell, Evelyne Heyer, Mathias Currat, David Reich, Zainolla Samashev, Hermann Parzinger, Vyacheslav I. Molodin, and Joachim Burger. 2017. Ancestry and demography and descendants of Iron Age nomads of the Eurasian Steppe. 8:14615.

Váczi, Gábor. 2013. Cultural connections and interactions of Eastern Transdanubia during the Urnfield period. *DissArch* 3 (1):205-230.

Valamoti, Soultana Maria. 2016. Millet, the late comer: on the tracks of Panicum miliaceum in prehistoric Greece. *Archaeological and Anthropological Sciences* 8 (1):51-63.

Valdiosera, Cristina, Torsten Günther, Juan Carlos Vera-Rodríguez, Irene Ureña, Eneko Iriarte, Ricardo Rodríguez-Varela, Luciana G. Simões, Rafael M. Martínez-Sánchez, Emma M. Svensson, Helena Malmström, Laura Rodríguez, José-María Bermúdez de Castro, Eudald Carbonell, Alfonso Alday, José Antonio Hernández Vera, Anders Götherström, José-Miguel Carretero, Juan Luis Arsuaga, Colin I. Smith, and Mattias Jakobsson. 2018. Four millennia of Iberian biomolecular prehistory illustrate the impact of prehistoric migrations at the far end of Eurasia. *Proceedings of the National Academy of Sciences* 115 (13):3428-3433.

Vallejo, José M. 2013. Hacia una definición del lusitano. *Acta Palaeohispanica* 13:273-291.

van den Brink, Edwin C. M., Ron Beeri, Dan Kirzner, Enno Bron, Anat Cohen-Weinberger, Elisheva Kamaisky, Tamar Gonen, Lilly Gershuny, Yossi Nagar, Daphna Ben-Tor, Naama Sukenik, Orit Shamir, Edward F. Maher, and David Reich. 2017. A Late Bronze Age II clay coffin from Tel Shaddud in the Central Jezreel Valley, Israel: context and historical implications AU - van den Brink, Edwin C. M. *Levant* 49 (2):105-135.

Vander Linden, Marc. 2007. For equalities are plural: reassessing the social in Europe during the third millenniumbc. *World Archaeology* 39 (2):177-193.

Vandkilde, Helle. 2005. A Review of the Early Late Neolithic Period in Denmark: Practice, Identity and Connectivity. *Journal of Neolithic Archaeology* 7.

Vanek, Daniel, Hana Brzobohata, Marcela Silerova, Zdenek Horak, Miriam Nyvltova Fisakova, Michaela Vasinova Galiova, Pavla Zednikova Mala, Vladislava Urbanova, Miluse Dobisikova, Michal Beran, and Petr Brestovansky. 2015. Complex Analysis of 700-Year-Old Skeletal Remains found in an Unusual Grave-Case Report. *Anthropology* 2 (5).

Vanhanen, Santeri, Stefan Gustafsson, Håkan Ranheden, Niclas Björck, Marianna Kemell, and Volker Heyd. 2019. Maritime Hunter-Gatherers Adopt Cultivation at the Farming Extreme of Northern Europe 5000 Years Ago. *Scientific Reports* 9 (1):4756.

Vasilyev, Stanislav Aleksandrovich. 2002. Iskusstvo drevnego naselenija Volgo-Kam'ja v Anan'inskuju epokhu (istoki i formirovanie), Sankt Peterburg.

Veeramah, Krishna R., Andreas Rott, Melanie Groß, Lucy van Dorp, Saioa López, Karola Kirsanow, Christian Sell, Jens Blöcher, Daniel Wegmann, Vivian Link, Zuzana Hofmanová, Joris Peters, Bernd Trautmann, Anja Gairhos, Jochen Haberstroh, Bernd Päffgen, Garrett Hellenthal, Brigitte Haas-Gebhard, Michaela Harbeck, and Joachim Burger. 2018. Population genomic analysis of elongated skulls reveals extensive female-biased immigration in Early Medieval Bavaria. *Proceedings of the National Academy of Sciences* 115 (13):3494-3499.

Villar Liébana, Francisco. 2014. *Indoeuropeos, iberos, vascos y sus parientes. Estratigrafía y cronología de las poblaciones prehistóricas.* Salamanca: Ediciones Universidad de Salamanca.

Vinogradov, N. B. 2018. Синташта как транскультурный феномен. *Поволжская археология* 23 (1):74-90.

Volkov, V.G., and A.N. Seslavin. 2019. Genetic study of the Rurik Dynasty. In *Centenary of Human Population Genetics.* Moscow.

Voskarides, K., S. Mazieres, D. Hadjipanagi, J. Di Cristofaro, A. Ignatiou, C. Stefanou, R. J. King, P. A. Underhill, J. Chiaroni, and C. Deltas. 2016. Y-chromosome phylogeographic analysis of the Greek-Cypriot population reveals elements consistent with Neolithic and Bronze Age settlements. *Investig Genet* 7:1.

Voutsaki, Sofia. 2010. Middle Bronze Age: Mainland Greece. In *The Oxford Handbook of the Bronze Age Aegean*, edited by E. H. Cline. Oxford: Oxford University Press.

Wang, Chuan-Chao, Sabine Reinhold, Alexey Kalmykov, Antje Wissgott, Guido Brandt, Choongwon Jeong, Olivia Cheronet, Matthew Ferry, Eadaoin Harney, Denise Keating, Swapan Mallick, Nadin Rohland, Kristin Stewardson, Anatoly R. Kantorovich, Vladimir E. Maslov, Vladimira G. Petrenko, Vladimir R. Erlikh, Biaslan Ch Atabiev, Rabadan G. Magomedov, Philipp L. Kohl, Kurt W. Alt, Sandra L. Pichler, Claudia Gerling, Harald Meller, Benik Vardanyan, Larisa Yeganyan, Alexey D. Rezepkin, Dirk Mariaschk, Natalia Berezina, Julia Gresky, Katharina Fuchs, Corina Knipper, Stephan Schiffels, Elena Balanovska, Oleg Balanovsky, Iain Mathieson, Thomas Higham, Yakov B.

Berezin, Alexandra Buzhilova, Viktor Trifonov, Ron Pinhasi, Andrej B. Belinskij, David Reich, Svend Hansen, Johannes Krause, and Wolfgang Haak. 2019. Ancient human genome-wide data from a 3000-year interval in the Caucasus corresponds with eco-geographic regions. *Nature Communications* 10 (1):590.

Wei, Lan-Hai, Shi Yan, Yan Lu, Shao-Qing Wen, Yun-Zhi Huang, Ling-Xiang Wang, Shi-Lin Li, Ya-Jun Yang, Xiao-Feng Wang, Chao Zhang, Shu-Hua Xu, Da-Li Yao, Li Jin, and Hui Li. 2018. Whole-sequence analysis indicates that the Y chromosome C2*-Star Cluster traces back to ordinary Mongols, rather than Genghis Khan. *European Journal of Human Genetics* 26 (2):230-237.

Wiik, Kalevi. 1997. The Uralic and Finno-Ugric phonetic substratum in Proto-Germanic. *Linguistica Uralica* 33 (4):258-280.

Witczak, Krzysztof. 2016. The earliest Alhanian loanwords in Greek. Paper read at First International Conference on Language Contact in the Balkans and Asia Minor, November 3rd-5th, at Thessaloniki.

Włodarczak, Piotr. 2017. Battle-axes and beakers. The Final Eneolithic societies. In *The Past Societies: Polish lands from the first evidence of human presence to the Early Middle Ages 2 (5500-2000 BC)*, edited by P. Urbańczyk. Warszawa: Institute of Archaeology and Ethnology, Polish Academy of Science.

Repeated Author. 2017. Małopolska at the beginning of the Bronze Age (2000-1600 BC) In *The Past Societies. Polish lands from the first evidence of human presence to the Early Middle Ages 3 (2000-500 BC)*, edited by U. Bugaj. Warszawa: Institute of Archaeology and Ethnology, Polish Academy of Science.

Repeated Author. 2017. Towards the Bronze Age in south-eastern Poland (2300-2000 BC). In *The Past Societies: Polish lands from the first evidence of human presence to the Early Middle Ages 2 (5500-2000 BC)*, edited by P. Urbańczyk. Warszawa: Institute of Archaeology and Ethnology, Polish Academy of Sciences.

Woudhuizen, Frederik Christiaan. 2006. The ethnicity of the Sea Peoples, College voor Promoties, Erasmus Universiteit Rotterdam, Rotterdam.

Yates, D. 2007. *Land, Power and Prestige: Bronze Age Field Systems in Southern England*. Oxford: Oxbow Books.

Yushkova, M. A. 2010. Metallicheskie izdelija epokhi bronzy na severo-zapade Rossii. *Известия Самарского научного центра Российской академии наук* 12 (2):272-277.

Zalloua, Pierre, Catherine J. Collins, Anna Gosling, Simone Andrea Biagini, Benjamí Costa, Olga Kardailsky, Lorenzo Nigro, Wissam Khalil, Francesc Calafell, and Elizabeth Matisoo-Smith. 2018. Ancient DNA of Phoenician remains indicates discontinuity in the settlement history of Ibiza. *Scientific Reports* 8 (1):17567.

Zavodny, Emily, Sarah B. McClure, Martin H. Welker, Brendan J. Culleton, Jacqueline Balen, and Douglas J. Kennett. 2018. Scaling up: Stable isotope evidence for the intensification of animal husbandry in Bronze-Iron Age Lika, Croatia. *Journal of Archaeological Science: Reports*.

Zhang, Ye, Xiyan Wu, Jiawei Li, Hongjie Li, Yongbin Zhao, and Hui Zhou. 2018. The Y-chromosome haplogroup C3*-F3918, likely attributed to the Mongol

Empire, can be traced to a 2500-year-old nomadic group. *Journal of Human Genetics* 63 (2):231-238.

Zhernakova, Daria V., Vladimir Brukhin, Sergey Malov, Taras K. Oleksyk, Klaus Peter Koepfli, Anna Zhuk, Pavel Dobrynin, Sergei Kliver, Nikolay Cherkasov, Gaik Tamazian, Mikhail Rotkevich, Ksenia Krasheninnikova, Igor Evsyukov, Sviatoslav Sidorov, Anna Gorbunova, Ekaterina Chernyaeva, Andrey Shevchenko, Sofia Kolchanova, Alexei Komissarov, Serguei Simonov, Alexey Antonik, Anton Logachev, Dmitrii E. Polev, Olga A. Pavlova, Andrey S. Glotov, Vladimir Ulantsev, Ekaterina Noskova, Tatyana K. Davydova, Tatyana M. Sivtseva, Svetlana Limborska, Oleg Balanovsky, Vladimir Osakovsky, Alexey Novozhilov, Valery Puzyrev, and Stephen J. O'Brien. 2019. Genome-wide sequence analyses of ethnic populations across Russia. *Genomics*.

Zhernakova, Daria V., Igor Evsyukov, Elena Lukianova, Anna Zhuk, Mikhail Rotkevich, Anton Logachev, Gaik Tamazian, Ksenia Krasheninnikova, Alexei Komissarov, Anna Gorbunova, Andrey Shevchenko, Sergey Malov, Nikolay Cherkasov, Dmitrii E. Polev, Genome Russia Consortium, Oleg Balanovsky, Vladimir Brukhin, and Stephen J. O'Brien. 2019. The Genome Russia Project: a reference database of whole genome sequences across Russia. In *Centenary of Human Population Genetics*. Moscow.

Zhivlov, Mikhail. 2015. Неиндоевропейский субстрат в финно-волжских языках. In *X Чтения памяти С.А. Старостина, 27 марта 2015*.

Zhong, Hua, Hong Shi, Xue-Bin Qi, Zi-Yuan Duan, Ping-Ping Tan, Li Jin, Bing Su, and Runlin Z. Ma. 2013. Extended Y chromosome investigation suggests postglacial migrations of modern humans into East Asia via the northern route. *Mol Biol Evol* 28 (1):717-727.

Made in the USA
Monee, IL
15 August 2021